IN THE NAME OF PHENOMENOLOGY

Simon Glendinning

Routledge
Taylor & Francis Group

LONDON AND NEW YORK

First published 2007
by Routledge
2 Park Square, Milton Park, Abingdon, Oxon OX14 4RN

Simultaneously published in the USA and Canada
by Routledge
270 Madison Ave, New York, NY 10016

Routledge is an imprint of the Taylor & Francis Group, an informa business

© 2007 Simon Glendinning

Typeset in Goudy by Taylor & Francis Books
Printed and bound in Great Britain by
Antony Rowe Ltd, Chippenham, Wiltshire

British Library Cataloguing in Publication Data
A catalogue record for this book is available from the British Library

Library of Congress Cataloging in Publication Data
A catalog record for this book has been requested

ISBN 10: 0-415-22337-7 (hbk)
ISBN 10: 0-415-22338-5 (pbk)
ISBN 10: 0-203-94670-7 (ebk)

ISBN 13: 978-0-415-22337-9 (hbk)
ISBN 13: 978-0-415-22338-6 (pbk)
ISBN 13: 978-0-203-94670-1 (ebk)

FOR ROBERT DENOON CUMMING

CONTENTS

CONTENTS

CONTENTS

ACKNOWLEDGEMENTS

The shape of this book began to emerge for me in the course of teaching undergraduate classes in Modern European Philosophy between 1995 and 2004 at the Universities of Kent and Reading. I would like to thank my former students for their participation, their interest and their ideas.

Some of the material in this book has appeared elsewhere in preliminary form. Part II of Chapter 1 works over material published as 'What Is Phenomenology?' in *Think* (no. 7, 2004); some of Part II of Chapter 3 draws on material in 'The End of Philosophy as Metaphysics' in *The Cambridge History of Philosophy 1870–1945* (Cambridge University Press, 2004) and Part III of Chapter 3 draws on material from 'Much Ado about Nothing' in *Ratio*, vol. XIV, no. 3, pp. 281–88; a version of Part III of Chapter 5 appears as 'Merleau-Ponty: The Genius of Man' in *Reading Merleau-Ponty* (Routledge, 2007); Parts II and III of Chapter 6 are a development of material in '*Le Plaisir de la lecture*: Reading the Other Animal' in *Parallax*, vol. 12, no. 1, 2006; Part II of Chapter 7 is a development of 'Language' in *Understanding Derrida* (Continuum, 2004). I am grateful to the editors of the various journals and books for permission to work with that material again here.

I have never yet worked in a philosophy department with colleagues whose own work took them regularly into the texts I have been reading. But I have never had a philosophy colleague who was not prepared to think about the things I have been thinking about either. At different stages in the development of this book I have had useful conversations with and advice from John Cottingham, Jonathan Dancy, Hanjo Glock, Brad Hooker, Richard Norman, Michael Proudfoot, Sean Sayers and Philip Stratton-Lake.

Various people have read or heard drafts of parts of the text as research papers, and I am particularly grateful to Simon Critchley, Paul Davies, Robert Eaglestone, Annabel Herzog, Christina Howells, Luke Mulhall, Bob Plant, Stella Sandford, Ali Shahrukhi and John Shand for comments and discussions. I would also like to thank the publisher's readers who read the first draft of this book and saved me from numerous errors, misunderstandings and certain embarrassment.

ACKNOWLEDGEMENTS

I am especially grateful to Daniel Whiting, who read early drafts of each chapter and made many detailed and helpful comments and criticisms.

Finally, I would like to thank Tony Bruce at Routledge for encouraging me to finish this book, and my family for making it impossible for me to finish it sooner.

Simon Glendinning
London, 2007

INTRODUCTION
Opening words

This book consists of a series of interconnected essays concerned primarily with 'beginnings' in phenomenology in Germany and France during the twentieth century. I have three kinds of beginning in view here. There are, first of all, issues about *origins*, questions concerning how phenomenology first emerged as an inheritance of philosophy. But there are also beginnings that are rather more internal to the texts that belong to that inheritance: *launches* and *re-launches*, new initiatives in the name of phenomenology. The third kind of beginning is more humdrum and relates to the kind of *starting points* one finds in prefaces, introductions, opening chapters, introductory lectures and so on.

For reasons I will explain in this introduction, while I will, at various stages, take an interest in each of these kinds of beginnings, I am especially concerned with an effort to examine beginnings of the second kind – or, more precisely, especially concerned to examine beginnings of the second kind as they are (for the most part, but I am not going to be obsessional about this) elaborated in beginnings of the third kind. I am not trying to introduce what is often called 'the phenomenological movement', still less to introduce the whole corpus or oeuvre of any of the authors who have contributed to its formation and re-formation. Rather, I follow textual openings that attempt to finesse headings from an inheritance and which thus show up the shifting trajectories of that inheritance.

My supplementary interest in beginnings of the third kind has two basic motivations: one theoretical and one pedagogical. My theoretical interest in such starting points is bound up with the way they tend to relate to the launches that characterise beginnings of the second kind. Philosophers may be distinguished by theses, by method or anything else you like. They themselves begin to distinguish themselves as soon as they begin to write. They distinguish themselves at that point, at the very point of departure, in terms of the way their writing responds (explicitly or implicitly) to what I think is an irreducibly ambiguous but nevertheless unavoidable demand: the (endless and endlessly circular) demand to inherit philosophy *philosophically*.

Of course, the issue of how to inherit philosophy philosophically is no more decided in advance or at the outset than any other issue in philosophy. Indeed, it has the character of a decision in play that is, if not prior to deliberation, then implied within every deliberative step. Moreover, since it remains in play from first to last there is no particular stage of writing which can radically arrogate the issue for itself and spare the rest. Nevertheless, it seems to me that there is a certain *intensity* of its taking place – in the choices, selections and deselections – in the moments where, as it were, one takes the plunge. Very often it is here that one can see most clearly how the determination of philosophical *priorities* simultaneously effects and transforms a philosophical inheritance.

With respect to this point, writings that belong to the inheritance of philosophy as phenomenology are particularly significant. As I will explain in Chapter 1, phenomenological philosophy is permeated with a sense that the kind of thinking that predominates in and as philosophy in our time – the kind of thinking which falls (more or less) squarely into the dominant intellectual culture of Western modernity, a culture preoccupied by the methods and achievements of natural science – has lost sight of philosophy's original motivations or originating sources. Typically, then, phenomenological writings aim to rekindle or repossess a dimension of our philosophical heritage which, it is felt, has been lost or left behind by what, following John McDowell, I will call the 'ordinary philosophy' of our time.[1] The question of how, in our time, even to begin in philosophy is one which phenomenology is particularly alive to, particularly shaped by.

Ordinary philosophy can be defined as an outlook which is in the 'grip' of the thought that an intellectually satisfactory 'conception of ourselves'[2] should be given exclusively in terms that 'belong to a natural-scientific depiction of nature'.[3] This is the frame of mind of what McDowell calls 'modern naturalism'.[4] 'Science has presented itself as the very exemplar of access to objective truth',[5] and so anything short of a rigorous naturalism in philosophy will always be suspected of trying to smuggle in something intellectually unrespectable. Ordinary philosophy in our time is thus the kind of thinking which, as Husserl puts it, looks for its inspiration and in certain respects also its method in 'the intellectual achievements of the sciences of a natural sort'.[6] The critique of this kind of distinctively modern naturalistic inheritance of philosophy will be a central theme throughout this book.

Following an introductory discussion of phenomenology in general, the essays track the Germanophone elaboration of phenomenology into the terrain of post-war France. Starting off with the legacy of the descriptive phenomenology of Franz Brentano and the development of transcendental phenomenology by Edmund Husserl, I examine in turn the re-elaboration of phenomenology by Martin Heidegger; the attempts to reconcile the differences between Husserl and Heidegger in new starts by Jean-Paul Sartre and Maurice Merleau-Ponty; and finally two radicalisations of phenomenology in work by Emmanuel Levinas and Jacques Derrida. As we shall see, in Derrida's case the radicalisation of phenomenology both interrupts the reconciling efforts of his French predecessors and, up to a point, interrupts phenomenology itself.

The shifting sequence concludes with Derrida, and the narrative line is, throughout, informed by that trajectory. However, since I do not read Derrida's interruption of phenomenology as simply bringing it to an end or breaking with it completely, ending with Derrida does not imply that I want to regard phenomenological philosophy as of historical significance only. Nevertheless, I accept that the understanding of phenomenology I want to defend robustly affirms that its future lies elsewhere than in what many of its foremost advocates have hoped to make out for it: namely, the formation of a unified philosophical movement or philosophical school.

I want this book to belong to a reconfiguration of the legacy of phenomenology, not to report on its demise. My view, a view which I will introduce in Chapter 1, is that phenomenology should be conceived less as a distinctive movement in European thought and more as a general title for a powerful force of resistance to contemporary ordinary philosophy. It is because I would like our intellectual culture to be better equipped to resist the appeal of ordinary philosophy that I want it to be better informed about and informed by philosophy written in the name of phenomenology.

So this book is not an introduction to the phenomenological movement and I am not setting out to introduce the entirety of anyone's philosophy either. Nevertheless, the focus of the book, tackling beginnings of the second kind (largely) through beginnings of the third, allows me to retain certain introductory ambitions and pedagogical motivations. I hope that people who are already familiar with the texts discussed here will be brought to see something new. However, this book has also been written with an eye to people with a philosophical education in the English-speaking world who have, as yet, made little or no headway with them. There are, I think, a number of reasons why those readers from the philosophical culture I belong to who turn away from these texts tend to stay away. Some of the reasons are more or less internal to the texts themselves (there is a distinctive demandingness to the texts discussed here that I will try to come to terms with) and some are more or less external to them (features of ordinary philosophy that would construe their formation as perversions of philosophy proper). I hope to tempt people to read on beyond the highly circumscribed and relatively short-run readings pursued in this book. For this reason I will start out myself with a sense that even readers new to phenomenology will already be, to some extent at least, underway. By taking advantage of some continuity with their previous experience in philosophy I want to encourage such readers to render themselves capable of opening texts that might otherwise remain closed. That is, by orienting my own work of reading towards those 'beginnings' that are textual openings I will try to provide an intro-duction (literally, *a leading inside*) to texts that will enable newcomers to get beyond the bit that they often find genuinely and frustratingly hard to get beyond: the start.

On that score let me add, finally, that I have not found it everywhere possible or indeed desirable to sustain a mode of discussion that is uniformly welcoming to the novice. I have no pretensions to having written a book that will be immediately accessible to all. As far as I am able I have tried to make room for those who are themselves starting out, but I see no advantage in trying to do justice to the texts I am reading in a way that would make it all seem just plain sailing, or disguised plain speaking. Having engaged in the struggle to come to terms with authors whose various starting points I will be opening up in this book, I have found, as Mary Warnock put it back in 1965 after reading Sartre's *Being and Nothingness*, that 'it is impossible not to feel that the struggle was worth while'.[7] Today, both professionally and personally the struggle continues. I (hereby) commend it to you.

1

WHAT IS PHENOMENOLOGY?

Faces of phenomenology

The texts explored in this book belong to what I have come to regard as *the* most significant and important development in philosophy during the twentieth century, a development that also includes some of *the* major figures in contemporary philosophy. I do not mean here to be talking up the achievements of what is often called the 'phenomenological movement' in twentieth-century philosophy in Continental Europe. Indeed, in my view the ongoing strength and coherence of phenomenology as a force within the contemporary philosophical culture is to be explained not by what Maurice Merleau-Ponty called the 'unity' of its 'manner of thinking' but by what he perhaps somewhat more faithfully called its (in his view only currently) 'unfinished nature'.[1] In order to affirm the ongoing capacity for phenomenology to have a future, a capacity perhaps already evident in the astonishing internal diversity that marks its existing legacy, I will want to regard this unfinished condition as a kind of constant. In my view, the diversity within philosophy pursued in the name of phenomenology is not to be explained away as an 'inchoative atmosphere' that 'inevitably' attends the early days of a 'movement' on its way to 'becoming a doctrine or philosophical system'.[2] On the contrary, it is properly internal to its philosophical character, internal to its affirmation of philosophy as an 'ever-renewed experiment in making its own beginning',[3] internal to what Jacques Derrida calls its prolific openness to 'self-interruption'.[4]

So I see no advantage in attempting to configure the development that the emergence of phenomenology has brought about in contemporary philosophy in terms of a movement on its way to becoming a doctrine. Moreover, for the same reason, I see no advantage in attempting to limit something like 'phenomenology proper' to the work from the European mainland standardly included in the 'phenomenological movement' either. On the contrary, and the scope of my opening sentence anticipates this point, we can and should make room for variations that greatly increase rather than decrease the diversity within this development. I am thinking here not only of the work of a 'radical phenomenologist' like Derrida,[5] but also of some of the very best and most influential writings in twentieth-century philosophy beyond the European mainland. Indeed, what one might call *phenomenology at large* patently includes figures central to philosophical developments in the English-speaking world: Ludwig Wittgenstein,[6] J.L. Austin[7] and Gilbert Ryle[8] are the three clearest cases here. And if we allow ourselves to look beyond thinkers who have explicitly taken phenomenology as a title for their own work and include thinkers with clear methodological affinities to those who reach for the title themselves, it is relatively easy to identify other important Anglo-American contributors too: Stanley Cavell, Cora Diamond, John McDowell, Hilary Putnam, David Wiggins; indeed most of the English-language inheritors of Wittgenstein are obvious candidates.[9]

What we have in view here, then, is a widespread proliferation of initiatives which have found in phenomenology 'the most convincing expression of a philosopher's claim on people's attention'.[10] Although the texts I will be exploring in the following chapters are drawn primarily from the work of a short line-up of philosophers working in Germany and France, I will not hide my interest in the elaboration of phenomenology at large. Indeed, this chapter concerns itself with the question of *what phenomenology is* in such a way as to warrant the fundamentally catholic embrace I have in view here.

In Part I of this chapter I will draw attention to two salient features of phenomenological philosophy in general. The first was touched on in the Introduction: namely, that it is a way of thinking for which questions concerning how one should, in our time, inherit the subject we call 'philosophy' has itself become a philosophical issue. There is an abiding sense in phenomenological philosophy that a distinctive and (let's say) spiritually crucial dimension of the philosophical heritage has been lost or left behind by ordinary philosophy in our time. According to phenomenological philosophers we live in an age in which philosophy requires a radical renewal.

As I indicated in the Introduction, ordinary philosophy can be characterised by its modern naturalism. It is a post-Enlightenment tradition in which philosophy is conducted in the spirit and sometimes even in the light of the methods and achievements of the natural sciences. This gives us a second salient feature of phenomenological philosophy: namely, its profoundly anti-scientistic stance.[11]

Perhaps neither of these features belongs exclusively to phenomenology, certainly not exclusively to the writings of phenomenological philosophers from the European mainland. Nevertheless, we can begin to get something like phenomenology as a distinctive philosophical orientation into view by noting that (and here is a first formulation) *those who have taken 'phenomenology' as the title for their work conceive it as a legitimate heir to the subject that used to be called 'philosophy'*. This first formulation is almost totally empty. It means little more than that phenomenological philosophers regard how they go on *in* philosophy as resolving questions about how (today) one should go on *with* philosophy.

Still, it does introduce a point of first importance about phenomenology in general: namely, that it relates to the method (the 'how') and not to the matter (the 'what') of a philosophical investigation. Near the outset of his major work of phenomenological philosophy, *Being and Time*, Martin Heidegger puts the point as follows: 'The expression "phenomenology" signifies primarily a methodological conception. This expression does not characterize the w h a t of the objects of philosophical research as subject-matter, but rather the *how* of that research'.[12]

It is helpful to get this point out straightaway since in recent English-language philosophy the opposite would more often be thought to be the case. In particular, 'phenomenology' is typically understood as 'the w h a t' that is studied or investigated in the philosophy of mind: it is 'the passing show', 'the flux of experience', 'experience as it is undergone', it is 'the w h a t' that makes it so that there is a '*what it is like*' to subjective experience. While we will see in all the texts explored in this book a distinctive commitment to something like an 'insider standpoint', phenomenology is definitely *not* philosophy which has a special interest in this conception of subjective experience. Indeed, phenomenologists – even the most Cartesian among them – are not, in general, warm to this conception at all. Edmund Husserl stresses that 'in its proper sense' the word 'phenomenon' relates to 'that which appears' and *not* the subjective phenomenon, 'the appearance'.[13] Heidegger is even more insistent: the term phenomenon as it shows up in the title phenomenology has, he states, 'nothing at all to do with what is called an "appearance", still less a "mere appearance"'.[14]

Nevertheless, while it directs us towards matters of method the first formulation remains largely uninformative. I hope the two further formulations proposed in this chapter will flesh out the idea somewhat, but even then I want to leave it somewhat skeletal. That is because I want to try to avoid something that seems always to happen when presentations of 'what phenomenology is' are drawn with more flesh on the bone: namely, a usually unnoticed but always distorting foregrounding of the writings and method of some one or other of the leading phenomenologists.

Such foregrounding is always distorting because it covers over the extent to which the nature of phenomenology is precisely not a finished issue, that the question 'What is phenomenology?' is a question in and for phenomenology. Without even trying to look for a more catholic embrace for the title, the exploration of beginnings conducted in this book will show up some quite dramatic deviations and shifts on this issue.

Now, as one interpreter (who was in the middle of trying to justify the domination of his own description of what phenomenology is by the work of a particular phenomenologist) has noted, most often one finds that in attempts to flesh out the idea of phenomenology 'the name that arises spontaneously' is 'that of Edmund Husserl'.[15] When this is what happens one tends to get a picture of phenomenology as a philosophical method which:

- insists that all consciousness is consciousness *of* something, and is, in that sense, essentially 'intentional' (see Chapter 2);
- involves 'bracketing' the natural attitude (see Chapter 2);
- engages in certain 'reductions' (see Chapter 2).

But running through these ideas does not give a sketch of phenomenology. It gives a sketch of Husserl's phenomenology.

Even if he was not the first to take the name as a title for work in philosophy, nor even the first to arrogate the title for a whole area of inquiry, Husserl was the self-conscious 'inaugurator' of what he hoped would be a communal programme of phenomenological research capable of completing all the tasks which belong to the subject that has hitherto been called 'philosophy'. So Husserl's phenomenology is, indeed, an obvious place to start. On the other hand, the idea of founding a philosophical school or movement is itself a quite specific heading for philosophy in the name of phenomenology, and the shifting inheritances examined in this book are, each in their own way, deviations from the direction marked out by Husserl. Furthermore, while Husserl may have wanted his work to launch phenomenology as a philosophical movement, he himself inherited the title from his inspirational mentor Franz Brentano. In Chapter 2 I will begin with Brentano, not Husserl.

Still, it is not surprising that Husserl's name usually arises 'spontaneously' first. Indeed, after Husserl, the spontaneity with which his name arises in the context of this question is profoundly predictable. But then how much more surprising it is that in Heidegger's lengthy discussion of phenomenology in the section of the introduction to *Being and Time* devoted to questions of method Husserl is hardly mentioned at all, spontaneously or otherwise. Just once in fact. And as for discussion of intentionality, bracketing and reductions (another way in which the name of Husserl might be said 'spontaneously' to arise) ... *not a word*.[16] There are one or two sideways glances at Husserl, such as a repetition of Husserl's rallying maxim that we can repossess what philosophy in our time has lost by redirecting ourselves back 'to the "things themselves"',[17] but in articulating his conception of this methodological direction Heidegger reaches back before Husserl, to Greek etymological sources. And the single mention of Husserl by name, while not in the least disrespectful to him, must, with regard to Husserl's theoretical and methodological contribution, count as one of the most backhanded compliments in the history of philosophical acknowledgements:

> The following investigation would not have been possible if the ground had not been prepared by Edmund Husserl, with whose *Logical Investigations* phenomenology first emerged. Our comments on the preliminary conception of phenomenology [which, let me stress again, reached back before Husserl, SG] have shown [since they had no need to make recourse to Husserl *at all*, SG] that what is essential in it does

not lie in its *actuality* as a philosophical 'movement' [does not, that is, lie in Husserl's work *at all* – the only actual phenomenology Heidegger is here acknowledging, SG]. Higher than actuality stands *possibility*. We can understand phenomenology only by seizing upon it as a possibility [and hence only if we do not let Husserl's name 'spontaneously' arise *at all* – except, in Heidegger's own case, where (as his attached footnote indicates) personal respect is due to the 'incisive guidance' of the man who first introduced him to 'the most diverse areas of phenomenological research' (p. 489), SG].[18]

Perhaps this is rather less disrespectful of Husserl's contribution than I am making out. For Husserl himself would emphasise a certain priority of possibility over actuality,[19] and he (Husserl) also takes his lead from the original Greek word 'Φαινόμενον' when he identifies the 'proper sense' of the word 'phenomenon'.[20] But Heidegger's acknowledgement remains dismissive. Husserl will insist, for example, that 'phenomenological research is *inseparable* from undeviating observance of the [phenomenological] reduction'.[21] Husserl's idea here (again, see Chapter 2 for details) is that what characterises the properly phenomenological approach is that the reflective philosopher should begin by completely stepping back from ('suspending' or 'bracketing') his or her ordinary convictions and assumptions regarding the transcendent being of the world as it is given in experience, suspend all assumptions regarding the existence-status of that which appears. So, for Husserl, no phenomenologist worthy of the name can accept a phenomenon that is ordinarily given as, say, 'actual' *as* actually actual, but must regard that mode of givenness as itself a phenomenon, in this case an 'actuality-phenomenon'.[22] Now, while Heidegger (not wholly unlike Husserl) will identify a main source of philosophical confusion in a tendency on our part to interpret the kind of actuality that belongs to our own existence in terms of the kind of actuality that belongs to the kind of objects in the world that unproblematically figure in many of our ordinary convictions and assumptions, he totally rejects the idea that our own 'being-actual' can be understood in terms of a 'subject' capable of such an actuality-bracketing performance. The 'how' of method and the 'what' of its matter are so closely entangled at this point that it is impossible to say whether this is, primarily, a methodological or a material interruption of the Husserlian elaboration of phenomenology. In any case, what Heidegger finds is, in my view, a way of going on *within* the inheritance of phenomenology that can do *without* the supposedly inseparable Husserlian requirement of a phenomenological reduction.[23]

So in order to avoid the trap of presenting phenomenological philosophy in terms which are, in fact, only the terms of so-and-so's phenomenology, the presentation of it has to be kept at a rather high level of generality. As I say, however, it should still put some flesh on the bones, and even the first formulation indicates that phenomenology is, primarily, a way of pursuing philosophy, a methodological conception, and not some exotic phenomenon to be investigated. Phenomenology is thus a title to be taken by philosophical research that intends to explore questions or approach philosophical problems *phenomenologically* – whatever that means.

In what follows I want to do what I can to clarify what this means. In order that it can be compatible with writings which genuinely conflict with each other, and indeed do so over the question of what it is to pursue philosophy phenomenologically, the characterisations will have to fit more than one kind of procedural, thematic and lexical garb. This approach will also allow us to see the fittingness of conceiving phenomenology at large as embracing thinkers working beyond the European mainland, and that is important for me too.

The rest of this chapter has two parts. In Part I I introduce the *outlook* of phenomenological philosophy; in Part II I identify a number of *theses* that summarily characterise phenomenological inquiries as such.

Part I: Outlook

Inheriting philosophy

Taking up some ideas already touched on, my aim in this part is to clarify and develop Dermot Moran's intriguing but largely unexplored suggestion that 'phenomenology as a way of doing philosophy' is marked by its having 'a thoroughly modernist outlook'.[24]

The idea that phenomenological philosophy has a modernist outlook applies a complex and quasi-literary sense of 'modernism' to philosophical texts. At its most basic level it expresses the idea that philosophers who have taken the title of phenomenology for their own work have found themselves, in quite radical ways, in conflict with philosophy as they found it, and yet have attempted, nevertheless, themselves to pursue philosophy. I will come back to this in a moment, but it is worth heading off a somewhat confusing aspect of Moran's suggestion that arises from the fact that the intellectual and philosophical milieu *against* which phenomenologists are reacting is usually called, and is so called by Moran too, the culture of Western 'modernity', by which he means the scientific culture of 'the modern technological world'.[25] Thus Moran's basic (but terminologically confusing) idea is that the modernist outlook of the phenomenologists is profoundly anti-modernist. This is not intended as some flashy paradox. For the idea is not that phenomenologists have a modernist outlook on their own modernist outlook. Rather, the point is that the kind of conflict with and opposition to the contemporary technical-scientific culture found in phenomenological writings has a broad connection with the kind of outlook that one finds in literary modernism. To facilitate the discussion and elaboration of this thought I will, in what follows, distinguish between the 'modernist outlook' of phenomenology with superscript[1] (modernist[1]) and the 'modernity' of contemporary Western scientific-technical culture with superscript[2] (modernist[2]).

In my view, discomfort with the implications for human life of the modern[2] age, and a serious dissatisfaction with the thought that science and scientific method offer the primary, if not sole, route to truth on all matters for thinking, does indeed run throughout phenomenological philosophy in general. It is a kind of philosophy which is everywhere (though in various ways) sensitive to the concern that, in our time, human beings have become somehow lost to themselves: in an age in which 'science is our passion'[26] we have become distanced from the understanding of ourselves and the world which is, in some way, genuinely closest to us. As Moran puts it, the modernist[1] outlook of phenomenology is inseparable from its attempt to develop a 'critique of the effect of the [modern[2]] natural scientific outlook on human being in the world'.[27]

For the phenomenological philosopher the dominance of the culture of scientific modernity[2] raises sharply the question of how one can, in our time, *begin* in philosophy, how one can inherit the tradition of writing and thinking that goes by the name 'philosophy'. This problem, which is essentially one of trying to find (distinctively) philosophical feet in the modern[2] world, is not further explored by Moran, but I think this idea – the idea that the modern[2] world presents philosophical thinking with a modernist[1] predicament concerning how even to begin – is well worth looking at more closely. For, in the concern rigorously to pursue a form of reflective, theoretical activity that could legitimately inherit the subject that was called 'philosophy', but which would be, as Heidegger puts it, *'neither metaphysics nor science'*,[28] I think phenomenological philosophy is responsive to its cultural situation in a way which connects closely to what has been called writing in a modernist[1] condition. As we shall see, the basic issue here is that the right way even to begin in philosophy is not something that one can simply take over from the dominant culture or spirit of the modern[2] world.

Modernism in philosophy

Stephen Mulhall's introductory discussion of the idea of modernism[1] in philosophy, situated at the start of his book *Inheritance and Originality* is, I think, a good place to begin.[29] In that discussion (a discussion which is constantly alive to itself as an example of writing in the modernist[1] mode) Mulhall's first words (words which ape Wittgenstein's first words in the *Philosophical Investigations*) initiate a response to the response to the first words of Stanley Cavell's (Wittgenstein-inspired) book *The Claim of Reason* from a *Times Literary Supplement* review of Cavell's book by (the acclaimed Wittgenstein scholar) Anthony Kenny.

Cavell's first words raise expressly the question or problem of finding an 'approach' to and making a start in reading Wittgenstein's *Philosophical Investigations*, a question that Cavell takes to be inseparable from finding a way of coming to terms with 'the way this work is written'.[30] The first words from Kenny that Mulhall's first words respond to express the profound *exasperation* that he (Kenny) experienced reading Cavell's first words. Mulhall takes this exasperation to be a characteristic expression of someone 'in the grip of a picture' of what it is for philosophical writing 'to be well shaped and disciplined'.[31] And, since one's way of writing philosophy cannot be independent of what one understands philosophy to be, it expresses a concern that Cavell does not (even) begin properly, does not pursue the writing of philosophy sufficiently philosophically. Thus Kenny writes as if he knows what (well-shaped and disciplined) philosophical writing should look like, and he seems blind to the thought that it is precisely the appropriateness of that form of expression which has become a problem for the text he is reading. Indeed, he seems blind to the thought that he is responding to writing which, quite precisely, regards 'the proper place and manner of its own commencement as a genuine question'.[32]

For Mulhall, then, the crucial mark of the modernist[1] condition in philosophy is that the question of the beginning, of how even to begin in philosophy, has itself become a philosophical problem. While it manifests itself as a condition of writing, it would, Mulhall insists, be quite wrong to conceive the modern[1] in terms of 'literary style'. Mulhall describes it, rather, as a condition in which

> neither writer nor reader possess[es] a common fund of agreed conventions which they might call upon or recall to control their sense of what a philosophical problem is, what might count as its solution, what resources might be used to discover those solutions, and what might count as a mistaken resolution; and the absence of such familiar landmarks or reference points puts the direction of any exercise of philosophical thinking, and so the task of predicting or recalling its progress, in the absence of a permanent record of it, essentially beyond us. In these conditions philosophical teaching must be written, and written in the face of the thought that the entire enterprise of creative thinking has become problematic, that thinkers in the present circumstances of human culture lack any grasp of what they want of thinking, let alone how to achieve it.[33]

Mulhall is writing immediately about the predicament facing the thinkers Cavell and Wittgenstein (and will progress, unpredictably enough, to the cases of Heidegger and Kierkegaard), and, moreover, he is writing as a reader for whom the problem of how even to begin responding to their writing is internal to his own undertaking too. As his own unpredictable progress suggests, what Mulhall says here about writing philosophy in the condition in which even beginning writing philosophy has itself become a philosophical problem is not intended to hold only for this more or less small corner of the contemporary inheritance of philosophy. Indeed, the heart of Moran's idea as I want to read it is that it pervades phenomenology at large.

While I think the idea of a modernist[1] predicament or condition is internal to the inheritance of philosophy as phenomenology, I am not sure that Mulhall's description of it is entirely satisfactory as it stands. In the quoted passage Mulhall depicts 'the present circumstances of human culture' as one where 'thinkers' 'lack *any* grasp of what they want of thinking', and he continues by insisting that the situation of modernist[1] writing in philosophy is one in which 'there are *no* given philosophical conventions', so that 'the present philosophical task is continuously to improvise them, and to do so through the writing of texts that offer statements *so personal* as to permit communication without convention, or the origination of new conventions'.[34]

This way of looking at the modernist[1] condition seems to me problematic not because it conceives statements that are made from out of it too personally but because it conceives them, as it were, too theologically: the condition is one which seems to call for heroically creative acts *ex nihilo*. Nevertheless there is, I think, an important and rather more general truth in the picture of radical isolation presented in Mulhall's description. It is that even for those 'thinkers' of today who, like Kenny for example, find that 'the resources of philosophical writing typically available' to them 'present themselves so strongly as the responsible way of going on',[35] the condition of inheritance in philosophy involves, for everyone and for each equally, an irrecusable responsibility. Being-an-heir to the subject that has been called 'philosophy' can never be reduced to the passive reception of something simply available (a given which presents itself strongly), and even those who endorse the currently dominant 'resources' do not do so, cannot do so, in utter ignorance of the fact that philosophy does not have one legitimate heir only. In question, then, is not the passive acquisition of a forceful fragment of what is available, but relatively confident acts of endorsement, what one might call the 'countersigning' of a particular way of going on. And the moment of such a countersignature is, I am suggesting, essentially a moment in which (even if one has numbers on one's side) one is on one's own.[36] I will come back to what phenomenological philosophy will tend to regard as 'the most convincing expression of a philosopher's claim on people's attention' in the final section of this chapter.[37]

The way this idea of a universal but not universally experienced modernist[1] condition of philosophical writing relates to the specific case of phenomenology can be further clarified by picking up Moran's implicit suggestion that the modernism[1] of phenomenology goes hand in hand with its attempt to provide 'a profound critique of naturalism as a philosophical programme'.[38]

For present purposes we can accept the idea that contemporary naturalism has two basic tendencies:

> Contemporary naturalists embrace either weak or strong scientism. According to the former, non-scientific fields are not worthless nor do they offer no intellectual results, but they are vastly inferior to science in their epistemic standing and do not merit full credence. According

to the latter, unqualified cognitive value resides in science and in nothing else.[39]

Clearly, contemporary naturalism in philosophy (especially in its strongly scientistic form) is that inheritance of philosophy that is most closely affiliated with contemporary modernity[2]. It is also contemporary naturalism – and its attendant understandings of the proprieties of well-disciplined philosophical writing – that finds least to admire in writings of phenomenology, European or otherwise.

The authors of the texts I will be exploring in this book are united in thinking that modern naturalism involves a kind of unnoticed false start for philosophy. Alive to the modernist[1] condition – alive, that is, to a self-responsibility which insists that the right way even to begin in philosophy cannot be supplied as a given inheritance from the modern[2] world – these writers sacrifice the perceived security which would accrue from engaging with and using 'the intellectual achievements of the sciences of a natural sort', and all affirm that 'philosophy lies in a radically different dimension than science'.[40]

At this point we can perhaps anticipate that (and here is a second formulation) *what distinguishes phenomenological philosophers is that, writing in an age dominated by the methods and achievements of sciences of a natural sort, they take themselves to have found some kind of 'solution' to the modernist[1] predicament by resolving to inherit philosophy as phenomenology.*

As I have already indicated, a thoroughly modernist[1] outlook is not the preserve of those authors who have taken the title of phenomenology for their work. I want now to specify more precisely what it means to inherit philosophy as phenomenology.

Part II: Theses

In this part I propose five theses that seem to me to articulate the (appropriately) general methodological conception of phenomenological philosophy. Discussion of the fifth will involve an extended assessment of what a phenomenological philosopher will regard as offering a '*convincing expression* of a philosopher's claim on people's attention'[41] and tackle the thorny question of whether it gives sufficient attention to the need for and value of a certain kind of argument in philosophy.

Thesis one: No 'theses in philosophy'[42]

The last section concluded with the thought that the kind of theoretical (in the sense of self-consciously reflective) activity that characterises phenomenology invariably aims to eschew the kind of constructive theoretical work one finds in the natural sciences, work of a sort which endeavours to develop a theory that explains how some phenomenon comes about or is as it is. Such constructive theorising is centrally characterised by the effort to *advance a thesis*. Making use of recognised research methods and often building on the work of others, one seeks to develop a convincing rationale for a particular position on some topic (something which might then be further explored, debated and tested), a position which could be made public as the 'outcome' or 'output' or 'result' of one's research activity.

Phenomenological research, even where it aims to be programmatic, is never like this. While phenomenological philosophers certainly look towards the production of a work of words intended to be made public – a text prepared with others in mind – they do not set out to develop a 'thesis' on some topic or to present a stand-alone 'result' at all (even one at a higher level of abstraction and generality than those normally found in the natural sciences). Phenomenological research does not have in view the defence of a 'position' in the sense of something which could be carried away with one *independently of the work of words in which such summary fragments might be formulated.* What you will *not* get from writings in phenomenology is a thesis that could be extracted and presented in a student textbook as a specific phenomenological 'thesis' on some question or problem. Or, rather, as Heidegger stresses, it belongs to philosophy that is pursued phenomenologically, that is alive to the threat that phenomenological investigations too 'may degenerate' into the kind of thesis-advancing constructive philosophy it opposes: its own theoretical work can itself get passed around as a 'standpoint' or 'direction', in this way 'losing its indigenous character, and becoming a free-floating thesis'.[43]

Heidegger represents the phenomenological standpoint on this matter (rather unfairly perhaps) like this:

> [Phenomenology] is opposed to all free-floating constructions and accidental findings; it is opposed to taking over any conceptions which only seem to have been demonstrated; it is opposed to those pseudo-questions which parade themselves as 'problems', often for generations at a time.[44]

One can hardly imagine anyone seriously affirming the opposite. Indeed, Heidegger continues, 'Why should anything so self-evident be taken up explicitly in giving a title to a branch of research?' And, anyway, isn't Heidegger presenting us here with something that (if it wasn't so undistinguishing) amounts to being a self-subverting thesis about supposedly thesis-free phenomenological research?

While it is hard not to regard this comment as a kind of metaphilosophical thesis, it is, I think, best thought of as a remark of the sort that J.L. Austin called (superbly) 'cackle'.[45] What it does is to give a pithy and representative fragment of the terms of criticism that will belong to the indigenous soil of the

15

phenomenologist's inquiry; it indicates what he or she will especially have his or her eye on in the philosophical writings of others.

With an eye to what I am doing in this chapter, and perhaps especially in my attempt to specify five phenomenological 'theses', one may well wonder if this whole effort of coming to terms with 'what phenomenology is' isn't itself a 'degenerate' enterprise. Aren't my five 'theses' a methodologically self-subverting distortion? Would it help to call them, instead, 'cackle' or 'maxims'?[46] What is achieved by their elaboration? My answer is that what I say aims to provide something akin to the underlining that can orient an ongoing reading: they are (by my lights) faithful résumés that make salient noteworthy aspects of the (various) ways that phenomenological philosophers go about their business.[47] But I accept that those ways are not equally or in every respect faithfully observed in the way I give summary expression to them.[48]

Thesis two: 'Description, not explanation or analysis'[49]

Foregoing theses does not mean that phenomenology cannot make use of theoretical distinctions or create its own terms or concepts. However, in phenomenology what such conceptual innovation aims at is not a work of theoretical explanation but, essentially, an effort or activity of *elucidation*: the bringing to concepts of something we (in some way) already know, rather than the attainment of or claim to new knowledge of some phenomenon. And if new concepts and distinctions are introduced in the course of such work their significance is inseparable from the purpose of the elucidations they subserve; they are tools for the achievement not of a new theory but of lucidity, of '*clarity*'.[50] What the phenomenologist aims at, then, is not a theory of this or that phenomenon – a theory which would be characterised by its distinctive positions and extractable theses – but an effort to come reflectively to terms with something that is, in some way, already 'evident'. It is in this sense a work of explication, elucidation, explicitation or description of something we, in some way, already understand, or with which we are already, in some way, familiar, but which, for some reason, we cannot get into clear focus for ourselves without more ado. As Husserl puts it:

> Phenomenological explication is nothing like 'metaphysical construction'; and it is neither overtly nor covertly a theorizing with adopted presuppositions or helpful thoughts drawn from the historical metaphysical tradition. It stands in sharpest contrast to all that . . . . Phenomenological explication does nothing but *explicate the sense this world has for us all, prior to any philosophising . . . a sense which philosophy can uncover but never alter.*[51]

In other words (Heidegger's words), 'the expression "descriptive phenomenology" . . . is at bottom tautological'.[52]

Thesis three: 'Re-look at the world without blinkers'[53]

I mentioned that Heidegger's 'cackle' offers a representative fragment of the terms of criticism that belongs to his phenomenology. What phenomenologists will criticise most continuously in contemporary ordinary philosophy are features that they regard as inherited theoretical prejudices, descriptive distortions and inadequacies, everything that prevents us from 'seeing' what (by the phenomenologist's lights) is there to be 'seen'. What is needed is a reflective re-visioning which frees us for 'what stands before our eyes'.[54]

Against the theoretical staples of ordinary philosophical explanations and accounts, phenomenological philosophers have consistently demanded that we 're-look at the world without blinkers' and 're-achieve a direct and primitive contact with the world'.[55] The idea here is not that we attempt to disregard the richly contentful ways in which 'that which appears' typically appears (the ways in which the phenomena show themselves) but, on the contrary, that we give theoretically unfettered regard to those ways: for they, unlike the prejudices of ordinary philosophy, actually express what is given as it is given, *as* phenomena.

Thus, for example, all the phenomenologists are united in their total rejection of the 'sensationalist prejudice' in the philosophy of perception: the idea that the primary given of perceptual experience is a meaningless throng of 'sense-data' – tone-data, colour-data, odour-data and so on – which are subsequently endowed with meaning by 'the mind'. It is important, of course, to make room for sensuous immediacy in a faithful phenomenology of perception, but there is nothing faithful about an interpretation that regards bare sense-data as the primary objects of awareness or the basic units of experience. Even the most cursory reflection on what is 'in the first instance' perceived is sufficient to remind us that awareness of colours and sounds belongs to modes of perception that are first and from the start perceptions of phenomena as such: what is given is, for example, the sound of drilling and hammering somewhere outside, the hiss and hum of an old gas boiler, the happy twittering of kid's TV presenters *still* audible from the next room, a passing taxi, and so on. And even if, through 'a very artificial and complicated frame of mind',[56] one manages to attend solely to the sensuous content of what is given, what one is attending to remains, essentially, a discriminable feature and not a detachable layer of that which appears.

Thesis four: No view 'from the sideways perspective'[57]

Not surprisingly, the descriptive phenomenology affirmed by the first three 'theses' meets with extremely strong resistance from contemporary ordinary philosophy. An ordinary philosopher might accept that the phenomena are, like pre-prepared meals, typically taken in stride without more ado. But then the phenomena include, among other things, those that are (given as) funny, fantastic, furry, fat, fit, floppy, flashy, foreign, foolish, fabricated, fateful – just to take some f-words – and whatever other kind of colourful human packaging one can think of. Hence, the phenomena of interest to phenomenology are simply objects and properties '*for us*' or even '*for me*', and – it will be urged – what philosophy has to consider is how such exotic phenomena relate to or are in some way set upon or within the non-human reality which stands at the back of or at the basis of the world of phenomena as given. Indeed, *that* issue, it might be thought, is both what really matters to philosophy and what really does not matter enough to phenomenology.

I have put the point in terms of the inclusion of human significance in the description of the phenomena. But one can motivate the worries of an ordinary philosopher without that in view. One might think only of the possibility of a perception and a hallucination having the same experiential ('phenomenological') content, or, to take an example we will look at again in the next chapter, of the sort of sceptical hypotheses that figure in Descartes' doubts about the existence of the world outside his own mind. These thoughts too can motivate an interest in questions concerning the 'fit' or 'lack of fit' between how things are '*for us*' or '*for me*' and 'how things are *simpliciter*', crucial issues which, again, it seems, phenomenology leaves untouched.

If phenomenology does not touch on these issues (directly), then that is because, without wishing to compromise or slight our existing notions of objectivity, phenomenologists of all stripes are deeply suspicious of the 'world-behind-the-scenes' idea which informs the ordinary philosopher's worry with phenomenology. What is at issue with this idea is a reality which would be as it is whether or not humans – or any living things – were around to catch a glimpse of it but which is not simply given (or not normally simply given) 'in person' in such glimpses. What is given 'in person' is normally given dressed up in terms of an alphabet of descriptive properties that obscure the naked truth. The objectivity required of philosophical investigations is, on this view, achieved only by *starting* with a thoroughly *dehumanised* representation of the phenomenon. This standpoint, so the ordinary philosopher's thought goes, is one that 'we philosophers' need to occupy if we are properly to assess the credentials of our unreflective thought and talk about the world. For, as human beings unselfconsciously inhabiting the world 'as it is given to us', we tend not to realise that much – perhaps all – that we might normally regard as unexceptional and even objective answers to questions about 'how things are' may, in fact, have *nothing* in reality to back it up at all (this is easy to appreciate – it will be said – if one considers what we say in moral and aesthetic judgements). Indeed, when it comes down to it, it seems that in philosophy phenomenology is *exactly* what we don't want: what we want is to ask 'what in reality there is to *justify* the answers we give when we are unselfconsciously inside the ordinary practice'?[58] It might be thought that the right answer in many, perhaps all, cases is, precisely, 'nothing' – in which case (it might be thought) we had better 'pull in our horns' about objectivity[59] and provide an idealist or some other kind of anti-realist explanation of our unselfconscious 'insider' answers in many domains. In any case, whether an ordinary philosopher winds up as an anti-realist about some region of our thinking or not, the proper job of philosophy is to develop explanatory accounts of our judgements in these regions, and to do so only in terms 'that already belong to a natural-scientific depiction of nature'.[60] On this view, in eschewing such naturalistic explanatory accounts phenomenology has not so much inherited philosophy as, in a modern[2] age, abandoned it.

What this objection fails to realise is that phenomenology is not a form of philosophy which denies that the attempt to take an external or 'dehumanised' position on the phenomena – and so to see them 'from the sideways perspective' – is humanly possible, as if it urges us to give up trying to do something we are insufficiently powerful or insufficiently clever to achieve. Phenomenology does not have an insight into human finitude which shows that sideways-on standpoints are beyond us and unavailable. (A totally contradictory idea!) On the contrary, as I will explain in greater detail in Chapter 2, the beating heart of phenomenology as a living philosophy – indeed, in my view a lastingly brilliant legacy of phenomenology – lies in the attempt consistently to rid us of the idea that a view of the phenomena from sideways on makes *sense*. That is, the ordinary philosopher's idea of getting sideways on *is* to be abandoned, *not because it is hopeless but because it is nonsense*. We cannot get to that external position on the phenomena *not* because we ain't up to getting to it but because there ain't no 'it' to get to here. Or, better: *there is no sense to be made of 'taking up a standpoint on the phenomena' that is not also some –* perhaps radically and dislocatingly new – *way of inhabiting the standpoint one occupies 'when we are unselfconsciously inside the ordinary practice'*.[61]

The 'thesis' that there is no sideways on perspective can seem to draw the phenomenologist into a troubling proximity to the phenomenalist. Phenomenalism is the view in ordinary philosophy that physical objects and physical properties are 'constructions', perhaps 'logical constructions', out of immediately given 'sense-data'. On this view, what we call experiences of the 'external' world are, one and all, reducible to statements about actual and possible perceptual sensory appearances. How things *are* is reducible to how things sensibly *seem* and could possibly seem – so phenomenalism also opposes the 'world behind the scenes' idea. Is phenomenology a form of phenomenalism? In my view, phenomenalist idealism is not a form of phenomenology so much as its standing *threat*. A thoroughgoing phenomenologist would not want to *deny* that there is, for each of us, 'a reality completely independent of the mind which conceives it, sees or feels it',[62] for the phenomenologist should not *slight* or *diminish* the *sense* of objectivity that we pre-reflectively affirm. Phenomenology should give a (faithful) explication and not a (reductive) explanation of that sense.

In fact, it is not only the empirical idealism of phenomenalism that is resisted by the phenomenologist's response to ordinary philosophy; so too is the form of transcendental idealism developed by Kant. Kant tried to retain the sense of objectivity that belongs to our 'insider' understanding of the world by affirming an analysis which claimed that the structures of objectivity of all empirical objects (all objects of experience) are constituted by *a priori* structures of rational subjectivity: so what we normally understand as 'objective reality' *just is* 'reality as it is *for us*'. However, Kant's analysis of the conditions of possibility of objective experience left him with the problematic contrasting notion of 'reality as it is *in itself*' independently of the subjective conditions under which we can have any objective experience (knowledge) of it. And not only is that reality something about which we can (by definition) *know* nothing, but it is hard not to regard it (whatever 'it' is) as answering to what we would want from a satisfactory explication of our sense of objectivity: for that is precisely a matter of *how things are anyway*. Kantian transcendental analysis, then, seems to give the world for us only an *ersatz* objectivity, a sense of objectivity where we 'pull in our horns', not the reality we thought we – at least sometimes – had available for us or might, for example through natural science, come to know.

How, or indeed whether, phenomenology has, in Sartre's words, 'realized considerable progress' over other kinds of philosophy,[63] perhaps especially phenomenalist and Kantian idealist philosophy, is something that will be taken up as we go along. Suffice to say for the moment that, on its own terms, phenomenological philosophy only succeeds when we are not left yearning for the ordinary philosopher's sideways-on perspective. One might well wonder how that can be achieved. This is the topic to be explored next.

Thesis five: 'We must go back to the "things themselves"'[64]

Where's the beef?

Philosophy (in general) has a constitutive relation to the distinction between legitimate and illegitimate forms of persuasion; between, say, being *reasonably convinced* (the aim of philosophy proper) and being *merely persuaded* (the upshot perhaps of being taken in by sophistry and illusion). Within philosophy today the understanding of this distinction is most often cast in terms of the presence or absence of (at least the attempt to advance) arguments. In the absence of (even the attempt to advance) arguments, what one does cannot be a genuinely '*convincing expression* of a philosopher's claim on people's attention'.[65]

Now, among the complaints one often hears directed against phenomenology is the perceived lack in it of explicit (or, anyhow, clear) arguments. Indeed, I think it is true that the writings of phenomenologists will not be well understood at all if one seeks out in them only arguments, arguments, that is, in the *narrow sense* of a discussion that moves through a series of inferential steps from premises to conclusions. On the other hand, and in another sense, I think that their writings really are *argument all the way down* – for they are all writing with the aim of *convincing* other people. But, yes, it is not only by way of argument in the narrow sense that they proceed. The worry, of course, is that in the absence of sufficient argument in the narrow sense their contribution is of limited philosophical interest. Even if their writings are persuasive, in the absence of sufficient step-by-step argument they cannot be said to offer the chance of bringing *reasonable conviction*. Consequently, many reckon such writings philosophically weak or questionable, or worse.

Socrates is often cited as a model of philosophical objectivity and integrity, famed for his willingness to '*follow the argument where it leads*'.[66] The phenomenological inheritance of philosophy is often thought to have departed from that main line of the dialogue of reason that takes Socrates as its model. On the other hand, however, Socrates is equally famed as the gadfly who *addressed himself to others*, the one who talked philosophically (directly) to (the) people. And, whether one cares to think about it much or not, it is clear that *who one is actually addressing* makes a huge difference to one's prospects of convincing by argument, particularly argument of the narrow sort typically found in ordinary philosophy. As Cora Diamond observes in the following passage, this issue is particularly acute in relation to thinking in moral philosophy, but I will want to develop her observations in relation to writings in phenomenology too:

> When we engage in philosophical discussion about such a subject as abortion, or the moral status of animals, *whom* should we think of ourselves as trying to convince? For if we proceed by giving *arguments*, we presumably do not expect to be able to convince anyone who is incapable of following our arguments, or who is too prejudiced to consider them. And if we are talking about convincing *human beings*, surely it is a fact about many of them that one certain way of *not* convincing them is to try arguing the case ... . No one who urges another philosopher to give arguments thinks of arguments as capable of convincing everybody. When we put forward arguments, or urge someone else to do so, we have a conception of what it would be to succeed in giving genuinely convincing arguments, and also of those who would nevertheless not be convinced, even should they attend to the arguments. Now, argument is simply one way people approach moral questions, and there are other ways of trying to convince someone of one's view of animals or foetuses or slaves or children or whatever it may be.[67]

This is not an argument utterly against narrow argument in moral philosophy. Diamond has no intention of suggesting any impropriety in the thought that developing such arguments is what '*all* [moral philosophers] do some or most of the time'.[68] Indeed, I think there are arguments (in the narrow sense) in *all* the (not-specifically-or-exclusively-moral) phenomenological writings explored in this book. However, what Diamond wants to encourage us to acknowledge is that it is actually quite perverse to think that this is all that moral philosophers can or should do, or that this is the only thing that moral philosophers can or should do which could lead others to be reasonably convinced of something; as if giving an argument in the narrow sense was the only thing which would qualify as a genuinely 'convincing expression of a philosopher's claim on people's attention'.

When he reflects on what many philosophers today would regard as such an expression, Bernard Williams does not find them much concerned that their way of going on in philosophy (including moral philosophy) would not actually convince many of those whose attention it claims. The idea is, rather, that the (science-inspired) plain-speaking argumentative mode is being held up as *exemplary*: this mode is worth shouting about even to others who, in fact, lack the interest or capacity to attend to the rigours of its procedures themselves.[69] With respect to work in moral philosophy Diamond puts the point as follows:

> If we think that philosophers should try to work out moral views with
> *that* kind of systematic generality, it is because we think that *people*
> should aim to order their own moral thought in something like this
> sort of way, even if we do not expect them to work out fully explicit
> systems.[70]

Diamond, however, is not convinced that this way of thinking is genuinely exemplary, for she is not convinced that it correctly identifies 'which human capacities are characteristically exercised in the development of someone's moral life, and more specifically of what it is for someone to exercise his capacities as a thinking being in that development'.[71] Ordinary moral philosophy identifies *ratiocinative capacities* as of first importance in our moral thinking, and thus thinks of argument in the narrow sense as the most (perhaps only) legitimate way of reasonably convincing others. Diamond (and, in fact, Williams himself to some extent) disagrees: to pursue moral thinking this way is massively to underestimate the place of *imaginative capacities* in our moral lives.

On this view, unless we pursue moral philosophy in ways that involve our capacity to 'bring imagination to bear on observation' or to 'recognise that that has been done',[72] the development of arguments will prove 'quite useless'[73] – what we do will have foregone the kind of thinking that can actually *touch us* or *turn us round*. So getting our imaginative capacities in play in moral thinking is not simply of assistance to developing a convincing argument but is the *sine qua non* of bringing about the kind of *lucid seeing* that goes with an alteration in a person's moral view, of bringing a person to see something they had (by their own lights) hitherto failed to see. It should come as no surprise, then, that for Diamond the best model for such an effort is not the argumentation of ordinary moral philosophy but imaginative literature. The sometimes simply astonishingly disciplined use of language that one finds in such writing is not to be regarded as a second-best means of developing one's moral vision or as a problematically questionable way of bringing about the kind of gestalt shift which might transform what Diamond cites Iris Murdoch calling 'the texture' of someone's being.[74] On the contrary, on this view the way imaginative capacities are both deployed (by writers) *and* demanded (of readers) in such works of words make them the gold standard of 'convincing expression' in this area.

It belongs to this conception of moral development that writings in moral philosophy will not be especially concerned with the evaluation of actions, or even the solution of practical problems, but with attempting to find a mode of addressing others in philosophy that can bring about changes akin to those that can be achieved by imaginative literature: changes to someone's 'vision of life' which will show up in *all* someone's 'reactions and conversation' – and not just in their 'ethical statements';[75] for example, making them into more sensitive and more refined readers of what legitimately goes on in philosophy that is not reducible to argument in the narrow sense.

Of course, philosophical writing about moral matters that regards it as properly disciplined only when it occupies itself with narrow argument is just as committed, at least implicitly, to a conception of the proper formation and moral development of human beings. However, if we take seriously Diamond's Murdochian objection to limiting moral matters to one corner of our lives (the part where we defend or contest 'ethical statements') we will not suppose that this, let's say, argumentocentric conception of moral development is something expressed only in relation to thinking in moral philosophy. Indeed, it belongs to this conception of the proper formation and moral development of human beings that it leaves no room for finding in *anything but* (narrow) *argument* a fully satisfactory expression of a philosopher's claim on people's attention anywhere in philosophy. It is a conception which closes one off from embracing other ways of going on in philosophy.[76]

Again, challenging the argumentocentric conception is not an invitation to abandon narrow argument. But I think that the idea that something that is judged to be convincing must, if one is to be reasonably convinced by it, be capable of being presented in the form of a narrow argument does need to be challenged. We need to learn better to resist the idea that meagreness of narrow argument in a work of (not-specifically-or-exclusively-moral) philosophy is incompatible with its striving to achieve the most philosophically convincing expression one could wish for. In my view, writings in phenomenology both are part of that resistance movement and provide a major motivation for it. For in writings of phenomenology the achievement of clarity is not conceived as the upshot of becoming convinced by an argument for an unambiguous statement or thesis but a matter of having come reflectively to terms with something pre-reflectively 'before one's eyes'. It is not at all obvious that this transformation of oneself with respect to matters for thinking in philosophy can be brought about by way of narrow argument alone. In the next section I want to take up this thought a little further by looking at the supposedly problematic 'quietism' of phenomenology.

Quietism

On Karl Marx's gravestone in London's Highgate Cemetery one can read two famous slogans. The first is the communist battle cry 'Workers of all lands unite.' The second is Marx's eleventh thesis on Feuerbach: 'The philosophers have only interpreted the world in various ways; the point is to change it.' This thesis has, of course, been the subject of all sorts of philosophical interpretations. Does it mean that Marx had no serious interest in philosophy? Does it mean that philosophers do what philosophers should do when they interpret the world, but that something more is also required of us? Or does it mean that philosophical problems are only really solved or resolved by changing the world? Whatever is made of it, however, for my purposes the precise content of the claim is not as important as its profoundly *activist* accent. For Marxists it is imperative that one gets actively involved in the 'class struggle', that one engages in *a certain kind of resistance* to the injustices of social inequality, exploitation, oppression and so on. Those who fail so to do are charged with *quietism*. In the face of a call to take strike action over pay, for example, the worker (or, better, the worker's official representative) who says, 'Why jeopardise the company's future? Five percent is better than nothing' will be admonished as a pessimist and a quietist, someone whose willingness to make concessions to the bosses and the social status quo should not be accepted without more ado.

Phenomenology has often felt the heat of Marxist critics, and accusations of *political* quietism have been made against nearly all of the thinkers included in this book, though it seems to me (despite the simply dreadful politics of some [most?] of them) always unfairly.[77] Still, there does seem to be considerable justice in accusations of *philosophical* quietism. Indeed, it is hard not to hear an ironic echo of Marx's eleventh thesis in Husserl's claim that phenomenological explication 'never alters ... the world', and also in Wittgenstein's (I think utterly phenomenological) suggestion that philosophy 'advances no theses' and 'leaves everything as it is';[78] an echo of Marx re-echoed in the title of Crispin Wright's paper 'Comrades against Quietism', in which Wittgenstein is taken to task for not doing nearly enough of the kind of thing that needs doing. Philosophers, as much as workers of all lands, are, it seems, liable to lapse into quietism.

Or at least that is how it looks as long as one is convinced that *something of a quite specific sort* needs to be done. For, of course, quietism is a rebuke, a complaint: it is something one might (perhaps even by one's own lights) lapse into but not something one is likely (activistically, as it were) to go in for and endorse. And the charge of quietism is made from a standpoint which may itself be questionable. Indeed, just as one might think, for example, that the Marxist charge of quietism, while connected to concerns with justice that are '*still absolutely indispensable*', is nevertheless made from a standpoint of a political economy and class struggle that '*belongs to another time*',[79] so also one might think, for example, that the philosophical charge of quietism, while connected to concerns with clarity that are '*the fixed point of our real need*',[80] nevertheless belongs to a standpoint of ordinary philosophy that seeks explanations for which we really '*have no use*'.[81] And the thesis in phenomenology that I am working towards (the 'maxim' that calls us back 'to "things themselves"') does not express a (snooty) quietist disdain for the hard labours of theory-construction, but expresses a full-throated (revolutionary) conviction that going in for these things is never going to lead us even towards the clarity that philosophy has always strived for. This contrast can be sharpened by looking at the contrasting responses to the absence of certain arguments in Wittgenstein's later philosophy by Crispin Wright and John McDowell.

Although himself influenced by Wittgenstein, Wright is suspicious of what he perceives as Wittgenstein's fundamentally underdefended (and maybe indefensible) hostility to the possibility of 'significant metaphysical debate'.[82] Unimpressed by Wittgenstein's refusal properly to develop his own theoretical insights, Wright persists where Wittgenstein stops, and attempts to forge out of scattered suggestions in Wittgenstein's work a substantive anti-realist alternative to the realist position he sees Wittgenstein so roundly and profoundly criticise. For Wright, then, Wittgenstein's quietism – his refusal to develop a properly worked out anti-realist alternative himself – is an annoyance that needs to be resisted and remedied.[83] Wittgenstein has brilliantly undermined the realist approach to meaning but winds up leaving us in the theoretical lurch, wondering how, then, meaning is possible after all. As John McDowell puts it, 'Wittgenstein's "quietism" looks like an embarrassing failure to acknowledge the character of his own philosophical achievement.'[84]

For McDowell, by contrast, Wright's conviction that Wittgenstein's battle with the realist 'points up a good question about how meaning is possible' is interpreted as a reflection of his (Wright's) having taken up – with the realist he officially opposes – 'the standpoint of a world-view that is inhospitable to meaning'.[85] The standpoint here is not the one we occupy 'when we are unselfconsciously inside the ordinary practice', a standpoint in which signs, words and sentences are first and from the start encountered as 'alive' with meaning, but rather that of a detached, scientific onlooker, a standpoint in which such signs are regarded as ('in themselves') normatively inert or 'dead'. And what McDowell is encouraging us to see is that the inhospitable standpoint that sustains the appearance of a 'good question' about how meaning is possible is not something that can be made more homely by supplying 'a philosophical construction in which we pull in our horns, about objectivity or whatever'.[86] On the contrary (and this is a perfect example-in-action of the orientation in philosophy marked by the fourth thesis on p. 19), the mistake is to think that one can make *sense* of investigating the phenomena of language and meaning from such a standpoint *at all*: for it is simply an illusion that – having given up the 'insider perspective' – what one has in view here can even *be* the phenomena of language and meaning.[87]

So what we need is not a way to make ourselves at home in the inhospitable standpoint but a way of getting ourselves (now self-consciously, as it were) out of such an 'uncongenial environment'[88] – a way of getting *back in philosophy* to the native land of an understanding that is not dominated by modern[2] prejudices about, for example, the primary data for a theory of meaning or perception or whatever. In philosophy, for McDowell, we do not need to 'answer' but to 'exorcise' the idea that we need to *explain how it can be* that something that is supposedly 'in itself' nothing more than a noise or a mark means something.[89]

Of course, *bringing it about that others see too that we do not need such explanations* in philosophy is also part of the philosopher's task. What, in this case, will be 'the most convincing expression' one could wish for? Can the kind of lucid 'seeing' that is required to release us from the felt need for explanations be achieved only or even primarily by means of narrow arguments alone? One lesson of the modernist[1] condition may be that the intellectual motivations of modernity[2] one must combat here run too deep for that. Or, better: these motivations are *not* simply intellectual but belong to the distinctive elaboration of 'the life of human beings living in communities with a history'[90] that weaves the fabric of modern[2] times. Hence, just as it is not clear that, when our moral convictions are at issue, narrow argument can be anything but 'in a sense quite useless', so also it is not clear that narrow argument alone can hope to answer to what will provide the *in its way* (judged to be) convincing appeal to our attention sought by writings of phenomenology. Narrow argument cannot be the exclusive mode of that inheritance of philosophy which aims to bring us back to an understanding of ourselves and the world denied to us by ordinary philosophy's inhospitable modern naturalistic standpoints.

How the phenomenological texts explored in this book attempt to loosen the grip of modernity[2] on our thinking in philosophy (that is to say, how each attempts to replace explanation and analysis with description without leaving us yearning for something more – or, again, how each attempts to pursue philosophy as 'neither metaphysics nor science' – how, then, each attempts to pursue philosophy as phenomenology) resides in the particular and sometimes strikingly novel ways they put words to work in their work.[91] And we should not expect that a talent for writing phenomenological philosophy will belong to everyone equally or that all who do attempt to pursue it will respond to questions concerning 'the proper place and manner of its own commencement' in the same way or a (judged to be) especially convincing way.[92] Nevertheless, it seems to me that something Husserl articulated as a shorthand for his not very maxim-like 'principle of principles' of phenomenology[93] struck a chord with many thinkers who felt out of tune with the dominant scientific spirit of our time: namely, his 'thesis' that going *on* in philosophy requires that one 'go *back* to "things themselves"'.[94]

In 1900 this shift *back* was essentially a shift *against* the then-dominant school of philosophy in Germany, whose slogan was 'Back to Kant'.[95] What Husserl had in mind with his alternative rallying call was not a kind of thinking which would concern itself with (obviously very Kantian) things-of-which-we-have-no-experience, but precisely to an awareness of phenomena that can in some way be directly or imaginatively presented to us, presented 'as it were in its bodily reality'. For all the deviations that mark the later inheritance of phenomenology after Husserl, something of his call remains everywhere in the work of those who follow him, especially those whose work would have been 'impossible without him', there in the effort to get rid of distorting pre-suppositions and assumptions not simply by narrow argument – and not by writing a novel or a poem either[96] – but by way of descriptions which offer some other kind of *in their way* (aiming to be) convincing appeal to people's attention, through writing whose distinctive discipline resides in its capacity to bring people *back* to what they already know, to *turn people round* so that they can *see clearly* what (by the phenomenologist's lights) – particularly in modern[2] times – we typically find it *hard to see*.

It is not news that writings in phenomenology typically pose a distinctive problem for readers acquainted only with mainstream philosophy in the English-speaking world: the texts – and not just the ideas – are distinctively demanding. But it should now be clearer why this is so. For *they are works of words whose capacity to work as philosophy is inseparable from their capacity to involve their reader's capacity to acknowledge the matter for thinking itself for themselves.* And, specifically, since what is at issue is essentially an effort at *self-explication*, and hence an inquiry in which one is oneself (called) in(to) question, their work demands the involvement of their readers' capacity to bring their own understanding to bear with respect to the conception of ourselves they are reading about, and also their capacity to recognise that that has been done in its writing. It is a work of words that strives, then, not for new knowledge but *your acknowledgement*. And so you can see that (and here is a third and final formulation) *what characterises an investigation in phenomenology is a work of convincing words which, in an age dominated by science, aims to cultivate and develop your capacity faithfully to retrieve (for) yourself (as from the inside) a radically re-vis(ion)ed understanding of yourself and your place in the world and with others.* In my view, then, those who take the name of phenomenology for their inheritance of philosophy see themselves as engaging with matters for thinking in such a way that, in the face of the grip of modernist[2] modes, others too might be turned around, turned back to 'see' what is right before their eyes.

Is phenomenology the right way to go on with philosophy? There is and can be no radical justification for phenomenology that is not itself phenomenological in character. Merleau-Ponty says: phenomenology 'rests on itself'.[97] Austin says: 'there is gold in them thar hills'.[98] But to affirm this for yourself you have to pass from a concern with the idea of phenomenology to actually reading some. You must, as Austin put it, 'cut the cackle' and move on to indigenous words. Taking the 'beginnings' noted in the Introduction as my cue, I will now turn to examine how phenomenology begins.

2

THE EMERGENCE OF PHENOMENOLOGY

Brentano and Husserl

The dream of phenomenology

It is still matter of course today to regard the history of phenomenology, with Maurice Merleau-Ponty, in terms of the steady emergence of a distinctive philosophical 'doctrine or system';[1] a way of going on in philosophy with a 'unity' sufficient that it 'can be practised and identified as a manner or style of thinking'.[2] While this conception may have taken time to take hold, it did not slowly dawn as a movement gradually took shape and grew. On the contrary, it belongs to the inaugural elaboration of philosophy as phenomenology in the work of Edmund Husserl. Husserl sought to present his work as an outset that would found a movement of just the sort that Merleau-Ponty describes.

I do not think that phenomenology needs to understand either its trajectory or its history in this way. Gilbert Ryle was quite right to insist that it is a mistake to think that 'the whole notion of phenomenology hinges on [Husserl's] theory' of meaningfulness.[3] And I think it is just as mistaken to think that the whole notion of phenomenology hinges on Husserl's (or anyone else's) conception of it as a unified movement or programme of philosophical research. In an implicit interruption of such a unitary conception, one of the first inheritors of the Husserlian legacy, and one of Husserl's own most able students, Martin Heidegger, countered that 'there is no such thing as *the one* phenomenology'.[4] Or, as I would rather put it, faithfulness to a single way of going on is neither the basic historical form of nor the basic philosophical imperative for philosophy written in the name of phenomenology. On the contrary, what is striking and impressive about phenomenology is not its increasingly unified character as a movement but its capacity to *go on* amidst ongoing interruption and deviance.

It is for this reason that I am presenting this book as following a circumscribed line of shifting inheritances and not an introduction to a philosophical movement. However, before stepping back to examine an idea of phenomenology that Husserl himself inherited from the philosophical psychology of Franz Brentano, and to help prepare for an examination of what I will want most of all to save and see saved in Husserl's conception of phenomenology, I want to begin this chapter with a brief excursus on Husserl's dream that his own accomplished deviance could and should found a philosophical movement. I will approach this issue by examining two kinds of 'difficulty' that Husserl saw as standing in the way of progress in philosophy. Difficulties of the first kind are those that demand philosophical work in the first place. Difficulties of the second kind are those that arise when one attempts persuasively to communicate that work to others.

We get a first indication of Husserl's view of philosophy in general when we note that the effort to deal with difficulties of the first kind was typically grasped by him as requiring the laborious '*work*' of overcoming 'ambiguities' in our usual forms of expression.[5] Such disambiguation was for Husserl a basic condition of 'making forward steps' towards 'complete reflective clarity' on 'fundamental questions' and 'great themes', in his view the only issues that really matter in philosophy, the real business of what from early in his career he would call 'philosophy as a rigorous science'.[6]

It is in view of understanding his work as, ideally, 'a rigorous science' that Husserl would conceive himself as the founder of a movement. For it belongs to his understanding of philosophy with this scientific character that it could become what A.D. Smith has called 'a communal enterprise'.[7] It needs to be stressed that the affirmation of this scientific character should not be taken to suggest that Husserl thinks of someone who pursues such phenomenological research as 'a student of nature', as Ryle once claimed.[8] There is, as we shall see in a moment, a certain relationship with what Husserl calls the 'positive sciences', but phenomenology as a rigorous science is not conceived as one kind of empirical investigation (an inquiry into what exists in the world) among others at all. Rather, it concerns a systematic investigation into the *essence* of everything empirical; it strives for complete clarity concerning the fundamental *grounds* of all positive sciences. Thus in claiming to pursue philosophy as 'a rigorous science' Husserl is precisely not 'assimilating' philosophy and science as Ryle thought.[9] Nothing could be further from the truth. Indeed, while Husserl is concerned to elaborate the relationship between a systematic investigation of essences and empirical studies of the world, what matters most for Husserl is holding fast to the essential distinction between the two different levels of inquiry, not levelling their differences.

Of course, Husserl might have avoided misunderstandings had he called his phenomenological research something other than a 'science' in the first place, and one can have sympathy with Ryle when he says, in a somewhat more sober mood, that it is 'an awkward terminological innovation'.[10] Jean-Paul Sartre also regarded it as a 'foolish' misnomer, letting it lie as a quirk of Husserl's 'genius'.[11] However, while it has nothing to do with the assimilation of philosophy and natural science, it is not a mere quirk either. Rather, it is inseparable from Husserl's philosophical commitment to what he calls a distinctively '*Cartesian* idea of science': the idea that positive sciences in various domains need to be 'grounded on an absolute foundation and absolutely justified'.[12] It is this radical grounding that would be supplied by an all-embracing 'rigorous science'. While profoundly connected to them – articulating their unity and providing their 'complete and ultimate grounding'[13] – such a 'science' is thus essentially different from *any* 'science of fact'.[14]

As we shall see in the final section of this chapter, in his mature thought Husserl came to conceive the grounding character of philosophy in robustly idealist terms: the ultimate grounds of all positive sciences in every domain are held to lie in the fundamental structures of rational subjectivity. On this view, the kind of complete clarification of essences sought through phenomenological research is conceived as, at the same time, the absolute self-elucidation of self-conscious rational life, that is to say, as the complete self-explication of the life-structure of 'man' as the distinctively 'rational animal'.

The achievement of complete clarity in this investigation would, for this reason, be a certain kind of end-game in the history of its object. For while (rather traditionally and not unproblematically) Husserl conceives 'man' as 'the rational animal', and so affirms that reason must, in some way, be something that 'functions in every man',[15] 'even the Papuan',[16] he also conceives this 'rational animal' (rather traditionally and not unproblematically) as the locus of the unfolding of 'a teleology of reason' in (as) human history.[17] For Husserl, this development reaches a new stage with the establishment in Ancient Greece of philosophy and science, and culminates, finally, in 'the conversion of philosophy into phenomenology' that is beginning to occur, he supposes, in his own work.[18] On this view, the realisation of phenomenology as a 'rigorous science' is not just the high point of human self-understanding but equally the high point of human historical development. As should be clear, the movement of self-understanding that is involved in this enterprise is not confined to the life of an individual mind, still less, as A.D. Smith stresses, 'to the groves of academe'. On the contrary, 'as a transformation of the human spirit, as the raising of humanity to a higher level of existence, it will resonate through, indeed transform, the culture in which it is genuinely alive'.[19]

Husserl's finding such wide cultural significance in and urgency for the development of a phenomenological movement was, in some respects, a late development in his thinking. However, regarding philosophy as in urgent need of a renewal through which it might finally attain an authentically scientific and communal character was a constant – as was his awareness that his own efforts to set philosophy off in this direction faced 'a further difficulty'. As I have indicated, the 'difficulty' here did not concern his own capacity to attain lucid 'results' in phenomenology (though he was far from confident of having himself provided the final answer to the 'great themes' he worked on) but his capacity convincingly to communicate them. Robert Cumming introduces the nature of Husserl's 'further difficulty' as follows:

'Ponderous,' 'involved,' 'diffuse,' 'opaque' – these are the epithets Edmund Husserl culled from a review of his *Logical Investigations*, [the book which] was to become one of the most propulsive works in twentieth century philosophy .... It ushered in the century; the first volume was published in 1900 and the second in 1901. In the jargon of historians, it 'founded' phenomenology, which eventually came to dominate Continental philosophy longer than any other philosophical movement in the past century .... The epithets were culled by Husserl in an introduction to the second edition (1913) of the *Logical Investigations*. This introduction he did not publish. Husserl had published an introduction to the first volume of the *Logical Investigations* – itself a prolegomena – and an introduction to the second volume. To the foreword for the first edition, he added in 1913 a second foreword for the second edition. In this second foreword he presented the *Logical Investigations* as an attempt to 'introduce the reader to the nature of genuinely phenomenological ... work.'

He also presented *Ideas I* (1913), with the subtitle *A General Introduction to a Pure Phenomenology*, but he was unable to follow it up with *Ideas II*, as he had planned. His next publication was the *Cartesian Meditations: An Introduction to Phenomenology*. These were lectures at the Sorbonne that were published in a French translation (1933), and Husserl eventually gave up his attempt to rework the lectures for publication in German. He began *The Crisis of European Sciences* [in 1934], which was once again called *An Introduction to Phenomenological Philosophy*. He was unable to finish it. I would accordingly take introductions as almost the characteristic genre of Husserl's philosophy. This can be taken in conjunction with ... what he describes as his 'inability to finish' and his remaining a 'miserable beginner.'[20]

In a passage from the *Logical Investigations* in which Husserl explicitly discusses the 'further difficulty' of providing a 'persuasive communication of our resultant insights', his response is already, and very characteristically, strictly impersonal: the difficulty arises from the shift in level implied by the inquiry; it arises, that is, from the fact that the phenomenologist is forced to use expressions that 'only fit familiar natural objects' in an inquiry whose 'thought-stance' is 'the unnatural attitude of reflection'.[21] Nevertheless, and precisely because of his sense of the communal character of 'philosophy as a rigorous science', Husserl never lost his conviction that 'the difficulties standing in the way of a pure phenomenology' could be 'overcome';[22] the situation was, in principle, 'by no means ... hopeless'.[23] As he put it at the turn of the twentieth century, 'resolute co-operation among a generation of research-workers, conscious of their goal and dedicated to the main issue' could succeed in establishing a genuinely '*scientific* philosophy'.[24]

As Husserl's career reached its end his growing sense of failure successfully to 'introduce' phenomenology was painfully compounded by the different, indeed by his lights completely deviant, direction being taken by others, and perhaps especially by Heidegger, his onetime star pupil. Husserl's various launching efforts seemed always to fall on stony ground or ill-suited ground. In the text of the *Crisis* composed at the end of the 1930s, Husserl writes: 'The dream is over.'[25]

Cumming presents these words as an 'announcement',[26] and his suggestion seems to be that Husserl, towards the end of his career, finally and openly admits defeat. That is, with regard to his hope of establishing a phenomenological programme in philosophy that would attain the status of 'a rigorous science' he has tried and tried, but he has, he here admits, failed and the dream of succeeding is now over. However, A.D. Smith reads these words rather differently, and rather more carefully. They are not in Husserl's voice at all but are the words of 'an imaginary objector' whom Husserl wants decisively to reject.[27] Cumming has not got the scene quite right. The 'announcement' expresses a view that Husserl himself, to the end, refuses to accept. On the other hand, the fact that Husserl has an imaginary objector voice, it certainly indicates how far he felt that the philosophical culture of his time was moving against him, and the objector's claim has something in view that Husserl would not for a moment deny: 'a torrent of philosophy which renounces its scientific character'. Husserl was utterly opposed to those who thought philosophy should renounce that character, and was in no way himself willing to give up on the 'dream'. On the contrary, Husserl clearly wants the dream to remain alive and to be realised. However, he knows that he had not himself succeeded in realising it, and he knows too that those who wish to keep the dream alive (Husserl + ?) are swimming against the prevailing 'inundating' torrent. Not only had none of his attempts to launch phenomenology managed to launch what he dreamt of launching, but the cultural current seemed to be moving in just the opposite direction. On this point it seems to me that Cumming's speculation that Husserl's eye may be focused most acutely in these passages of the *Crisis* on Heidegger's rising star *within the inheritance of phenomenology* – the very conception of philosophy which was meant to realise the dream – has a tragic plausibility.[28] The 'way of phenomenology' was taking a course radically different from the one the inaugural launch had planned to set it on. For Husserl, Heidegger was 'a defector' from phenomenology,[29] in a certain way ending it before it had hardly begun.

But, of course, this defection can be spun in terms more favourable to Heidegger too (i.e. in something more like Heidegger's own terms). We might equally think that 'what Husserl has actually accomplished is to be superseded by the new possibility opened up for phenomenology by Heidegger'.[30] Indeed, as I have indicated, I would want to see this succession of accomplished deviance generalised: we need to get rid of the idea that the most significant accomplishments in phenomenology are bound up with their communal faithfulness to a single way of going on. Indeed, in my view continued interest in (and so concern for the future of) phenomenology does not depend on the flourishing of a faithfulness of that kind. Or, again, as I argued in Chapter 1, the inheritance of philosophy in the name of phenomenology can do without what many of its foremost advocates hoped to make out for it: a unified movement or a single programme of philosophical research.

This is not a point of view that Husserl, above all, could be remotely content with. Nevertheless, despite the fact that the inheritance of phenomenology is, as we shall see in this book, positively littered with deviance, there are aspects of Husserl's thought which seem to me to return again and again, returning, indeed, even in conceptions of phenomenology, like Heidegger's, that have also wanted to distance themselves most decisively from Husserl's. In this chapter I aim both to identify the central impetus for that force of philosophical longevity and also to bring to the fore a feature internal to Husserl's conception that, in my view, really prevented it from having the kind of future he himself dreamt of.

The examination in Part III of this chapter of the opening phases of one of Husserl's last efforts to 'introduce' phenomenology, the *Cartesian Meditations* (original text 1929), will try to bring out these points. For my purposes this text has a further privilege on two counts. First, it starts somewhere that is familiar to most students of philosophy today, somewhere I take it that we can all start out: namely, via a critical engagement with 'the remarkable train of thoughts contained in [Descartes'] *Meditations*'.[31] Second, this Husserlian starting point – what is often referred to by Husserl specialists as 'the Cartesian way' to a distinctively transcendental form of phenomenology – is notable also for its explicit engagement with the problem of how to begin in philosophy. It will be through an examination of what is opened up by this introductory text that I will explore the somewhat mixed legacy of Husserl's elaboration of a new beginning for philosophy in the name of phenomenology.

In my view, for the reasons just given, following Husserl's 'Cartesian way' to transcendental phenomenology can be a particularly helpful point of departure for readers new to phenomenological philosophy in general. However, this way of presenting a Husserlian launch into phenomenology also covers over the motivations which specifically launched it in that name in the first place. Indeed, Husserl's launching of transcendental phenomenology via the beginning steps to be found in Descartes' *Meditations* is something he arrived at only after he had already launched away not only from an existing idea of phenomenology in the work of Franz Brentano, but also from his own first (as he called it) 'break-through' to phenomenology in the *Logical Investigations*.[32]

So we have three beginnings vying for attention here, indeed the very three outlined in the Introduction. The first comes into view when we note that 'Husserl's phenomenology takes its *beginning* from a certain project of describing mental acts and their parts initiated by Brentano'.[33] But we need to be clear that *none* of Husserl's texts *begins* in this way. The second beginning then

comes into view with the achievement of a first 'break-through' to phenomenology. And finally we can turn to a beginning of the third kind, the opening
of Husserl's 'Cartesian way' into transcendental phenomenology, as a text particularly well suited to readers new to phenomenology, a text which is also
precisely oriented towards 'the question of the beginning' itself.[34]

With the intention of setting the scene for the initial phases of 'the Cartesian way', I will first explore the other two beginnings. Accordingly, this
chapter has three parts. In Part I I sketch the legacy of Brentano, and do so
with a view to providing a background to the problematic that Husserl
addresses in the *Cartesian Meditations*. Taking advantage of a confluence of
thematic concerns, Part II will take up the launching topic from Husserl's
'break-through' work in the *Logical Investigations*: his analysis of signs. Taking in
Heidegger's and Derrida's responses to that early launch, the discussion of the
second part aims both to show how far the turn to the transcendental view-
point of the *Cartesian Meditations* was already prepared for in Husserl's earlier
text and to give a preliminary indication of what, after Husserl, becomes a
central problem within the inheritance of phenomenology itself. As I will
indicate, since the second part leaps ahead of the sequence of beginnings followed up in this book, it can be passed over by readers new to the subject. Part
III of the chapter picks up on the problematic legacy of Brentano and turns to
the early stages of the *Cartesian Meditations* for the development of a new
beginning for phenomenology.

Part I: The legacy of Brentano

The subjectivity of the mental

Pursuing 'the Cartesian way' into transcendental phenomenology will allow us
to see how Husserl's thought mounts a remarkable challenge to fundamental
assumptions of contemporary ordinary philosophy. However, to appreciate this
challenge we need to work our way into the framework of his reflections. And I
will begin by briefly examining the discipline of 'descriptive psychology' or
'descriptive phenomenology' pioneered by Franz Brentano, the supposedly *a
priori* science of the fundamental laws of our mental lives, which provided the
basic conceptuality of Husserl's thought.

Brentano conceived his new discipline as serving to provide an absolutely
secure foundation for empirical studies in '*genetic* psychology', studies which
would pursue physiological investigations of the dependence of our mental
lives on occurrences in the brain. The order of priority here may seem odd in
that the founding discipline is concerned with states and processes which are
held to depend on states and processes studied by the founded discipline.
However, in the special case of investigations in psychology there is a long-
standing assumption which would explain away this priority oddness: namely,
the assumption that the essential features of our mental lives are revealed to us

as they are 'in themselves' only from within. It is this (supposed) immediate 'self-evidence' of the mental that would make the primary and founding study of 'psychical reality' a descriptive and not a genetic one. Indeed, the long-standing assumption gives us reason to think that a genetic inquiry has and can have no genuinely adequate idea *what* it is investigating (thought processes, conscious states and acts, the different mental phenomena) without the prior descriptive one.[35]

The longstanding assumption concerns a feature of mental phenomena which is often thought to rule out the very idea of a physical account of them altogether. This feature concerns what can be called the subjectivity of con-sciousness. This is the idea – not one accepted by every philosophy of psychology – that all conscious states are 'present to oneself' in a radically unique way: there is a *'something that it is like'* feature to all mental phenomena, and this feature is only revealed 'from the inside'.

This (supposedly) ubiquitous feature of mental phenomena has profound consequences for what a positive science of them might involve. A physical thing, a stone for example, has many properties, many states that it can be in: it might be hot, cracked, made of sediment, touching another stone, held lightly in the beak of an ostrich and so on. But, so the idea goes, there is nothing that it is like for the stone to have any of these properties. There is, that is to say, no 'something that it is like' property that belongs *to* the stone which is also a property *for* the stone. All mental phenomena, by contrast, have properties that are or involve features that are only manifest 'from the inside'; properties which cannot then be fully captured (if captured at all) in the objective forms of thought belonging to the sciences of the physical world.[36] Although real properties, they do not belong to the reality that is investigated by physical sciences. They can be grasped as the phenomena they are only with reference to what it is like for a subject to instantiate them, and in that sense are irreducibly subjective. Or, again: ultimately these phenomena are what they are only by virtue of the fact that there is something that it is like to be the subject of them. As should be clear, whether and in what sense there can be a genuine science of such phenomena seems to be a serious problem.

Brentano completely accepts the idea that this conception identifies an essential and irreducible feature of mental phenomena. However, to this long-standing idea he adds (or rather, retrieves from medieval scholastic philosophy) a second, he supposes equally intractable, feature of mental phenomena, and one which he regards as central to his project of descriptive psychology: namely, their intentionality, which means their 'directedness' or 'aboutness'. This is the feature of mental phenomena identified when we say that they have something as their 'content'. As Husserl later put it, 'in perception something is perceived, in imagination something imagined; in judging something judged, in love something loved, in hate hated, in desire desired, etc.'.[37] In each case the mental phenomena are characterised, as such, by an essential relation to a content or direction to an object. Thus the intentionality doctrine is that consciousness is essentially consciousness-of-something. Brentano's central claim is that all and only subjective phenomena possess intentionality, and that a science of the mind is thus essentially a study of the different kinds of intentional phenomena. In the next section I want briefly to examine the problems and possibilities that Brentano's central doctrine opens up for philosophy.

The intentionality doctrine

Typical of many thinkers after Kant, Brentano kept a foot in both empiricist and rationalist camps. On the one hand he fundamentally agreed with the empiricists that original experiential 'presentations' or impressions form the basis of all mental contents. On the other hand, however, like the rationalists he believed that our understanding of the mind's own activity was not a matter of forming empirical generalisations by introspective observation – Locke's knowledge by reflection; rather, through what he calls 'inner perception' we have a capacity directly to grasp truths about the mind that have the status of necessary *a priori* laws. For Brentano, then, descriptive psychology, or what he also called 'descriptive phenomenology', the science which specifies the laws governing the essential nature and structure of 'psychical realities', would have a rigour and certainty unobtainable by the generalisations of an empirical science. We can simply come to 'see' the undeniable truth of certain psychological propositions regarding what he called 'the properties and laws of the soul'.[38]

First among all these universal psychological laws is that there are no mental acts that do not involve a presentation. When I hear a tone I have a presentation of a sound; when I see something red I have a presentation of red, etc. A presentation provides the basic object or content of a mental act. This is the core of Brentano's intentionality doctrine.

The traditional distinction between the mental and the physical permeates Brentano's conception. In fact he explicitly uses the idea of intentionality to draw this distinction. That is, as I have indicated, he insists not only that every subjective phenomenon displays intentionality but also that only such states do: no physical phenomena have this property. For Brentano, then, this object-directedness is ubiquitous in and exclusive to the mind. Thus, he took the intentionality of mental phenomena to be a reason for endorsing a form of dualism. Indeed, from the point of view of a descriptive phenomenology of consciousness this is first and foremost a dualism concerning two basic kinds of intentional content: 'All the appearances of our consciousness are divided into two great classes – the class of physical and the class of mental phenomena.'[39]

Brentano appealed to a distinction between what we know directly (what is given in experience) and what we know only indirectly (what is inferred on the basis of what is given experience) in further elaborating this fundamental division of classes. When he talks about physical phenomena he means objects as we know them, as they are presented in perception. As to what exists independently of such presentations, he concedes that our epistemic reach falls sadly short: we simply 'have no experience of that which truly exists, in and of itself'.[40] On the other hand, however, mental phenomena are as they appear. And of course this is supposed to be the peculiar advantage of descriptive phenomenology. The mind can grasp itself as it is 'in and of itself', and in principle it can do so immediately and with absolute certainty.

Preparing for Husserl's entry it is important to note that this supposed benefit can be construed equally plausibly as a profound problem for the Brentanian conception. For there is an obvious sceptical threat implied by it, a threat Brentano acknowledges when he recognises that the real existence of objects 'outside us' must be, on his account, 'initially hypothetical'.[41] Nevertheless, like a no-nonsense man of science, and rather like a commonsense empiricist philosopher, Brentano does not dwell on this issue and regards it as a 'hypothesis' which is obviously well established, and he supposes that, without further need for proofs, we are justified in inferring, as we do, the existence of objects 'outside us'. Yet, it is by no means obvious that a satisfactory philosophy can endorse the very conception of the mind affirmed by the traditional sceptic. Husserl certainly regarded the sceptical implications of both 'extreme empiricism' and what he called 'the usual post-Cartesian way of thinking' as utterly unacceptable.[42] Whether he (Husserl) was able, though his own 'Cartesian way', to offer a satisfactory response in turn is, as we shall see, hotly disputed.

Nevertheless, with the questionable conception of mind in place, the first and most important point to note about Brentano's appeal to the intentionality doctrine is that he does not regard intentionality as a relation between two independently existing things, a mind and an external physical thing. The object of an intentional act is always something immanent to consciousness: a phenomenon of some kind. Thus, for example, the mental phenomenon of hearing is related to a heard sound, not to, say, sound waves in the outer, external world. In general, then, the intentional object of consciousness is for Brentano always a presented object, an 'immanent objectivity', or an object as it shows itself to consciousness. Brentano calls these accusatives of mental phenomena intentional contents, and since they exist as such only (immanently) *in* mental phenomena he states that presented contents have what he calls intentional 'inexistence':

> Every mental phenomenon is characterised by what the Scholastics of the Middle Ages called the intentional (or mental) inexistence of an object, and what we might call, though not wholly unambiguously, reference to a content, direction towards an object (by which a reality is not to be understood) or an imminent objectivity. Each mental phenomenon contains something as object within itself, although they do not all do so in the same way.[43]

'Inexistence' here does not mean *non*-existence but existence *in* the mind or 'existence-as-an-object-of-consciousness'.

As I have indicated, Brentano's intentionality doctrine is composed of two separable claims, and we should consider them separately. The first is that all mental phenomena exhibit intentionality. This seems plausible for perception, conception and emotion, but how about bodily sensation? Is the experience of feeling pain in one's foot, for example, a consciousness *of*, say, foot pain or, rather differently, are pains a form in which consciousness is directed at certain physical phenomena? This second option is quite attractive. All pains are felt as coming from certain parts of the body-as-experienced (even in the cases where one actually lacks the appropriate body part). A pain is not just a nasty 'sensory presence' in consciousness but is clearly related to a location on or in one's experienced body. We clutch at or can point to the painful place. And so one might argue for a certain intentionality of sensations; they too are to be understood as 'directed towards' something: namely, the injured place on or in one's experienced body. Pain might thus be regarded as the form or mode that consciousness of an injured part of the experienced body takes. So at first blush it seems that the first claim may be defensible.[44]

The second claim central to Brentano's intentionality doctrine is that *only* mental phenomena exhibit intentionality. This claim seems rather less plausible than the first. For aren't maps and pictures – and indeed ordinary linguistic signs such as the ones you are reading right now – just as much characterised by their intentionality, their 'directedness' or 'aboutness', as are states and acts of consciousness? And since what we might call 'the general phenomena of signs', maps, pictures, speech, writing and the like, are all obviously 'outer', 'in the world' or 'physical' phenomena, they look like clear counterexamples to the idea that intentionality belongs only to mental phenomena.

With this objection we are standing strikingly close to the theme of Husserl's first launch into phenomenology, indeed at the very first launching point of his programme of phenomenology. For the analysis of signs that opens the first part proper of the *Logical Investigations* can be read as offering a robust response to this objection. Significantly, however, the whole field of Husserl's analysis of signs is also the target of fundamental criticisms by both Heidegger[45] and Derrida.[46] Indeed, both attempt *at this very point* (the very first starting point of Husserlian phenomenology) a deviation from Husserl's thought which would prevent it from launching off in the way he wanted. Since it is clearly a moment of special importance to the inheritance of phenomenology we should pause to get this early but arguably most determining starting point of Husserl's into clearer view. In doing so we will be jumping ahead of ourselves somewhat and first-time readers may prefer to skip this as a detour and pass on directly to the summary of the Husserlian response to the intentionality objection which will be set down without further argument at the start of the section that follows it.

Part II: Husserl's analysis of signs

Indication and expression

'From *indicative* signs we distinguish *meaningful* signs, i.e. *expressions*.'[47] The distinction or (as Heidegger and Derrida tend to put it) the opposition between indicative signs and expressions which dominates the First Investigation in Husserl's *Logical Investigations* would, from this sort of formulation, seem to be a contrast between *two kinds of sign*. Christopher Norris tends to read Husserl this way, presenting the indication/expression distinction as a contrast between a kind of sign that 'functions merely as a "lifeless" token in a system of arbitrary sense' (indicative signs) and a kind of sign that is 'endowed with meaning' in the sense that it 'represents the communicative purpose or intentional force which "animates" language' (expressive signs).[48] However, a closer examination of Husserl's discussion makes it clear that the contrast at issue does not relate to a distinction between kinds of sign at all, and especially not to a contrast between, as it were, the 'lifeless' and the 'lively' ones. It is true that there are for Husserl cases of signs, even signs which we ordinarily call 'expressions', which on his view indicate something but do not themselves express anything at all: facial expressions like smiles and frowns, for example.[49] And it is equally true that there are for Husserl cases of signs which express something but which do not indicate anything at all: the imagined words which play a part in one's 'solitary and interior' mental life are an example, *the* unique example in fact, of such signs. However, first of all, in *both* of these cases we are dealing with signs which are, to use Norris's metaphors, enlivened or alive. And second, and more significantly, in what Husserl presents as the key and central case of the use of signs, namely in interpersonal linguistic communication, the two uses of the term 'sign' that Husserl wants to *distinguish* are, in fact, *always both in play*, and are fundamentally interwoven or entangled with one another. In other words, what Husserl claims to identify is what could be called a purely *grammatical* difference: a contrast between *different uses of the term 'sign'*, uses which in the key and central case are always both somehow involved together. As the quotation which began this section makes plain, only expressive signs are, for Husserl, to be understood as strictly speaking meaningful, and yet 'meaning – in communicative speech – is always bound up with an indicative relation'.[50] Husserl represents the work of teasing out or unbinding this grammatical tangle by presenting his First Investigation as concerned with the identification of an 'essential distinction' that resides, as he puts it, in 'an ambiguity in the term "sign"'.[51]

Despite appearances, therefore, the suggestion of a distinction between kinds of sign is not quite right. As Derrida notes, 'the difference between indication and expression very quickly appears ... to be a difference more *functional* than *substantial*': not a type difference in kinds of sign but a differentiation of use, *within* the use of the term 'sign'. And this difference is thus one which 'may be interwoven or entangled in the same concatenation of signs'.[52]

40

But now, however, if there really is such ubiquitous *Verflechtung* (entanglement) in the key and central case, is it so certain that there is an 'essential distinction' to be drawn here at all? As we shall see, both Heidegger and Derrida will question Husserl's claims in this area. Nevertheless, if we are to see how they interrupt Husserl's analysis of signs – and thus interrupt this inaugural launch of phenomenology – we need first to understand Husserl's analysis itself. What, in particular, is he trying to achieve with it?

A good and (more or less) noncommittal start of an answer can be found in Heidegger's pre-*Being and Time* discussion of Husserl's work where he describes the analysis of signs as one that aims at 'the delineation of the phenomenon of *linguistic meaning* as opposed to the general phenomena (as he says) of signs'.[53] Again, we have to be careful not to assume that the opposition here is between two species in a genus or two subsets of a general set. The crucial idea is rather that of delineation, and above all else the theoretical *isolation* of the phenomenon of expression, by which Husserl always means a 'sense-informed expression' as it is given 'when we live in the understanding of a *word*'.[54] By 'expression' Husserl always means the linguistic expression of meaning. Not at all unreasonably, Husserl regards this phenomenon as fundamental to our life with signs, but he is also aware that this is not all that is normally meant by the term 'sign'. His aim, then, is *completely* to isolate, and in this way *completely* to clarify, what shows itself in that most fundamental aspect of our life with signs. And he claims to be able to do so by completely *setting aside* a different sense of the word 'sign', setting aside the indicative sense of signs.

Although we have to keep the *Verflechtung* of uses in view, it is not difficult to grasp the principle of Husserl's distinction, even if, with Heidegger and Derrida, one may come to regard his whole analysis as a kind of false start. The fundamental question is whether or not, in any case of the use of the word 'sign', what we mean by 'sign' is something which stands in the (non-natural) relation 'means' to what it signifies.[55] Husserl's analytic clarification of what he takes to be the essential distinction here runs as follows: If by 'sign' is meant something which stands in the (non-natural) relation 'means' to what it signifies, then the sign can be called an *expression*. An expression simply *is* a meaningful linguistic sign, so that if A is an expression of B, then A just *is* the meaningful linguistic sign which means B. On the other hand, if by 'sign' is meant something which does *not* stand in the (non-natural) relation 'means' to what it signifies, then the sign can be called an *indication*. An indicative sign involves a mediating structure that Husserl calls 'motivation', which is utterly different to the purely internal or logical relation between an expression and its meaning. If A indicates B, then, according to Husserl, that is so only because, for some 'thinking being', the 'belief in the reality of A' *motivates* a 'belief in (or at least a surmise of) the reality of B'.[56] The structures in the two cases are quite different but one can see why we might be strongly inclined to call them both signs, for there is an experienced unity of indicative signs, just as there is an experienced unity of a sign with its meaning. In the case of indications this is essentially a *descriptive* unity in which A and B are (for the 'thinking being' for whom the connections are established) in view *as* indicating/indicated. What we experience here is thus given as a whole, as an objective connection between one thing and another thing. Consequently, the sign is (for the 'thinking being') 'alive' despite the fact that in its indicative function it does not 'mean' anything at all. In other words, in virtue of the descriptive unity forged by the motivational relation the structure of, for example, 'something-in-the-world *pointing* to something-else-in-the-world' is experienced *in* the first something, *in* the 'apparent object' (an exit arrow on a cinema wall, for example), or, again, the connection 'endows contents with a new phenomenological character'.[57] Hence, we *see* that 'a brand is the sign of a slave, a flag the sign of a nation', and we see them *as such*.

The primacy of expression: Husserl

As I have mentioned, while Husserl wants to recognise two senses of the term 'sign', he does not regard them as having equal significance. If, as he suggests, 'the terms "expression" and "sign" are often treated as synonyms'[58] that is a reflection of the fact that *for us* the use of the term 'sign' that relates to expressions, to words and sentences, is *fundamental*. Nevertheless (and the 'nevertheless' here marks the 'difficulty' that is the impetus behind the whole analysis) they are not true synonyms. We use the term 'sign' in connection with indicative relations too. Moreover, such relations are involved in *every* actual communication of expressions. How so? The problematic *Verflechtung* of uses is due to the fact that, in interpersonal communication, *the linguistic expression always also serves as an indication for others*: 'they serve the hearer as signs of the "thoughts" of the speaker'.[59] Indeed, it is only by virtue of this indicative function of the sign that the ordinary communicative situation is not one of someone witnessing another person 'uttering sounds', but, precisely, of a person '*speaking to him*':[60]

> I perceive him as a speaker, I hear him recounting, demonstrating, doubting, wishing etc ... I 'see' his anger, his pain etc. Such talk is quite correct [even though] I do not experience them myself: I have not an 'inner' but an 'outer' percept of them.[61]

So even in the case of the ordinary use of signs in interpersonal linguistic communication there are crucial and *irreducible* indicative relations bound up with them. However, Husserl does not give up on the project of *isolating* the phenomenon of expression, and, by a further essential contrast, proposes that *in solitary mental life* – in interior monologue – indicative functions *completely* fall away and yet the signs continue to function, indeed continue to function *purely* as expressions. Hence, Husserl concludes that in its essence an expression *as such* has nothing at all to do with, does not depend upon and can do without

42

the 'in the world' structures of indication with which it is normally entangled: 'Shall one say that in soliloquy one speaks to oneself, and employs words as signs i.e. as indications, of one's own inner experiences? I cannot think such a view is acceptable.'[62] Here, then, the isolation of a *purely* expressive stratum is finally achieved.

Husserl regards this purely expressive stratum as a feature *common* to both soliloquy and dialogue, indeed as a feature that is essential to every experience of a sign '*as a word*'.[63] The basic idea here is that *what we recognise* when we recognise a sign as a word is something that we know can be expressed as *precisely the same* by someone else, indeed by 'whomsoever'; our experience is thus not merely of a specific sound pattern but of a specific word. 'And the same holds', Husserl immediately insists, 'of talk about the [word's] meaning': in the situation that concerns us, that too is something that *we recognise* can be recognised as *the same* by 'whomsoever'.[64] But this means that the unity of 'sign and signified' in the case of expressions is in no way (as it is with indications) *the unity of two realities* (*qua* existents in the world) but, essentially, *the unity of two idealities*, in each aspect experienced as *essentially* 'repeatable as the same' by 'whomsoever'. Thus, in interpersonal communication 'when a subjective act is *intimated* [by the signs in their indicative function], something objective and ideal is brought to *expression*'.[65] In this way the thinking or judging that we 'see' in the other's behaviour brings to expression a thought or judgement that we can *share*.[66] And thus, for Husserl, it is in the 'reduced' scenario of interior monologue, where all structures of indication have been set aside, that the essence of expression as *the intending of a pure ideality* is clearly revealed 'in person': the essence of expression itself is lucidly disclosed. But what is disclosed there is something that therefore belongs to the essence of the expression of linguistic meaning *simpliciter*, in every case, monological or not.

In the situation that is *basic* to our lives with signs our experience is of words that (immediately) express something as their meaning.[67] As we have seen, that situation is one in which our interest does not 'stop at the sensory contour' of the sign: we are not confronted by 'a mere sound pattern' which we then have to interpret but 'we live in the understanding of a word'.[68] However, since the expression that is understood here is *essentially unaffected* by the 'reduction' to the interior monologue, what Husserl continues to designate as 'the physical phenomenon' in this structure, the ex-pressive moment of expression, is conceived in terms which can essentially do without reference to a *physical*, or 'in the world', outside. Indeed, according to Husserl's analysis, *that* 'relation to outside' can, as Derrida puts it, precisely be 'suspended'.[69] Nevertheless (and, as we shall see in Part III of this chapter, this 'nevertheless' opens on to a constant figure of Husserlian thought), for Husserl even in this moment in which everything relating to what exists in the world is set aside – 'bracketed', as he will later put it – a certain 'relation to outside' still remains in view. As Derrida notes, 'this reduction does not eliminate but rather reveals, within pure expression, a relation to an object, namely, the intending of an objective ideality'.[70] The act in which this relation takes place, what Husserl calls a 'meaning-intention', is not intentional in the sense that one is aware of a meaning as the object of one's consciousness. As Husserl puts it, 'in the act of meaning we are not conscious of meaning as an object'.[71] On the contrary, what we are intentionally conscious of or directed towards when we 'perform the act and live in it' is not the 'thought' but 'what we are thinking about' in the sense of the object judged (the red square, the end of the summer or whatever).[72] Nevertheless, according to Husserl, in reflection we may turn our attention to and become intuitively aware of meanings 'in themselves'. I find the Husserlian quasi-perceptual language of intuitions very difficult to follow here, but the idea is not, I think, that one observes independently subsisting Platonic objects but rather that one has an immediate awareness of essentially repeatable and sharable contents of possible acts of thinking, what he calls, for that reason, ideal identities.

It would be wrong to think that the work of setting aside the indicative sense of signs is an inward withdrawal that achieves in everything but name what Husserl will later call a 'phenomenological reduction'. Moreover, as we shall see in Part III of this chapter, the final stage on Husserl's journey towards a rigorously transcendental phenomenology of the kind one finds in *Cartesian Mediations* is only reached when the 'externality' of the existing world posited by the early analysis is itself grasped in terms of an intentional 'relation to outside' to be described 'from the standpoint of "interiority"'.[73] Nevertheless, even if there are further steps to be taken on Husserl's path to his mature conception, I think Derrida is right to suggest that the analysis of signs can be seen 'to show the germinal structure of the whole of Husserl's thought'.[74] Indeed, the two major *shifts of level* undertaken in the analysis of signs (the shift from various *empirical examples* of signs to the identification of their *essence* and the shift from the *in the world* phenomenon of interpersonal communica- tion to the *purely subjective field* of internal monologue) certainly foreshadow the shifts of level that will later become the centrepieces of his phenomen- ological method: namely, what is called the 'eidetic' reduction from empirical examples to essences and the 'phenomenological' reduction from a pre-reflective 'in the world' perspective (or 'natural attitude') to a transcendental perspective in which we can explore how the pre-reflective sense of the externality of the world is originally constituted.[75]

In fact, the possibility of setting factual and 'in the world' matters *completely* to one side in the case of expressions not only is an example of the early Husserl's conception of attaining the proper level in a phenomenological investigation but is, by his lights, the condition *sine qua non* of such an inves- tigation in general. For if the isolation of a purely expressive stratum were *not* achievable, if we could not set everything that concerns existence in the world to one side, that would be tantamount to supposing that there is no level of investigation of phenomena in general which would not presuppose or be beholden to findings in the positive sciences – it would not be a *purely non-empirical investigation*; indeed, it would not be philosophy as a rigorous science. Thus, as Derrida further pointedly notes, 'Husserl's whole enterprise – and far beyond the *Investigations* – would be threatened if the *Verflechtung* [entanglement] ... were absolutely irreducible, if it were in principle inextricable and if indication were essentially *internal* to the movement of expression'.[76] As I will briefly explain in the next section, it belongs to a 'deconstructive' critique of the Husserlian analysis that, while faithful to the traditional philosophical concern for what is essential, seeks to describe the structure and functioning of signs (in general) in a way which makes perspicuous that 'indication' really is, in an irreducible way, 'essentially internal to the movement of expression'. In the deconstruction of Husserl's analysis of signs philosophy returns, as philosophy, to the world.

The primacy of indication: Heidegger and Derrida

For Husserl, the inclusion of references to what is irreducibly 'in the world' inevitably corrupts the pure ideality of expressions. It is as an attempt to produce a line of deviation away from *this* understanding of philosophy's strictly non-empirical or non-scientific character that Heidegger and Derrida would (in Derrida's words) 'rehabilitate the indicative sign':[77] a deviation that would bring us back within philosophy, and indeed still in the name of phenomenology, to the inhabited world worked over with marks, traces, writing, signposts, boundary stones, signals, flags – the genuine motley of signs that Derrida (not without crucial debts to the Husserlian emphasis on essential structures) calls, one and all, kinds of *writing*, and that Heidegger (also in the interest of an analysis concerned with essential structures) analyses by attention to a *single* 'exemplary instance' of 'in the world' signs; the little flag that served in his day as (n.b.) a car *indicator*. Husserl will want to set indicative signs – and with them every kind of writing or directional indicator – aside. Heidegger and Derrida stake out another inheritance of phenomenology by setting them back on board: in Heidegger in the guise of an indicator which, on reflection, shows something of the 'taking a direction' which is *essential* to our being-in-the-world as such,[78] and in Derrida in the guise of a (general) writing which would be the very element of *every* trait and gesture of human (and, in fact, not only human) life.[79] Philosophy, it will then be suggested, need not give up on its essential concern with essence when it is, in this way, brought back to the world.[80]

It is easy to miss quite how much damage this interruption of the Husserlian analysis of signs would do to the structure of Husserl's philosophy generally. Yet if the so-called indicative function is supposed to relate to 'everything that falls subject to [i.e. is "set aside" by] the [Husserlian] reductions',[81] if, that is, Husserlian phenomenological method in general profoundly depends on the in principle isolability of a *purely* 'expressive core',[82] then the impossibility of drawing this first 'essential distinction' would, in turn, ruin the possibility of the Husserlian conception of phenomenology *tout court*. Of course, independently of Husserl's analysis we might still wish to acknowledge an important difference between uses of signs which are 'expressions' and uses which are 'indications', but that difference would now be philosophically innocuous since it would be drawn *within* a space of signification which would be, as it were, a space of indication in general in the sense that it (signification in general) would everywhere remain irreducibly tied to 'in the world' items, irreducibly tied, then, to what is, for Husserl, the existing world in general. Heidegger robustly affirms this deconstruction of Husserl's analysis of signs, proposing a fundamentally relational and 'in the world' analysis in which, 'in the first instance', *all* signs are conceived of as 'items of equipment', items in the world 'whose specific character as equipment consists in *showing* or *indicating*' [*Zeigen*].[83] Any contrast one might then make between specifically indicative signs (*Anzeichen*) and expressions (*Ausdruck*) would then be just one contrast among a slew of various, and variously contrasting, uses of such equipment, one among a number of different '*ways of indicating*'.[84] This 'deconstructive' reversal and displacement of the Husserlian 'opposition' is evident too in Derrida's (as we shall see, in some respects rather Merleau-Pontian) suggestion that the rehabilitation of the indicative sign will allow us to overturn the Husserlian privilege accorded to linguistic expression and to conceive it as a (no doubt distinctive) form of expressive behaviour in general, indeed as a form of expression of a (general) sort that Husserl had identified as, essentially, indication: 'the spoken word, whatever dignity or originality we still accord it, is but a form of gesture'.[85]

As we have seen, Husserl aims to separate out (i.e. separate without residue) the tangled use of the term 'sign' and to draw an essential distinction between indication and expression. The stark contrast between Husserl's separating procedure and Heidegger's affirmation of the 'multiplicity of possible signs' as so many 'ways of indicating' is implicitly in view in Heidegger's two illustrative lists of signs:

> Among signs [*Zeichen*] there are indicative signs [*Anzeichen*], warning signals [*Vorzeichen*], signs of things that have happened already [*Rückzeichen*], signs by which things are recognised; these have different ways of indicating, regardless of what may be serving as such a sign. Among these 'signs' are to be distinguished trace, remains, commemorative monument, document, testimony, symbol, expression, appearances, significations.[86]

While Heidegger is clearly keen to acknowledge the intrinsic variety of signs here, his lists are not a mere miscellany. First of all, as Robert Cumming notes, Heidegger's first list brings to the fore examples that stress 'the "horizon" of time':[87] 'warning signals' and 'signs of things that have happened already'. Heidegger thus draws in precisely the kind of worldly temporal references to the future and past that are obscured in Husserl's 'essential' analysis. We might note in addition that Heidegger's first list is led off with 'indicative signs' [*Anzeichen*][88] and that his second list, which is clearly subordinate to the first in the sense that it comprises items that are to be distinguished from 'among' the first, as if rooted in them, includes Husserl's privileged term 'expression', and includes it without special comment and very near the end. With only a footnote reference to the Husserlian analysis of signs to mark the conjunction, a major parting of the phenomenological ways is being brought very quietly into view.[89]

I will return to Heidegger's deviation from Husserlian phenomenology, the movement back to the world, at the end of this chapter, and will pursue it in more detail in Chapter 3. At this point, however, the detour into the early Husserlian analysis of signs has reached a point where it can turn back into the road we had been travelling on beforehand. First, we need to recall that, for Husserl, insofar as signs are caught up in 'in the world' relations ('the general phenomena (as he says) of signs', as Heidegger rather pointedly says) the application of the term 'sign' will nowhere be simply separable from (will everywhere be tangled up with) indicative relations. However, as should be clear, the opposite point holds too: purely indicative signs in the world – a smile, a flag or a chalk mark on a door, for example – are also everywhere caught up in the field of linguistic meaning. The point here is that (in Husserl's terms) a purely indicative sign such as a smile can be recognised *as such*, as a smile, only within a distinctively discursive horizon of significance, a sense of significance, then, which, for Husserl, cannot be properly grasped in terms that retain the trace of indicative relations *at all*. Indeed, this is a sense of significance which only comes into clear (untangled) view for Husserl when we home in on an application of the term 'sign' that is, in its essence, utterly free of any dependence on 'in the world' structures. In short, according to Husserl, no 'in the world' item to which we apply the term 'sign' could be apprehended as *what in itself it is* unless it appeared within the ideal horizon of pure expression, within a space opened up, therefore, by the ideal intelligibility of the *word*.[90] Hence (and now the roads of this chapter come together again), whether the focus is on maps, pictures, chalk marks or indeed 'outward' speech and writing, the 'life' of any such 'in the world' signs will be essentially *dependent* on intentional structures which can be fully described even if we suspend every reference to the totality of the existing world, and which anything in the world can only indicate through intimation. Thus, although it would be wrong to say, with Christopher Norris, that the indicative sign is, unlike the expressive word, 'lifeless', one might well summarise Husserl's position in the *Logical Investigations* with the idea that the 'life' of any sign in the world is not *original* but essentially *derived* from intentional structures that in themselves can do without the relation to anything in the existing world. The primacy given to expressive signs and linguistic meaning is ultimately, for Husserl, a logical primacy; it is not merely a mark of its being humanly distinctive.

Part III: Husserl's *Cartesian Meditations*

The Cartesian starting point

We were considering an objection to the idea that intentionality may be a feature only of mental states. The counterexample of maps, pictures and other 'in the world' signs in general was presented. An intuitively plausible, if not unproblematic, reply to this (the detour of Part II suggests) would be to argue that the recognition of any presented sign as the specific sign it is depends on an original directedness to *essentially* intentional ('inexisting') contents, contents that can do without anything in the existing world.[91] We might then attempt to sustain Brentano's conception by arguing that only mental acts can have this *original* rather than *derived* intentionality.[92]

Although Brentano takes his lead from medieval scholastic philosophy, his conception of the mind as characterised by intrinsically subjective phenomena with intrinsically 'inexisting' intentional content is one which is, in many respects, powerfully prefigured in the work of Descartes. Think about the sceptical phase of Descartes' inquiry at the start of his *Meditations* and ask: what difference is there, for the Cartesian meditating subject, between what is given to the mind in the case of genuine knowledge and in the case of universal illusion? And Descartes' answer is surely: nothing. On such an understanding, even if we restrict ourselves to what is given to the mind we might say that the whole 'external world' *as it is given to us* is actually included in the 'cogito', as the intentional correlate of the 'I think'. In full, that is, the Cartesian cogito should read 'I think (*of* something) therefore I am', where the accusative is a 'something' that can be as it is even if the 'initial hypothesis' of the existence of an external world is, in fact, false.

Is this (basically) Cartesian conception of the mind and its inexistent objects really acceptable? As I have noted already, there seems to belong to it a standing threat of scepticism. Indeed, the conception would seem to resolve ultimately into solipsism. Since I cannot be present to the subjective states and acts of others (as an 'inner percept', as Husserl puts it), I cannot really know what is going on in someone else's mind. Moreover, since I can never really know the subjective character of their experience – indeed perhaps I finally cannot be wholly sure whether they have what I call 'experience' at all – maybe I alone have genuinely subjective and intentional experiences .... In the end can I even conceive of experiences which are not *my* experiences?[93]

As I have indicated, the sceptical and ultimately solipsistic implications of the Cartesian conception of the mind do not unduly bother Brentano. He sees it as a matter of having sufficient evidence, and regards himself as having all the evidence he needs to dismiss the doubts of the sceptic and the bizarre conclusion of the solipsist. As I hope to show in this part, in his *Cartesian Meditations* Husserl aims to leave this kind of Cartesian problematic totally behind him, regarding such a standing threat of scepticism or solipsism as fundamentally incompatible with our pre-reflective understanding of the world. Husserl will not be remotely content with a philosophy so out of kilter with 'the sense this world has for us, prior to any philosophising',[94] not remotely content, then, with belief in the objective world or belief in the existence of others as mere hypotheses. The question is, however, whether a philosophy which embarks from certain Cartesian shores can ever radically haul itself off what Sartre calls 'the reef of solipsism'.[95] That is the problem which haunts Husserl's own analysis the *Cartesian Meditations*, and it is to that text that I will now turn.

The opening of transcendental phenomenology

Husserl began preparing the text of the *Meditations* for publication in around 1930, as a development of two lectures delivered at the Sorbonne in Paris a year earlier and whose title became the subtitle to the published text: 'An Introduction to Transcendental Phenomenology'. In what follows I will map the opening stretches of this text to see how it negotiates a new beginning for phenomenology. I will conclude by taking note of its closing conclusions for the future of phenomenology, conclusions which were profoundly challenged by Heidegger, the 'deviant disciple' who, despite his debts to Husserl, was to take up anew the task of an inheritance of philosophy in the name of phenomenology.

In the first seven sections or so of Husserl's text, Descartes is presented as a crucial forerunner to phenomenology, in some respects a phenomenologist *avant la lettre*. However, because of a certain (important) analogy between the movement of the sceptical phase of Descartes' *Meditations* and the world-bracketing that leads to what Husserl will call the 'phenomenological reduction' it is very easy to misunderstand this suggestion. In particular, it is tempting to read into the tribute to Descartes a view of Husserl as a philosopher who shares the Cartesian project of seeking to overcome sceptical doubts from a starting point of the 'inner world' of the mind.

Such a view has been encouraged by the typical 'Heideggerian' representation of Husserl as a merely Cartesian philosopher. Indeed, in Heidegger's own writings Husserl's views seem often to be simply absorbed into a more general representation of something like the Cartesian view. And when Heidegger wants to engage in *gigantomachia* (γιγαντομαχία), with 'the opposite extreme' to his phenomenology he is likely to identify the French philosophical giant he sees behind Husserl, and quietly sweep his teacher up along the way.[96] As we shall see, this flattening out of philosophical differences into a homogeneous tradition invites us to pass over aspects of Husserl's thought which are not so easily swept under a Cartesian carpet.

On the other hand, this is a flattening out with respect to Descartes that Husserl also sometimes invites, and he does so in writings Heidegger knew. Significantly, however, a crucial aspect of the specifically Husserlian invitation to regard oneself as following in Descartes' wake – and this is the invitation that comes to the fore at the start of the *Cartesian Meditations* – might also sweep up Heidegger:

> All modern philosophy originates in the Cartesian *Meditations* ... . This historical proposition means that every genuine beginning of philosophy issues from meditations, from solitary self-reflection. Autonomous philosophy ... comes into being in the solitary, radical taking responsibility for himself on the part of the philosopher. Through isolation and meditation alone does a philosopher come into being, does philosophy begin in him.[97]

What Husserl embraces here is, of course, for each of us, a solitary meditation 'carried out in the first person singular'. The 'isolation' of the philosopher insisted upon here might seem to contradict the earlier affirmation of the communal character of philosophy pursued as a rigorous science. But that is not so. Rather, it specifies the nature of that community as, precisely, an *ethical* one, that is, as a community of self-responsible singularities.[98] Moreover, the idea of specifying a distinctively 'Cartesian Mediation' primarily as a matter of 'solitary self-reflection' is not in any case what we might expect. Indeed, what is strikingly missing in Husserl's representation of that idea is *any* invitation to engage with the epistemological problematic arising from 'the egocentric predicament' that we are generally used to treating as the basic Cartesian legacy. What Husserl emphasises with his gesture towards Descartes is not the legacy of an epistemological problematic but the idea of a 'presuppositionless' or 'neutral' starting point in philosophy: a radically self-reliant breaking off from all traditional assumptions and presuppositions. Not at all a development of the Cartesian problem of knowledge or the Cartesian conception of mind, but the rekindling, for each of us, of the irrecusable responsibility entailed by '*the question of the beginning*'.[99]

Heidegger could hardly object to the gesture Husserl identifies as Cartesian here since it is one that he also makes himself, inherits himself, pursuing, as we shall see in Chapter 3, his own work in phenomenology through an analysis of what he calls 'Dasein', a term used to designate 'man himself' in a way which he hoped would be, precisely, 'neutral'.[100] On the other hand, as we shall see, the neutrality that Heidegger seeks here is *also* a neutrality with respect to what he identifies as the fundamentally Cartesian understanding which interprets the entity that we ourselves are as, in each case, an isolated and worldless 'subject' or 'ego'. That is, what is to be neutralised by Heidegger is, in some way, *also* connected to what Husserl calls 'modern philosophy' in view of its specific twist to the turn to the first-person singular: the twist that opens on to the idea of an 'inner space' of subjectivity, a subjective field, whose 'being as it is' is compatible with the non-existence of the physical world.

This is a Cartesianism that Heidegger wants decisively to oppose, and his (Heidegger's) importance today still lies largely in the astonishing rigour of this opposition. The question is, however, whether this is a Cartesianism that Husserl surreptitiously inherits, perhaps inherits through the very beginning gesture that would hope to break with every inheritance. While I am inclined to think it is – there are further levels of faithfulness to Descartes in Husserl than the renewal of the (modernist[1]) idea that philosophical self-responsibility demands 'we make a new beginning' by 'put[ting] out of action all the convictions we have been accepting up to now'[101] – it is also clear that his *Cartesian Mediations* aim precisely to free us from what he thinks of as the fatal flaw in Descartes' own 'reduction' to the ego-cogito. Moreover, as I hope to show in what follows, ridding us of this flaw will turn out to be inseparable from achieving a 'transcendental turn' that would (Husserl hopes) arm us against the real bugbear of Cartesian philosophy – meaning by that its modern[2] not its modernist[1] character, its finding philosophical satisfaction from what, in Chapter 1, I called an account from the sideways-on perspective.

Husserl's new beginning for phenomenology, the crucial 'transcendental turn', starts to emerge at the end of section 7. Starting out with a classically Cartesian way of responding to the question of the beginning – embracing the classically Cartesian search for a presuppositionless and yet absolutely certain point of departure in the theory of knowledge – Husserl lurches away from Descartes:[102] 'But what if the world were not the absolutely first basis for judgments, and a being that is intrinsically prior to the world were the *already presupposed* basis for the existence of the world?'[103] In this unflagged but unmistakable shift to a *Kantian* transcendental perspective, Husserl now goes beyond Descartes even as he forms his own variation of the cogito argument.

The variation is superficially very close to Descartes' formulation at the start of the Second Meditation, where the Cartesian meditating thinker (heroically) affirms: 'let the demon deceive me as much as he can, he will never bring it about that I am nothing so long as I think I am something'. However, as A.D. Smith notes in his reading of Husserl's variation, we should not be fooled by the analogies between the Husserlian 'phenomenological *epoché*' that realises the turn to the solitude of a transcendental ego (as I suggested in Part II, this turn is prefigured by but not transcendentally conceived in his effort to 'set aside the totality of the existing world' in his first 'break-through' to phenomenology in the *Logical Investigations*) and what Descartes achieves with the hyperbolic doubts of the First Mediation:

> The phenomenological *epoché* is not and does not involve *any* process of doubt . . . . In the phenomenological *epoché* we have [an] operation [of 'setting aside' or 'bracketing' the world] in its purity, [and] doubt *excludes* [that operation]. For doubt is a certain 'position', as Husserl puts it, *vis-à-vis* the existence of something, other positions being certainty (the positive limit), disbelief (the negative limit), regarding as likely, etc. 'Bracketing' is a matter of putting *all* such positions out of

play, it is not a matter of cleaving universally to one of them – namely, doubt or certainty. Since doubt is precisely a matter of holding a position on the reality of something, it is a particular way in which bracketing, disconnection, has *not* been effected. Hence, Husserl insists over and over again that if we initially believe something, such belief *remains* when we effect the bracketing.[104]

The new Husserlian *epoché* that leads to the phenomenological reduction or 'regress to the ego' is thus not an expression of one's starting *uncertainty*, but fundamentally an expression of one's starting *freedom*: an expression – in Husserl's view the purest and most radical possible – of our capacity to 'step back from the natural impulse',[105] specifically to step back from what Husserl calls the 'natural attitude' of ordinary life, in which we have always already taken (and inhabit) various stepped-back 'positions'. But now, Smith's point in his reading of Husserl is that even if I thus 'abstain' or step back (by the *epoché*) from *every* such stepped-back 'position', I do not thereby *annul* any of them: *all previous positions remain* but I step back from them; they are set aside, bracketed. Hence Smith notes that for Husserl, 'as far as the content of our natural experience is concerned, the *epoché* leaves everything exactly as it is', *including* 'belief in a real world'.[106] In first-person terms that again mark a lurch away from Descartes towards the Kantian appeal to the cogito ('It must be possible for the "I think" to accompany all my representations'),[107] Husserl thus concludes that after the *epoché* 'the whole stream of my experiencing life ... is continually there *for me*'.[108]

Thus the crucial transition effected by the Husserlian *epoché* is not to the Cartesian idea that perhaps the world does not exist but to the Kantian idea that the world is in every respect something *for me*. We thereby make possible the distinctively 'transcendental reduction' which consists in a shift in focus to, or regress to, the subject *for whom* there is a world given as it is given in everyday 'positional' consciousness.

Could this (still) be a regress that takes Husserl towards a Cartesian conception of the mind as the typical Heideggerian reading of Husserl would suggest? We shall soon have decisive reason see that, in certain crucial respects, it does not.

Precisely in order to retain the distance to Descartes, Husserl calls the subject or ego reached in his Kantian-style version of the 'cogito' argument the transcendental ego, i.e. the subject that is presupposed in all my experience of the world (including my embodied or 'objectivated' self in the world). However, Descartes is not now a negligible figure. The existence of the transcendental ego, like a Cartesian 'thinking being', is something Husserl thinks one can affirm with 'apodictic' (that is, absolutely justified) certainty. And Husserl clearly thinks that, with Descartes' implicit awareness that for this subject there is no difference between what is given to the mind in the case of genuine knowledge and in the case of universal illusion, Cartesian philosophy stood on the on the very brink of 'insight' concerning 'the intrinsically first field of knowledge' that, in Husserl's view, it rightly sought.[109]

However, though standing on the brink of this supposed insight, 'on the threshold of the greatest of all discoveries', Descartes was also 'standing on the brink of a precipice',[110] and according to Husserl he made a mistake which plunged him right into it: from the revelation of the ego 'Descartes introduced the apparently insignificant but actually fateful change whereby the ego becomes a *substantia cogitans*, a separate human "*mens sive animus*" [mind or intelligence]'.[111] Portentously, Husserl remarks that, having performed the *epoché*, 'we remain aloof from all that'.[112] Indeed, Husserl now stands squarely against the Cartesian conception of the subjective field – the conception still at work in both Brentano and his own early thought – by insisting that the ego-cogito is not to be understood as the one bit of reality about which we have absolutely certain knowledge, or which remains somehow unbracketed, but, since the ego is a presupposition of every positional consciousness of existing reality (and so is not itself something that belongs to 'existing reality' as it appears *to me*), it must be understood in what Husserl calls 'its proper sense': 'namely of transcendental subjectivity'.[113]

Husserl's new transcendental conception hinges on the thought that the phenomenological reduction to the transcendental ego (with its entire life-stream) arrived at by the *epoché* is not itself the disclosure of a realm or region of reality – that of '*purely internal experience*', for example – with the rest of reality lying (perhaps, we hope) 'outside' it. On the contrary, from the new standpoint, in which one is focused exclusively on one's ego and its intentional contents, one comes to see that *every* intentional content within the life-stream of one's own ego, contents which include both one's own life as a human being in the world and the rest of the world one perceives, 'derives its whole sense and its existential status from me myself, *from me as the trans-cendental ego*, the ego who comes to the fore only with the transcendental-phenomenological *epoché*'.[114]

Descartes thinks that, starting with his own 'mind' as the one bit of reality he can be sure exists and having thus seemed to himself to have 'rescued a little *tag end of the world*',[115] his task is one of proving (on pain of regarding the rest of reality as perhaps nothing but a subjective illusion) that, as Heidegger would put it, 'independently of it and "outside" of it, a "world" is to be proved as present-at-hand'.[116] Husserl's phenomenological reduction aims, by contrast, to allow us to see that it is as mistaken to regard the ego as a substantial pre-sence or 'a piece of the world' as it is to conceive the world as a subjective illusion or 'a piece of my ego'. The inner and outer *both* need to be radically rethought on the basis of the reduction. We need to acknowledge both that the idea of the transcendence (the 'outsideness') of anything in the world is part of any object's intrinsic sense *as it is given* and that 'anything worldly necessarily acquires all the sense determining it, along with its existential status, ... only from my grounding acts'.[117]

Husserl speaks of such grounding acts as *constitutive* of the sense, including the existential sense, of the phenomena. The phenomena are thus 'constituted' *as* whatever type of existing thing they are (given as) *by* acts of consciousness that (for the most part passively) give unity to the pre-personal data of sensation so as to fabricate (synthesise) something objective *for me*: intentional objectivities. Obviously, talk of 'data' here is misleading insofar as it suggests an experientially given sense-stratum which is subsequently given meaning by subjective acts of mind. But that is not part of Husserl's picture. Indeed, it is a fundamental tenet of Husserlian phenomenology that what is 'first given' – which is what one might properly regard as 'basic experiential data' – is always *an intentional object*, and thus something that *already* has some *intentional content* or other. There is, therefore, no experientially given sense-data or, as Husserl calls it, 'hyletic data' (*hylé* is the Greek for matter or stuff) that is not an abstraction from constituted intentional objectivities which already have (various levels of *at least some* enriched) *sense* (for me). We can work backwards in experience to a stratum of sensuous contents – indeed to what Husserl calls 'a sphere of pure sensuousness'[118] – but that does not reveal a non-intentional stratum within experience. If anything is experientially given *at all* there is already a structure of intentionality involving the synthetic constitution of a sense-endowed (intentional) 'object-pole' for the subject.

There is, therefore, nothing in experience which corresponds to the classical empiricist's Given and Husserl fully endorses the essentially Kantian critique of empiricism. This critique turns on the claim that it is never sufficient for something to be true *for* one (for one to be sensorily aware of something), merely that something is true *of* one (that one is sensorily affected). This is the fundamental lesson of what Husserl calls the Kantian 'Copernican shift'. I will come back to this in the final section.

Descartes finds (correctly in Husserl's view) that the two basic cognitive situations he considers for the ego (the veridical and radically illusory scenarios) are, for the ego, identical. However, he still thinks it makes *sense* to conceive of a world 'outside' the world which, for that ego, is *given* with the sense 'outside'. Husserl's Kantian argument, by contrast, insists that the sense of what is given can only be derived from the (constitutive acts of the) ego to whom it is given. And hence, as he will come to put it, '*if* transcendental subjectivity is the universe of possible sense, then an outside is precisely – *nonsense*'.[119] This, in my view, is a remarkably important and profoundly influential argument for phenomenology, and in the next section I want to look at a formulation of it more closely.

Husserl's master argument and the inward turn

For later phenomenologists the 'if' we came to at the end of the last section will seem pretty big, and there is a serious question whether the very idea of a regress back from of the natural attitude (and so back from 'the answers we

54

give when we are unselfconsciously inside the ordinary practice') to non-worldly structures of a transcendental subject *still* builds an insuperably problematic subjectivism or even solipsism into one's reflective terms of trade. However, while we will see considerable resistance to accepting Husserl's '*if*' from within the shifting sequence of texts explored in this book, it is crucial to see that the form of argument he deploys against a scientific (or, as he sometimes puts it, 'transcendental') realist like Descartes is one that no subsequent phenomenologist will forswear. It is here we find an impulse in the inheritance of philosophy as phenomenology that seems to me to have survived in every re-launching of philosophy in the name of phenomenology after Husserl.

It is an argument which aims radically to question the *intelligibility* of the idea of reflectively shifting from what one might call 'the insider standpoint' to one which conceives that standpoint from sideways on and hence as related, as Husserl puts it, 'merely externally by a rigid law' to something (hopefully) lying outside it.[120] In other words, for Husserl the wriggle room required by the attempt reflectively to come to terms with (what Husserl conceives of as) the positional consciousness of the natural attitude is not one that can countenance its loss from view.

While this idea is implicit in the movement of the phenomenological *epoché* as I have presented it, Husserl only draws it into an explicit argument towards the end of the book. As a conclusion to this chapter, I will briefly turn to this closing presentation of this crucial phenomenological challenge to the outlook of ordinary modern[2] philosophy.

Philosophising within the presuppositions of the dominant tradition of ordinary philosophy, one tends to think that the essential task is to explain, for example, *how it is possible* to 'get outside my island of consciousness' or *how it is possible* that 'a subjective evidence-process can acquire objective significance'.[121] What I am regarding as Husserl's phenomenological 'master argument' aims to convince us that there are no good 'how possible' questions to be asked here.

Husserl tries to bring into relief the distinctively problematic status of ordinary philosophy's 'how possible' questions by putting his readers on the line and asking directly 'who ... can rightly ask such ... questions?' One might be inclined to answer robustly: I can! Husserl then seeks to clarify who this 'I' might be who says here 'I can'.[122] We know, first of all, that these are not questions for a 'natural man'.[123] This is not, as one might think, because common sense prevails for such a man but, if we follow Husserl to this point, because a 'natural man' is precisely someone for whom 'the validity of world-apperception has already been presupposed'.[124] Thus, for 'natural man' 'the psyche' is precisely *not* regarded as 'my island of consciousness', *not* regarded as the given point of departure for every relationship to 'transcendent' objects 'outside me'. On the contrary, in terms of the everyday phenomenological situation, in terms, that is, of one's ordinary spatial and temporal orientation in the world, each one of us is such that 'I *already have* an Outside Me'.[125]

So the 'how possible' questions can only be asked by someone for whom the validity of world-apperception has *not* already been presupposed. That is, the 'who' who can ask such questions must be the one who has more or less explicitly taken up (as Husserl put it in the *Logical Investigations*) an inquiry whose 'thought-stance' is 'the unnatural attitude of reflection',[126] someone who has, therefore, stepped back from the 'natural attitude' of ordinary life and hence has executed something like a phenomenological reduction. But a moment's reflection shows that the 'how possible' questions cannot belong to *that* ego either, since the very 'transcendency' which was in view to the 'natural man' is for *that* ego revealed *not* as something open to doubt (a 'position' that still belongs to the natural attitude) but as 'an immanent existential characteristic'.[127] For Husserl, then, the 'how possible' questions that emerge from what he pointedly calls 'the usual post-Cartesian way of thinking' are really just *senseless pseudo-questions* which trade entirely on what he takes to be the crucial post-Cartesian misunderstanding 'of the genuine sense of the reduction to the indubitable',[128] a misunderstanding which regards the revealed ego as 'a bit of reality', a misunderstanding which alone can spur us to the explanatory sideways-on theorizing called for by the 'how possible' questions. But the very idea of taking up such a theoretical perspective is, according to Husserl's master argument, not simply false; it is *strictly nonsensical.*

The argument here demands that you (the reader) engage your own capacity faithfully to retrieve (for) yourself (as from the inside) an understanding of yourself and of the world that really does not come easily to you *at all*, does not, that is, belong *either* to the usual outlook of your natural attitude *or* to the usual outlook of the dominant, sedimented tradition of philosophy that has come down to you. Thus it takes a peculiar discipline of the reader and not only of the philosophising writer to liberate oneself from this 'cruder' Cartesian way[129] and to break free from thinking one has asked a good 'how possible' question. The *work* of phenomenology thus involves an irreducible reference to the reader. However, Husserl's hope was that the reader's task could be massively simplified by the possibility of following what he (Husserl) regarded as the proper methodological procedures, procedures that lay down a systematic path that can take philosophy forward.

The fundamental movements of Husserl's phenomenological procedures, prefigured as we have seen in his early 'break-through' writings, involve a meditation which aims to set aside *every* dimension or structural aspect of one's own life-stream which presupposes *any* factual peculiarities or in the world commitments, whether in relation to things or to others. It involves, then, a distinctively 'inward' withdrawal which seeks to disclose the primordial basis of the constitution of the *sense* of an 'existing world' or of a 'truly existing other' within the purely subjective field of the transcendental ego. Husserl explicitly draws on Kantian resources to describe the general 'Copernican shift' effected by his phenomenological method, a shift which aims to demonstrate 'the essential rootedness of any objective world in transcendental subjectivity'.[130]

In other (equally Kantian) words, the ultimate grounds of the objectivity of all objects (of whatever type; 'for example: of Nature, psychophysical being, humanness, sociality of various levels, and culture')[131] are claimed to lie in the essential structures of subjectivity of the transcendental subject.[132] The *sense* of objectivity of all objects (what it means to be an object of whatever type) is thus disclosed everywhere 'as a *constituted* sense'.[133] Phenomenology as Husserl practices it is thus a method for 'going back into the constitutive' which seeks, like the 'first philosophy' of classical Greek metaphysics, 'ultimate cognitions of being'.[134]

As I have indicated, the inheritance of phenomenology after Husserl that I will be following in this book is largely unpersuaded that the regress to the subject, albeit a transcendental subject, that characterises the Husserlian conception of phenomenological method can prevent what Husserl identifies as the lingering worry that it inevitably 'lapses into a transcendental solipsism'.[135] Husserl himself was confident that this lingering worry could be fully answered. While admitting that there is a sense in which there is something right in the solipsist's view, he regards it as involving a crucial and avoidable error. Thus, *on the one hand*, it is true that I constitute the *sense* of the objectivity of all objects, and constitute too the sense of the 'alter ego' *as* a 'truly existing other'. And Husserl embraces the idea that the proper mode of phenomenological research is nothing but an explication of this sense. However, *on the other hand*, it is, he insists, a fundamental error to suppose that 'what I constitute' must be regarded as 'belonging to me', as something that is merely 'for me'.[136] On the contrary, what is constituted in me, for me, is the sense of objectivity of objects and of the alterity of others as, precisely, 'outside me' and as another 'me' who is *not* me (another subject who, like me, has its *own* point of view on an objective world). And this is so 'even though the proposition that everything existing for me must derive its existential sense exclusively from me myself ... retains its validity and importance'.[137]

For Husserl, then, transcendental phenomenology is essentially an explication of the (consitituted) *sense* of the world we live in with others, not 'theory-building' with regard to how it might be possible, for example, to have knowledge of objects or of other subjects on the basis of experience. In a crucial respect, then, Husserlian transcendental phenomenology fundamentally interrupts the movement of ordinary modern[2] philosophy that pretends to be able to take such questions seriously and tries to answer them. And transcendental phenomenology effects this profound interruption of ordinary philosophy precisely by leaving everything as it is:[138] *'Phenomenological explication does nothing but explicate the sense this world has for us, prior to any philosophising ... – a sense which philosophy can uncover but never alter.'*[139]

While the pursuit of such phenomenological explication should, in this way, precisely *not* leave ordinary modern[2] philosophy, and so, for Husserl, not leave our contemporary culture, as it is, it remains characteristic of Husserl's method that it presupposes an inward withdrawal that belongs unmistakeably to the

Cartesian tradition of philosophies of the cogito. The path involves a regress to a subject in order, from that apodictic starting point, to return once more, although now within philosophy, to our pre-reflective point of departure. The path is conceived, therefore, as 'the path of universal *self*-knowledge' which, as Husserl puts it, takes one in a direction in which 'I must lose the world by *epoché* in order to regain it by a universal self-examination.'[140] Husserl closes the *Cartesian Meditations* by citing St Augustine, the author of the first cogito: 'truth dwells in the inner man'.[141]

While the inheritance of phenomenology after Husserl that I will be exploring in this book is sometimes marked by a certain Cartesianism, none go along with Husserl on the particular inward path he laid down for his phe-nomenological followers. Indeed, most would affirm what Merleau-Ponty came to affirm: truth does not dwell in the inner man because '*there is no inner man, man is in the world, and only in the world does he know himself*'.[142] After Husserl, the first and most radical step in this deviant direction came from Heidegger. In Heidegger's work there would be no going back to the solitude of an ego, transcendental or otherwise, but, as Merleau-Ponty's comment suggests, a turn around for phenomenology that would re-launch it as an interpretative engagement with our existence as, essentially and irreducibly, *in the world*. Indeed, we find with Heidegger a phenomenologist who fills out the cogito by precisely reversing and displacing (and hence 'deconstructing') the direction of Husserl's more traditional filling out of it. In a passage that is directly responsive to the Husserlian point of departure in intentional structures of consciousness, Heidegger insists that

> if the '*cogito sum*' is to serve as the point of departure for the existen-tial analytic of Dasein, then it needs to be turned around [*Umkehrung*] ... The '*sum*' is then asserted first, and indeed in the sense that 'I am in a world'.[143]

It is to the beginnings of this about-turn in the inheritance of phenomenology that I will now turn.

3

PHENOMENOLOGY AS FUNDAMENTAL ONTOLOGY

Martin Heidegger

The new beginning again

Martin Heidegger's *Being and Time* (1927), the early work on which his reputation as a major phenomenologist largely rests, is a hugely ambitious undertaking. Against the grain of modern[2] times it does not seek merely to articulate
an original response to this or that problem in this or that area of philosophical
research,[1] but to achieve that by engaging anew in a 'battle of the giants' (a
gigantomachia [γιγαντομαχία]) over what must strike many today as the most
baffling of questions: the 'question of Being' [*Seinsfrage*], the question 'What is
the meaning of Being?'[2] Could there be a less contemporary theme, at least for
our contemporaries who feel most contemporary?

Heidegger's text raises specific problems for a book that takes up 'beginnings'
too. As we shall see, Heidegger does not start out by presenting a worked-out
conception that will be opposed to those of others, but with an admission that,
at the beginning of the inquiry, one does not quite know what to say or even
know how to begin. And his progress is marked less by the sureness of a single
path than by a series of new beginnings and restarts each taking on board,
developing, enriching and reinterpreting earlier departures. In fact, given the
unfinished state in which it was to remain, the text comprises a series of
beginnings without end.[3]

With respect to the departures made in *Being and Time* I will restrict myself
to those from the initial phases of the book and to the modernist[1] question of
the beginning that comes into view there. Yet even in the book's opening we
find a start that very rapidly calls for a radical restart. Setting off with a preliminary plunge into the question of Being – the 'theme of ontology'[4] that
remains throughout Heidegger's *primary* concern – the text rapidly re-launches
into what Heidegger calls 'a phenomenology of *Dasein*'.[5] As we shall see, the
shift from one point of departure to another does not mark a retreat from the
primary concern but, for Heidegger, is a matter of getting involved with it in
the right way. As he will put it, '*only as phenomenology, is ontology possible*'.[6]
Taking in this segue at the opening of *Being and Time*, Parts I and II of this

chapter will follow this double departure, a double departure that will also effect the turnaround from the starting point of Husserlian phenomenology noted at the end of Chapter 2. Part III will try to bring out the distinctive manner in which Heidegger's project in *Being and Time* engages with contemporary modernity[2] by examining one of his most audacious deviations from what he regards as the contemporary passion for science, his inaugural lecture at Freiburg University in 1929. That lecture also marks Heidegger's taking up of the chair which had been previously held by Husserl. As we shall see, Heidegger doesn't miss the opportunity to turn away from Husserl there either.

Part I: Fundamental ontology

The question of Being

In view of its leading off with a citation from Plato's *Sophist* it has been remarked that *Being and Time* begins 'in the middle of a Platonic dialogue'.[7] However, what that *co*-locating of texts passes over is the insistence in Heidegger's opening words of a fundamental *dis*-location of times: a contrast between the situation that belonged to a certain 'we ... now' in Plato's time and a very different one that belongs to the 'we ... in our time' in ours.[8] This opening contrast is elaborated as a puzzle: namely, that, unlike 'the ancient philosophers' who found 'what you mean when you use the expression "being"' 'continually disturbing' and were 'perplexed' by what it means, 'we ... today' are not puzzled by it at all, 'not at all'.[9] Heidegger begins, then, with a puzzle about the absence of a puzzle, an absence that marks our time as contemporary, as distinctively ours. It is a kind of 'riddle'[10] that, as he puts it, 'we already live in an understanding of Being' – and yet today we are utterly untroubled by the fact that the meaning of Being 'is still veiled in darkness'.[11]

This is an intriguing but no doubt also perplexing opening for a reader today. For even if one accepts that Heidegger is right to say 'this question has today been forgotten',[12] and even if one accepts that it 'provided a stimulus for the researches of Plato and Aristotle',[13] indeed, even if one accepts that 'what sanctions its complete neglect' in our time is rooted in the very tradition of analysis of the concept 'Being' that has come down to us from those non-contemporary Greek sources,[14] a contemporary reader might still wonder whether the absence of a puzzle is really so puzzling. Indeed, one might well think today that the so-called 'question of Being' is itself, *as a question*, fundamentally *questionable*. I mean: a reader in our time is likely to have concerns that it is not clear what the question means or even if it means anything at all, and have concerns too that Heidegger does not seem all that concerned to help his readers out on this score. One might recall here the British philosopher R.M. Hare's annoyance at 'German philosophers ... who do not even seem worried about convincing the sceptic that their philosophical propositions mean something',[15] philosophers who 'have chosen to ignore [the] important developments made by Vienna Circle positivism' and who 'carry on in their old ways as if nothing had happened'.[16] As if nothing had happened, Heidegger is, right from the start, up and running, resolutely committed to what the title of the very first section of *Being and Time* dramatically calls 'The Necessity for Explicitly Restating the Question of Being'.

The impatience shown towards philosophical writings that retain a certain patience towards questions that Vienna Circle positivism sought to foreclose seems to have a particularly pointed relevance to the opening of *Being and Time* and its openness to the question of Being. Indeed, Heidegger knows that 'if anyone continues to ask it he is charged with an error of method'.[17] Hare's impatience with a willingness to pursue such (as he calls them) 'metaphysical' questions has just that kind of ground: philosophers who 'carry on in their old ways' are not just taking a different philosophical path but overlooking what we (a certain 'we ... in our time') have come to recognise as the *logically prior* question of whether their 'statements' on such topics actually 'mean something'.[18] If they do not, then one should just stop advancing them as if they do; and if they do, this meaning should be clearly explained and not left in a dark and enigmatic obscurity. On this view, the best one can say is that a philosopher who in our times carries on with such matters 'as if nothing had happened' shows an annoying willingness to use words whose meaning is (at least) not clear. The fact that Heidegger anticipates that others will come who will charge him with an error of method doesn't mean he hasn't made one.

But it is not obvious that it is incumbent on Heidegger to give an answer to the question of what 'Being' means at the *outset* of the inquiry since, after all, that is meant to be the basic question *for* the inquiry. And that is not all. Though it will require a certain patience to come to terms with it, there is also a philosophical significance to his manner of launching. Heidegger does not want simply to present 'results' to a passive reader but, in a profoundly phenomenological gesture, wants to commence *with* his reader, indeed, in a manner that he will identify later in the book as a distinctively 'authentic' mode of 'being-with' an other. For if we jump to the analysis of being with others in the fourth chapter of *Being and Time*, we find Heidegger contrasting there 'two extreme possibilities' for 'Being-with-one-another' that for all the world look like relations between a teacher and a pupil or between a guide and one who is guided. In the first case the one who has taken the position of teacher or guide attempts to '*leap in*' for the other and thus 'take over for the other that with which he is to concern himself'. In the second case, by contrast, the teacher or guide 'does not so much leap in for the other as *leap ahead* of him'.[19] In keeping with what in Chapter 1 I called the essential demand-ingness of phenomenological philosophy Heidegger's own understanding of *the kind of question* he is engaging with is such that he finds it crucial not to position the reader as someone who is simply under instruction, as someone who can come to terms with the matter for thinking without having to work through it for themselves. Heidegger's understanding of the starting condition of his reader – the reader in our time who lacks being puzzled by the meaning of Being – is not external to the way the book starts.

I will return to Heidegger's conception of the starting position of his reader again, but for the moment I want to take advantage of his not 'leaping in' concerning the meaning of Being to ask, not what his propositions about Being mean but, in what I think is a far more profitable turn, what justification one might offer for thinking that there is anything that one might legitimately call 'an *inquiry* into the meaning of Being' in the first place.

Cora Diamond nicely summarises an idea central to Wittgenstein's thought in the 'nutshell' that 'what it is that we are talking about is shown in how we talk about it, and in how that talk enters our lives, the shape – the "face" – that life containing such talk has'.[20] This nutshell has its own nutshell in the slogan 'Tell me how you are looking and I will tell you what you are looking for'. The question I want to raise with respect to Heidegger's text is whether it provides any basis for the idea that there is some way of looking or seeking, some way of going about one's business, that might intelligibly be called 'undertaking an inquiry into the meaning of Being'. Do we have *any idea at all* how to distinguish going about *that* inquiry 'rightly' and going about it in 'the wrong way altogether'? Is there anything that I am willing to call doing or failing to do *that*? And if not, then the very idea of such an inquiry, as yet, has no sense – and hence also (according to the nutshell) the idea that there is a distinctive 'what' that we are inquiring about has, as yet, no sense either. The first opening of *Being and Time* that I want to follow is concerned precisely with the question of finding the right way (even) to begin. The course of this chapter as a whole aims to gain a sense of 'the shape – the "face" – that life containing talk' about Being might have, and have for us today.

The inquiry into the meaning of 'Being'

Hare's impatience with what he calls 'German philosophy' is the upshot of his concern with a lack of concern for engaging in the first instance with questions about meaning. True enough, Heidegger does not begin by laying out a theory of meaning.[21] On the other hand, with respect to the question of Being, questions concerning the meaning of the words we use and our understanding or non-understanding of them are absolutely central to his point of departure. Indeed, it is striking that Heidegger immediately identifies the question of Being in terms of what we *mean* and *understand* by 'Being'. The question Heidegger wishes to 'raise anew' is precisely '*the question of the meaning* [Sinn] *of Being*'.[22] He is interested, therefore, in *what is understood* in 'any understanding of Being whatsoever'.[23]

So Heidegger is concerned straightaway with issues of meaning and understanding. Nevertheless, one might still baulk at the assumption that there is some 'what' that is the 'what is understood' in the particular case Heidegger is concerned with. Or, as I am urging that we look at this, one might still want to ask what sense there is, if any, to undertaking an inquiry that would take up this question.

We have a recognisably modernist[1] predicament at this point – a problem with the question of how even to begin. In the second section of *Being and Time*, and on the basis of little more than a previous and, of course, itself baffling assertion that 'we already live in an understanding of Being',[24] Heidegger outlines what would make it possible to get things going in the following terms:

> Inquiry, as a kind of seeking, must be guided beforehand by what is sought. So the meaning of Being must already be available to us in some way. As we have intimated, we always conduct our activities in an understanding of Being. Out of this understanding arise both the explicit question of the meaning of Being and the tendency that leads towards its conception.[25]

The questionableness of the question is held at bay here with a barely supported assurance that what is asked about in the question is, in fact, already 'available to us in some way'. But then that should be enough: we should be able to tell 'in some way' what will and what will not be 'appropriate conduct' for an inquiry in this case.

Yet he immediately goes on to state, or confesses on our behalf, that things are not nearly so simple:

> As we have intimated, we always conduct our activities in an understanding of Being. Out of this understanding arise both the explicit question of the meaning of Being and the tendency that leads towards its conception. We do not *know* what 'Being' means.

Heidegger's first remarks about the conditions of an inquiry suggest, however shakily, why he thinks he may be able to address the question of Being in an appropriately focused way. But then suddenly the road seems closed again: we do not know what 'Being' means, and so we do not know what we mean by the question of Being. However, according to Heidegger the fact that 'we do not know what "Being" means' does not mean that in attempting to address the question we are simply talking nonsense and should give up. We may not *know* it, but we are not, he thinks, in a condition of utter ignorance either:

> We do not *know* what 'Being' means. But even if we ask, 'What *is* "Being"?', we keep within an understanding of the 'is', though we are unable to fix conceptually what that 'is' signifies. We do not even know the horizon in terms of which that meaning is to be grasped and fixed. *But this vague average understanding of Being is still a fact.*[26]

Hare declared himself unwilling 'to read or discuss philosophy' with people who are, by his lights, insensitive to the problem of 'convincing the sceptic that their philosophical propositions mean something'. But, as should now be clear, Heidegger does not ride roughshod over the question of what, if anything, his question means. Quite the reverse. On the other hand, perhaps Hare would be no happier reading or discussing philosophy with someone who confesses that, with respect to what is asked about, they do not know what they mean. I can well understand impatience in the first kind of situation, but, as I will explain, impatience in the second is far from obviously appropriate in philosophy.

Hare takes exception to philosophical discussions which are not (for well-trained philosophers) more or less immediately 'clear and to the point'.[27] They can be difficult, of course, but should not be unclear. Heidegger, by contrast, seems to begin by stressing (clearly enough) how unclear the meaning of his question is. To put it another way, Hare's worry is that a philosopher is going about his business in the *wrong* way when he is prepared to use words whose meaning is (at best) not clear, and, as we have just confirmed, Heidegger is clearly willing to do just that. But, for Heidegger, at the start of the inquiry this 'being prepared to use words whose meaning is unclear' is a state of affairs that the inquirer experiences as strictly *undeniable* and not a reflection of an inquirer who is somehow *unconscientious* – and that shifts the weight of the observation. That is, it is no longer a criticism of a philosophical inquiry but an affirmation of its first condition. It is, Heidegger thinks, precisely because the meaning of 'Being' is 'in some way' available to us and yet cannot be brought to concepts without more ado that he wants explicitly to undertake 'an investigation of the meaning of Being'.[28]

Rendering what is already in some way available to us conceptually transparent is the form of clarification that Heidegger attempts in *Being and Time*. And, as we saw in Chapters 1 and 2, it is precisely in view of this form of difficulty that phenomenology is elaborated as a method of philosophical analysis. The sense of 'unclarity' at issue here is one which contrasts sharply with the state of pre-theoretical ignorance that comes before making discoveries or building theories in natural science, and for Heidegger it is this contrast which brings into view what he will want us to acknowledge as the contour of a distinctively *philosophical* question. Wittgenstein's discussion of philosophical questions in *Philosophical Investigations* invites us to acknowledge this difference too. He cites Augustine's condition of estranged puzzlement in the face of the question of time ('What, therefore, is time?') as a characteristic example: If no one questions me I have no problem; if I am questioned I am at a loss.[29] 'This could not be said about a question in natural science', Wittgenstein notes.[30] Heidegger's conception of our starting unclarity with respect to the question of Being has a fundamentally similar shape: it concerns something which is, in one way, 'closest and well known' but, in another way, 'the farthest and not known at all'.[31] Heidegger's phenomenological clarification is thus oriented towards bringing something that is, in what he calls 'an egregious sense', 'hidden' into clear view, to 'let us see' it.[32] Significantly, the Augustinian reference that Wittgenstein draws on to illustrate the sense of something that can be 'hidden' precisely because of its 'familiarity'[33] also belongs to Heidegger's elaboration of this point, although the issue has (on the face of it) shifted. He (Heidegger) cites Augustine's estrangement from his own being: 'But what is closer to me than myself? Assuredly I labour here and I labour within myself; I have become to myself a land of trouble and inordinate sweat.'[34] The theme may appear to have changed but the avowal of estranged puzzlement in the face of a question is the same.[35]

So there is, if not knowledge, then at least some pre-reflective *familiarity* that should make it possible to get an investigation started and, indeed, motivates doing so not 'just casually' but on the basis of an 'explicitly formulated' question.[36] On the other hand, however, if Heidegger really does not know what 'Being' means, how can he *be* so sure that there *is* anything at all that *is* 'what is asked about' in this question? How can he *be* so sure that an investigation of any kind could possibly be undertaken on this question? Heidegger's first answer, his first argument, is: look at the questions just posed; the very questions themselves can only be asked, you yourself can only ask them, from within an understanding of the meaning of the 'is' and of 'being'. Of course, we have no problem with this understanding when no one questions us and no special difficulty when we are questioned just casually about what is understood in this understanding. The *problem* is, however, that when we come *explicitly* to ask ourselves about what is understood here, we are, if we are not already 'infiltrated with traditional theories',[37] far from surefooted and, in the face of being utterly unprepared to engage in an inquiry with respect to an estranged puzzlement of this 'distinctive character',[38] more than likely tempted to elaborate 'ideas' based on a 'picture' of Being (as Wittgenstein might put it) rather than pursue an investigation that unfolds our pre-reflective familiarity with the meaning of the 'is'.[39]

The picture here, Heidegger suggests, is one in which Being is interpreted, without more ado, with '*time* as its standpoint'.[40] Heidegger does not dispute the correctness of this picture *at all* but takes issue with the traditional ideas which have grown from it, ideas which consistently privilege 'a definite mode of time – the "Present"'.[41] In the ontological tradition that Heidegger engages with, 'entities are grasped in their Being as "presence"'.[42] And, according to Heidegger, this tradition, as it has come down to us, not only does not assist but positively stands in the way of rightly seeing the 'temporal character' of Being,[43] stands in the way of coming to temporal terms with the question of Being in an adequate manner.

Heidegger's claims about the starting point in his inquiry come to this, then. On his view, the fact that we cannot *know* that our way of going on is taking the right path or not is not to be conceived as a radically disabling defect but the basic (and, as we have seen, modernist[1]) condition of our starting situation with the question of Being: 'what we seek when we inquire into Being is not something entirely unfamiliar, even if proximally we cannot grasp it at all'.[44] To begin with we are not adequately prepared – indeed we are profoundly ill prepared – for the task of putting into words or fixing conceptually what it is that we are asking about. And that despite the 'fact' that we seem 'in some way' to have an understanding of it – some kind of familiarity with it – already.

In the next section I want to bring the idea of an inquiry appropriate to the question of Being – what Heidegger will call a phenomenological inquiry – into sharper relief by looking more closely at its *relationship* with inquiries of kinds which, according to Heidegger, it essentially is *not*; namely, with (what he will call) 'metaphysics' and with 'science'.[45]

The essence and end of philosophy

Despite his opening references to 'the researches of Plato and Aristotle', it is easy to see Heidegger as an out-and-out critic of the Western philosophical tradition. His talk of '*destroying the history of ontology*' can encourage the idea that he simply *rejects* what has come down to us, that he wants to bring philosophy as we know it to an end.[46] However, a glance at the context of Heidegger's remarks here makes it clear that he does not regard 'having a tradition' as an optional extra for us, as something we might simply reject or rid ourselves of. So his notion of 'destruction' does not and cannot have 'the negative sense' of 'shaking a tradition off', but a 'positive' one: namely, of 'making the past our own'. 'On its negative side', Heidegger insists, 'its criticism is aimed at "today" and at the prevalent way of treating the history of ontology.'[47] We have already broached the way the opening of *Being and Time* is framed by a dislocation of times that serves to specify our 'today'. In this section the examination of contrasting kinds of inquiries will help us span the period of this dislocation and see its connection to 'the prevalent way of treating the history of ontology'. In Part III of this chapter I will engage more directly with what is at stake in a 'criticism aimed at "today"'.

Although it would be a mistake to think that Heidegger wants simply to reject our philosophical heritage or bring it to an end, it is also true that, according to Heidegger, the subject that we call 'philosophy' *is*, in our time, coming to an end. However, this is not at all a piece of braggadocio on Heidegger's part, since he does not think it is coming to an end under the pressure of his own critique. No, it is coming to an end under its own steam. For by 'the end of philosophy' Heidegger does not mean its *disposal* or elimination through a new kind of criticism (what could be more philosophical than a critique of philosophy?), but rather its *dissolution* into positive empirical science. As we shall see, this view has been put forward by others, but where the movement towards such a 'completion' is typically regarded as a sign of progress, for Heidegger it is not something to be championed or cheered. For unlike most defenders of this view of the end of philosophy, Heidegger thinks that something was left behind at the start of philosophy and its ending only makes more urgent a new beginning for another task for thinking. As I hope to show in this section, the history of philosophy as Heidegger understands it *is* this constant leaving behind of what it is nonetheless open to on the way to completion as positive science – and Heidegger's inquiry aims precisely to speak about what the philosophical tradition has consistently passed over in silence.

But what does Heidegger understand by philosophy here? In *Being and Time* Heidegger typically identifies the history of the subject that goes by that name with the history of ontology, and he typically calls it, simply, metaphysics. For reasons I will explain, Heidegger's basic understanding is that 'philosophy *is* metaphysics'.[48]

What, then, is metaphysics? This question supplies the title for the inaugural lecture that I will look at in Part III of this chapter, a lecture in which he also identifies philosophy with metaphysics.[49] However, as we shall see, while Heidegger wants fundamentally to *distinguish* what he does from metaphysics he remains also, in a certain way, decisively *on the side* of metaphysics.

The point is that there is to be, with Heidegger's thinking, a displacement of the subject we call 'philosophy' – a displacement of metaphysics – but not simply a departure from it altogether. The kind of displacing move in view here can again be brought out by considering a comparable gesture in Wittgenstein's thought. Having just called into question the idea that the use of words is governed by definite rules, Wittgenstein specifies the ultimate motivation for his reflections on the structure and functioning of language in terms of its relation to a long-cherished understanding of a 'logical investigation':

> These considerations bring us up to the problem: In what sense is logic something sublime.
>
> For there seemed to pertain to logic a peculiar depth – a universal significance. Logic lay, it seemed, at the bottom of all the sciences. — For logical investigation explores the nature of all things. It seeks to see to the bottom of things and is not meant to concern itself whether what actually happens is this or that. — It takes its rise, not from an interest in the facts of nature, nor from a need to grasp causal connexions: but from an urge to understand the basis, or essence, of everything empirical. Not, however, as if to this end we had to hunt out new facts; it is, rather, of the essence of our investigation that we do not seek to learn anything *new* by it. We want to *understand* something that is already in plain view. For *this* is what we seem in some sense not to understand.[50]

This passage helpfully specifies the idea of philosophy as metaphysics that, in my view, Heidegger wants to move away from. However, it also shows why we should be wary of reading Wittgenstein or, as I am suggesting here, Heidegger as simply *opposed* to this traditional ('metaphysical') conception. In Wittgenstein's case the very long dash in the middle of the quoted passage marks a silent turn to terms of description which also and increasingly belong to his own inheritance of the subject called 'philosophy'. He starts to speak, that is to say, not simply against but, as it were, in a way that moves alongside and even inside the traditional philosophical voice. And this is something one finds in Heidegger too. Even as he calls into question the long-cherished 'metaphysical' understanding of philosophical investigations, even as his own work of words seeks to free our responsiveness to a question he thinks that understanding is unable to hear, Heidegger does not simply reject the philosophical tradition. Indeed, as the discussion of the last section should suggest, Wittgenstein's segueing description of 'the essence of our investigation' (as concerned with something already familiar) is something Heidegger clearly embraces too.

As I say, however, it is equally clear that 'metaphysics' is the title for the historical form of philosophical inquiry which *contrasts* with what Heidegger wants to do. In this respect 'metaphysics' is the title Heidegger uses to identify the kind of philosophy which has dominated since Greek times, the kind of philosophy which, Heidegger supposes, is coming to an end in our own. Specifically, it is philosophy as an inquiry into the foundations of science, or into 'the essence of everything empirical'; an inquiry into *everything* insofar as it *is*; an inquiry which aims finally to understand the *whole* universe of *beings*; an inquiry aiming to grasp the essence (as ground or foundation) of everything empirical; an inquiry into the Being (as ground or foundation) of *all* beings; an inquiry which concerns itself with beings as beings or beings-as-a-whole, and thus is an inquiry '*over* beings' – *that* is '*meta*-physics'.[51]

It is not difficult, I think, to see how this understanding of philosophical inquiry fits with a view of it as finding its final 'completion' when it has opened up fields of empirical study for *every* type of being (Heidegger's clear view of the end of philosophy as metaphysics). However, and this is crucial, Heidegger does not envisage this achievement positivistically; that is, as a victory for or validation of positive, empirical science as, finally, the only legitimate mode of inquiry. Indeed, my hope of getting any sort of handle on the inquiry into Being in this chapter depends entirely on making a case for Heidegger's claim that what first calls for philosophy is something which can neither be grasped by philosophy as metaphysics nor answered by natural scientific studies. What Heidegger is committed to is a way of (non-empirical) thinking for which the (now no doubt also misleading) title 'philosophy' remains irresistibly appropriate, but it will be thinking which would belong 'neither to ... metaphysics ... nor [to] the sciences'.[52] So what is it? I will take my bearings on this question by first considering the relationship between those inquiries which it is not.

That Heidegger regards metaphysics and science as importantly related belongs to the idea that metaphysics finds its 'legitimate completion' in the formation of natural or positive sciences. As I have mentioned, this is not an especially unusual or unorthodox idea. The British proponent of linguistic phenomenology J.L. Austin also affirmed it, and it is worth reminding oneself how plausible an idea it is:

> In the history of human inquiry, philosophy has the place of the initial sun, seminal and tumultuous: from time to time it throws off some portion of itself to take station as a science, a planet cool and well regulated, progressing steadily towards a distant final state. This happened long ago at the birth of mathematics, and again at the birth of physics: only in the last century we have witnessed the same process once again, slow and at the same time almost imperceptible, in the birth of the science of mathematical logic . . . . Is it not possible that the next century may see the birth ... of a true and comprehensive *science of language*? Then we shall have rid ourselves of one more part of philosophy (there will be plenty left) in the only way we ever can get rid of philosophy, by kicking it upstairs.[53]

The idea that Austin so vividly captures here, that philosophy has its end in a kind of promotion into science, is precisely what Heidegger envisages as the proper end, the 'dissolution' which is also the 'legitimate completion', of philosophy as metaphysics.[54] The notable contrast between Austin and Heidegger (besides the fundamental fact that Heidegger envisages a continuing task for a distinctively non-scientific kind of thinking at the end of philosophy as metaphysics) is that, while Austin seems to think that there is a long way to go before the philosophical sun is exhausted, Heidegger believes that the end is nigh: 'in the present age', says Heidegger, 'philosophy is coming to an end'.[55]

On the face of it one might be strongly inclined to side with Austin here. But, to take Austin's own example, many contemporary linguists after Chomsky would want to claim that we have already seen 'the birth of a true and comprehensive science of language'. Furthermore, it is not implausible to suppose that for *every* area of inquiry which continues to be investigated in philosophy today there is not some scientist (or some philosopher who is gripped by the idea of scientific inquiry) who believes that the proper way to settle the questions will be through the development of a baldly natural, scientific theory, and who believes that philosophers who are still going on 'in their old ways' are dinosaurs soon to disappear.

It is the cultural dominance today of this naturalistic point of view which informs Heidegger's assessment of the idea of the imminent end of philosophy. It is a point of view which wants not merely to 'assimilate' philosophical inquiry to inquiries in the natural sciences, but (at least on the 'strongly scientistic' version identified in Chapter 1) to disqualify the claims of non-scientific inquiries altogether. Like Husserl, and indeed to a significant extent shoulder to shoulder with him, Heidegger is totally opposed to this view. We noted at the beginning of Chapter 2 that Ryle was quite wrong to criticise Husserl for assimilating philosophy and science. However, it is true that

Husserl has a serious interest in the historical *relationship* between philosophy and science. And, following Husserl quite closely, this is something that Heidegger examines too, drawing (as Husserl does) a distinctive tripartite division of related but radically different *levels* of inquiry.

On the Husserlian model accepted by Heidegger, the highest level is that of the empirical or positive sciences: inquiries that want to concern themselves with 'what actually happens' and which have their primary focus of interest 'in the facts'. At the next level down there are those inquiries which *found* such sciences: what Husserl calls 'regional ontologies'.[56] While Heidegger would not subscribe to the Husserlian idea that a positive science presupposes 'the apprehending in its purity' of an '*eidos*' that would specify the 'essence' of beings of a certain type,[57] he does affirm the idea of 'ontology in its widest sense' as that inquiry which lays the foundations for the positive sciences by 'leaping ahead, as it were, into some area of Being'.[58] This running ahead of positive scientific inquiries involves the 'disclosure' *in advance of empirical investigation* of some 'definite area of subject-matter', thus opening up the possibility for a science which examines beings 'as beings of such and such a type'.[59]

In the last section I touched on the thought that inquiries in general must be guided beforehand by some kind of prior understanding of what is inquired about. Thus, even if a regional ontology has not been explicitly undertaken, every positive science, what Heidegger includes within what he calls 'ontical inquiry' in general, presumes, as its founding condition of possibility, either an explicit 'ontological inquiry' or at least a 'pre-ontological understanding' of its subject matter: a supply of (more or less well-worked-out) 'basic concepts' which articulate some 'area' or 'region' within the domain of beings as a whole.[60] And the thought is, to use Austin's image, that 'in the history of human inquiry, philosophy has the place of the initial sun' which has done the most far-reaching spadework for opening up fields for positive sciences, and which has, in the first instance, supplied their basic, subject-specifying concepts. 'Such research', Heidegger states, 'must run ahead of the positive sciences, and it *can*.' And he suggests that, on this score, 'the work of Plato and Aristotle is evidence enough'.[61] Their inquiries 'seminal and tumultuous' have, over time, given rise to sciences which can, in a certain way, get on alone. Heidegger calls this 'more primordial' and 'preliminary' work of 'ontology in its widest sense', the work of 'laying the foundations for the sciences'.[62]

So Heidegger follows Husserl in drawing a distinction between positive or ontical science, on the one hand, and a foundational discipline, 'regional ontology' or 'ontology in its widest sense', on the other. However, as I have indicated, Husserl wants to go further and ultimately draws a tripartite division. In his view, the regress from positive science to regional ontology does not reach bedrock. As we saw in Chapter 2, there is, for Husserl, a more basic level a further stage back: the regress to 'transcendental phenomenology'. The latter inquiry would have as its concern the disclosure of the foundations of *all* regional ontology.

As we have seen, following in the tradition of philosophies of the cogito after Descartes and Kant, for Husserl this further regress would be to that inquiry which brings to full presence the presence of a *transcendental subject*. That is, transcendental phenomenology is conceived as the 'universal science', identifying the constitution of the objectivity of all objects (the Being of *all* beings, in *all* 'regions') as having its ultimate ground in the structures of 'absolute' subjectivity.[63]

It is precisely characteristic of the major shift in Heidegger's inheritance of phenomenology to call into question the idealistic regress to a subject that Husserl invokes here, and I will explore this further in the next section. However, and despite this shift, Heidegger does retain something of the regress outlined by Husserl. For, according to Heidegger, 'ontology in its widest sense' also 'requires a further clue':

> Ontological inquiry is indeed more primordial, as over against the ontical inquiry of the positive sciences. But it remains naïve and opaque if in its researches into the Being of beings it fails to discuss the meaning of Being in general ... . The question of Being aims therefore at ascertaining the a priori conditions not only for the possibility of the sciences ... but also for the possibility of those ontologies themselves which are prior to the ontical sciences and provide their foundations. Basically all ontology ... remains blind and perverted from its ownmost aim, if it has not first adequately clarified the meaning of Being, and conceived this clarification as its fundamental task.[64]

Complicating still further Heidegger's break from Husserl and the tradition of philosophies of the cogito, Heidegger's attempt to develop philosophy as '*fundamental* ontology' (inquiry into Being as such) and not merely regional ontology (inquiry into the Being of beings of such and such a type) is carried out not only by pursuing a specific regional ontology, but quite precisely through a phenomenology of the being which, in each case, *we ourselves* are. At this point, the following out of the fundamental task of philosophy requires a turn to an investigation or testamentary interrogation of the entity which, according to Heidegger, is already in possession of an understanding of Being, a distinctively phenomenological investigation of the (already familiar) entity 'in which a pre-ontological understanding of Being is comprised as a definite characteristic'.[65] Phenomenological clarification of our own Being is now taken to supply the right way of access to the fundamental matter for thinking, Being as such, and thus becomes the exemplary theme of the inquiry that 'makes up fundamental ontology'.[66]

As I indicated at the end of Chapter 2, even if we ourselves remain the entity to be analysed, the Heideggerian text also turns away from the Husserlian legacy in phenomenology:

if the 'cogito sum' is to serve as the point of departure for the existential analytic of Dasein, then it needs to be turned around [*Umkehrung*] .... The 'sum' is then asserted first, and indeed in the sense that 'I am in a world'.[67]

In the next part of this chapter I will follow Heidegger's path to this new beginning.

Part II: The phenomenology of Dasein

The forgotten question

We are confronted with a tripartite division of levels of inquiry. Starting this time from the bottom, we have, first, the most 'primordial' inquiry possible for us, the one which is possible before all empirical discoveries and technological innovations, fundamental ontology (*the inquiry into Being as such*); moving up one level we have the inquiry which a (tacit and unclarified) understanding of the subject matter of the first makes possible, metaphysics as 'ontology in the widest sense' or regional ontology (*the inquiry into the Being of beings in various domains*); and, finally, up one more level, we have that inquiry which develops within the field that the second has opened up, science as the ontical inquiry oriented to everything that is (*the inquiry into beings of all types*).

But now note: given that we do not have at our disposal the explicit development of an inquiry of the first kind, indeed given that such an inquiry concerns a question which 'has today been forgotten', in effect the second kind of inquiry is the *only* site at which there is, within Western humanity today, *some* openness to the question of Being: the marks of the pre-ontological understanding of Being are particularly readable – if fundamentally unread – there. And, as we have seen, that kind of inquiry is, according to Heidegger, 'ending in the present age' by virtue of the very way in which it has in fact been pursued:

> In the age of Greek philosophy a decisive characteristic of philosophy appears: the development of the sciences within the field that philosophy opened up. The development of the sciences is at the same time their separation from philosophy and the establishment of their independence. This process belongs to the completion of philosophy. Its development is in full swing today in all regions of beings. This development looks like the mere dissolution of philosophy, yet in truth is precisely its completion.[68]

While philosophy as metaphysics is conceived as having its 'legitimate completion' in the development of positive sciences, and so is not its 'mere dissolution', it should not be forgotten that it is *also* its dissolution. For in achieving independence from philosophy (or at least supposing – or feigning to suppose – that such independence could be fully achieved) the sciences then 'interpret everything in their structure that is still reminiscent of their prove-nance from philosophy in accordance with the rules of science'.[69] In other words, sciences themselves suppose that all questions, including basic ontolo-gical questions, must ultimately (if they are genuine questions at all) have an appropriate scientific response and treatment.

Joanna Hodge has called this 'a loss of sense of there being anything other than a domain of fact'.[70] Finding the right words for that with which science – quite properly – does *not* deal or for that which 'is' but is not a being is, as I will explain in Part III of this chapter, another way of putting the central dif-ficulty for Heideggerian thinking concerning the question of Being. And Hodge's formulation, perhaps like any other, is misleading insofar as it suggests that over and above the domain of 'what there is' there is something more: that there is somehow more to what there is than what (in fact) there is. But Heidegger does not think that science has missed or lost sight of another domain when it says: we are concerned with 'what there is' and nothing else. The Heideggerian concern with science is not that it fails to see that there is more to what there is than what, in fact, there is, but that the exclusive orientation towards *beings* that rightly marks science can, for just that reason, make no sense of a sense of 'is' that cannot be interpreted scientifically – that is, otherwise than in relation to what can be investigated by the apprehension, measurement and manipulation of beings. But Hodge's basic point is right: even though '"Being" means the Being of beings',[71] questions about Being are precisely not *about* beings: the Being of beings 'is' not itself a being.[72] And so science, as that inquiry devoted 'solely [to] beings and beyond that – nothing'[73] is closed to precisely those questions which, according to Heidegger, are *the* most fundamental for the being that we ourselves are.

And perhaps we can now begin to see what motivates Heidegger's passion for the question of Being. For within the domain of everything that is, *we* (the questioners) are unique in that what we *are* in our Being (the meaning of our 'to be') is – according to what one might call the wager that opens of *Being and Time* – fundamentally indissociable from having already some understanding of Being. Yet with the end of philosophy as metaphysics there threatens to dis-appear from human life, even a concealed opening to the question of Being, a question which positive sciences, including those which are human or humane or historiological, simply cannot find intelligible (or can only find intelligible by interpreting it as if it were, after all, able to be settled by the measurement or manipulation of beings) and yet which, as responsive to our very being-what-we-are, 'speaks in the destiny man'.[74] Its loss is not one among others for us.

So it is in order to retrieve an opening to the question of Being that Hei-degger commits himself, still in the opening pages of *Being and Time*, to effect a regress from metaphysics to fundamental ontology, a regress to be pursued through a clarification of the entity that we are, the entity that exists already in an understanding of Being, through a 'phenomenology of Dasein'.

As I mentioned in Chapter 2, taking 'Dasein' as the name for the entity we are is, in one respect, a distinctively Cartesian moment of Heidegger's philosophical investigation since it aims at a self-reliant breaking off from and neutralisation of traditional assumptions and presuppositions. On the other hand, it is also a profoundly anti-Cartesian gesture since it aims, in addition, to break off from the conception of ourselves in terms of a 'subject' that has come down to us from Descartes, and in particular the idea of a notional solitude of the subject or 'inner space of subjectivity' whose 'being as it is' is compatible with the non-existence of the physical world. For Heidegger, the incorporation of a still basically Cartesian conception of a purely subjective field fundamentally undermines the claimed radicality of the new beginning launched by the Husserlian regress to transcendental phenomenology. The movement back to the world implied by the Heideggerian Dasein is intended as an adjustment that can fulfil the properly radical character of phenomenology.

The Heideggerian deviation fundamentally calls into question the Husserlian idea of a reduction to a purely subjective field. As I noted in Chapter 1, it was obvious to Husserl that Heidegger had failed to understand the necessary shift of point of view entailed by the phenomenological reduction. Indeed, Husserl regarded the Heideggerian movement back to the world as a 'translation' (*Übertragung*) which 'transposes or transfers' (*transponiert oder transversiert*) his (Husserl's) pure phenomenology 'into the anthropological'.[75] And this shift does seem to be implied by Heidegger's own insistence that Dasein's existence must be grasped as being and remaining always '"outside" alongside entities which it encounters'.[76] However, Husserl's anthropological reading is, from Heidegger's point of view, a limited trans-lation that is itself a transposing of the analytic of Dasein – the worldly entity that is only in an understanding of Being – back into an *ontic* register that is meant to be totally alien to it. For the fact that 'a pre-ontological understanding of Being' is 'a definite characteristic' of Dasein's Being[77] cannot but enroot itself into the idea that Dasein is 'always "outside" alongside'. Indeed, Heidegger immediately qualifies that apparently ontic and anthropological description with the transposing thought that in such 'Being-outside' we are 'still "inside"'.[78] The idea of an 'inside' here is not of an interior world with an exterior world 'outside' it, but of our 'being there' in such a way that entities are, in the 'there' where Dasein finds itself, encountered in their Being, *as* entities.

It is certainly plausible to suppose that it is something quite like this, something comparable to this, that Husserl wants to get in view *via* the phenomenological reduction. That is, what the reduction aims at is ridding us of a distorted understanding of interiority as an inner space with a real world outside it. Perhaps it is with this comparison in view that Merleau-Ponty describes Heidegger's 'being-in-the-world' as appearing 'only against the background of the phenomenological reduction'.[79] On the other hand, the idea of Dasein being still 'inside' is not simply an alternative way of putting Husserl's insistence that the phenomenological reduction achieves the isolation or solitude of an ego of some sort. On the contrary, it is a reconfiguration of the Husserlian idea that fundamentally calls into question its terms of trade. Thus, when, much later in the book, Heidegger describes how Dasein is 'individualised' by 'anxiety', and affirms that this discloses an 'existential "solipsism"',[80] he immediately stresses (à la Wittgenstein of the *Tractatus*) that this solipsism brings Dasein 'face to face with its world *as* world' and is not at all the disclosure of 'an isolated subject-Thing'.[81] In other words, Husserl and Heidegger are *both* concerned (*pace* Husserl) to effect a fundamental shift of level in their reflections on our worldly existence. But the Heideggerian identification of anxiety as fit to 'take over a *methodological function* in principle for the existential analytic' does not isolate an even notionally reducible field of pure subjectivity.[82] Indeed, it serves only to mark the worldly character of Dasein even more strongly. Nevertheless, the *functional equivalence* in view here is an important reminder of the fact that while Dasein is precisely *not* the 'subject' or 'ego' of Husserlian transcendental philosophy – and so, *pace* Merleau-Ponty, there can be no question of an even implicit phenomenological reduction to an ego in Heidegger's analysis of Dasein's being-in-the-world – still, as Derrida notes, 'Dasein comes to occupy ... the place of the subject, the cogito or the classical "*Ich denke*". From these it retains certain essential traits.'[83]

I will come back to this functional equivalence in Chapter 7. However, even accepting this point should not lead us to suppose that Heidegger's new beginning for ontology via a phenomenology of Dasein is yet another idealistic regress to a 'subject'. The analysis really is (to borrow Derrida's assessment of the Levinasian conception of human solitude and separateness that I will examine in Chapter 6) 'new, quite new'.[84] That the disclosure of Being as such is sought in this regional way is not to be explained by reference to 'man' as being the fundamental 'substance of beings', or of finding with 'man' a being through which 'the possibility of grounding the objectivity of all objects' can be 'given and secured'.[85] On the contrary, the regress to Dasein is justified solely by the fact that a 'pre-ontological understanding of Being' – our familiarity with the 'is' – is given (gifted) there. The interest in Dasein lies, that is to say, in the fact that, in advance of the development of an explicit fundamental ontology, Dasein possesses already ('pre-ontologically') an understanding of Being. For Heidegger, the analytic of Dasein, for all its considerable intrinsic interest, has its fundamental *raison d'être* in the effort to achieve a conceptual clarification of *what is understood* in this understanding (namely, the meaning of 'Being' as such). This and this alone is the ultimate matter for thinking for Heidegger. It is, that is to say, the question of Being as such and not a question concerning the Being of a particular being (even the being that we are) which stands, for Heidegger, as *the* fundamental, *the* pre-eminent question of philosophy.[86] Yet it is the question which philosophy as metaphysics, even while it must constantly open on to it, equally constantly fails to address. And in the time of contemporary Western humanity, that is, for the 'we ... in our time' identified at the start of *Being and Time*, that inquiry is coming to an end. I will come back to the contemporary significance of Heidegger's thought in Part III of this chapter. First, however, I want to look at the distinctively phenomenological form of Heidegger's analytic of Dasein.

The analytic of Dasein

Following in the wake of positivism, R.M. Hare saw his task in philosophy as one of eliminating 'unnecessary confusion' and avoiding the 'verbiage' of traditional metaphysical speculation by making his language as completely unambiguous, clear and, in this sense, as scientific as possible. For Hare and philosophers like Hare, philosophical conduct should be carried out in an understanding of clear meaning. As we can now see, this is not a conception of philosophical investigations which Heidegger can embrace without question. Indeed, for Heidegger, as for Husserl and Wittgenstein, a first requirement of avoiding confusion in our thinking is to see that the kind of question that belongs to the subject we call 'philosophy' is *essentially* different from ontic questions, questions about entities of the sort one finds in science. But this raises considerable problems for the inquiry. Our everyday language is, as Husserl suggests, ontically oriented, 'only fit[s] familiar natural objects', so in an inquiry whose 'thought-stance' is 'the unnatural attitude of reflection'[87] there are special demands not just on us but on our language. As Heidegger introduces the analytic of Dasein he explicitly acknowledges this problem:

> With regard to the awkwardness and 'inelegance' of expression in the analyses to come, we may remark that it is one thing to give a report in which we tell about entities, but another to grasp entities in their Being. For the latter task we lack not only most of the words but, above all, the 'grammar'.[88]

Unlike Husserl, however – and quite unlike Hare and his ilk – Heidegger does not understand his task as making language as unambiguous and scientific as possible, but as seeking to give language the greatest chance of bringing to concepts the ontological matter for thinking, something which 'pre-ontologically' we, uniquely, have some familiarity with already. And it is with this in view that the concept of Dasein is elaborated. Thus Dasein is not the name of a living thing that has, in addition, an understanding of Being. On the contrary, if it *is* at all, Dasein can be said to be at all *only* insofar as there is this understanding. For the sake of conceptual clarity on this point, Heidegger reserves the term 'exists' for this *phenomenological happening* that occurs when 'there is' Dasein, thereby sharply distinguishing it from entities which do *not* have this character of Being.[89] The Being of other entities is characterised not by 'existence' but, he states, by '"presence-at-hand"'.[90] The Heideggerian 'analytic of Dasein' is precisely not, as Husserl had mistakenly thought, 'anthropological', precisely not the study of the presence-at-hand in the world of a certain animal.

Heidegger's apology for the unconventional language of his analysis appeals to its difference of *level* from that of everyday and scientific uses of language. On the other hand, however, the (understandable) tendency for us to *neglect* any such difference and so to regard ourselves anthropologically (as, in the first instance, 'an animal entity (present in the world) with certain properties') belongs to the very phenomenological event that Heidegger is trying to get into clearer view. That we are largely 'out of tune with that with which [we are] nonetheless most fundamentally attuned'[91] is not simply an intellectual error but a definite characteristic of the kind of entity that Dasein is. Indeed, the Heideggerian suggestion seems to be that when the kind of entity which we are 'is' it will tend constantly to be tempted to draw its self-understanding in distorting anthropological terms. This is what Heidegger conceives as the strange fatality of the entity that we are. For Heidegger, we are distinguished by the fact that we *are* only insofar as we have an understanding of Being – and this includes a familiarity with our *own* Being, a familiarity with *existence* – and yet our tempting tendency is precisely to interpret ourselves as if we were 'reporting about entities', that is, as if we were describing a (no doubt rather exotic) object which we encounter as, in the first instance, present-at-hand in the world. But that means that we are interpreting ourselves on the basis of an implicit understanding of the kind of Being that belongs to entities which we, precisely, are *not*.

So Heidegger presents what he is calling Dasein as marked by a definite tendency to affirm inadequate and distorting conceptions of its own Being, distorting conceptions of *what it is to be* the entity we ourselves are. In the opening chapter of *Being and Time*, Heidegger broaches a historical interpretation of the way 'we ... in our time' have become disoriented: 'What stands in the way of the basic question of our Being (or leads it off the track) is', he suggests, 'an orientation thoroughly coloured by the anthropology of the ancient [Greek] world [the conception of man as the *zoon logon echon* (*animal rationale*)] and Christianity [the conception of man as made in God's image]'.[92] Following Heidegger, I will refer to the disorientating anthropology of our time as 'humanism'.[93]

Heidegger characterizes humanism as that tradition in which what it calls 'man' is defined by setting it off as one kind of entity present in the world among other entities. Of course, human beings are not then simply equated with mere things in the world or even with other living creatures. On the contrary, 'man' is accorded a specific and special difference or dignity: 'man' is the animal endowed with the capacity to reason or for language; or 'man' is the *ens finitum* made in God's image.

According to Heidegger, philosophy since Descartes has inherited the essential features of this classical humanist anthropology. That is, post-Cartesian philosophy too conceives human existence primarily in terms of presence and only then supplies it with a distinctive trait. Thus, although it rejects the fully naturalistic idea that 'the essence of man simply consists in being an animal organism' it proposes that 'this insufficient definition of man's essence [can] be overcome or offset' merely by adding on to it the idea of man having 'an immortal soul'; or by 'adjoining a mind to the human body' and saying that we are a thinking thing, a self-conscious subject.[94] Thus Heidegger's view is that in post-Cartesian philosophy, where consciousness is the point of departure, humanism remains the background conception: 'In principle we are still thinking of *homo animalis* – even when ... this is later posited as subject, person or spirit.'[95]

For Heidegger, then, classical humanist anthropologies are the source of the ordinary philosophy which expresses Dasein's contemporary misalignment. So what is different about Heidegger's alternative? As I will try to explain, the basic difference lies in the way our 'dwelling in' or 'inhabitation of' the world is conceived.

It should be clear that if your point of departure in philosophy is consciousness and 'what is going on within an individual consciousness' you are beginning with something that is being conceived as a subject that is, in itself, *worldless and isolated.* The idea of it having 'access to entities in the world' or 'access to others' emerges as something requiring further investigation and possibly even as an insuperable problem. Heidegger's alternative *begins* not by giving a new answer to these great questions but by rejecting the idea that something like 'access to entities and others in the world' is merely a fortunate, secondary supplement, a supplementary benefit, to our existence: for the entity that we are, an entity which in Heidegger's sense 'exists', 'Being in a world is something that belongs *essentially*.'[96] To emphasise that this is a basic state of our Being, Heidegger coins the compound expression 'Being-in-the-world' to describe it, stressing thereby that the 'worldly' aspect of our existence is not an added extra but an essential and irreducible feature of it. To 'exist' is to have this 'unitary phenomenon' as one's basic state of Being.[97]

Heidegger's view, then, and in this respect he remains close to Husserl, is that the problems of ordinary philosophy (especially epistemological problems) are fundamentally *pseudo-problems*. And it belongs to Heidegger's conception of them as arising from Dasein's misalignment that he sees his task not as supplying new solutions to such problems but as enabling Dasein to resist the disorientating conceptions of our Being which alone sustain them as problems in the first place.

Heidegger's approach, then, is to clarify the phenomenological happening that occurs when there is an understanding of Being, when, that is, Dasein exists. And what occurs with this event is, first of all, the phenomenon of 'something like a "world"'[98] – and a world here not as the totality of entities (a field that might be investigated by sciences of various kinds), but a 'wherein', a 'whereabouts' or a 'there' where Dasein always already finds itself and within which it encounters entities as such.

To describe the 'worldly' character of Dasein's Being-in-the-world, Heidegger introduces a further contrast to the traditional ontological category of presence-at-hand. Or, rather, he draws that category into a contrast drawn *within* the field of entities that he had previously been characterising in terms only of presence-at-hand: namely, a contrast between 'presence-at-hand' and 'readiness-to-hand'.[99] The latter category does not denote a different kind of entity in the world, but interpretively articulates a distinctive mode in which entities within the world are *encountered*, a mode internally related to Dasein's own everyday ways of going about. This everyday way of Dasein's going about can be provisionally denoted as active (or practical) and contrasts with a contemplative (or theoretical) stance in which entities can be said to be perceived as just there or merely present-at-hand.

Heidegger famously introduces the idea of encounters with entities in their readiness-to-hand through an analysis of equipment or kit (*Zeug*), and with an example of someone using a hammer:

> In dealings ... our concern subordinates itself to the 'in-order-to' which is constitutive for the equipment we are employing at the time; the less we just stare at the hammer-Thing and the more we seize hold of it and use it, the more primordial does our relationship to it become, and the more unveiledly is it encountered as that which it is – as equipment. The hammering itself uncovers the specific 'manipulability' [*Handlichkeit*] of the hammer.[100]

In such circumstances the hammer is paradigmatically encountered in its readiness-to-hand. Now, in Heidegger's view, if we begin with the presence of a 'perceiving subject' we will typically conceive the hammer (as Husserl explicitly does) as something 'given beforehand' *without* what Husserl calls 'the "spiritual" or "cultural" characteristics that make it knowable as, for example, a hammer'.[101] The 'active grasping' that would disclose the mere object as a hammer would thus be secondary to and based upon the prior disclosure of an entity in its presence-at-hand, as an 'existent mere physical thing'.[102] Heidegger regards the starting point that characterises this conception, the conception that always begins with consciousness and consciousness of an object (staring at the hammer-Thing), as radically deficient: 'No matter how sharply we just look at the "outward appearance" of Things in whatever form this takes, we cannot discover anything ready-to-hand.'[103]

Heidegger's claim here is that one simply cannot get in view what shows itself as the specific character of the hammer *qua* hammer if one regards that character as a secondary (or, say, spiritual or cultural) grasp of an object which is given in the first instance as present-at-hand. And his basic argument for this claim is that one's appreciation of the specific hammer-character of the hammer is not a matter of attending to or grasping attributes of an object at all but of being familiar with its place in a structure of relationships or 'involvements', relationships which are themselves simply not explicable in terms of the spatio-temporal layout of present-at-hand configurations. In the work required for the making of a pair of shoes, for example, there is indeed a chain of inter-connected spatio-temporal relations: to animals from which comes the leather for the shoes; to the wood and steel which compose the hammers and tools; to the foundry where the steel was forged; to the various stages of production and design and the totality of equipment required to complete them; to others for whom the shoes are made; and so on. But none of these *relations* is or could be, as it were, *given* with the mere spatial and temporal *arrangement* of the entities mentioned conceived in their presence-at-hand. The structure of involvements is not, that is to say, something which could be manifest to just anyone you please, and, specifically, not something that is or could be manifest to a per-ceptual cognition (however sophisticated) that grasps properties of an entity present-at-hand. On the contrary, the seeing that belongs to the disclosure of an entity in its readiness-to-hand, and hence the seeing that is receptive to the 'that which it is' of things as they are encountered in Dasein's everyday going about, presupposes Dasein's familiarity with a matrix of relations and involve-ments, a matrix which always come back to and is shaped by Dasein as Being-in-the-world:

> In a workshop, for example, the totality of involvements which is constitutive for the ready-to-hand in its readiness-to-hand, is 'earlier' than any single item of equipment; so too for the farmstead with its utensils and outlying lands. But the totality of involvements goes back ultimately to a 'towards-which' in which there is no further involve-ment: this 'towards-which' is not an entity with the kind of Being that belongs to what is ready-to-hand within a world; it is rather an entity whose Being is defined as Being-in-the-world, and to whose state of Being worldhood itself belongs.[104]

As we have seen, describing an entity in its readiness-to-hand requires that we include in its description the structure of involvements which are constitutive of it. Encountering such an entity thus presupposes a familiarity with that structure. It can, that is, only be encountered *in view* of that structure. But what is 'in view' here is not a further entity. It is, rather, that 'wherein concern always dwells';[105] something 'constantly sighted' when Dasein is going about and getting something done, but not thematically, and never as an object. The 'what' that Dasein is familiar with here is what Heidegger is calling the 'world'. And, as I have indicated, the world relates not to the totality of entities but to a constitutive part of Dasein's own 'worldly' state of Being as Being-in-the-world. At issue, then, is familiarity with existence.

At this point we can begin to see how Heidegger's phenomenology of Dasein opens a path for fundamental ontology. For the issue of articulating Dasein's understanding of Being has taken a theoretically novel turn. The understanding of Being is not to be interpreted as a specific 'mental' achievement, the grasping of a sense by the mind, but rather as a way of characterising the fundamental structure of existence itself, the very fabric of our lives, its shape, its "face" – a 'primordial' existential structure that has its most basic expression in the fact that existence, as such, articulates 'an understanding of something like a "world"'.[106]

I will take up again this linkage between 'the understanding of Being' and 'an understanding of something like a "world"' in Part III of this chapter. What I have tried to bring out in this part is that Heidegger's 'inelegant' phenomenology of Dasein is an attempt reflectively to come to terms with something that is already pre-reflectively familiar to his readers, indeed it should interpretively articulate something that is 'closest' to us or right before our eyes: our own basic state of Being. It is for this reason that the appropriate form of inquiry will be phenomenological explication not scientific theorizing. However, the fundamental misalignment problem is that our own basic state of Being *itself* also constantly invites us to conceive ourselves wrongly and in inappropriate terms, terms that would lead to anthropological misunderstandings of Dasein as a distinctive kind of presence in the world:

> For the most part the phenomenon [of Being-in-the-world] has been explained in a way which is basically wrong, or interpreted in an inadequate manner. On the other hand, this ... is itself based upon nothing else but this very state of Dasein's Being, which is such that Dasein itself ... gets its understanding of itself in the first instance from those entities which it itself is *not* but which it encounters 'within' its world, and from the Being which they possess.[107]

Nevertheless, and this is where I want to draw this brief excursion into the early stages of Heidegger's phenomenology of Dasein to a close, a satisfactory interpretation of our existence is *a priori* possible. We are able to reject anthropological interpretations, not because we can disprove them or refute them, but

> because this phenomenon [Being-in-the-world] itself always gets 'seen' in a certain way in every Dasein. And it thus gets 'seen' because it makes up a basic state of Dasein, and in every case is already disclosed for Dasein's understanding of Being, and disclosed along with that Being itself.[108]

Thus the force, the capacity to convince, that belongs to the phenomenological explication of Dasein's familiarity with existence will not accrue from the rigour of arguments in the narrow sense but through demonstrations that are marked by what one might call the exegetical faithfulness of its testimony or attestation.[109] In order to attain clarity Dasein must attest to its

Being-in-the-world. And it must be able to do so because, *as* Dasein, it is, in every case, *already* disclosed as such. Hence, an explicit understanding of existence does not require an account that is as unambiguous, clear and in this sense as scientific as possible. Understanding Dasein is more like interpreting a text than reporting on a thing, and Heidegger's aim in the phenomenological analytic of Dasein is to enable that great text of Dasein to undertake an explicit and rigorous self-explication in terms of fundamental and primordial structures of its Being as Being-in-the-world, an analysis which will lead us towards a clarification of what it means to be an entity that *is* only in an understanding of Being.

In the next part of this chapter I want to examine a text by Heidegger that presents a highly condensed attempt at such self-explication. As we shall see, in that text Heidegger attempts to provide a phenomenological attestation of our understanding of Being. Again Heidegger will not try to invoke some kind of *intellectual* apprehension of Being but to identify a fundamental *existential* structure, indeed an existentially basic kind of *affective* condition. In doing so Heidegger hopes to mount a fundamental challenge to the (roughly speaking 'intellectualistic') understanding of ourselves which dominates in our time, a time when, as he puts it, 'science [has] become our passion'.[110] To highlight this latter aspect it will prove helpful to read the text along with a response to it that belongs *squarely* within the modern[2] passion of our time. In what follows I will attend not only to Heidegger's text but, in addition, to the critical reading of it presented by the linguistic analyst Herman Philipse in his book *Heidegger's Philosophy of Being*.

Part III: Being and the Nothing

Conceding nothing

The text I will examine in this part was originally a lecture; and not just any lecture. As Simon Critchley points out in a recent discussion of it, when it was delivered by Heidegger in 1929

> he was 39 years old and at the height of his intellectual powers. He was returning to his home university after several enormously productive years in Marburg to take up the chair of his teacher, Edmund Husserl .... It was a moment of clear personal triumph.[111]

It is also, I think, a clear triumph of his philosophical personality, a work of words as rich and provocative as anything he wrote.

It begins rather modestly and soberly, the kind of business-like start that Heidegger's audience at the inaugural lecture, those who made up 'the community of researchers, teachers and students' at Freiburg University, might have hoped for and would suppose proper to its own practice. Speaking under the simple title 'What is Metaphysics?', Heidegger announces his apparently plain intentions in the lecture in the following words: 'Our plan begins with the unfolding of a metaphysical inquiry, then tries to elaborate the question, and concludes by answering it.'[112] It looks as if we are going to get something very straightforward indeed: the elaboration of a question and then the provision of an answer. And in view of this straightforwardness it will, then, surely prove something of a surprise to find Heidegger later insisting that 'at least the first and the only essential [answer]' to the question he is posing will have been 'won' simply by getting to the stage where we can acknowledge that it is a genuine and legitimate question at all.[113] Not so straightforward after all …

As we shall see, the orthodox point of departure quickly gives way to a line of thinking in which our contemporary idea of ourselves as 'scientific man' is fundamentally called into question. For that reason we would do well to pause and to think seriously about the fact that Heidegger is, in an inaugural lecture, addressing the (broadly speaking) scientific community as a whole and not a meeting of philosophers. Heidegger has the platform, and in front of the community of researchers, teachers and students he proceeds to call into question the contemporary understanding of the kind of being that poses questions and seeks answers to them, the 'who' that we in this community are: 'What is happening to us', Heidegger asks, 'in the grounds of our existence, when science becomes our passion?'[114] Heidegger's immediate response to this question in the first part of the lecture is that the only thing that now holds together the various fields of inquiry represented in this community is the 'technical organisation' of universities: a managerial-scientific-technical answer to the question of the ground of scientific activity. Heidegger will want to find something deeper, and in a literal sense something more passionate, at the bottom of all of this.

So it is clear that from the start that Heidegger is not going to leave his audience confident or at ease with its typical self-understanding. Its 'leadership in the whole of human existence' is, he will frankly declare, 'proper but *limited*'.[115] Man as the knower, man as the animal that pursues science, is not, Heidegger will argue, the highest or most fundamental understanding of the 'who' that we are. His strategy will be, as we shall see, to try to show that science itself depends on the prior disclosure to 'man' of a matter for thinking which simply *cannot* be an issue for scientific inquiry.

There are, then, two points in the inaugural lecture that I want particularly to focus on in this part: first, a certain interruption or displacement by Heidegger of the authority of the scientific community and its worldview; and, second, a rigorous, if not simply scientific, concern on his part to show the essential legitimacy and primordiality of a strictly non-scientific inquiry.

In his reading of Heidegger's lecture, Herman Philipse, a philosopher who is a self-consciously modern[2] defender of the superiority of the scientific worldview, acknowledges that the 'argument' of the first part of the lecture identifies a crucial limit of science:

Heidegger says in 1929 that science is characterized by a specific relation (*Bezug*) to the world, by an attitude (*Haltung*) in which we freely choose to let things speak for themselves, and by the fact that in science one being, namely, man, 'breaks into the totality of beings' (*Einbruch*) in such a manner that Being 'breaks open' and 'is restored to what and how it is'. [Philipse's translation is mistaken here. It is not Being (*Sein*) but 'beings' (*Seienden*) which 'break open and show what they are and how they are'. This is very important given that the next sentence runs:] In all three respects, *Bezug*, *Haltung*, and *Einbruch*, the scientist is concerned with beings and with nothing else. Heidegger repeats the phrase 'and with nothing else' six times in different variations in order to prepare his conclusion: that when the scientist tries to say what he is up to, he inevitably speaks of something else, namely, the Nothing, or nothingness (*das Nichts*). It follows that in reflecting on science we cannot avoid the metaphysical question: What about the Nothing?[116]

As we shall see, it is a mistake to think that the first part of the lecture aims to show that 'we cannot avoid' a certain question. What is 'unfolded' there is simply a suggestion that there *may* be a legitimate matter for thinking which, strictly speaking, could not be a concern for science: a question that science can hear, if at all, in only the most backhanded kind of way, through what Heidegger calls a 'concession' regarding *that with which science does not deal*.[117]

Philipse does not attend to the crucial notion of 'concession' which organises Heidegger's discussion at this point. The kind of concession at issue here can be clarified by looking again at the passage from J.P. Moreland on weak and strong scientism:

Contemporary naturalists embrace either weak or strong scientism. According to the former, non-scientific fields are not worthless nor do they offer no intellectual results, but they are vastly inferior to science in their epistemic standing and do not merit full credence. According to the latter, unqualified cognitive value resides in science and in nothing else.[118]

So weak scientism concedes x (something), and strong scientism concedes y (nothing). Of course, as Heidegger notes, it is questionable whether 'we [can] ... speak of concession when we concede nothing'.[119] However, since Heidegger will want to argue that there is a legitimate question which should concern us here, a question which, moreover, concerns precisely that with which science does not deal, he resists the scientist's understandable conviction that 'science must reassert its seriousness and soberness of mind'.[120] Thus Heidegger will (extremely provocatively) *affirm* the scientist's 'concession' that 'that with which science does not deal' is, precisely, 'nothing'.

A comparison will help clarify the movement of Heidegger's discussion. Let us imagine a botanist saying 'what he is up to' and someone else (a proto-geologist, say) replying in the following way:

A: We are interested in plants – and not rocks and stones.
B: So what about this other kind of thing, what about this 'rocks and stones' topic? How is it with the rocks and stones?

We might now (try to) apply this schema to the more general case of a scientist (in the broad sense of science that one finds with the German term *Wissenschaft*) saying 'what he is up to' and a syntactically parallel reply from this scientist's inquisitive other:

A*: We are interested in beings, in what is – and besides that nothing.
B*: So what about this 'other' to beings, what about this 'nothing' topic? How is it with the nothing?[121]

Of course, as Heidegger acknowledges, in A* (unlike A), 'what we are interested in' is meant to be *everything that is*. So, it seems, there is (can be) no further inquiry – as there is in B – which one might go in for. But Heidegger thinks there is, and in the next part of the lecture he will try to demonstrate that there is. He thinks one can inquire into beings (science) and one can at least come to the point where one sees that one can ask the question of Being (which on its own would be quite a breakthrough in Heidegger's view). This latter 'matter for thinking' is the 'what we do not deal with' which *quite properly* belongs to science. And, as we shall see, there is something deeply appropriate about the choice of word that Heidegger takes from the scientist's 'concession' at this point. For, if, as we noted in the last part, 'the Being of beings "is" not itself a being',[122] then what Heidegger regards as the fundamental matter for thinking in philosophy is, one might say, precisely *the* no(t-a-)thing, or the Nothing.

Thus, although Heidegger does not in the least think it 'follows' that 'in reflecting on science we cannot avoid the metaphysical question' (in fact *avoiding* it is what he thinks we do best today), he resists avoiding it by attempting to formulate an *essentially* non-scientific question. Of course, whether Heidegger has raised an *intelligible* or *legitimate* question in doing so has not, at this point in the lecture, been settled *at all*.

Philipse clearly thinks Heidegger is getting ahead of himself, however, and following his summary of the first part of the lecture he immediately continues: 'Is this argument sound? Rudolf Carnap criticized Heidegger's *Was ist Metaphysik?* in his 1931 essay on "The Elimination of Metaphysics through Logical Analysis of Language"'.[123] Philipse then recalls Carnap's famous account of metaphysics as consisting of meaningless pseudo-sentences of two sorts: sentences with no empirical significance and sentences that violate logical syntax.

As far as Heidegger's text is concerned, Philipse's subsequent concession to opponents of verificationism concedes nothing at all: 'It is important to distinguish these two sources of meaninglessness, for even if one rejects the verification principle, one still has to admit that violations of logical grammar may generate meaningless pseudo-sentences.'[124]

'One still has to admit that ... ' Does one? Philipse here declares, without declaring it, a profound dependence or debt in his entire analysis and its code on a substantive orientation to language (a quite specific understanding of what a sentence with sense must be like) which claims to be able to identify, *independently of every context*, cases where sentences which are, as he puts it, 'correct according to the rules of ordinary grammar' are nevertheless 'violations of logical grammar'.[125] However, if one takes the role of context as *fundamental* to any string of words having sense, then one will 'have to admit' that *no* words or chains of words are *in themselves* meaningless and must be so *whatever* the context, and that consequently it is only within a quite specific theoretico-metaphysical horizon that such decisions concerning what, according to Philipse, 'one still has to admit' have the force of necessity. Nevertheless, for Philipse Heidegger may have to be condemned: 'Clearly, then, Heidegger's conclusion does not follow from his premise, and it is meaningless because it violates the rules of logical syntax.'[126]

And it is certainly true that Heidegger produces sentences which shift the use of 'nothing' from a quantifier to a noun phrase – when he writes, for example: 'What should be examined [according to science] are beings only ... and beyond that – nothing. What about this nothing?'[127] But, as we have seen, this is no more or less legitimate, grammatically speaking, than when our proto-geologist says to the botanist: 'What about the rocks?' The noun phrase 'the rocks' here simply picks up on, and is a placeholder or variable for, whatever it is that the concession concedes as 'that with which we do not deal'. Heidegger is not supposing that it is as if there were some 'thing' that is 'conceded' by the scientist. Indeed, he is precisely opening a space for questions which are not about *any* kind of beings, even of a very weird kind called the Nothing.

Philipse also knows that Heidegger is fully aware of the problems that arise in the very formulation of his question about the Nothing. He (Philipse) continues:

> Does this settle the matter of Heidegger's question of Being and Nothingness? Should we conclude that it is a pseudo-question? We are tempted to do so. Yet this would be rash, for Heidegger seems to have anticipated Carnap's critique, albeit in an informal way.[128]

We now turn to the second part of the lecture, in which, in my view, Heidegger attempts to show that what *may* be a legitimate question *is* one.

Anxiety and the Nothing

Summarising the start of the second part, Philipse again acknowledges Heidegger's acknowledgement that the very form of the question, asking what the nothing *is*, 'presupposes that there is something whose nature we might investigate'.[129] Philipse speculates in a footnote that Heidegger may actually have Carnap's point in mind here. It is more likely to be Husserl, since the objection that Heidegger presents to the idea that the question is legitimate explicitly invokes the intentionality doctrine central to Husserlian phenomenology. As Heidegger puts it: 'Universal "logic" itself lays low this question. For thinking, which is essentially thinking *about* something, must act in a way contrary to its own essence when it thinks of the nothing.'[130] From the point of view of this 'logical' understanding of thought, every attempt to formulate the question is necessarily thwarted by the fact that we can only succeed in actually thinking (at all) by failing to think at all about the nothing *as* nothing. The mere expression of the thought 'turns what is interrogated into its opposite'[131] – into something (weird).

Heidegger's conclusion at this point seems unexceptional: 'Assuming that in this question "logic" is of supreme importance, that the intellect is the means, and thought the way, ... have we not already come to the end of our inquiry into the nothing.'[132] These (Husserlian but clearly not only Husserlian) assumptions are for Heidegger the crucial presupposition for rejecting the legitimacy of the question. And we here reach the point at which many readers of Heidegger will feel close to Philipse when he expresses the worry that Heidegger's lecture 'undermines the authority of logic'. For a challenge to the 'supreme importance' of 'logic' in this matter looks tantamount to a challenge to reason and reasonableness as such. It is a leap into irrationality. In view of that take on Heidegger's text, it is surprising that Philipse makes so little of the fact that Heidegger makes every effort to proceed here with great caution. Indeed, for Heidegger, at this point the new question, indeed what he calls 'the basic demand for the possible advancing of every question',[133] is this: is there any other kind of access, any other means than the power of the intellect and its logic, for establishing the legitimacy of the question? Heidegger gives himself a clear and I would think reasonable criterion for this: '[The] legitimacy [of our search] ... can be demonstrated only on the basis of a fundamental experience of the nothing.'[134]

As the point of departure to a response to this challenge, Heidegger then introduces the idea (an idea developed at length in *Being and Time*) that the 'intellect' and *its* logic (what Kant would call the faculty of understanding through concepts) is not the only form of *discursive receptivity* – or understanding in general – that belongs to the entity that we are. Specifically, what Heidegger calls '*Befindlichkeit*' (unhappily translated as 'state of mind' by Macquarrie and Robinson) designates modes of receptive attunement, instantiated by moods, in which, he claims, we are discursively disclosed both to the world and to ourselves '*prior* to all cognition and volition, and *beyond* their range of disclosure'.[135] Philipse again fails to examine the logic of Heidegger's discussion here. In this case he fails to acknowledge Heidegger's appeal to a distinction *within* the sphere of discursive receptivity (within understanding in general) between intellect and attunement and, moreover, within each between what Heidegger calls fundamental and founded modes of such disclosure.

In the second part of the lecture Heidegger offers two examples of supposedly 'fundamental' moods, examples where what is disclosed can never be comprehended by a purely intentional act or 'consciousness of something'. These moods are, first, 'profound boredom' and, second, 'joy in the presence of the Dasein – and not simply the person – of a human being whom we love'.[136] According to Heidegger, neither mood has an in-the-world state of affairs as its intentional content since both concern the disclosure of beings-as-a-whole, indeed of that 'whole' in the midst of which our everyday existence is 'stationed'. However, for Heidegger, these examples, in their very disclosure of, precisely, *everything*, 'conceal from us the nothing we are seeking'.[137] So, again, the question is: is there an experience or mood which discloses that with which science does not deal, 'the nothing itself'?

As Philipse notes, Heidegger answers positively: 'There is a fundamental experience or fundamental mood of *Angst*, and in *Angst* we experience the Nothing.'[138] Despite his worries with the logical syntax, Philipse again tries to give some kind of charitable support for what he clearly regards as the absurd illogicality of Heidegger's discussion:

> But, one might ask, does Heidegger not ostensively define the word *Nichts* (nothingness) in the second part? Should we not apply the principle of charity and assume that Heidegger meant *Nichts* from the outset in the sense given by this ostensive definition, so that his introduction of the question of nothingness is needlessly misleading?[139]

I do not find this suggestion charitably helpful at all. As we have seen, Heidegger takes the 'conceded' word 'nothing' from the scientist in order to attempt to formulate a question concerning that with which science does not deal. The problem, then, is whether we can make sense of 'encountering' such a not-a-thing at all given that we cannot even coherently frame the question by reference to the intellect and its logic. In the second part of the lecture anxiety is identified as the 'fundamental mood' that might allow the inquiry to continue nonetheless. Indeed, Heidegger finds a certain attestation of the pertinence of anxiety in the words of everyday life: 'In the lucid vision sustained by fresh remembrance we say that that in the face of which and for which we were anxious was "properly" nothing.'[140] It helps, I think, to note that Heidegger's recourse to everyday ways of speaking about anxiety here borrows from a parallel passage in *Being and Time*:

When anxiety has subsided, then in our everyday way of talking we are accustomed to say that 'it was really nothing'. And what it was, indeed, does get reached ontically by such a way of talking. Everyday discourse tends towards concerning itself with the ready-to-hand and talking about it. That in the face of which anxiety is anxious is nothing ready-to-hand-within-the-world. But this 'nothing-ready-to-hand', which our everyday circumspective discourse understands, is not totally nothing. The 'nothing' of readiness-to-hand is grounded in the most primordial 'something' – in the *world*. Ontologically, however, the world belongs essentially to Dasein's Being as Being-in-the-world. So if the 'nothing' – that is, the world as such – exhibits itself as that in the face of which one has anxiety, this means that *Being-in-the-world itself is that in the face of which anxiety is anxious*.[141]

Now, the ordinary notion of 'ostensive definition' that Philipse appeals to is clearly ruled out in this case. Indeed, just as Kant would object to the idea that we could define our concept of causality by ostensive definition, it would be better to say that 'what we experience in *Angst*', while it is the transcendental condition of every ostensive definition, is not itself something we might intelligibly 'point at' within the world at all. (This makes anxiety, like Kant's transcendental horizon of all experience, a permanent, if sometimes imperceptible, feature of all existence.) What we are 'brought before' in anxiety is ourselves *qua* Dasein, that is, ourselves *not* as an entity within the world but as that entity which *is* only insofar as 'the world' is disclosed to it as the 'wherein' of its 'understanding of itself', an understanding Heidegger has, as we have seen, from the start related to 'familiarity'. Later in *Being and Time* the familiarity he set out with emerges as the very heart of Dasein's existence: 'and this familiarity [with existence], in turn, is *constitutive* for Dasein, and goes to make up Dasein's understanding of Being'.[142] What we are familiar with here, then, is a primordial 'something' that both science and everyday talk grasp, quite 'properly' and appropriately as 'nothing' – and it is *for that reason alone* that Heidegger takes this as the name of his theme in 'What is Metaphysics?'

None of this seems to interest Philipse, but it should now be clearer why Heidegger's strategy in the lecture is to take the Nothing as his matter for thinking. Taking up the word 'nothing', as found in the 'concession' where science declares what it does not deal with and as found in the everyday talk of the 'what' of anxiety, it designates precisely:

1 that with which science does not deal, and
2 that which is not a being in the world.

That is, he uses the term 'the Nothing' because it is *as* nothing that we preontologically understand (1) and (2), i.e. *Being itself*. Here we see the kernel of Heidegger's non-scientific understanding of what happens to us 'when science becomes our passion': what happens is that (1) and (2), i.e. Being itself, are understood as negligible and are forgotten. This is why, at the end of the lecture, he reinscribes in a fundamentally new context the famous 'metaphysical' question: 'Why is there something and not nothing?' And what he is doing here is not expressing anew a traditional wonder at the presence of the world, but attempting to enact a transition in philosophy from representational and intentional 'thinking of beings' to another kind of thinking, what he calls a thinking of 'the truth of Being', which will overcome it.

Twilight of the idols

Heidegger's lecture is an attempt to show that 'the power of the intellect and its logic' cannot take the role of taskmaster in the field of inquiry into Being. This does not seek to abolish, liquidate or reject logic or reason, but only, as one might put it, a certain vision or inheritance of logic and reason: namely, one which is sure that proper reasoning requires that a certain intellectualistic *formal logicity* (not 'logic' as opposed to the 'illogical' pure and simple) must be the master in every legitimate inquiry.

Struggling to make sense of a text that challenges the modernist[2] worldview he is wedded to, Philipse claims that 'Heidegger's views on logic' can be 'explained' only according to an interpretation which locates them within an 'attempt to replace the Christian religion by a different variety of religious discourse'.[143] I do not think this is the best and it is certainly not the only way of understanding Heidegger's engagement with modern[2] thought. To put it very schematically, the essential contrast here is between Heidegger, who makes moves within our language which aim to cultivate its greatest *expressive* power regarding our familiarity with existence, and 'scientific man', who wants ideally, as Philipse puts it himself, to 'make language … as unambiguous, clear and "scientific" as possible'.[144]

The motivation behind what Philipse calls his 'postmonotheist explanation' of Heidegger's views on the intellect and logic is, I think, as familiar as it is dubious: Philipse wants to discredit Heidegger's critique of the modern[2] conception of 'man' by placing *all* the emphasis in 'explaining' it on quasi-religious, and thus potentially irrational and presumably supernaturalistic, grounds. Indeed, Philipse will urge that the 'atmosphere' of 'What is Metaphysics?' 'is markedly religious'.[145]

Philipse's basic claim here is that the strategy of Heidegger's lecture is to 'first destroy the dominance of reason and logic' in order to make way, in the closing paragraph, for a 'leap of faith'[146] or 'leap to religion'.[147] But this reading of the lecture is far from obvious or obviously sound. What is clear is that the closing paragraph of the essay, the closing of the lecture, invites us to 'liberate ourselves from those idols (*Götzen*) everyone has and to which they are wont to go cringing'.[148] I think the idols Heidegger has in mind are of the sort Sartre lists as 'the great explanatory idols of our epoch':[149] 'heredity, education, environment, physiological constitution' – ways of giving scientific or naturalistic 'explanations' of *every* aspect of human existence. No doubt Heidegger's idol-hammering suggestion aims to open a 'spiritual' path for philosophy quite distinct from the one envisaged in the explicit affirmation of 'linguistics' and 'linguistic analysis' that marks Philipse's (in the sense I am using it here equally 'spiritual') closing paragraph,[150] but it is distorting to claim that Heidegger's has a 'clearly religious meaning'[151] or aims to prepare us for a 'religious conversion',[152] in the way that Philipse would have us have it. It shows a distinct narrowness of vision to suppose that the only alternative to the scientific world picture must be, in some way, a form of religious supernaturalism.

What Heidegger wanted from his inaugural lecture was to make plausible a radical attempt to question the 'who' that, in each case, we are. Today we understand ourselves primarily as 'man the knower' (or 'the animal with the capacity for knowledge') as 'scientific man' or the 'rational animal'. Philipse is, without a shadow of a doubt, a man of today, 'a man of affairs' in whose clear and decisive '"Oh, yes" and "Oh, no"' anxiety is almost imperceptible.[153] He is decided on deciding the fate of Heidegger, and in his view Heidegger is not just a philosopher it is hard to take seriously but, ultimately, not a serious philosopher at all.[154] Ironically, perhaps it is true, perhaps it really is hard for someone like Philipse to take Heidegger seriously, or at least hard for him to do so and to remain a man of science. For while Heidegger should not be read as developing what, historically, has tended to be called a 'religious discourse', following his thinking does demand that one be prepared to engage in a passionate deconstruction of the understanding of oneself and one's condition in the world with others which prevails today.

In this chapter I have wanted to say something about Heidegger's efforts to launch philosophy back to the question of Being through the pursuit of a phenomenology of Dasein. Taking my direction from Cora Diamond, I looked towards clarifying the idea of an *inquiry* into this question to see what sense we could make of that. Cora Diamond's Wittgensteinian 'nutshell' was that 'what it is that we are talking about is shown in how we talk about it, and in how that talk enters our lives, the shape – the "face" – that life containing such talk has'. Looking at Heidegger's launching of an inquiry into Being has, I hope, shed some light on what the inquiry is 'talking about'. Having said that, Heidegger does not pretend to know what an ordinary life 'containing such talk' would look like. Certainly it was never Heidegger's motivation for 'restating the question of Being' that ordinary people would start engaging *en masse* in 'original philosophy'.[155] On the other hand, however, it is precisely in view of the shape or 'face' of a life *without* such talk, indeed in view of *a world that has forgotten the question*, and which he regards as (non-coincidentally) 'darkening',[156] that 'in the limits within which philosophy can accomplish anything'[157] Heidegger resolutely puts this talk back into circulation.[158]

4

EXISTENTIAL PHENOMENOLOGY

Jean-Paul Sartre

The 'has been'

Along with his contemporary Maurice Merleau-Ponty, Jean-Paul Sartre was at the forefront of attempts to conceive the work of Husserl and Heidegger as the nascent formation of a 'phenomenological movement'. Convinced that the differences between Husserl and Heidegger were capable of being reconciled, Sartre's own major work of phenomenology *Being and Nothingness* (1943) fashioned an inheritance of phenomenology that attempted seamlessly to pass from an analysis of the essential intentionality of consciousness to a conception of consciousness as fundamentally 'an abstraction' from the 'concrete totality' of 'Being-in-the-world'.[1] In this distinctive deviation, a deviation which would recast the phenomenological call 'back to things themselves' as a call to 'start with the concrete',[2] Sartre would attempt to cover over the differences between Husserl and Heidegger on the terms in which phenomenology should be conducted. Sartre was to pay a high price for his reconciling efforts, becoming in his own (English) words a 'has been'.[3]

I am completely convinced that the Sartrean project of reconciliation is slated to disappoint. However, I also completely reject the idea that Sartre's own writings in the name of phenomenology should be cursorily dismissed as a result. While one might retain a deep Heideggerian question mark over the very idea of the philosophy of mind, it seems to me that Gregory McCulloch was right to suggest that 'people working in the philosophy of mind ... would do well to study the early Sartre carefully'.[4] And I am inclined to say something similar about people working in moral philosophy too. Robert Cumming, usually a very generous reader of Sartre's work, regards Sartre's famous public lecture, published in English under the title *Existentialism and Humanism* (1948, original text 1945), as 'shoddy'.[5] But I will want to make a case in defence of that little text too. The public lecture that launched Sartre as a major intellectual force in post-war Europe launches into moral phenomenology from an unconditional affirmation of human freedom. In Part III of this chapter I will argue that the case for his claims in that lecture are strongest when they are seen in the light of the phenomenological arguments which lead up to that

92

unconditional affirmation in the opening phases of *Being and Nothingness*. Unfortunately, there is some difficult material to engage with here, and despite the fact that the 'beginnings' that occupy my attention in Part I and Part II of this chapter are an introduction and opening chapter, respectively, the content is not very introductory and not very open either. Readers new to Sartre might prefer – as Sartre's little lecture implicitly recognised they might – to start with the engagement with Sartre's discussion of moral themes in Part III.

Part I: The assault on idealism

Realism and idealism

That Sartre's work is a backward step from the advances made by Heidegger is for many today part of the exegetical furniture. The radical core of Heidegger's attack on the premises of Cartesianism and philosophies of the subject seems somehow to pass Sartre by. While knowing full well that in his phenomenological elaboration of the entity that, in each case, 'I am' Heidegger 'speaks of Dasein, not of consciousness',[6] Sartre is, as we shall see, unhesitating in his willingness to develop his own analysis of our Being in terms of consciousness. And it is not just consciousness. The general privileging of presence in what, in Chapter 3, I called the problematic elaboration of an 'idea' of Being is retained without a flinch. One can see why Derrida, the inheritor of everything in Heidegger which would want to resist such an idea, might want to say so bluntly 'I do not need Sartre'.[7]

And yet this blunt dismissal, the suggestion that Sartre has not learnt well from the very text he regards as so 'important',[8] can readily make one blind to the profound richness of Sartre's *anti*-Cartesian views, the considerable subtlety of his argumentation and what is in some ways an admirable effort to come to terms with novelty of some of Heidegger's most enigmatic formulations. While my project rather goes against the grain of contemporary assessments, I hope what follows will improve visibility on all these points. However, as I have indicated, I also want the investigation of 'beginnings' in Sartre in this chapter to align the opening phases of *Being and Nothingness* with the introductory lecture on moral philosophy. And that looks like a simply hopeless project. For example, while the former engages in a systematic *critique* of idealism, the latter seeks to *affirm* such fundamentally idealist-sounding claims as 'there is no other universe except the human universe, the universe of human subjectivity'.[9] Worse still, while the former advances a profoundly *individualistic* conception of existence,[10] the latter seems to offer an essentially '*universalist* critique of individualism'.[11] Showing that the two are fundamentally continuous may seem implausible. But my view is that both texts look very much better when one can see that they are.

Exegetical challenges like these are not helped by the fact that *Being and Nothingness* is in any case a difficult book to navigate, and to get things going it leads off with what must be one of the most misleading first lines of any major text of philosophy: 'Modern thought', Sartre begins, 'has realized considerable progress by reducing the existent to the series of appearances which manifest it.'[12] Someone who has heard the idealist-sounding notes of the public lecture might not be surprised to come across this suggestion – but then any such reader will be totally at sea in the discussion that follows it. For whatever 'considerable progress' the development of the phenomenalist reduction might be thought to have achieved (for example in overcoming the traditional realist's embarrassment in the face of the threat of scepticism),[13] it is, according to Sartre's opening arguments, a thoroughly erroneous view.[14] For Sartre, a phenomenalist account trades in second-rate goods, 'dealing with a false transcendence',[15] and cannot be accepted: 'the *esse* of the phenomenon cannot be its *percipi*'.[16] The breaking of a fragile vase, for example, is simply 'an irreversible absolute event which [one] could only verify',[17] not something whose happening or not happening is reducible to (actual or possible) experiences or judgements. Thus, far from regarding phenomenalism as the new way to go in philosophy, if we focus on what Heidegger calls 'the ordinary conception of phenomenon'[18] we will find Sartre, in the opening stretch of *Being and Nothingness*, arguing for the very opposite thought and developing a robust affirmation of the transcendent *reality* of the phenomena. That is, Sartre argues that the phenomena *qua* phenomena – whether we are concerned with what *is* the case or indeed with what *is not* the case – cannot coherently be understood in terms which reduce them or make them in any way dependent in their Being (or, with respect to what *is not* the case, their non-Being) on our experiences or judgements. Indeed, throughout the opening discussion Sartre aims to affirm, quite generally, that nothing *is* so (or *is not* so) because thinking makes it so (or *not* so).

One might easily be thrown off the track of these opening lines of argument by Sartre's first sentence. Equally, however, once one gets back on track it is hard to align the relentless critique of phenomenalist idealism with the idealist-sounding claims in the public lecture. But it can be done. Sartre's affirmation of what he calls *the transphenomenality of the phenomena* (having a Being beyond their perceived Being) is so uncompromising that Gregory McCulloch talks about Sartre's 'realism' in this context.[19] However, Sartre's conception of the phenomena is a little more complicated than this suggests. First, traditional realism is a position that gets 'ruled out' by Sartre as completely as he rules out phenomenalism.[20] And, second (and this is where I will want to mark the text in a way which will help us interpret the apparent idealism of the public lecture), he develops an account of the *identity conditions* of phenomena (what I will call – following Stanley Cavell[21] – the conditions of their 'being *so*' as opposed to their '*being* so') which gives his conception of them a distinctively idealist-sounding twist. Nevertheless, McCulloch is right to resist the suggestion that Sartre is really some kind of idealist,[22] and we need to tread carefully if the idealist-sounding twist is not to be read naïvely as the residual trace of an idealist (or even transcendental idealist) outlook. In order to understand Sartre's conception of the phenomena with any interpretive rigour we need to see how his affirmation of their transphenomenal *reality* hangs together with an affirmation of their irreducibly human *meaning*. In what follows I will try to get this conception into clearer view.

Sartre's critique of phenomenalism in the introduction to *Being and Nothingness* has two main parts. In the first he aims to show the impossibility of carrying out a phenomenalist reduction with respect to *the Being of the subject* to whom objects appear. In the second he aims to show the impossibility of carrying out a phenomenalist reduction with respect to *the Being of the objects* which appear to that subject. As we shall see, as Sartre turns from the introduction to chapter 1 he introduces a surprising third part to his critique, aiming to show the impossibility of carrying out a phenomenalist reduction with respect to phenomena of *non-Being*. It is in this part that he gives his account the idealist-sounding twist. In order to understand the movement of this opening stretch I will run through the argument of each part in turn.

The Being of the subject

Sartre begins with a classic transcendental argument against his phenomenalist opponent: the argument the phenomenalist uses presupposes in its premises precisely that which it denies in its own conclusion. Specifically, the phenomenalist who claims to demonstrate that the Being of every perceived being can be reduced to the series of appearances which manifest it presupposes that the Being of the perceiving subject is not itself subject to the reduction. As the condition of every appearance, consciousness cannot itself be subject to the phenomenalist condition: it has to have a Being that is independent of its appearing-to-itself to be. 'Consciousness', Sartre will argue, 'is the dimension of transphenomenal Being in the subject.'[23] This objection to a phenomenalist reduction with respect to the Being of the subject (having a Being that is independent of its appearing-to-itself to be) is not intended to deny that we have self-knowledge, his claim is only that what consciousness *is* 'in itself' is not reducible to its being perceived or known.[24]

But what does it mean to talk about what consciousness *is* 'in itself' independently of its being conscious of itself? Isn't the idea of a consciousness that exists but which is not somehow aware of itself existing a pure absurdity? Sartre does not suppose that there can be a kind of consciousness which is not, in some way, revealed to itself. However, while he fully accepts the idea that consciousness can exist at all only insofar as it exists (in some way) *for itself* (and further – and here Sartre explicitly endorses Husserl[25] – exists for itself *as* an intentional consciousness *of* something or other), he denies that such 'self-consciousness' is a matter of consciousness constantly having itself *as* an intentional object for itself. Consciousness is, Sartre proposes, in itself *'pure "appearance"'* but not because it is, for itself, a constant 'object of knowledge'.[26]

Consciousness is thus transphenomenal in the sense that it does not exist only insofar as it is (in the intentional sense) perceived or known. Nevertheless, as *pure* 'appearance' it is not something hidden *behind* its appearances to itself either. But then in what way is consciousness revealed to itself? What is self-consciousness if not consciousness' reflective awareness of itself as something known? Sartre offers a Kantian-style 'condition of possibility' argument for an alternative conception: if reflective or intentional awareness of itself is to be possible – the kind of intentional awareness of oneself as thinking that Sartre thinks Descartes affirms in the cogito – there must be a *'pre-reflective cogito'* as its condition:[27] a prior non-thetic,[28] non-cognitive self-relation that Sartre sometimes calls (totally problematically from a Heideggerian perspective) being 'present to itself'.[29]

Sartre offers a typically well-drawn example of counting cigarettes to illustrate his conception of pre-reflective awareness.[30] I am counting cigarettes. What I am primarily (intentionally) aware of is: how many cigarettes there are. But if I am asked: 'What are you doing?', then 'I should reply at once' that I am counting, adding up the number of cigarettes. This is self-reflection – self-knowledge – but it is not what first reveals the consciousness reflected on. 'Quite the contrary, it is the non-reflective consciousness which renders the reflection possible.'[31] It is because I am *already* non-reflectively conscious of myself as counting that I can (typically) reflect so authoritatively on my own consciousness. Thus, Sartre concludes that consciousness is, as such, a consciousness 'of' itself, but that this is not a reflective or intentional awareness of itself; rather, it is to exist in such a way that one *is* a pre-reflective awareness of existing: consciousness is, precisely 'non-thetically aware of itself *as* thetically aware of intentional objects'.[32] At this point Sartre borrows (and surely at once betrays) a Heideggerian formula to affirm that the 'essence' of consciousness lies in 'existence through and through'.[33]

Heidegger attempts to steer thinking away from the distortions produced by the Cartesian idea of consciousness as (in itself) 'isolated and worldless' by taking his point of departure from the basic state of Being of the entity which 'is' only in an understanding of Being: Dasein's basic state of Being-in-the-world. By endorsing Husserl's conception of consciousness as essentially intentional, Sartre risks jeopardising the robustly 'worldly' orientation he found so compelling in Heidegger. If consciousness only exists at all insofar as it is pre-reflectively aware of existing, is it not thereby closed in or wrapped up in its relation to itself and its intentional objects? It is to the Being of such intentional objects (a much more attractive prospect for the phenomenalist reduction, one might think) that Sartre turns next.

The Being of the object

Perhaps no phenomenalist would want to deny the transphenomenal Being of the subject. However, this by no means precludes affirming a phenomenalist reduction concerning the Being of 'existents' which appear to such a subject. Indeed, since what is apprehended is on Sartre's own admission always an intentional object, a being-for-consciousness, he cannot easily rule out the possibility of conducting a satisfactory reduction here. Moreover, as I have suggested, since it would prevent the traditional realist's admission into philosophy of 'worlds behind the scene', such a reduction might even seem philosophically attractive, an advance. For example, one might try to show with Kant and post-Kantian idealists like Husserl that the conditions of possibility for anything to be *an object of experience* are at the same time the conditions of possibility for anything to be *an object as such*.

Sartre thus focuses on the question whether consciousness and its Being are 'sufficient to provide the foundation for the appearance qua appearance' – where appearances here are perceivings whose contents are phenomena in the ordinary sense.[34] Again, he totally rejects the idea, and seeks to affirm that 'the Being of that which appears does not exist only in so far as it appears'.[35]

Forging a path to this conclusion is not as straightforward as it might seem. For Sartre does not want to take a step back from the phenomenalist's minor advance by reinstalling the traditional realist's assumption that the 'true being' of phenomena is something hidden behind its appearances, as an unperceived noumenal cause to the perceived phenomenal effect. In basic cases the intentional contents of appearances just *are*, Sartre wants to be able to say, genuinely transcendent realities. Of course, they only appear by appearing to a subject in appearances, but Sartre wants to avoid construing that either as a kind of dependence of the Being of the object on the perceiving subject or (in a traditional-realist recoil from that) as a shortfall in our access to the transcendent reality. Sartre's strategy is to try to show that, far from it being the case that the object that appears is dependent in its Being on the subject to whom it appears, *the very opposite is true*. Consciousness is, *essentially*, consciousness *of* something, and *if* that something must be (at least in the basic cases) a something which transcends consciousness, then we will be able to say that consciousness itself could not be or exist (and we know *it can* exist because, as every post-Cartesian knows, *it certainly does*) unless objects which are not part of consciousness exist. The proposal, then, is that, in its Being, consciousness is dependent on something which, in its Being, is not dependent on consciousness.

Demonstrating this is what Sartre calls 'the ontological proof'.[36] It begins with an either/or choice between interpreting the object that appears as something constituted by the subject (as it is, for example, in Husserl) or as something which is a genuinely transcendent reality. From that starting point Sartre attempts to show that the first option is always insufficient, that it is 'futile . . . to attempt to found the reality of the object on the subjective plenitude of impressions'.[37] This then leaves him free to make a 'radical reversal' of the phenomenalist position and affirm that consciousness is dependent on a transphenomenal Being, something which *is* anyway, something which *is* so without consciousness.

Sartre's discussion of the futility of the claim that the Being of the object might be constituted by objectifying acts of the subject is not a simple one. The aim is to make implausible the idea that one can derive a satisfactory conception of the Being of an object from the idea of the infinite non-fulfilment of meaning-intentions. Accepting as completely innocuous the thought that 'things give themselves in profile', Sartre claims that the phenomenalist needlessly misconstrues it.[38] According to the phenomenalist, since what appears are 'only' 'fleeting and successive profiles', the fact that what we experience is given as *an object* cannot be based on appearances alone.[39] And if the Being of the phenomenon cannot be construed as something manifest in 'the plenitude of impressions' it must be constituted by the perceiving subject through 'objectifying intentions' which aim beyond them.[40] Sartre accepts that what we experience (the object) transcends its appearing here and now, but totally rejects the phenomenalist's assumption that this experience can only arise from (subjectively) regarding what appears as a finite part of the 'infinite totality of the series of appearances'.[41] For that assumption 'does not bring us out of the subjective' at all and so ruins the whole idea of grasping 'consciousness precisely as a transcendence'.[42] A merely 'imminent objectivity' of the sort one finds in Husserl is a reconstruction of the sense of what is subjectively given as 'outside me' that winds up, as McDowell might put it, forcing one to 'pull in one's horns about objectivity'[43] and denying that appearances are, 'in themselves', glimpses of things that are genuinely 'outside me'. The error is to construe an appearance as a given profile that must fall short of a genuine glimpse.

I do not intend to dwell further on this argument here, but assuming that it disrupts the cause of the phenomenalist we now arrive at a point at which Sartre is in a position to affirm the transphenomenality of two radically different types of phenomena, two distinct senses or 'regions of Being':[44] the transphenomenal Being of the subject and now also the transphenomenal Being of objects. The first has the sense of 'presence to itself' (which Sartre calls 'Being for-itself'); the second has the sense of simple 'presence' (which Sartre calls 'Being in-itself'). Sartre, in part following Heidegger, also identifies a *non-cognitive* mode in which we have 'immediate access'[45] to Being in both regions: in both cases Being is experientially attested by certain (non-objectual) phenomena of Being.[46] In the case of the Being of the subject the disclosing experience is *anxiety*, and in the case of the Being of the object this experience is *nausea*. The former case is discussed at some length at the end of chapter 1 in *Being and Nothingness*[47] and it will be a major issue in Part II of this chapter; the latter, however, is mentioned only in passing and is not examined in any detail at all.[48] This omission is a shame since that experience brings to the fore a distinction which lies at the heart of Sartre's conception of the phenomena in the ordinary sense, and which allows us to see what is going on when his text seems to make the idealist-sounding turns mentioned at the start: the distinction between their existence (*being* so or *not being* so) and their identity (being *so* or not being *so*).

To bring out the significance of nausea to this issue I want to cite a crucial passage from Sartre's eponymous novel. On a tram journey to he doesn't really know where, Sartre's protagonist Roquentin begins to undergo an experience in which *the sense of the world* slips away, leaving only the suffocating *presence of what is there* all around him:

> I lean my hand on the seat, but I pull it away hurriedly: the thing exists. This thing on which I'm sitting, on which I leaned my hand just now, is called a seat. They made it on purpose for people to sit on, they took some leather, some springs, some cloth, they set to work with the idea of making a seat, and when they had finished, *this* was what they had made .... I murmur: 'It's a seat,' rather like an exorcism. But the word remains on my lips, it refuses to settle on the thing .... Things have broken free from their names. They are there, grotesque, stubborn, gigantic, and it seems ridiculous to call them seats or to say anything at all about them: I am in the midst of Things, which cannot be given names .... They demand nothing, they don't impose themselves, they are there.[49]

Soon enough Roquentin has to jump off the tram. He finds himself at the municipal park, where he flops on to a bench for a while, sitting 'between the great black trunks' of the trees,[50] and where again he feels 'the meaning of things' evaporate.[51] Later he collects himself somewhat and reflects on what he experienced that day:

> Words had disappeared, and with them the meaning of things, the methods of using them, the feeble landmarks which men have traced on their surface .... Never, until these last few days, had I suspected what it meant to 'exist'. I was like the others .... I used to say like them: 'The sea *is* green; that white speck up there *is* a sea gull', but I didn't feel that it existed, that the seagull was an 'existing seagull'; usually existence hides itself ... [but with the onset of nausea] existence had suddenly unveiled itself ... The root, the park gates, the bench, the sparse grass on the lawn, all that had vanished; the diversity of things, their individuality, was only an appearance, a veneer. This veneer had melted, leaving soft, monstrous masses, in disorder – naked with a frightening, obscene nakedness.[52]

As he puts it in *Being and Nothingness* (again with an obvious debt to Heidegger), the Being of things must *already* be manifest to us *in some way* 'since we can speak of it and have a certain comprehension of it'.[53] But, for Sartre, this (as Heidegger calls it) *familiarity* with the *meaning of Being* is an understanding that is subordinated to our efforts to be at home in the world, subordinated, that is, to our everyday interest in the human *meaning of beings*. In

Nausea Sartre gives figurative expression to the phenomenon of Being as the disclosure of a soft, monstrous mass. The idea is not that the Being of things is a sort of viscous porridge but that what is meant by Being is not a specific being (thing) with a human meaning: it is – and here Sartre again rather blithely repeats the fundamental idea of the ontological tradition that Heidegger sought to 'destroy' – sheer (undifferentiated, unstructured) *presence*. And Sartre's claim is that, in certain circumstances, beings can find themselves stripped of their familiar *meanings* and be disclosed simply in their *Being*. The differential structures, 'the human world of measures',[54] within which we make ourselves at home in Being can collapse. What we discover in such circumstances is that the meaning of things is like a veneer which can fall away. Yet when it does, when the world in which we are at home collapses, we are precisely *not* left with nothing – I remain in the midst of things, 'they are there': an existent can lose its *meaning*, but it 'cannot be stripped of its *Being*'.[55]

As I have indicated, there are two dimensions within the structure of the phenomena that Sartre is identifying here: on the one hand their existence (*being* so) and on the other hand their identity (being *so*). Normally these dimensions form an experientially concrete whole: what is given to experience is typically 'the phenomena in the ordinary sense', something's *being so* (or *not being so*). To understand how Sartre accounts for the normal integration of these two dimensions, *how it can come about that consciousness can be at home in Being*, we need to turn to his third and most surprising affirmation of transphenomenal phenomena: 'the transphenomenality of non-Being' introduced in chapter 1 of *Being and Nothingness*.[56]

Part II: Being and nothingness[57]

Sartre's négatités

It is sometimes thought that Sartre's investigation of the transphenomenality of non-Being in chapter 1 of *Being and Nothingness* involves major revisions of the discussion of the two kinds of transphenomenal Being – the Being for-itself of consciousness and the Being in-itself of things – presented in the introduction. I don't think that is right at all. On the contrary, it seems to me that chapter 1 attempts to resolve the central issue left hanging by the analysis of Being in the introduction: namely, how two radically different regions of Being, 'two regions without communication', can be concretely united, or, again, how consciousness can be at home in Being.[58]

At the start of chapter 1, without retracting anything from his previous analysis, Sartre notes that there is no prospect of getting the two regions of Being back together once they have been analytically separated out. However, while he thinks there is no way of 'restoring the concrete by the summation or organization of the elements we have abstracted',[59] we can anticipate that the relation of the two regions is precisely what is achieved in the concrete phenomenon of 'man in the world' (or, to use and abuse Heidegger's termi-nology, the 'unified phenomenon' of 'Being-in-the-world'). And so by examin-ing such worldly conduct it should be possible to get clearer on the question of how consciousness can be at home in Being. This is what Sartre attempts in chapter 1.

Although the relation of the two regions of Being he is concerned with will be manifest 'in each type of human conduct',[60] Sartre does not develop his inquiry by attending to just any arbitrary example. On the contrary, he selects a type which he believes will most perspicuously reveal the structure of the (essentially) concrete phenomenon at issue. For reasons which will become clearer as we proceed, Sartre's surprising strategy is to focus not on examples in which the conduct of 'man' is oriented towards 'what *is*' but rather on those that introduce the possibility of an intentional consciousness of 'what *is not*' – a relation to what he calls 'non-Being'.

Now it is often thought that, strictly speaking, there is no such 'relation'. There is only relation to Being, to what is – and so *the world* disclosed to us would be, in its Being, a space of pure Being, a space of pure presence or pure plenitude. Any *lack* of Being, any *absence* of presence, must be, as it were, added on in thought, by negative judgements – a logical but wholly psychic activity which is projected on Being from outside it.

Sartre certainly does not deny that phenomena of non-Being appear only in the context of human expectations, anticipations and projects. As he puts it, 'it would be in vain to deny that negation appears on the original basis of a rela-tion of man to the world'.[61] However, he does question whether the disclosure of what is *not* the case can be reduced to a purely subjective addition, to something added in thought. As demanded by the inquiry itself, Sartre devel-ops his argument by looking at concrete examples. I will mention two of them.

First, a scene in which I am fixing my car. Suppose I think that there may be a blockage in the carburettor. On the basis of that thought I might investigate the carburettor and look for the stuff blocking it. However, as Sartre notes, from the very start of such an investigation, an investigation in which I seek in the carburettor the stuff causing a blockage, and hence an investigation in which I am prepared for a disclosure of a being, 'I am prepared at the same time for the eventuality of a disclosure of a non-Being': 'if I question the car-burettor, it is because I consider it possible that "there is nothing there" in the carburettor'.[62]

Are we to say that the 'being there' of stuff blocking the carburettor is a 'more real' *feature of the world* that I am investigating than the 'nothing there' that I am also prepared to find? Are not both possibilities precisely *possibilities* that belong (equally) to *the world*? Is it not precisely because it may be true that there is nothing in the carburettor that I might see and think just that? Why should we say that the thought 'There is stuff in the carburettor' might be true because of the possibility which happens to have been realised in the world, and not say exactly the same for the thought 'There is nothing in the carburettor'?

To borrow from the early Wittgenstein, if the space of the world is 'the totality of facts', then that really must include *all* the facts, positive *and* negative.[63]

To sharpen his objection to the idea that it is only in thought (in a subjective act of the mind) that non-Being figures in our encounters with phenomena in the world, Sartre considers a meeting with a friend in a café:

> I have an appointment with Pierre at four o'clock. I arrive at the café a quarter of an hour late. Pierre is always punctual. Will he have waited for me? I look at the room, and the patrons, and I say, 'He is not here'. Is there an intuition of Pierre's absence, or does negation indeed enter in only with judgement?[64]

And Sartre wants to affirm the former. Indeed, he wants to affirm that it is precisely because the real situation in the world is one in which Pierre is *not* in the café that one might (truly) think or judge 'Pierre is not here':

> To be sure Pierre's absence supposes an original relation between me and this café; there is an infinity of people who are without any relation with this café for want of a real expectation which establishes their absence. But, to be exact, I myself expected to see Pierre, and my expectation has caused the absence of Pierre *to happen* as a real event concerning this café. It is an objective fact at present that I have *discovered* this absence, and it presents itself as a synthetic relation between Pierre and the setting in which I am looking for him. Pierre absent haunts this café . . . . By contrast, judgements which I can make subsequently to amuse myself, such as, 'Wellington is not in this café, Paul Valéry is no longer here, etc.' – these have a purely abstract meaning; they are pure applications of the principle of negation without real or efficacious foundation, and they never succeed in establishing a *real* relation between the café and Wellington or Valéry. Here the relation 'is not' is merely *thought*. This example is sufficient to show that non-Being does not come to things by a negative judgement; it is the negative judgement, on the contrary, which is conditioned and supported by non-Being.[65]

The judgements 'Pierre is not in the café' and 'Wellington is not in the café' are, one might say, *logically* on a par (and, moreover, they are both apt to be true or false). However, for Sartre this equivalence should not be taken to show that phenomena of non-Being are all of a piece as, like the Wellington case, mere shadows of a negative judgement. On the contrary, by virtue of the 'real expectation' of seeing Pierre (and not Wellington), the presence and absence of Pierre (and not Wellington) are equally real features of the disclosed world. And here we can see a basic *symmetry* between the experienced Being and the experienced non-Being of phenomena. In neither case will we say that they *are* so or are *not* so because thinking makes them so or not so. In short, as Sartre notes, 'there is a transphenomenality of non-Being as of Being'.[66]

Taking a term from the influential French philosopher Henri Bergson, Sartre calls the ubiquitous 'presence' of non-Being in the world the 'haunting' of 'Being' by 'nothingness'.[67] I'm not sure any more whether this sounds more bizarre than the (not particularly bizarre) idea it expresses. Obviously if you choose to ignore the surrounding discussion of transphenomenality in this case, then, yes, this way of affirming the reality of phenomena of non-Being is likely to look like a very weird affirmation of an 'insubstantial and mysterious' or 'invisible and intangible' kind of Being.[68] In fact, however, Sartre is perfectly clear that the 'being there' of nothingness is precisely *not* the 'being there' of a kind of being, and he is equally clear that every phenomena of non-Being is profoundly and irreducibly connected to human affairs, so that *negative realities*, what Sartre calls by the neat neologism '*négatités*', while they are (in the sense outlined above) genuinely 'transcendent realities', nevertheless 'indicate an essential relation of human reality to the world'.[69]

At home in the world

It is a mistake to conceive Sartre's position with regard to non-Being as a mysterious kind of realism about some weird kind of being. A better approach is to treat it as more like a form of *projectivism*, a construal that sits well with Sartre's two central metaphors: that nothingness 'haunts' Being and that it 'exists only on the surface of Being'.[70] However, I will say 'more like' projectivism because, strictly speaking, that must also be a misconstrual since, as we have seen, what we experience with *négatités* are precisely not shadows projected by subjective acts of thought upon independently specifiable beings. No, they are genuine features of and are discovered *in the world*. Nevertheless, the projectivist metaphor is not entirely inappropriate. While we do not have 'man' on one side projecting nothingness on to 'the world' on the other,[71] there is a crucial contrast between 'the world' and 'Being' – where the former and not the latter is a human whereabouts in which *négatités* can be discovered. This is why the parallelism between Being and nothingness is not in all respects symmetrical:[72] for every phenomenon of non-Being, every worldly *négatité*, is essentially caught up in structures of expectation and the projects of human beings through which alone 'that which is not' is 'made-to-be', and so, in general, nothingness, unlike Being, 'is' only as long as 'man' is.

With the contrast between the world and Being in view, we can now understand why the investigation of nothingness serves to clarify the basic issue Sartre is addressing in this chapter: namely, how consciousness can be at home in Being. And his basic answer to that is that *consciousness can be at home in Being by virtue of man being at home in the world*, where the world, though 'supported' by Being, is precisely *not* simply Being. On the contrary, and this is the idealist-sounding twist to Sartre's affirmation of the transphenomenality of phenomenon that we have been preparing for, the world is a 'man-centred' space in which Being is 'disposed around human reality' as 'an organized totality' (the 'human universe', as he puts it in the public lecture).[73] In what is clearly intended to be a development and partial correction of Heidegger's conception of 'the world' in terms of references and relations constitutive of *Zeug* as *Zeug*, as 'a synthetic complex of instrumental realities',[74] Sartre argues that the disclosure of worldly objects presupposes a distinctive kind of human conduct in the midst of Being, conduct in which 'Being is surpassed' through various negation-involving acts and projects:[75]

> We are no longer dealing with those relations of instrumentality by which, according to Heidegger, objects in the world disclose themselves to 'human reality' . . . . In order for the totality of Being to order itself around us as instruments, in order for it to parcel itself into differentiated complexes that refer to one another and which can *be used*, it is necessary that negation rise up not as a thing among things but as the rubric of a category which presides over the arrangement and the redistribution of great masses of Being in things. Thus the rise of man in the midst of the Being which 'invests' him causes a world to be discovered.[76]

The idea here is that the 'relations of instrumentality' which characterise the world in its differential structure presuppose 'empirical activity' of a distinctive kind; specifically, they presuppose 'acts, expectations and projects of human beings'[77] which are essentially negation-involving in the sense that they make it so that something is disclosed as, for example, (precisely) a seat – and *not* a table and *not* a bed, and so on.

Thus it is not only *négatités* but the determination of *the meaning* (the identity) *of all things* – as being *so* and *not so* – that depend on man. For the world is not the totality of things that *are* but a space of human meaning in Being. Hence there is, as Sartre puts it, 'no world' without man;[78] 'the world is human'.[79] This is *not* an idealism since it says nothing at all that would compromise the transcendent *reality* of the phenomena in their *Being* – but it *is* an affirmation of the *ideality* of their *meaning*.[80]

But, now, what must 'we' be in our Being if 'with the rise of man in the midst of Being' a world is to be disclosed in Being? Somehow, Sartre concludes, we must be capable of a definite kind of 'nihilating' [nothing-making] conduct[81] which effects for us a 'withdrawal' in relation to pure Being, a 'dissociation' from 'the causal series which constitutes Being', a causal series which can, in its own right, produce only more Being. In other words, in the midst of Being we must be a being capable of something like a *step back* from Being, a step back in which we 'wrench' ourselves from Being and are no longer simply or exclusively subject to natural causality.[82] This possibility of stepping back from the causal order of things, of 'disengaging from Being', is, as we saw in the chapter on Husserl, precisely what philosophy has always understood by *free-dom*.[83]

In other words, to be a being that can be at home in the world – and in this way at home in Being – is, essentially, *to be free*. To freely have one's Being *to be* – this, for Sartre, is the fundamental meaning of the Heideggerian formula that the 'how' (*essentia*) of this being 'must be conceived in terms of existence'; it is what it means to be 'a being which is existence through and through'. But now if *Being* a 'human subject' is, according to this (as we might now put it) *existentialist* phenomenology, to be a being that has its Being to be, then this implies that such a being is also irrecusably *responsible* for its Being. It is at this point that Sartre's phenomenology passes naturally from issues in the philosophy of mind to issues in moral philosophy. This is a transition that is not taken up by Sartre at the start of *Being and Nothingness*. However, it comes sharply to the fore in the public lecture he delivered in Paris in 1945, a lecture which established his reputation as *the* philosophical voice of post-war France. It is to questions concerning the ethical significance of existentialist phenomenology, as Sartre presented it in that introductory lecture, that I will now turn.

Part III: Moral phenomenology

Freedom

As I mentioned at the start of this chapter, the starting point of Sartre's discussion of moral phenomenology is a conception of human nature drawn from the understanding of 'man' arrived at in the opening stretch of *Being and Nothingness*.[84] The understanding is that man is *free* (in the philosophical sense of this word) or that the *primary* form of *determination* in human life is *self-determination*.[85] Appealing again to the Heideggerian formula that for 'man' ('or as Heidegger has it, the human reality', but the qualification is never returned to) 'existence precedes essence',[86] Sartre concludes that there is, therefore, *no human nature* that determines our existence. In terms that are also reminiscent of Heidegger's 'What is Metaphysics?', Sartre offers the following explication of this thought:

> What do we mean by saying that existence precedes essence? We mean that man first of all exists, encounters himself, surges up in the world – and defines himself afterwards. If man as the existentialist sees him is not definable, it is because to begin with he is nothing. He will not be anything until later, and then he will be what he makes of himself. Thus there is no human nature.[87]

The order of words here does not identify a lengthy order of events. Sartre is not saying: first of all there is existing, which is followed by encountering, followed next by surging, followed finally by defining. The sentence is rather more compressed. Beginning with the idea that, for man, 'to exist' *means* something like surging-up-in-the-world-as-a-self-encountering-point-of-view-on-the-world, Sartre ends up with the idea that *what* is in the world here cannot be an entity or substance with a specific or identifiable nature.

I will come back to this conclusion in a moment, but it is important to recognise that what is situated here as the *beginning* ('first of all') is in fact already a step beyond what one might have thought was the real first step here: the bipedal stepping in the midst of Being of an upright human animal.[88] That is, when Sartre says that 'Man first of all exists', he is not, as Heidegger unfairly interpreted him, simply giving an affirmative answer to 'the question of whether man actually exists or not', but, rather, specifying a distinctive, and not wholly un-Heideggerian, sense of man's Being.[89] Indeed, what Sartre is suggesting with his multiple gloss on the phrase is that to say 'man exists' is precisely *not* to assert the mere 'presence in Being' of a human animal. On the other hand, the contrast here is instructive. For that human animal (and presumably there was something that was merely that once upon a time), like any other animal, would have been quite properly characterised by its distinctive *nature*. Perhaps it naturally lived socially in groups; perhaps it was naturally polygamous or naturally plurisexual or naturally aggressive or naturally gregarious, or whatever. However, the essential premise introduced by the 'first of all' condition is that this human animal nature would have been *totally suspended* once it happened that 'man exists'. For – and this was what we arrived at in the last part of this chapter – according to Sartre, to be in such a way that one's 'substance' is 'existence through and through' is inseparable from being such that one *is* at all only *as* a 'stepping back' from Being (including every natural animal mode of being) in a 'nihilating withdrawal' from Being, and hence being in such a way that one is *not* determined to do merely 'what comes naturally'. In this new beginning, to say 'man exists' is to specify that this being has its Being to be: each man or woman is essentially a freedom that can define or determine *for itself* the meaning(s) of the '*who*' that (in each case) I am – as (say) 'a father' or 'a philosopher' or 'a European'. In general, then, 'man' *is* precisely by making the human *otherwise* than a merely natural being.[90] Hence, even to say that 'man exists' is already to assume that there has been this phenomenological happening in which man comes to be by (as) stepping back from Being, breaking out of the order of nature, and thus distancing itself from the life-patterns which would have otherwise belonged to the human animal, *the animal which therefore I am not*.[91]

So 'man first exists' (in the indicated way) and thus *is* (already) in such a way that 'man' has no given nature but rather has its own Being to be. As such a being, there can be in this new beginning no trace which could be taken to determine any specific direction or definite tendency for the 'who' that I am, no trace or tendency that one cannot step back from: man is a fundamentally *self-creative* subject.[92]

While Sartre's appeal to the 'existence precedes essence' idea is for this reason a radical reversal of the Christian creationist understanding of man's Being,[93] he clearly continues to endorse the (originally theological) idea that 'there is at least one being' who falls radically outside the scope of a wholly naturalistic understanding. For Sartre, there is no more a question of treating the animal kingdom as being, like man, self-created than there is of treating the human kingdom as, like animals, part of nature: 'our aim is precisely to establish the human kingdom as a pattern of values in distinction from the material world'.[94] So for Sartre the Christian humanists were right about one thing: human beings really are special. Indeed, in a certain way man as the existential phenomenologist sees him is, as Heidegger also supposed,[95] closer to divinity than he is to beasts – for the 'dignity of man' is that he *cannot* be understood fully in naturalistic terms, in terms, that is, of a distinctive (for example rational) nature, but only in terms which acknowledge the creative freedom of man to fashion his own essence: 'Man makes himself; he is not found ready-made.'[96]

The idea that there is no trace of a 'ready-made' nature to man is obviously controversial, but it is worth noting that Sartre does not regard his view as entailing an absurd denial of limitations to our choices. For Sartre, while our choices are always absolutely free they are not made in a vacuum but are essentially situated in a distinctive socio-historical time and space, situated, that is, in what was identified in the previous part of this chapter as *a human world*. Indeed, Sartre affirms a universality of a shared 'human condition' for everyone, the condition of 'Being in the world', as something that we all face.[97] And it must have been one of the most pointed moments in Sartre's lecture when he insisted that 'we Europeans of 1945' understand that no human life could be so 'wholly foreign' to 'us' that 'we' could not reconceive in ourselves the strivings and purposes that are manifest in such a life.[98] The universal human condition ensures, Sartre thinks, that the choices that any human being actually makes will always be in principle comprehensible to every other human being.

In fact, Sartre goes further than merely affirming the *intelligibility* of the world-inhabiting choices made by those who are not 'us'. Far more radically, and especially so for 'we Europeans of 1945', Sartre completely rejects the classical humanist and very European idea that a particular form of human life could, by virtue of its adherence to or respect for certain values, realise something that would be the ideal or truly human community, a form of social life that would represent the highest and best for humanity. Whatever else he may say about different ways of living a human life, Sartre regards *every* way of living a human life as a free self-creation, and none can be judged as appreciating better its objective significance. In that sense there is no room in Sartre's outlook for belief in an idea of the progress of man as European thinkers had for so long supposed. For Sartre, 'man is always the same, facing a situation which is always changing, and choice remains always a choice in the situation'.[99]

Yet, for all that, Sartre regards his own work as constituting a kind of humanist reminder for contemporary European humanity – a reminder which will show 'we Europeans' that there really is a possibility of realising a 'truly human' existence.[100] Of course, this reminder will not take the form of identifying certain eternal moral or spiritual truths to which everyone should adhere. On the contrary, it involves an attempt to find our feet with the idea that there are no such truths – that values are *entirely* our own creation: they are invented not discovered. For Sartre, any significance we find in our life, anything that we might say 'confers meaning' upon it or makes it 'worth living' is an essentially free construct: it is not fashioned in a manner that is answerable to anything external to what we ourselves make. As we shall see, in Sartre's view if human beings (in general) could live comfortably with that truth about their responsibility for meaning and value, that would be as close as one could get to what European humanists of the past regarded as creating the best way of life for humanity.

Our moral situation

Sartre says that his project is nothing but 'an attempt to draw the full conclusions from a consistently atheistic position'.[101] This may seem to be one problem among others in moral philosophy, and one that only arises for those who *want* a consistently atheistic position in the first place. However, Sartre regards it as *the* central problem of European humanity, not just for 'we Europeans of 1945' but a distinctive inheritance for every heir of the European Enlightenment. And I think he is right about that. It concerns the problem of how we – we *whoevers* who today live in (more or less) secular democracies – should think about what it is to be human in a place and time for which an appeal to the idea that there exists a divine being who ordains certain specific duties or ends for us can no longer be taken for granted. David Wiggins puts the point as follows:

> Unless we are Marxists, we are more resistant [today] than the eighteenth- or nineteenth-centuries knew how to be [to] attempts to locate the meaning of human life or human history in mystical or metaphysical conceptions – in the emancipation of mankind, or progress, or the onward advance of Absolute Spirit. It is not that we have lost interest in emancipation or progress themselves. But whether temporarily or permanently, we have more or less abandoned the idea that the importance of emancipation or progress (or a correct conception of spiritual advance) is that these are marks by which our minute speck in the universe can distinguish itself as the spiritual focus of the cosmos.[102]

Sartre (even Sartre-the-Marxist) would surely concur with most of that. In particular he regards us as living in an epoch (what Wiggins quite appropriately calls a time 'after Darwin') in which the traditional idea that man has a special place in the cosmos is no longer something simply available, or at least is not readily available to most of us around here. I think Sartre and Wiggins are right about this, and while I think Sartre's thought belongs to a movement which has made the very idea of Europe and 'we Europeans' questionable, I think it remains *in its origins* a profoundly European issue, and it is 'ours' today. For the *we whoevers* that are the inheritors of the world bequeathed by those last men and women who could confidently speak in European public spaces and say, simply, 'we Europeans', I think there is reason to accept that 'an attempt to draw the full conclusions from a consistently atheistic position' really is an attempt to confront our 'real problem' today – whether we are confident atheists or not, demonstrably European or not.

On the other hand, as I have indicated, one of the most striking things about Sartre is that he does not think that the very idea of a special dignity of man is simply a futile illusion. This is not, of course, because he regards us as, say, having been created by God in God's image, but, on the contrary, precisely because he regards us as, in each case, fundamentally self-creative. Needless to say, however, this new atheistic creationism really does put paid to traditional religious and metaphysical ideas about the objectivity of moral values. For Sartre, there is no question of getting things right morally speaking by adjusting one's moral outlook to how things really are in the moral universe. Indeed, the choice between different answers to what we should do or what we should value is not a matter of getting things right about 'reality in itself' at all; there is nothing radically outside us, no transcendent reality – not God, not Reason, not moral reality (whatever that might mean) – that our moral judgements or decisions might conform to: every moral judgement and decision is *essentially subjective* in the sense that, in each case, each one of us is profoundly alone.

This is all extremely exciting. But it is also very extreme, and it can be difficult to know how to handle Sartre's claims. On the one hand, I confess that I find the idea that values are created not discovered very attractive. Some find it plausible to affirm a robust realism in ethical matters but I really cannot make head nor tail of that idea. Moreover, it seems right to say that the 'who' that I am is something I have a hand in through the choices I make and the values I affirm. On the other hand, however, the extreme subjectivism looks worrying. While Sartre leaves us in a good position to embrace a healthy pluralism in moral matters (we can all agree to disagree), it seems he has only achieved that at the price of totally abandoning the idea that some moral stances are in *substantially better shape* than others. Since values are essentially subjective it seems that for Sartre *anything goes*. It doesn't matter what you decide, and it doesn't matter how you arrived at your decision. The only thing that matters is that you freely commit yourself to it. And that's just not a remotely acceptable description of moral phenomenology.[103]

The problem being put to Sartre here is not that by getting rid of objective values he fails to do justice to the difference between the life of a mere animal and the life of a human being. He clearly wants to acknowledge that difference with the thought that man is, uniquely, a self-creative being. But, as David Wiggins notes, there is another kind of difference which we, as participants in a human community, also insist upon and which Sartre's conception seems totally to undermine. This is the sort of difference we might introduce by contrasting 'the life of a man who contributes something to a society with a continuing history and a life lived on the plan of a southern pig-breeder who buys more land to grow more corn to feed more hogs to buy more land, to grow more corn to feed more hogs ... '.[104] Does Sartre give an account of life choices which can do anything to persuade us reflectively to take seriously this kind of (for participants undoubtedly important) difference?

For a start I think Sartre would want to insist that the contrast of cases that Wiggins is presenting here is in fact not just a contrast 'for participants' but responds to differences that are genuinely objective. It is surely a matter of plain fact that, in the example, one man's life, as Wiggins nicely puts it, 'fans out with a whole arborescence of concerns' while the other's has 'nowhere to go but round and round in circles'.[105] But then the crucial thing is not that this contrast is objective but that it *matters* to participants. And Sartre has to accept that, on his view, acknowledgement of the objective difference is *not decisive* in this regard. According to Sartre, if we live lives which 'fan out with a whole arborescence of concerns' that is simply because such differences *do* matter to us. However, that such differences *should* matter to us is not, on his view, something one can make a case for independently of living or striving for such a life.

Yet that doesn't seem to be enough. Sartre himself was the kind of man who tried to contribute something to his society – and he was also a constant critic of the shortcomings of others. The idea that we should attempt to *improve* our lives was really important to him. That we become less racist and less nationalistic in particular mattered to him profoundly. Now, as I noted in Chapter 1, the crucial issue in philosophy, and what has certainly mattered most in moral philosophy in our time, is whether it is possible to draw a substantial distinction between different methods of inducing people to take a particular view on such topics. We want to know, as John McDowell has put, if there is a distinction 'between making reasons available to them on the one hand and manipulating them in other ways that have nothing in particular to do with rationality on the other'.[106] If being of a certain mind in one's ethical thinking, being anti-racist for example, is *just* a matter of a subjective stance or personal commitment, then there seems to be no room for a distinction between someone who, say, offers a warm welcome to visitors because they have been convinced by the power of someone's (perhaps their own) thinking about hospitality and someone who holds the same view because they have been convinced by the power of someone's (perhaps their own) oratory on this topic. We want to be able to affirm this distinction, but isn't it possible that we are, as Levinas puts it, 'duped by morality'?[107] The question we need to put to Sartre is this: can he offer a convincing way of arriving at the idea that the ethical stances and commitments taken by some participants in our communities are in *substantially better shape* than those taken by others *by virtue of the way they have been arrived at*?[108] In the next section I will explore the little lecture's famous account of 'choosing for man' with a view to working out a Sartrean route of response to this question.

Kierkegaardian exemplarism

'Thus the first effect of existentialism is that it puts every man in possession of himself as he is, and places the entire responsibility for his existence squarely upon his own shoulders.'[109] This burden of radical self-responsibility is the upshot of accepting that, for every man or woman, 'to exist' at all is to have one's Being to be – to exist such that one is, as Sartre puts it, 'the incontestable author' of one's own Being.[110] While this *dictates* precisely *nothing* to anyone else, Sartre's whole outlook is aimed at stressing that *you* are, at every step, totally responsible for the life choices you actually make. Indeed it is for Sartre 'senseless to think of complaining' about your life 'since nothing foreign has decided what we feel, what we live, what we are'.[111]

Not surprisingly, Sartre is aware that this kind of thought 'may seem comfortless to one who has not made a success of his life'.[112] And many readers of Sartre have felt him drawing uncomfortably close to an unforgiving ruthlessness here. Of course, it is not intended to be a thought that *oppresses* by insisting that we deserve everything we get, but rather a thought that *liberates* by reminding us that we are always free to take the initiative. But the line between these alternatives can seem very fine indeed. On the other hand, I am not at all satisfied by the idea, suggested by a recent interpreter, that, with respect to the alternatives, one can say only that it is 'in tone ... that they differ'.[113] No, what is decisive here is not 'tone' but whether you relate to Sartre's thought as a claim made on you by *another* or, ultimately, as an acknowledgement of self-responsibility that comes from *yourself* and which is itself carried 'squarely upon [your] own shoulders'. In short, *what matters is whether you assume your self-responsibility autonomously*. In this part of the chapter I want to see how, if at all, this Sartrean demand bears on the question of whether we may be duped by morality.

The Sartrean demand is that you come to assume your own self-responsibility autonomously. Sartre's main argument to convince you to accept this demand for yourself is bound up with a proposal that seems at first sight to have nothing at all to do with it: namely, that to choose a way of being for yourself is always also *to choose for man* in general: 'When a man commits himself to anything ... he is not only choosing what he will be, but is thereby at the same time a legislator deciding for the whole of mankind.'[114] In what follows I will explain how this argument is connected to the Sartrean demand.

The usual, and I think thoroughly erroneous, reading of Sartre's argument is to see it as a variation of the Kantian argument for the universalisability of moral maxims. One can certainly see why Sartre is usually read this way. For one thing he concludes his discussion with the thoroughly Kantian idea that someone who judges without self-deception has to acknowledge that 'to make freedom *my* aim' is incoherent or 'impossible' without making that of others 'equally my aim'.[115] Or, again, since I cannot in fact do other than will my freedom, then in principle, if I am not self-deceived, 'I cannot not will the freedom of others'.[116] Moreover, in this same paragraph Sartre *explicitly* acknowledges agreement with Kant on this, endorsing the Kantian idea 'that freedom is a will both to itself and to the freedom of others'.[117]

On the face of it, then, the Kantian reading looks more than merely plausible. Cranston is sure that in *Existentialism and Humanism* Sartre advances 'the Kantian principle of treating persons as ends';[118] Caws is convinced that to say that when a man chooses for himself he chooses for all men 'is clearly a form of what is known in ethical theory as the "generalisation argument", the classical statement of which is found in Kant'.[119] Warnock too declares that 'Sartre expressly compares [his] doctrine with Kant's moral theory', urging that it involves a 'universalising' of the 'desire' for one's own freedom such that one is 'including in it the freedom of all.'[120]

In order to get at what is wrong with this 'universalising' reading, let us first very briefly sketch the Kantian version of the argument that Sartre is supposed to be (no doubt non-classically) advancing. For Kant, understanding moral agency is essentially a matter of appreciating an agent's *motivations* for action, and in particular the possibility that she is motivated to act in ways that she might not *want* to. There is no suggestion of external coercion here, simply the idea that her actions are constrained by the thought that she has a *duty* to obey what Kant calls 'the moral law'. Actions are thus conceived by Kant as morally right insofar as they are made in *obedience to the moral law*. Now, very roughly, the moral law here is a kind of voice of rational conscience speaking against the temptations of our non-rational and animal inclinations. For Kant, then, as for Sartre in fact, the distinction of human life is deeply connected to our freedom to *step back* from our natural condition and autonomously to select alternative ways of behaving, ways that one might not (naturally) *want* to. On the other hand, however, for Kant the possibility of making one's choices *rationally* invariably requires deciding *not* to do what is particular to oneself. What I will for myself *qua* rational being must be something I see as applying to *any* rational creature. This is why Kant states that the test of whether something is morally permissible is that one can universalise it: 'There is, therefore, only one categorical imperative. It is: Act only according to that maxim by which you can at the same time will that it should become a universal law.'[121]

The idea that this categorical imperative (self-)imposes a limitation on choice can thus be put like this: if I am to relate to *myself* as a rational agent, then *no* maxim which subjects *any other rational agent* to conditions in which he or she is reduced to a kind of an object or means to an end can be consistently affirmed. And – so the usual reading of Sartre goes – this is just the kind of reasoning that Sartre wants to affirm as well.

It would certainly seem to make things easier for Sartre if it was so. Instead of being mired by the threat of moral anarchy, the requirement of universalisability would provide for a genuinely compelling constraint on the choices of those who are not self-deceived. In willing one's own freedom one must also will the freedom of others, and so any image of man I choose for myself which results in oppressive conditions for others, conditions in which they are regarded as an object, cannot be consistently affirmed.

But one only has to recall that Sartre's conception of freedom is the technical 'philosophical' one and not the 'popular' one to realise that this reading cannot be right. Sartre is quite clear that in the sense he uses for the expression a slave is just as free as a master, and that in general one is never 'more free' in some situations than in others.[122] So 'willing the freedom of others' cannot mean willing that they are no longer oppressed, enslaved, discriminated against and so on. Sartre himself was 'a man of the left' and was consistently on the side of the oppressed – but the ethical significance of existentialism is not, as one might perhaps like to think, a nice wish for widespread freedom from oppression. No, Sartre's thought is both more complex and, I think, much more interesting than that. For when he says that willing one's own freedom requires that one also will the liberty of others this means: *If I choose to assume my own self-responsibility autonomously, then I am always also choosing that others do the same.* I am, therefore, willing a 'truly human' life for all, not, however, because we are now all the same (*vis-à-vis* our political and social freedoms in the popular sense) but because we are now all living *as* self-responsible individuals.

There is a major shift here from a form of egalitarianism to a form of individualism, a shift that is most readily brought out by following the replacement of the Kantian idea of man as a free rational subject with the Sartrean idea of man as a free creative subject. The crucial effect of this replacement is that, in a certain way, it produces an experienced *ungrounding* of whatever one affirms: taking a law to be binding, taking a procedure as rational, taking something as a proof, regarding something as one's duty . . . for Sartre, these are all ultimately *my* choices – they are not authorised, as it were, by the inherent nature of things or a transcendent structure of reason. One must, on each occasion, decide, and decide without recourse to an independently authoritative body or calculus of rules. There is no covenant in reality or reason which, independently of my commitments, forces me to go in the way I do.

So Sartre replaces a rational subject – a subject who autonomously sets aside his or her personal desires and inclinations to act in a way that should be accepted by any rational being – with a creative subject – a subject who can, under his or her own steam, choose or fail to choose to assume his or her own self-responsibility. This brings about, I want to suggest, a shift from a *Kantian universalism* to what I want to call a *Kierkegaardian exemplarism*. Indeed, it seems to me essential to understanding the ethical significance of Sartre's existentialism that when he introduces his view he does *not*, as Warnock's wording suggests he does, 'expressly compare his doctrine with Kant's', but in fact compares it with something that could hardly be less Kantian (or less abstract and formal): namely, 'the anguish that Kierkegaard called "the anguish of Abraham"'.[123] What Sartre clearly intends to pick up on in this reference to Kierkegaard's reading of the biblical story of Abraham and Isaac is that when we are confronted with a choice or dilemma we are *essentially alone* in our decision on *what to do* – 'and with this', Sartre insists, 'goes anguish'.[124] It is not surprising, then, that, far from being dependent on or lending itself to a Kantian moral theory, Sartre's primary reference to Kant is essentially *negative*:

> We cannot decide *a priori* what it is that should be done. I think it was made sufficiently clear to you in the case of that student who came to see me, that to whatever ethical system he might appeal, the Kantian or any other, he could find no sort of guidance whatever; he was obliged to invent the law for himself.[125]

When one sees that the central feature of Sartre's account is that each one of us is alone in deciding on what to do it becomes clear that Sartre's understanding of the ethical significance of existentialism is that it implies that every step we take along the way is an Abrahamic moment.

As the 1945 lecture makes clear, Sartre, like Kierkegaard, is totally unconvinced by the Kantian conception of ethical duty and profoundly impressed by the astonishing absence of hesitation in Abraham's singular conduct. As he puts it, 'anyone in such a case would wonder, first, whether it was indeed an angel and, secondly, whether I am really Abraham'.[126] In other words, what impresses Sartre is that Abraham acts *without* calculable proof. Not only is it 'I myself who must decide whether the voice is or is not that of an angel', but equally 'there is nothing to show that I am Abraham'.[127] The scene is one in which 'it came to pass that God did tempt Abraham, and said unto him, Abraham: and he said, Behold, here I am'. It is a scene in which a man *assumes unhesitating responsibility for his own 'here I am'*.

Here I am. This is the Kierkegaardian exemplarism that Sartre *opposes* to Kantian universalism. Not that, for Sartre, the 'leap' to a decision is informed by a specifically religious outlook either; it is not a leap of *religious* faith. 'You are free to choose – that is to say, invent', Sartre says; 'no general morality can show what you ought to do: no signs are vouchsafed in this world. The Catholics will reply, "Oh but they are!" Very well; still, it is I myself, in every case, who have to interpret the signs.'[128]

As we shall see, the individualism of this starting point is as irreducible as anything demanded by *Being and Nothingness*; moreover, there are passages in the earlier text that clearly prefigure but also clarify the apparently universalising wording of the lecture. Thus, for example, towards the end of the book, having just noted that our freedom is always a freedom related to a (human) condition, Sartre notes that, nevertheless,

> one is not man first in order to be oneself subsequently and one does not constitute oneself as oneself in terms of a human essence given a priori. Quite the contrary, it is in its effort to choose itself as a personal self that the for-itself sustains in existence certain social and abstract characteristics which make of it *a man* (or a woman); and the necessary connections which accompany the essential elements of man appear only on the foundation of a free choice; in this sense each for-itself is responsible in its being for the existence of a human race.[129]

As this passage indicates, the Sartrean idea of choosing for 'mankind' (whether one is a man or a woman) never was a Kantian gesture based on the universalisability of one's choices. On the contrary, the movement beyond oneself emerges only on the basis of appreciating that, for human beings at least, 'to exist' means that one has one's Being to be, and so one cannot *be* and not at once be under a constant Abrahamic obligation to take a stand on what it is to be human: 'at every instant I am obliged to perform actions which are *examples*. Everything happens to man as though the whole human race has its eyes fixed upon what he is doing and regulates its conduct accordingly'.[130]

Disappointed by Sartre's supposedly Kantian argument, Peter Caws suggests that the anguish of freedom is 'surely enough' to give content to Sartre's claims concerning the ethical significance of existentialism and does not 'require ... any universal warrant'.[131] Quite so, but nor did Sartre seek any such warrant for it. The point is that if I (and it is best that I speak in the first person here) accept the Sartrean version of the 'existence precedes essence' idea, then in everything that I do I must recognise that I am making a creative contribution to what it *means* to be, say, a father, a son, a brother, a teacher, a philosopher ... – and ultimately what it *means* to be 'a man (or a woman)'. You are the son or daughter of your parents. But even if this is (typically) also a kind of biological connectedness we also have a non-biological concept of 'being a son' or 'being a daughter': there is *what we have made* of a lived relationship. And what you *do* – whether you speak to your parents often, whether you regard them as past it or whatever – is implicitly to take a stand on what it is to *be* a son or daughter. Because we have our Being to be, everyone at every moment is obliged *to be an example* and not just *an instance* of the 'human race'. I am fated to being, at every step I take, 'a legislator deciding for the whole of mankind'.[132] *This* is what it means to be a human being. In other words, it is only in one's consciousness (of) being absolutely alone and absolutely self-responsible that every man or woman, in their local lives in England, in France, in Nova Scotia or wherever, finds him- or herself always already obliged to surpass that locality towards the 'human race' in general.[133] The agreement with Kant is simply an insistence on the *invariability* of this obligation.

So there is an acknowledgement of an agreement with Kant that there is indeed a universal form of morality connected to freedom: an unavoidable *normativity*, beyond rules, intrinsic to choices – a normativity that prevents them remaining, *simply*, one's own alone. However, while what Kant's *universalism* offered was regarded as sufficient 'for the constitution of morality' in that in any situation what is right is that act which would be willed by any rational creature, Sartre's *exemplarism* precisely denies that formal considerations can provide any clue whatsoever to the content of morality. No rules of moral theorising can supply a means of judging: the content of one's deliberations is 'always concrete', so the route to the decision 'always has to be invented'.[134]

Ultimately, the only issue that matters to Sartre is whether in pursuing your deliberations (in, say, forming an argument or forming some other kind of – by your lights – convincing work of words, or indeed in avoiding certain kinds of deliberation altogether) you take on the burden of exemplary self-responsibility autonomously or not. Of course, if you do, then, *eo ipso*, you are also willing that others do the same. But this is a formal structure which precisely does not provide a way of judging the proper conduct on any issue on any occasion. It leaves everyone, precisely, alone.

Mündig *man*

While the move away from Kant is profound there is of course something still rather Kantian about the stress on autonomy. Indeed, if one wanted a concept to capture the Sartrean oxymoron of exemplary self-responsibility the Kantian idea of *Mündigkeit*, the capacity to use one's own understanding, to act by one's own lights, might serve very well.[135] Of course, Sartre thinks that we always are already unavoidably *mündig* – thinking and deciding for ourselves – but our tendency is not to take on that self-responsibility autonomously; our tendency is to flee the anguish of Abraham, flee from our understanding of ourselves as freely inventive or creative (and hence responsible) for what it *means* to be (a) human. For the *mündig* man or woman, by contrast, self-responsibility is assumed autonomously, and hence in an awareness that 'the eyes of the world are upon you'. For Sartre, the anguish of Abraham is not the anguish of a man or a woman who must give voice to something universal and not just personal – but simply a man or a woman who must really speak for himself or herself.

The fact that we are radically alone in this does not mean that the *mündig* man or woman will never criticise others. On the contrary, the *mündig* man or woman is precisely the one who will want to arrive at his or her ethical stances and commitments by way of what are, by his or her lights, *convincing deliberations*, and it is for that reason that they *do* regard their choices as in *substantially better shape* than those that are arrived at through modes of manipulation that, by their lights, would call into question their claim to be speaking for themselves. However, what will not be accepted here is an attempt to give a *grounding* for these choices that claims they are everywhere 'adjusted to how things are', or that they are ultimately made on the basis of, say, an 'intuition' or 'revelation' of an objective moral truth. Nevertheless, the *mündig* man and woman certainly strive for objectivity in the sense that they simply will not accept that just anything goes. To be *mündig* implies that one puts one's own mind (and not the mind of the other or the mind of the crowd) where one's mouth is.

Still, it might be thought that this kind of refusal to accept that anything goes may nevertheless *not* give us any reason for supposing we have a conclusive answer to the worry about forms of persuasion raised by McDowell. And I think that is right: we don't. Indeed, I think there is no general answer as to what counts as making up one's mind, *Mündigkeit* – at least no answer from outside the evaluative discourse that the *mündig* man or woman endorses. There is no 'sideways-on' view which would show that our choices really were made for 'the best possible reasons', or show that we certainly had not been inappropriately manipulated or inappropriately influenced by someone's (perhaps our own) smooth talk. On the other hand, we should note too that the *mündig* man and woman cannot be both *mündig* and *indifferent* to whether their minds are made up by (what they regard as) appropriately convincing words and by knowledge of all kinds. On the contrary, that is something that will, in every case, strike them as crucial matters. You are condemned to judge by your own lights – but that does not make what you affirm the result of a purely personal sensibility that is really just 'pushing' you to decide one way or the other.[136] One's freedom implies that it is always possible to choose otherwise. And the *mündig* man and woman do not simply plump for one option or another either. When they are confronted by 'a real situation' their choice can have nothing to do with 'caprice' (a change of opinion without reason or on a whim).[137] Indeed, on Sartre's understanding of how consciousness can be at home in Being we are *all* more or less reflectively, and certainly pre-reflectively, *involved* in the situations we find ourselves in. The *mündig* man or woman knows that when there is more than one possibility open to him or her, he or she *must choose without excuse*. And so the question of whether they have made up their mind by appropriate persuasion or inappropriate manipulation is just the sort of thing that matters to them.

But how can one tell? There is no answer, or, again, no answer that does not already presuppose the evaluative discourse that the *mündig* man or woman endorses. There is nothing anyone could say that would guarantee you might not come to think you had been 'duped'. That kind of good conscience is not to be had. Of course, we must not present this situation overly abstractly. For even this 'nothing anyone could say' situation remains, precisely, situated. As I have indicated, the kind of evaluative discourse that is available to *me* has not simply fallen from the sky and is not simply my own fabrication. As Sartre puts it, 'men depend upon their epoch'.[138] And perhaps where we stand today is not somewhere well placed to meet McDowell's challenge: perhaps the resources available to us today cannot readily or satisfactorily show that the ethical stances taken by the *mündig* man or woman of today – or we *whoevers* of the twenty-first century – are in a substantially better shape than stances arrived at by merely manipulative persuasion. So the worry I took from McDowell is, perhaps, not one *we* can radically or totally despatch. And *that* will be a mark of our time, of our epoch. Some will regard that as the tragedy of our time. Perhaps, however, it is better seen as the enlightenment granted it.

I will return to moral issues in Chapter 6 in the context of Emmanuel Levinas' phenomenology of the other person. In the next chapter I will examine the new beginning in phenomenology launched by Maurice Merleau-Ponty. This new beginning, like Sartre's, conceives itself as reconciling the differences between Husserl and Heidegger. However, as we shall see, in Merleau-Ponty's case the work of reconciliation leads not to a new philosophy of consciousness in which we are 'condemned' to freedom,[139] but to a new philosophy of the body in which we are 'condemned' to meaning.[140]

5

PHENOMENOLOGY OF PERCEPTION
Maurice Merleau-Ponty

Ever-renewed beginnings

At the start of the last chapter I mentioned that Maurice Merleau-Ponty belongs with Sartre at the forefront of those who wanted to conceive the work of Husserl and Heidegger as inaugurating a new movement in philosophy. For Merleau-Ponty, this movement is bringing phenomenology into being as a distinctive 'doctrine or philosophical system'.[1] Out of the mists of an 'inchoate' emergence it has come to have a 'unity' sufficient that it 'can be practised and identified as a manner or style of thinking'.[2] Indeed, Merleau-Ponty regards himself as writing at a time in which it has finally become possible to engage with some confidence with the question of what phenomenology is. Merleau-Ponty's response to this question is presented as the Preface to his major work *Phenomenology of Perception* (1945), and I will begin this chapter by taking a look at some of the issues raised by this prefatory text.

As we shall see, in situating the emergence of phenomenology, Merleau-Ponty draws it into the wider movement of 'modern thought' in general, citing Balzac, Proust, Valéry and Cézanne as an exemplary quartet of (French) heroes who are in important respects fellow travellers here. The sense of 'modern' in play in this claim should, I think, be understood in terms of the modernist[1] predicament outlined in Chapter 1: it is work which finds itself, in quite radical ways, in conflict with the modern[2] modes which dominate our time. This conflict does not provoke modern[1] authors simply to abandon the field altogether but spurs those in its throes only more urgently to attempt to 'seize the meaning of the world or of history' that they find granted to them.[3] In this way, as Merleau-Ponty puts it, 'modern thought' attempts to become reflectively self-responsible by taking a 'decision' with regard to the current formation of the field, a decision which will inaugurate a new beginning, or 'performs' a new departure.[4] As far as philosophy is concerned, Merleau-Ponty finds in phenomenology the resources for just such a renewal of philosophy. In particular, he wants us to find it as an inheritance of philosophy that can acknowledge, through and through, the fundamentally worldly character of existence, hence as an inheritance which interrupts the traditional philosophical aspiration to achieve a point of view that transcends the 'facticity' of its own historical inscription.[5] For Merleau-Ponty, what we need to incorporate into philosophy in our time is proper appreciation that thinking of *every* kind remains always in the stream of history, and so there can be 'no thought which embraces all our thought'.[6] The task of philosophy in the name of phenomenology is thus to enable philosophical writing to suspend traditional certainties concerning what (inheriting) philosophy (philosophically) demands of us. It is a demand that 'philosophy itself must not take itself for granted' and hence conceives its own elaboration as 'an ever-renewed experiment in making its own beginning'.[7] A classic modernist[1] gesture.

Following an examination of the preface in Part I of this chapter, I will subsequently attend to two further 'beginnings' to be found in *Phenomenology of Perception*, two decisive renewals of the inheritance of phenomenology: first, a new elaboration of the idea of a phenomenological reduction and, second, a re-launching of phenomenology through an analysis of the living human body.

Part I: A preface for phenomenology

What we have been waiting for

Since it is presented before what he calls 'the outset' of his phenomenological study,[8] and because of the metaphilosophical topic it treats, it is tempting to read the preface to *Phenomenology of Perception* as a text which is not itself fully phenomenological in character. It can readily seem, that is, that in his preface (rather like in my presentation of phenomenology in Chapter 1) Merleau-Ponty aims faithfully to encapsulate the ways in which phenomenological philosophers go about their business, but without himself at that moment attempting to do business in that way.

The excellence – and the difficulty – of Merleau-Ponty's prefatory essay on the phenomenological method and movement lies in the fact that this tempting conception of it is quite mistaken. Indeed, if we are to follow one recent interpreter in supposing that Merleau-Ponty 'aptly describes the essence of this method' in the preface,[9] we had better place a heavy stress on 'aptly', otherwise the emphasis on it as offering a description of essence will make it seem that its mode is precisely a betrayal of the method it describes. For while (as we shall confirm in a moment) the very first gesture of Merleau-Ponty's answer to the question concerning 'what phenomenology *is*' is one which firmly aligns phenomenology with the fundamental characteristic of traditional philosophical inquiries in general – namely, its having a concern with questions of essence, a concern with 'what something, essentially, *is*' – he immediately turns on this gesture to insist that what distinguishes the phenomenological understanding of such questions is that the purity of its philosophical aim goes hand in hand with an apparently contradictory impurity of its method: phenomenology is a philosophy which 'puts essences back into existence'.[10] Thus a phenomenologically 'apt' description of the essence of phenomenological method will be one which aims to affirm, as thinkers such as Marx, Nietzsche and Freud have also affirmed, that this essence did not fall from the sky ready-made but that there was, on the contrary, what one might call a process of idealisation, a history of phenomenology, *a movement of formation of its meaning* which is not simply external to or radically abstractable from what it essentially is. In other words, a phenomenologically 'apt' description of the essence of phenomenology cannot be written in an exclusively ahistorical, baldly objective, 'thesis'-like mode.[11] What it is concerned with will be utterly *objective* all right since it aims to describe something that, in our time, really exists. However, what exists here is also something profoundly *subjective* since it only exists insofar as it has come concretely to be 'lived' *'for ourselves'* as this becoming-increasingly-meaningful phenomenon.[12] It *is* at all only *as* such a phenomenon. And the basic claim of the preface is that it is for this reason a phenomenon that can be made 'accessible' to us *as it is* only through the phenomenological method the preface describes.[13] The preface is thus intended to be itself, already, a fully-fledged phenomenological study: it is a phenomenology of the movement of phenomenology. As we shall see in a moment, the in some ways extremely equivocal opening makes the point unequivocally.

The preface begins by wondering at the historical fact that at the time of its writing in 1945, 'half a century after the first works of Husserl', the question 'What is phenomenology?' 'has by no means been answered'.[14] Through a series of contradictory assertions Merleau-Ponty reflexively suggests both that he will attempt to give an account of the essence of phenomenology and that he will be able aptly to do so only if, in the very form of his account of this essence, he acknowledges that it belongs to and emerges in a movement in history which makes phenomenology in the 'present day' both objectively actual and yet only subjectively determinate:

> What is phenomenology? It may seem strange that this question has still to be asked half a century after the first works of Husserl. The fact remains that it has by no means been answered. Phenomenology is the study of essences; and according to it, all problems amount to finding definitions of essences: the essence of perception, or the essence of consciousness, for example. But phenomenology is also a philosophy which puts essences back into existence, and does not expect to arrive at an understanding of man and the world from any starting point other than of their 'facticity'. It is a transcendental philosophy which places in abeyance the assertions arising out of the natural attitude, the better to understand them; but it is also a philosophy for which the world is always 'already there' before reflection begins – as an inalienable presence; and all its efforts are concentrated upon re-achieving a direct and primitive contact with the world, and endowing that contact with a philosophical status. It is the search for a

philosophy which shall be a 'rigorous science', but it also offers an account of space, time and the world as we 'live' them .... The reader pressed for time will be inclined to give up the idea of covering a doctrine which says everything, and will wonder whether a philosophy which cannot define its scope deserves all the discussion which has gone on around it, and whether he is not faced rather by a myth or a fashion.

Even if this were the case, there would still be a need to understand the prestige of the myth and the origin of the fashion, and the opinion of the responsible philosopher must be *that phenomenology can be practised and identified as a manner or a style of thinking, that it existed as a movement before arriving at complete awareness of itself as a philosophy.* It has been long on the way, and its adherents have discovered it in every quarter, certainly in Hegel and Kierkegaard, but equally in Marx, Nietzsche and Freud. A purely linguistic examination of the texts in question would yield no proof; we find in texts only what we put in them, and if ever any kind of history has suggested the interpretations which should be put on it, it is the history of philosophy. We shall find in ourselves and nowhere else, the unity and true meaning of phenomenology. It is less a question of counting up quotations than of determining and expressing in concrete form this *phenomenology for ourselves* which has given a number of present-day readers the impression ... not so much of encountering a new philosophy as of recognising what they had been waiting for. Phenomenology is accessible only through a phenomenological method. Let us, therefore, try systematically to bring together the celebrated phenomenological themes as they have grown spontaneously together in life. Perhaps we shall then understand why phenomenology has for so long remained at this initial stage as a problem to be solved and a hope to be realized.[15]

The movement in the lines of this long opening remark develops through a series of oscillating shifts between apparently contradictory poles: between essence and existence, objectivity and subjectivity, method and movement, themes and growth, problems and hopes. And those very shifts have their meta-level acknowledgement: on the one hand, they make phenomenology look empty because unlimited; on the other hand, finding a way of pursuing philosophy which is not sitting on one end or the other of traditional dialectical seesaws seems to be exactly what we want.

Of all of these contradictions it is the last meta-level opposition that the preface itself would seek to address. Not, we can be sure, by sitting proudly on one end of the seesaw, happily supposing it could be established that the phenomenological method is obviously the right way of going on in philosophy. On the contrary, at the end of the preface Merleau-Ponty closes his 'description of essence' with the thought that phenomenology cannot be validated by recourse to anything outside itself: it 'rests on itself' or 'provides it own foundation'.[16] More radically still, since it can only exploit 'the world and constituted reason' which are the gift of history at any time, its determining itself to go on in a certain way – its grasp of its essence – remains itself always in question: it must go on 'never knowing where it is going'.[17]

So the preface opens with an anticipation that it will close the question concerning the essence of phenomenology. It closes, aptly, by leaving it open: 'the unfinished nature of phenomenology and the inchoative atmosphere which has surrounded it are not to be taken as a sign of failure'.[18] It is not a sign of failure because it is nothing other than the ongoing, never-ending attempt to 'seize the meaning of the world or of history as that meaning comes into being'.[19] And hence as long as the world worlds or history happens there will be an always new task of expressing phenomenology as we find it for ourselves.[20]

It is a stirring song for a Socratic renewal of philosophy as constantly self-questioning (and hence self-responsible) 'radical reflection'.[21] In fact, as I have already indicated, it doesn't end there. Merleau-Ponty does not regard such reflection as having only an intra-philosophical historical significance, or as the mark only of a movement within philosophy. On the contrary, it belongs, he supposes, to a 'will to seize' one's time which 'merges into the general effort of modern thought'.[22]

So, it is also, in effect, a stirring song for the modernist[1] spirit in European thought in general. There is, however, a dimension of its strictly intra-philosophical significance that I have not touched on, and I should come clean concerning some lines in the opening of the preface that I deliberately left out. For there is a much shorter way of coming reflectively to terms with the oscillating contradictions that launch Merleau-Ponty's own much longer attempt to express phenomenology for himself, a route that he knows is available to him and which his contradictory formulations deliberately invite. At the heart of the material I have cut from the long opening paragraphs we find Merleau-Ponty frankly admitting that 'one may try to do away with these contradictions by making a distinction between Husserl's and Heidegger's phenomenologies'.[23]

Quite. Yet for Merleau-Ponty these contradictions do not point towards two distinct faces or phases in the inheritance of phenomenology. Indeed, according to Merleau-Ponty 'the whole of *Being and Time* springs from an indication given by Husserl',[24] and he goes on to insist that 'Heidegger's "Being-in-the-world" appears only against the background of the phenomenological reduction'.[25] If we take Merleau-Ponty at his word and accept that texts contain only what we put into them we can't complain too much if he finds Husserl and Heidegger capable of being reconciled in this way.[26] But the abiding interest in Merleau-Ponty's work is that his real effort of reconciliation is not pursued through interpretive exegesis but, like Sartre's, through the formation of his own phenomenology. And in this respect what one finds in his text is quite astonishing. For whereas Sartre would reconcile Husserl and Heidegger by regarding the intentionality of consciousness as an abstraction from the primordial and concrete 'relation' of Being-in-the-world, Merleau-Ponty reconciles them by regarding intentionality as fundamental to the in-the-world behaviour of *a living human body*. With this irreducibly bodily intentionality, he will argue, we catch sight of 'an imposition of meaning which is not the work of a constituting consciousness' but which nevertheless saturates experience and 'clings to certain contents'.[27] In other words, at the heart of the structure of meaning-endowment, the structure through which every one of us is always 'already there' in a historical and meaningful world, is not a transcendental ego or Dasein or the for-itself of consciousness but, precisely, a living human body in the world, a body which, in each case, '*I have*'.[28] According to Merleau-Ponty, then, the most fundamental form of intentionality is not to be grasped as a basic mode of the mind or Dasein's basic state or an essential property of consciousness but the basic dimension of the living human body's '*ek-static*' standing in the world.[29]

So the reconciliation of Husserl and Heidegger that becomes in Sartre's work a distinctive philosophy of mind becomes in Merleau-Ponty's work a distinctive philosophy of body. In order to prepare for an examination of some of the basic motifs of this new deviation in the inheritance of phenomenology, I want first to outline Merleau-Ponty's conception of the approaches to 'my existence' which, in his view, stand in the way of his new departure; stand in the way, that is, of achieving a phenomenologically apt description of one's existence as an essentially 'incarnate' subject.[30] These are conceptions drawn, on the one hand, on a scientific realist model and, on the other hand, on an intellectual idealist model. Through the double-handed critique of these rival conceptions we will find Merleau-Ponty developing a new and I think extremely compelling reconstrual of the idea of a phenomenological reduction.

Part II: A new phenomenological reduction

The forswearing of science

Following the long opening remark at the start of the preface, Merleau-Ponty takes up the challenge to offer a systematic expression of phenomenology as he finds it with a methodological slogan: 'It is a matter of describing, not of explaining or analysing.'[31] When I touched on the descriptive orientation of phenomenological investigations in Chapter 1 I also noted that 'the what' that is to be described by them itself undergoes profound shifts of understanding within the writings explored in this book. We can see such a shift occurring again in Merleau-Ponty's distinctive take on what phenomenology is to return to in its 'return to "things themselves"'.[32] For what Merleau-Ponty seeks from the Husserlian rallying call is a return, first of all, to perception as it is immediately enjoyed. And his basic argument for this returning shift aims at distinguishing *orders of priority on the same level* and not, as in Husserl, *different levels of inquiry*. So whereas Husserl, for example, regards phenomenology as requiring 'a forswearing' of all factual and in the world sciences because its proper 'things themselves' are intuited ideal essences to be reached by the reductions, Merleau-Ponty demands a shift away from scientific investigations because the meaning of their theorems and equations is dependent on a prior acquaintance with the kind of 'things themselves' that are given in one's own pre-theoretical, immediate perception of the world – 'things themselves' like forests, prairies and rivers:

> All my knowledge of the world, even my scientific knowledge, is gained from my own particular point of view, or from some experience of the world without which the symbols of science would be meaningless. The whole universe of science is built upon the world as directly experienced . . . . To return to things themselves is to return to that world which precedes knowledge, of which knowledge always *speaks*, and in relation to which every scientific schematization is an abstract and derivative sign-language, as is geography in relation to the countryside in which we have learnt beforehand what a forest, a prairie or a river is.[33]

There is obviously something rather Heideggerian about this return to the world as it is encountered prior to its being theoretically known.[34] However, and having said that, the phenomenological call back to 'things themselves' is not, for Heidegger either, a plea for philosophy to return to 'the world as directly experienced'. Indeed, although Heidegger interprets it differently from Husserl, coming to terms with 'the "phenomena" of phenomenology' involves, for Heidegger too, a fundamental shift of level away from all 'ontic' affairs and 'the "phenomenon" as ordinarily understood': it concerns an effort to 'see' 'that which shows itself in the appearance as prior to the "phenomenon" as ordinarily understood', i.e. an effort to describe the '*a priori*' structure of existence that is an understanding of Being.[35] For Heidegger, then, as we have seen, the basic task for phenomenology is to bring to concepts what is understood in this understanding of Being, the understanding which (as Heidegger cites Aquinas putting it) 'is already included in conceiving anything which one apprehends as an entity'.[36]

Merleau-Ponty's return to the immediately perceived world is, therefore, neither particularly Husserlian nor particularly Heideggerian. Nevertheless, in demanding a shift away from the point of view of science by calling for a *shift back* to its 'primordial'[37] conditions of intelligibility, he clearly strikes a related gesture. This is most obviously the case when he affirms that factual scientific research is utterly incapable, on its own, of coming to terms with the very entity which pursues such research: *the who* that (for example) *I am*. 'I cannot', he insists, 'conceive myself as nothing but a bit of world, a mere object of biological, psychological or sociological investigation.'[38] According to Merleau-Ponty, to understand what takes place when 'I exist' calls for an inquiry which is not scientific in the sense that it would grasp the who that I am as 'the outcome or the meeting-point of numerous causal agencies which determine my bodily or psychological make-up'.[39] As illustrated by the passage on the return to things themselves just cited, we can identify Merleau-Ponty's fundamental justification for this anti-naturalistic claim in terms of what we might call a priority argument: the terms of the sciences, including the so-called sciences of man, presuppose, as a condition of their intelligibility, a more 'basic experience' of that which they (the sciences) are 'the second order expression'.[40] Hence the appropriate mode for a fully satisfactory account of 'my existence' must be founded on a descriptive 'return' to 'my actual presence to myself':[41] a return to a cogito which precedes any scientific knowledge of myself 'and in relation to which every scientific schematisation is an abstract and derivative sign-language'.[42] In the next section I want to take a closer look at Merleau-Ponty's priority argument by considering some recent objections posed to it by Thomas Baldwin.

The priority argument

In his discussion of the priority argument Baldwin raises the general worry that 'Merleau-Ponty seems to be committing himself to a problematic foundationalist epistemology and philosophy of language; to the "myth of the given", indeed.'[43] The worry here arises from the thought that by regarding scientific explanations in general as founded on a prior 'immediate perception' of the world, Merleau-Ponty is committing himself to the problematic idea of 'an observation language uncontaminated by theory'.[44] Indeed, as that worry unfolds one might even come to see Merleau-Ponty as thinking that the 'direct and primitive contact with the world' that the sciences (supposedly) presuppose – the contact which it is the task of writings in the name of phenomenology to endow 'with a philosophical status' – is, in itself, not endowed with any meaning at all: it is a sensuous 'given' free of all conceptual content. And, as Baldwin makes clear, we are now confident that this traditional empiricist conception of 'the given' is a 'myth'.[45]

Although he does not register the connection, Baldwin clearly knows that the worry he is raising is totally removed in the very first chapter of the introduction to *Phenomenology of Perception*. For in that chapter Merleau-Ponty engages in a sustained *critique* of the traditional empiricist idea of intrinsically meaningless 'sensations' as the basic unit of experience. Indeed, against this 'traditional prejudice' – precisely the 'myth' of the given[46] – Merleau-Ponty defends the central claim of Gestalt psychology that even the most rudimentary of sense-experiences already has some articulate or articulable structure and involves a perception *of* something or other, a perception that thus already has *some* conceptual content or other. And so, as Baldwin himself elsewhere notes, for Merleau-Ponty's 'experience is not a mosaic of simple ideas which we somehow organise or interpret as representations of the world; it is, on the contrary the appearance of things in a world'.[47] Hence, as Merleau-Ponty puts it, when we try 'to seize "sensation" ... we find not a psychic individual ... but a formation already bound up with a larger whole, *already endowed with a meaning*'.[48]

So Baldwin's worry can be readily prevented from fully unfolding. However, its initial stage may still seem problematic enough. Can one defend, as Baldwin puts it, 'a foundationalist theory of meaning which ties the meaning of our words ... back to some "pre-scientific experience" in such a way that the "valid meaning" of sentences [which make use of scientific-theoretical terms] includes a reference to the pre-scientific life-world'? Baldwin thinks such an approach 'can no longer command serious assent'.[49]

Without developing the objection towards difficulties concerning a problematic empiricist commitment to the idea of the given, Baldwin offers the following complaint against Merleau-Ponty's priority argument, a complaint informed by certain arguments from the work of Saul Kripke: 'Even though we may rely on ordinary pre-scientific experience to help fix the reference of [scientific-theoretical terms], this method of reference fixing is just a ladder we climb before we dispose of it.'[50] The idea is that, after an initial 'baptism' of an object or type of object in referential contexts which will not be wholly experience independent, we are then able to refer to that very (type of) object in contexts that may well be wholly independent of experience. So within theoretical work in the sciences – in 'every equation in physics', to take Merleau-Ponty's example – the ladder that links its terms to human experience drops away and we are left with an understanding that is precisely an understanding of *how things are anyway*, 'wholly independent of human beings' and their experiences.[51]

Is this analysis of scientific-theoretical terms telling against Merleau-Ponty's priority argument? Since it explicitly retains the idea of a founding recourse to pre-scientific experience to fix the reference of such terms, I do not see that it can be. In fact, the Kripkean way of throwing away the ladder nicely illustrates how Merleau-Ponty's argument replays the classical phenomenological response to what, in Chapter 2, I called the 'priority oddness' objection. To recall, Brentano claims that the genetic studies which would show the dependence of our mental lives on occurrences in the brain must be founded on a prior descriptive inquiry. The problematic oddness of this priority is that the phenomena identified in the founding inquiry are held to *depend* on states and processes studied by the founded discipline. It seems to me that the basic answer given by Brentano to remove this priority oddness is precisely what Merleau-Ponty has in mind with his priority argument: the answer was that a genetic inquiry has and can have no genuinely adequate idea *what* it is investigating without the prior descriptive one.

The idea, then, is that Merleau-Ponty's presentation of the secondary status of the sciences is a generalisation of the earlier phenomenological response to the priority oddness objection. For example, the claim would be that appreciation that certain equations relate to, say, *the course of a river* (and not some other thing) is not something that can be achieved independently of the kind of acquaintance with rivers obtained in our pre-scientific lives. That it is a *river* that the sentences and equations of the theoretical study are about (and not some other thing) is not something that can be fully grasped by attending to the theoretical study alone.[52] And this is true *even if, once the identification has been made, one no longer has to make any appeal to the founding level in one's use of the theoretical apparatus* (Kripke's point) and *even if that apparatus is now brought to bear to explain features that are manifest at the founding level* (Brentano's point): the founding level still belongs to a fully explicit account of the formation of the meaning of the terms of the explanatory theoretical apparatus.

I will come back to the priority oddness issue again shortly, but it is worth mentioning that, while Baldwin's Kripkean objection to Merleau-Ponty does not unfold towards the worry about a commitment to the myth of the given, we might still want to restate the worry in terms which are further on the way to doing so. That is, we might still want to challenge Merleau-Ponty's priority argument on the grounds that there simply is no such thing as pre-scientific experience that is 'uncontaminated by theory'.[53] Baldwin presents this further challenge in a pointed comparison between Merleau-Ponty's conception of pre-scientific experience and Wittgenstein's *On Certainty* conception of the propositions which 'stand fast' for us 'prior to any reflective method we have for justifying our beliefs'.[54] As Baldwin notes, the view of the world articulated by such propositions is not 'unchallengeable in detail' but is, to use Wittgenstein's simile, like a river bed that only slowly shifts and changes over time. Crucially, however, it is not a structure whose formation is 'uninfected by our scientific beliefs' either.[55] The conception of the earth as a ball and the belief that water boils at 100°C, for example, are fairly recent developments in the formation of our world picture, but they certainly belong today to the unquestioned framework, the riverbed of contemporary world-inquiries, and they can hardly be said to be 'pre-scientific'.

In considering this objection Baldwin concedes that Wittgenstein's non-empiricist conception of the 'primitive trust' that underlies our system of beliefs is, in fact, 'similar in spirit' to the 'primordial faith' that Merleau-Ponty identifies at the basis of theoretical inquiry.[56] I'm sure that is right,[57] but I think that Wittgenstein's historical and cultural conception of the structure and formation of our world picture can also be readily absorbed by Merleau-Ponty without difficulty. For Merleau-Ponty's claim is not at all that our *non*-theoretical lives and perceptions are radically free of cultural acquisitions. On the contrary, as we shall see, for Merleau-Ponty our distinctive form of 'incarnate' existence is as it is only by virtue of the fact that 'it finds its sustenance' not only in the fruits of nature but also, and for most of us primarily, in the fruits of 'the cultural world'.[58] No, what Merleau-Ponty is insisting on in the priority argument is not an *impoverished* conception of experience, a conception that would be radically 'uncontaminated' by the achievements of culture and science, but, on the contrary, one which is pre-theoretical in the sense that *my* perception of the world is not, *by me*, arrived at through systematic scientific research; indeed it is not arrived at by intellectual acts in general *at all* (it is not arrived at by thinking or judging): 'Perception is not a science of the world, it is not even an act, a deliberate taking up of a position; it is the background from which all acts stand out and is presupposed by them.'[59]

The true cogito

Taking these points on board and returning again to Merleau-Ponty's deployment of the priority argument, let us now consider the case where there is scientific research not into a *river* but into (any) *me*. The crucial question for Merleau-Ponty is this: can we obtain any genuinely adequate idea of 'the what' that the various kinds of scientific research one might conduct in this case are investigating without recourse to (in Merleau-Ponty's sense of this idea) a prior non-scientific, non-theoretical acquaintance with it? According to Merleau-Ponty, the claims of the priority argument in this case are doubly telling. In the case of a river, there is nothing in principle wrong with conceiving 'what is investigated' as in itself 'a bit of the world', the only naïvety would be to think that the terms of the scientific investigation were totally self-standing. When what is at issue is the 'who' that I am, however, Merleau-Ponty regards the scientistic interpretation (the interpretation which thinks it can do without recourse to the non-theoretical point of view of immediate perception) as not only 'naïve' but also 'at the same time dishonest';[60] naïve because it tacitly presupposes the non-theoretical point of view 'without which the symbols of science would be meaningless', but also dishonest because in this case (unlike the river case) what we are studying is itself the zero-point or 'source' of the non-theoretical point of view that science itself depends on. Scientific points of view of every 'me' must thus feign to do without what they must, in fact and in principle, take for granted: 'the other point of view, namely that of consciousness, through which from the outset a world forms itself round me and begins to exist for me'.[61]

The basic claim, then, is that it is a fundamental distortion to suppose that we can come to terms with the 'who' that I am if we apprehend 'my existence' as just a part of the world's, as if I were merely a thing in the world, a thing among things. Indeed, what Merleau-Ponty's argument brings into view is the experientially undeniable fact that *when I am there* (when what occurs is 'my existence') *the perceived world is also there for me*. I am or I exist in the world *as* an openness to the world. Moreover, this 'facticity' of my existence, its irreducible in-the-world dimension, belongs to and is given in the immediate perception of *myself* which (implicitly or explicitly) provides the *sine qua non* of every scientific investigation into 'the what' that I am. As Merleau-Ponty puts it, 'the *cogito* must reveal me in a situation'.[62]

So, and this is now just a reiteration of the basic phenomenological response to the priority oddness objection, even if the phenomena identified in the founding experience are held to *depend* on states and processes studied by the founded scientific disciplines, the latter 'genetic' studies have and can have no genuinely adequate idea what (or, in this case, who) they are investigating without at least a tacit grasp of what is pre-theoretically given.

The suggestion that any understanding of 'my existence' presupposes a pre-theoretical disclosure of myself to myself in the world of immediate perception can readily seem to involve a problematic recoil from *scientific realism* to *idealism*: a recoil to a conception of the 'who' that I am as 'the subject' that will be 'a condition of possibility [of the world] ... and without which there would be no world'.[63] We reach here the second moment of Merleau-Ponty's first methodological slogan. The demand for pure description not only excludes scientific explanations but 'excludes equally' he states, 'the procedure of analytic reflection' of the sort one finds in idealistic philosophies of the cogito since Kant.[64]

As we shall see, Merleau-Ponty's major argument against idealism aims to show that the return to the pre-theoretical given that he (Merleau-Ponty) is urging is totally misunderstood if it is taken as a retreat to a layer or level of experience that, in itself, falls short of genuine 'contact with the world'. This is precisely what he thinks idealist treatments of 'my existence' do, and for this reason he regards the core fault of idealism as the exact mirror-image of scientific treatments that interpret 'my existence' as merely 'a moment of the world's': the core fault of idealism is that it '*detached* the subject' from the world.[65]

The complaint here is not that post-Kantian philosophies (or even post-Cartesian philosophies) leave the subject utterly bereft and worldless, but that a world is won for the subject only after a detaching retreat from the standpoint of immediate experience. In immediate experience the world is, unquestionably, simply there for us, and we are ourselves bodily there for ourselves too. For the idealist, by contrast, the world – and myself as having a bodily presence in the world – is supposedly only constituted as such by the activity of a non-worldly 'thinking subject', by 'the inner man'. As I noted in Chapter 2, in a quiet repudiation of what he knows to be the profoundly idealist orientation of Husserl's transcendental phenomenology, Merleau-Ponty affirms that 'truth does not "inhabit" only "the inner man"' because 'there is no inner man, man is in the world, and *only in the world does he know himself*'.[66] *Pace* idealism, then, Merleau-Ponty affirms that our most fundamental, pre-theoretical 'self experience' is not 'the *cogito*' understood as 'the thought I have of myself' or 'my bare awareness of existing'.[67] On the contrary, 'the true *cogito* ... does away with any kind of idealism in revealing me as "Being-in-the-world"'.[68]

Of course, this is not intended to offer a shred of consolation to the scientific realist who wants to regard me as 'part of the world' since the scientific conception does not so much *attach* the subject to the world (in the way the facticity internal to Merleau-Ponty's 'true *cogito*' would want to) as *abolish* the subject altogether: by virtue of the loss from view in naturalistic sciences of *the emergence of meaning*, of what Merleau-Ponty calls the 'inherence of subjectivity in history',[69] scientific (causal) explanations provide accounts which present only 'a semblance of subjectivity'.[70] On the other hand, however, Merleau-Ponty regards the same point as telling against idealism too. As I have indicated, it is a central feature of Merleau-Ponty's understanding of man and the world that he regards us as, in each case, 'always already' situated within an ongoing historical-cultural drama-without-end.[71] On such a view, it is not only absurd to suppose that the 'who' that I am is the constituting maker of the world *in its Being* but equally absurd to suppose I am the constituting maker of the world *in its meaning*.[72] I do not have the power to make the meaning of things *ex nihilo*, and I cannot radically escape or suspend their historical meanings either. Indeed, in clear contrast to Sartre, who insisted that we are 'condemned' to freedom,[73] Merleau-Ponty insists that prior to any exercise of our freedom, and as its condition, 'we are *condemned to meaning*'.[74] There is a kind of irreducible *thrownness* into a meaningful historical world of things and others here that cannot be grasped in either the impersonal terms of scientific explanation or the idealistic terms of analytic reflection: 'my existence' is stationed in a historical-cultural world that 'I live through' 'in direct and primitive contact' with things and others.[75] In the next section I will show how this conception of 'my existence' develops into a full-blown critique of both scientific realism and intellectualist idealism.

The critique of objective thought

In the last section I stressed that the conceptions of 'my existence' that one finds in the scientific realist's explanations and the idealist's analytic reconstructions are mirror-images of each other. The point was that while the former regards my existence as a moment of the world's and hence as 'the outcome or the meeting point of numerous causal agencies which determine my bodily or psychological make up', the latter, in an understandable recoil from the bald naturalism of the scientific point of view, detaches the subject from the world and regards it as profoundly involved in the very constitution of objectivity. Crucially, however, this mirroring relationship turns around a common axis: both positions share precisely the same conception of the world. Whether we are dealing with realism or idealism the world is understood as 'the totality of spatio-temporal events',[76] a 'precise and entirely determinate'[77] realm of law 'defined by the absolute mutual exteriority of its parts'.[78] In the realist framework of classical empiricism the goings-on in this objective world will be regarded as the *cause* of our perceptions;[79] in the intellectualist framework of classical idealism, by contrast, this objective world is understood as the *constituted* product of the activity of consciousness. Nevertheless, what is regarded as ready-made in one and constituted in the other is precisely the same:

Empiricism retained an absolute belief in the world as the totality of spatio-temporal events, and treated consciousness as a province of this world. Analytical reflection, it is true, breaks with the world in itself, since it constitutes it through the working of consciousness, but this constituting consciousness is built up in such a way as to make possible the idea of an absolutely determinate being.[80]

In shifting from realism to idealism we shift 'from absolute objectivity to absolute subjectivity',[81] but for Merleau-Ponty the shifting ontological status is of less importance than the shared understanding of the world that underlies them, and his new 'return to "things themselves"', the return to the immediately given, is intended to effect a reorientation that will make it possible for us to 'reject them both as false'.[82]

The 'complete reform of understanding'[83] that Merleau-Ponty undertakes here seeks to show that the idea of 'the objective world' that belongs to both realism and idealism is a 'prejudice' invited by the very structure of perception itself. In the 'natural attitude' our interest is (quite properly) held by the objects presented in perception: we are 'caught up in the world' and do not notice that the things we perceive are 'perceived things', things made accessible to us 'through perception'. Of course, since Merleau-Ponty conceives perception as an immediate openness to the world, he does not regard the fact of perception itself, the immediately enjoyed undergoing of perceptual consciousness, as itself a possible object of perception: it is not an inner state of consciousness that a subject might introspect. Nevertheless, it is something we can, he supposes, awaken ourselves to through what he calls 'a true phenomenological reduction':[84] a shift from the 'natural or dogmatic attitude'[85] in which one is unquestioningly involved with other people and things, to a reflective interest in 'the layer of living experience through which other people and things are first given to us':[86] 'one turns away from the object to its mode of presentation'.[87]

As I say, this shift does not involve a retreat to senseless impressions as quasi-perceptual objects occupying an 'inner world':[88] Merleau-Ponty is definitely not just repeating once more the traditional conception of subjectivity as an interiority outside of which would be the objective external world. On the contrary, what one is reflecting upon remains, precisely, a consciousness of an in the world object, indeed an object that 'always has a meaning'.[89] Merleau-Ponty calls what one is reflecting upon here 'the phenomenal field'.[90]

The 'inventory of the perceived world' given in this layer of 'living experience' will certainly offend a scientific realist since it is a world in which the 'intrinsic characteristics' of 'a landscape, an object or a body' can be directly perceived as, for example, '"gay" or "sad", "lively" or "dreary", "elegant" or "coarse"'. For the scientific realist, such contents are rejected as just so much 'projection' and 'association' or 'transference': the intrinsic characteristics of the world are essentially free of such 'human' meaning.[91] And the 'tacit thesis' would be that any indeterminacy and ambiguity in the content of perception could always be removed if we achieved 'a more complete knowledge'.[92] Significantly, however, the phenomenal field is equally unacceptable to an idealist philosophy. It is at this point that Merleau-Ponty develops his main argument against idealism, and I will briefly run through it.

As we have seen, the idealist is committed to the idea that the experienced world is constituted as such by the activity of the thinking subject. The most radical step involved in such an idea is its implicit effort to reveal the immediately perceived facticity of 'my existence' *too* as constituted by an 'autonomous transcendental subjectivity'.[93] Through his new 'phenomenological reduction' to the phenomenal field and the attendant attempt to 'make explicit or bring to light the pre-scientific life of consciousness' that is revealed there,[94] Merleau-Ponty claims to find an *essential limit* to the Husserlian project of complete thematic 'explicitation'. Indeed, as he puts it in the preface, on his construal of it 'the most important lesson which the reduction teaches us is the impossibility of a complete reduction'.[95]

The basic thought here is that if we cleave to the phenomenal field we are compelled to acknowledge perceptual contents that the natural attitude invites us reflectively to forget: for example, the demand for pure description would enjoin us to acknowledge that what is perceived is sometimes indeterminately given as merely '*something or other*';[96] and that what serves as a point of orientation may be presented simply as '*a vaguely located spot*';[97] and in general that the perceived world as it is given 'admits of the ambiguous, the shifting, and is shaped by context'.[98] Merleau-Ponty's main argument against the idealist is that what is in view here is not a 'logical space' which we can hope to render completely explicit or completely clear in terms of the (constituted) contents of ideally '*objective thoughts*'. On the contrary, reflective clarity requires accepting that, for the most part, we exist among the pluri-dimensional and ambiguous displays and many-layered manifestations of '*objective spirit*'.[99] Our life is led, that is to say, not in the fully determinate 'objective world' beloved by philosophy but '"the cultural world" or "human world"':[100] the world of 'cities, roads, houses and above all the presence of other people'; a world which *includes* 'the anger or the pain which I read in a face, the religion whose essence I seize in some hesitation or reticence, the city whose temper I recognise in the attitude of a policeman or the style of a public building'.[101] This world is, without question, 'the *homeland* of our thoughts',[102] and yet it is not the reduced realm of Husserlian *noemata*[103] or a realm of Fregean senses, emphatically not the 'world of the exact'.[104] On the contrary, it is the multi-textured 'fabric' that comprises the fundamentally 'ambiguous domain'[105] of the '"lived through" world'.[106]

Thus, in the 'phenomenological reduction' as it is newly elaborated by Merleau-Ponty what is *bracketed* is not at all the facticity of my Being-in-the-world, but *only* 'the idea of "the world"' embraced by traditional philosophical theory.[107] Hence what we are left with after the reduction is not so much a reformed experience as a reformed understanding: an understanding freed from the prejudice that the world is objective in the sense of being populated by causally interacting, externally related things which are unambiguously identifiable, determinate and exact. In Merleau-Ponty's hands, then, the project of a phenomenological reduction is displaced: it no longer aims to reveal a universal constituting consciousness underlying the formation of experience, but, still certainly in the spirit of Husserl, to enable a new beginning for philosophy: to engage in *unprejudiced reflection* on a mode of worldly existence which is prior to all reflection and makes it possible.

In the preface to *Phenomenology of Perception* Merleau-Ponty calls the most fundamental, pre-theoretical 'self experience' of such an in-the-world existence 'the true *cogito*'. As I will explain in the next section, the point of departure for phenomenological analysis takes a radically new turn at this point. On the back of the re-elaboration of the phenomenological reduction, the analysis of 'self experience' begins not with self-consciousness, nor even with Dasein as Heidegger understands that, but with the factical existence of the living human body.

Part III: The body prior to science

Towards the incarnate subject

For Merleau-Ponty there is no question of subjecting the facticity of 'my existence' to a Husserlian reduction, no question then of 'detaching the subject' or effecting a radical shift of level to a purely transcendental ego. On the other hand, and as we have seen, the affirmation of the facticity of one's individual existence offers no support whatever to the idea that subjectivity can be understood wholly naturalistically either. Indeed, the total inadequacy of any conception of 'my existence' which attempts to grasp it exclusively in terms of the presence of a complex physico-chemical system in the world is precisely what motivates the idealist recoil in the first place. However, what this recoil totally passes over is that the same profoundly unsatisfactory objective conception of the facticity of one's existence is in view in both scientific realism and idealism: in both cases that facticity can be conceived only in terms of one's bodily presence in the world – and in neither case could that bodily presence 'escape the determinations which alone made the object into an object'.[108]

It is hard to imagine a more significant example of the conflict between philosophical theorising and what is given in the phenomenal field than that of the living human body, whether one's own or that of an other. What is at issue here poses a special problem for objective thought since it precisely concerns 'not the practical difficulties of a complex object' but the special problem of *understanding* a fundamentally 'meaningful being'.[109] And, as we have already seen, Merleau-Ponty regards 'the objectification of the living body'[110] as

134

massively foreclosing the possibility of achieving a satisfactory conception of ourselves as an irreducibly worldly existence: the resources needed for coming to terms with the facticity of one's existence are totally lacking, totally invisible to philosophical theorising which regards the living body as a psychophysiological mechanism or a biological organism in the world. And yet, in each case, every thought and judgement that belongs to such theorising emerges precisely from an 'incarnate subject'[111] given immediately to itself in a 'true *cogito*' that gives the lie to every objectifying word of the theory.

There is a conflict here which, at some level, no theorist can fail to appreciate. Indeed, it is significant in this respect that no psychology has ever actually been able to proceed by treating the body as an object pure and simple. As Merleau-Ponty notes, 'in its descriptions of the body from the point of view of the self, classical psychology was already wont to attribute to it "characteristics" incompatible with the status of an object'.[112] Nevertheless, as long as it is understood as 'one more among external objects'[113] it was never going to be possible for psychology to develop a satisfactory account of the living body. Indeed, it was condemned to thinking of the facticity of existence either (with the realist) in terms of a bit of the world that has 'the peculiarity of always being there'[114] or (with the idealist) as that bit of the world which is directly subject to my will.[115] Neither comes close to providing an understanding of one's body not as one among other objects perceived in the world but precisely 'that which perceives'.[116] For Merleau-Ponty, then, the first imperative for a renewed phenomenology is to rethink the sense of our worldly existence: to see that our bodily presence is not 'an object of the world' but, on the contrary, 'our means of communication with it'.[117]

A being which is 'through and through compounded of relationships with the world'[118] is not present in the world 'as a collection of physico-chemical processes'.[119] Indeed, the distinctive *unity* of this being is not the physico-chemical unity of a complex object or even the biological unity of a living organism: it is a unity that expresses a 'nexus of living meanings'[120] and not a nexus of causal relations. In an effort to come reflectively to terms with such an original and distinctive mode of being, Merleau-Ponty proposes that the human body 'is to be compared, not to a physical object, but rather to a work of art':[121] it is not a unity *in* space and *in* time, but a mode of *inhabitation* of space and time[122] informed by what Merleau-Ponty calls 'a certain style'.[123]

To regard the living body as akin to a work of art is not to see it as an external representation (work) of an internal consciousness (artist), not the in the world site of a hidden (but nevertheless factually objective) 'psychic reality'. Rather, it is to see the body as '*the visible expression of a concrete Ego*',[124] or again as 'the outward expression of a certain manner of Being-in-the-world'.[125] It is, that is, the place where what takes place is an ongoing – though finite – expressive performance of a distinctive manner or style;[126] something that others appreciate when they 'find a fittingness and meaningful relationship between the gesture, the smile and the tone of the speaker'.[127] In the next section I will explore this idea further by looking at Merleau-Ponty's discussion of our most distinctive expressive capacity: the capacity for language.

Language and gesture

The vast bulk of the fairly vast bulk that is *Phenomenology of Perception* is devoted to an elucidation of the body as it is disclosed to us prior to its thematisation in science. However, as is obvious from even the most cursory glance at its pages, perhaps the most unusual feature of this elucidation, unusual at least for most philosophers, is that it is developed through the close examination of case studies in empirical psychology. For readers used to philosophy that is at best 'science lite', Merleau-Ponty's keenness to acknowledge that one should not pursue philosophy of psychology 'without psychology' is profoundly refreshing.[128] It would be a mistake, however, to regard this as a surreptitious reintroduction of the naturalism he has been at such pains to resist. Indeed, it is ultimately the implicit philosophy within such empirical psychology that he engages with – and often takes issue with – and his efforts to achieve a clarification of the facticity of 'my existence' is not itself pursued as an empirical investigation. Thus, even if he disapproves of the idea of pursuing a philosophy of the body without psychology, he is equally clear that such an inquiry cannot be conducted 'with psychology alone'.[129]

An exemplary case of this complex mode of inquiry is found in his attempt to shed light on the fundamental relation '*having a body*' through an analysis of bodily expression and the crucially connected and widely empirically studied phenomenon of '*having a language*'.[130]

As a preliminary to his inquiry, Merleau-Ponty identifies a grammatical difference between two uses of the relation 'having' that we need to keep in view. In ordinary language we speak indifferently of someone, for example, 'having an idea' or 'having a dog' or 'having a desire' or 'having a hat' or 'having a pain' or 'having a house' or 'having a bad temper'. But, despite the uniformity of this way of talking, the use of these expressions is clearly not equally uniform. As Merleau-Ponty notes, on the one hand there are cases in which the term simply designates a proprietary relationship of a given subject to an independently given object. At issue here is an external relation between two distinct items in the world. On the other hand, however, there are cases where the subject and object are not merely externally related but, as Merleau-Ponty puts it, the subject 'projects itself' into the possessed term: the sense of possession or 'belonging to me' involved here expresses an *existential involvement* of myself with or in something.[131] Borrowing (and reversing) a distinction introduced by his contemporary Gabriel Marcel, Merleau-Ponty attempts to 'take account' of an aspect of the 'usage' of the term 'being' to help mark out these two uses.[132] The recommendation is that in the former kind of case we should replace the relation 'having' with what he calls 'the weak sense' of being as existence or predication. So instead of using the expression 'I have a hat' we will use instead 'The hat is mine'. Now, nothing prevents us from using this way of speaking in the latter kind of case too (it is not pure nonsense), however, in those cases that replacement effectively 'conceals' the internal or 'existential' relation involved by presenting it on the model of external or 'ontic' relations obtaining between existents in the world.[133] So wherever one does *not* want to say that the case concerns two specifiable items that independently 'are', then one should retain 'having'.[134] Hence, taking the examples above, one will (I should say) produce the following lists:

1   'I have an idea', 'I have a pain', 'I have a desire', 'I have a bad temper'.
2   'The hat is mine', 'The house is mine', 'The dog is mine'.[135]

If the first list is formulated in the grammar of the second we produce a set of reifying objectifications which, although not mere nonsense, are clearly more likely to produce misunderstandings:[136]

1* 'The idea is mine', 'The pain is mine', 'The desire is mine', 'The bad temper is mine'.

It is with this distinction in view that Merleau-Ponty attempts to clarify a crucial aspect of the relation 'having a body' by pursuing an analysis of bodily expression, the phenomenon of 'having a language' and, in a related sense, of a word's 'having a meaning'.

Turning, then, to studies in empirical psychology, Merleau-Ponty notes that the standard interpretation of the idea of the possession of language was drawn, in the first instance, in exclusively naturalistic and objective terms: in terms of the real presence in the body of a stock of 'verbal images' (it is of no special significance whether these were understood as physical or psychic traces); images which would be mechanically produced as speech through neurological mechanisms or psychological associations by virtue of which 'a flow of words' occurs.[137] Such a mechanistic view might seem to be able to make sense of the fact that speaking is going on, but it is far less clear that it can make room for the idea of what one might call a 'speaking subject'. For on this understanding of speech the emission of sounds is not an intentional action by some 'who' who has something to say, and whose various sayings are thus pointedly telling with regard to who they are. As before, then, an empiricist psychology committed to scientific realism does not put the subject back into the world, but simply abolishes it: 'there is no speaker ... , speech occurs in a circuit of third person phenomena ... : man can speak as the electric lamp can become incandescent'.[138]

Fully naturalistic explanations of speech do not only run into conceptual worries, however, and in any case, one could imagine a theoretical scientist urging us to resist 'the myth of the speaker'. Things become more difficult for such a view, though, when the theory has to face empirical research into cases where patients do not simply lose the power of articulate speech (*anarthria*) – a phenomenon which could obviously be explained in terms of a loss of 'verbal images' from the previously possessed 'stock' – but lose it only in certain contexts (*aphasia*). Under pressure from such research, psychological theory has tended to flip over from fully naturalistic, empiricist explanations to intellectualist ones. The fact that a patient cannot identify certain colour samples in certain contexts, for example, is interpreted as a genuinely intellectual and not merely functional or mechanistic disorder. Take the case of a person who is able to identify coloured objects with reference to given colour samples but is unable, or no longer able, to classify the colour samples when taken on their own. Here, so the intellectualist suggestion goes, the problem is 'not that he has lost the verbal image of the words 'red' or 'blue', but that he has lost the general ability to subsume a sensory given under a category'.[139]

This alternative theory appears to be the antithesis of the fully naturalistic account 'since language now appears as conditioned by thought', and hence there is at least a return to a subject here.[140] The truth is, however, that this subject does not utter intrinsically meaningful words but rather has intrinsically meaningful thoughts. So we have a subject all right, but it is fundamentally 'a thinking subject not a speaking one'. The absurd situation, then, is that neither empiricism nor intellectualism can make sense of the idea of the living human body as itself a speaking subject. In what can now be seen as a classic gesture on Merleau-Ponty's part, and drawing on the distinction between 'having' and 'being' outlined earlier, he identifies the fundamental 'kinship' in the two standard positions in a way that will enable him to dismount from the seesaw and move towards a genuinely satisfactory conception: 'These two conceptions are at one', he notes, 'in holding that the word *has* no significance.'[141] His reasoning in the first case (that of mechanistic psychology) run as follows:

> In the first case this is obvious since the word is not summoned up through the medium of any concept, and since the given stimuli or 'states of mind' call it up in accordance with the laws of neurological mechanics or those of association, and thus that the word is not the bearer of its own meaning, has no inner power, and is merely a psychic, physiological or even physical phenomenon set alongside others, and thrown up by the working of an objective causality.[142]

The second case, the intellectualist psychology of categorial operations of thought, fares no better:

> The word is still bereft of any effectiveness of its own, this time because it is only the external sign of an internal recognition which could take place without it, and to which it makes no contribution. It

is not without meaning, since behind it there is a categorial operation, but this meaning is something which it does not *have*, does not possess, since it is thought which has a meaning, the word remaining an empty container. It is merely a phenomenon of articulation, of sound, or the consciousness of such a phenomenon, but in any case language is but an external accompaniment of thought.[143]

He then lays out the absurdity of the two approaches' failure to come to terms with the idea of a speaking subject, and points out again that intellectualism shares the same baleful objective conception of the body and its behaviour as does its empiricist rival. Merleau-Ponty concludes by reminding us of something we all already know, and in doing so powerfully refutes both cases at once:

> In the first case, we are on this side of the word as meaningful; in the second we are beyond it. In the first there is nobody to speak; in the second, there is certainly a subject, but a thinking one, not a speaking one. As far as speech is concerned, intellectualism is hardly any different from empiricism, and is no better able than the latter to dispense with an explanation in terms of involuntary action. Once the categorial operation is performed, the appearance of the word which completes the process still has to be explained, and this will still be done by recourse to a physiological or psychic mechanism, since the word is a passive shell. Thus we refute both intellectualism and empiricism by simply saying that *the word has a meaning.*[144]

Thus at the heart of Merleau-Ponty's attempt to develop a satisfactory conception of the speaking subject is an effort to avoid construals of speech which conceive it either as an external accompaniment of genuinely meaningful phenomena or as a natural event which is in itself insignificant. Against such views, Merleau-Ponty affirms that my possession of language is not a matter of the presence in my body of a store of verbal images but a matter of me having under my belt the 'articulatory style' of each word as 'one of the possible uses of my body'.[145] In this way, Merleau-Ponty's analysis makes viable an analysis of speech which situates it within a general field of intrinsically significant *bodily expression*, and thus opens up the possibility for a coherent conception of the living body as a speaking subject.

Although he does not acknowledge the point, or even show any indication that he is cognisant of it (which he certainly is), it is well worth noting that Merleau-Ponty's basic line of thought here is one which fundamentally challenges the distinction that launched Husserl's earliest phenomenological analysis. For whereas Husserl regards it as acceptable to stipulate that there are cases of signs which (he acknowledged) we ordinarily call 'expressions' but which on his theoretical view only 'indicate' something and do not themselves 'express' anything – facial expressions and gestures like smiles, frowns, winking, gesticulated obscenities and waving, for example – it is central to Merleau-Ponty's conception that the use of language in speech (the paradigm case of 'expression' for Husserl), though fundamentally original in many respects, is itself, essentially, a form of *gesture*: 'The spoken word is a genuine gesture, and it contains its meaning in the same way as the gesture contains its.'[146]

On this view, the work of words we produce when we utter a novel sentence is neither a mere 'flow of words' nor just the external 'clothing' of an original thought,[147] but for anyone who 'possesses' the vocabulary and syntax of the language in question a 'new gesture' comes into being: 'a fresh cultural entity has taken on existence'.[148] And when I grasp the meaning of such gestures formed by others this is not due to the fact that the words used arouse associated representations in me or lead me to form meaningful thoughts in myself. On the contrary, what is made manifest to me is 'the presence of that thought in the phenomenal world'.[149] Hence also, the other with whom I am talking is not just there for me as some 'exterior' bodily surface which supplies the indicating 'data' for his or her hidden thoughts and feelings; on the contrary, the other is manifest precisely as he or she is: as a bodily presence that *is* 'a speaking subject'.[150] It is not a meeting of external surfaces but an authentic meeting of minds. As Merleau-Ponty puts it somewhat earlier in the book, when I 'read' their 'gestures'[151] 'the mental life of others becomes an immediate object, a whole charged with immanent meaning'.[152] Here we have available a notion of the intrinsic *visibility* of the other utterly unavailable to objective thought. Towards the end of the book, Merleau-Ponty summarises his position with great clarity:

> We must learn to distinguish the body from the objective body as set forth in works of physiology. This is not the body which is capable of being inhabited by consciousness. We must grasp again on visible bodies those forms of behaviour which are outlined there and which appear on them, but are not really contained in them.[153]

By virtue of its distinctive emphasis on the body it seems plausible to characterise Merleau-Ponty's philosophy of psychology as having a fundamentally 'naturalistic' outlook.[154] However, if we do want to apply this label we need to recognise that it is not a naturalism of even the weakly scientistic form that was presented in Chapter 1. On the contrary, the naturalism in question is rather of the kind often associated with the later Wittgenstein: what I want to call a fundamentally *privative* naturalism which implies a steady resistance to supernatural explanations but without itself speculatively anticipating or uncritically embracing the results of empirical inquiry.[155] In the next section I will identify what seems to me a problematic limit to Merleau-Ponty's adherence to this non-scientific sense of naturalism in philosophy.

A genius for ambiguity

My own view is that a privative naturalism is just what a satisfactory phenomenology should aim at. It will be the kind of descriptive inquiry capable of working with scientific studies but which also recognises that the assumption of scientific status and method does nothing to protect such studies against confusions and prejudices which careful *a priori* reflection may show up.[156] This being said, however, there is an aspect of Merleau-Ponty's own discussion of the expressive body which seems to me to involve it in a problematic step beyond the merely privative naturalism appropriate to a purely descriptive phenomenology: namely, its implicit adherence to a basic *cognitivism* concerning *the difference between human beings and animals*. Thus, for example (although this is not one example among others), despite offering an analysis of language that invites comparisons with the gestural traits of animals, Merleau-Ponty affirms the rather more traditional idea that the possession of language involves (what he calls) 'man' in a form of life that is utterly unique, fundamentally different from that of any animal. Language, he notes, is something that we 'ordinarily' take to be 'in a peculiar category'.[157] True enough. However, Merleau-Ponty appeals to this ordinary take not in order to acknowledge the significance we ordinarily attach to the concept of '*the difference* between human beings and animals' but as marking an objective feature of human life that would (as it were from sideways on) *justify* it: it marks that the life of 'man' lies radically apart from the life of a merely animal being.[158]

I do not suppose and am not suggesting at all that Merleau-Ponty follows the Cartesian tradition and regards non-human animals as mere automata. Indeed, he does not altogether disregard what we might equally well call 'the view that we ordinarily take' that expressive behaviour can be found in the lives of a great many living things and not only in 'man'. Animal life is, he suggests, 'poor in expressive means' but not utterly non-expressive.[159] Similarly, he acknowledges that 'animals lead their lives in' what he calls 'a sort of *ekstase*',[160] so that 'the mere presence of a living being transforms the physical world, bringing to view here "food", there a "hiding place", and giving to "stimuli" a sense which they have not hitherto possessed'.[161] Nevertheless, there is no suggestion whatsoever that what is called 'history' or 'culture' might belong to what he, I think, far too blithely and uncritically calls 'the simplicity of animal life'. Indeed, at this point we might bring Merleau-Ponty against himself to affirm that philosophical anthropology would benefit from an engagement with empirical studies of the lives of non-human animals, with ethology. However, we know too that such studies are swarming with philosophy and so, again, there is no question of going on here with ethology alone.

But, largely in the absence of such supporting work, and despite his usual adherence to a merely privative naturalism, it seems to me that Merleau-Ponty holds fast to a more or less traditional *humanistic* prejudice:[162] a basic and uncritical *cognitivism* about the human difference. At issue is a conception of the lives of animals, on the one hand, as 'pre-ordained' by nature and a fundamentally contrasting view of the life of 'man', on the other, as a natural life radically or fundamentally transformed. In other words, he endorses the distinction, familiar in the work of Heidegger, Gadamer and McDowell, between animal inhabitation of an environment or 'setting' (*Umwelt*) and man living in a world (*Welt*). It is, I think, typical of Merleau-Ponty's usual resistance to philosophy's traditional binary oppositions, and his sensitivity to ambiguity, that he actually states that man 'has *not only* a setting, *but also* a world'.[163] Nevertheless, 'man' can, he speculatively suggests, be defined by 'a genius for ambiguity' which confers on human life and human behaviour a status that, while never purely cultural, is nevertheless radically unlike any animal: uniquely, it is not purely natural through and through. Man is unique; the nature of man alone is touched by culture, by spirit:

> It is impossible to superimpose on man a lower layer of behaviour which one chooses to call natural, followed by a manufactured cultural or spiritual world. Everything is both manufactured and natural in man, as it were, in the sense that there is not a word, not a form of behaviour which does not owe something to purely biological being – and which at the same time does not elude the simplicity of animal life, and causes forms of vital behaviour to deviate from their pre-ordained direction, through a sort of *leakage* and through a genius for ambiguity which might serve to define man.[164]

Thus, as he puts it, human inhabitation in a culture results in the fact that, for humans alone, 'behaviour creates meanings which are transcendent in relation to the anatomical apparatus, and yet immanent to the behaviour as such'.[165] Merleau-Ponty illustrates this idea with a nice – if, in this context, very rare – example from scientific literature: Darwin's thought-provoking suggestion of a cultural adaptation of the natural behaviour of knitting the brows. Such behaviour, which serves naturally simply to protect the eyes from the sun, is transformed by 'man's genius for ambiguity' into a visible part of 'the human act of meditation'.[166]

There is a good deal to admire here. However, and despite its advances over more inflexible dualistic views, I think this conception is still highly problematic. I will try to bring this out by looking at how adherence to the idea of a rigorous and fundamental distinction (in the nature of things) between nature and culture, even one which is, in the special case of 'man', radically undifferentiated,[167] gives Merleau-Ponty's analysis a profound difficulty concerning what must in some way be, on his own terms, the *naturally impossible* event of 'the origin of man'.[168]

In certain respects my claim here poses something of a challenge to Tom Baldwin's suggestion that the absence of 'any reference to evolutionary theory' in Merleau-Ponty's account is due simply to its 'familiarity'.[169] Holding to one side what Merleau-Ponty might have wanted to affirm here, my point is that, *however* he thinks 'man' comes into being, he regards what comes about with this coming into being as a state of affairs in which we have, on the one hand, merely natural life and, on the other hand, something which is *essentially more* than merely natural. And my worry is that this (supposed) state of affairs is not something that could have come about merely naturally.

The basic difficulty here can be seen as a generalisation of the 'insistent problem' that Merleau-Ponty himself acknowledges regarding the origin of language.[170] In the case of language (again not one case among others in this context), he knows, for example, that when he looks to 'culture' to supply 'what nature does not provide' this merely pushes the problem 'one stage further back'.[171] And at this stage further back, with the question of the origin of culture he cannot not, I am suggesting, encounter the 'insistent problem' (for his analysis) of 'the origin of man'.

Merleau-Ponty is not without a response. In an effort to resolve the paradox that the linguistic expressions of the 'first' speaker can function as such only if they communicate already available meanings from 'former acts of expression',[172] Merleau-Ponty appeals to what he calls an 'emotional content' that is retained in language and which links it to 'an earlier means of communication'.[173] Such content, he suggests, makes the wonderful and distinctive sonorousness of different so-called 'natural languages' amount to 'so many ways of "singing" the world', ways in which a people express in sound the experienced 'emotional essence' of things: 'ways for the body to sing the world's praises'.[174]

It is not clear, however, that this (perhaps rather more typically German than French) proposal resolves the paradox rather than simply pushes it one stage further back again. Indeed, his totally anti-naturalistic insistence that 'there is here *nothing* resembling the famous naturalistic conceptions which equate the artificial sign with the natural one, and try to reduce language to emotional expression', only serves to heighten the problem:[175] for if world-praising emotional contents *too* are no more natural in man than they are cultural, then it will already be a 'man' who is the subject of the 'acts of expression' which the first 'singing' words presuppose.

The basic difficulty, then, is this: as long as one sticks to the idea that there is in the nature of things a fundamental difference or split between animal life and human life, anything one appeals to in order to explain how 'man' became not-merely-an-animal is *a priori* inadequate to the task and destined to offend the idea of phenomenology as a privative naturalism: *either* the explanation will involve exclusively *natural* structures, in which case it is not clear how or why it could do more than put an animal on a new 'pre-ordained' natural path (rather than be the origin of a creature without one); *or* the explanation will appeal to something that is already *not-merely-natural*, in which case it only pushes the problem one step further back by presupposing what it is meant to explain, or it would have to involve an implicit appeal to the kind of *non-*

natural or *supernatural* explanation (the Genius of God, as it were) that a consistent (even if only privative) naturalism aims to eschew. It seems, then, that as long as what he rightly calls 'the ordinary view' of the 'peculiarity' of language is interpreted in terms which presume that one being, called 'man', has achieved some kind of radical break from the rest of animal nature (resulting, for example, in a definite and unique 'surplus of our existence over natural being')[176] such theoretical embarrassment over *the necessity and impossibility* of finding an 'origin of man' will prevail.[177]

In Chapter 7 I will examine Derrida's effort to think through the human/animal difference without recourse to traditional humanist cognitivism. As we shall see, this effort profoundly interrupts the dominant inheritance of phenomenology. Before that, however, I will turn to an examination of 'beginnings' in the work of a phenomenologist who himself, in asking profoundly searching questions about the visibility of the other, powerfully exposes the limits of phenomenology as a phenomenology of perception. I will turn next to Emmanuel Levinas.

6
PHENOMENOLOGY AND THE OTHER
Emmanuel Levinas

Levinas arrives

Speaking about his friend Maurice Blanchot, Emmanuel Levinas said that 'he gave the impression of a man without opportunism'.[1] The same could surely be said of Levinas himself. For most of his career he taught and worked in the shadow of others, in particular in the shadow of his French contemporaries Jean-Paul Sartre and Maurice Merleau-Ponty. He took pleasure in the 'new tone' and 'speculative power'[2] of their work and watched with admiration as French existentialist phenomenology blossomed. Sartre had a 'dynamism' he admired and Merleau-Ponty especially 'held my interest'.[3] Jacques Derrida was typically content to regard phenomenology as an inheritance that could do without its two most famous French exponents. Levinas, by contrast, retained a genuine admiration for them, and his own work does not ignore their presence or contribution.

Levinas' gracious acknowledgement of the achievements of Sartre and Merleau-Ponty was not much reciprocated, however. As we shall see, although Levinas more or less single-handedly brought phenomenology to France in the first place, his own work remained thoroughly in the background of post-war developments in French thought, typically mentioned only in marginal recollections and reminiscences of the early days of French phenomenology. His later essays and books made little impact either, at least not initially. Nor did Levinas attempt to make waves on his own behalf, preferring to pursue his own research rather than involve himself in the seductions of French cultural life. He was, in his own words, a 'reader and spectator rather than *engagé*'.[4]

For these reasons Levinas is mercurially hard to place in the swim of twentieth-century French thought. Robert Cumming presents him as someone whose own intellectual development followed rather closely the shifting history of the French reception of German phenomenology. Derrida, on the other hand (whose deeply appreciative, near book-length essay on Levinas in the early 1960s, 'Violence and Metaphysics', would eventually play a pivotal role in the development of this shifting history), regards Levinas' view of Husserl and Heidegger as largely continuous, consistently worthy of serious attention and, for many years, well ahead of its time. So where was Levinas?

The French swim in which Levinas participated is, in very general terms, fairly easy to characterise, at least as it concerns the reception of German phenomenology. Without prejudicing the case, I think we can follow Cumming in identifying three basic phases as concerns '"France"'.[5] First, during the pre-war period phenomenology arrived as a more or less coherent, more or less fully formed philosophical anthropology, and, as Cumming notes, 'there was no general attention to the differences between Husserl and Heidegger'.[6] During and in the immediate post-war period, however, differences between them were recognised, but the dominant assumption – the assumption, as we saw in Chapter 4 and Chapter 5, of Sartre and Merleau-Ponty in particular – was that these differences were fundamentally reconcilable. This phase finally gave way to Derrida's high-octane critique of the 'humanistic' and 'anthropologistic' mis-understandings of both Husserl and Heidegger by a 'France' that was dominated by Sartre's (in Derrida's view) baleful influence, a critique which went along with an equally strident insistence that the differences between Husserl's and Heidegger's phenomenologies were not just significant but strictly irreconcilable.

Cumming thinks that Derrida's unfailing interest in Levinas' thought blinds him to the extent that Levinas' conception of and relation to the German inaugurators of phenomenology itself took the course of – and indeed is in part responsible for – this shifting sequence. A brief run through some of the details of the young Levinas' life certainly shows him as intimately involved with the understanding of phenomenology with which the sequence starts.

Levinas was born in 1906 and his culturally enlightened Jewish family lived during his youth first in Lithuania and then, during the First World War, as migrant refugees in the Ukraine. His early education was conducted in Russian, and Russian literature and ideas were central to his home life too. However, in 1923, three years after returning to Lithuania, Levinas chose, apparently simply 'on account of the prestige of the French',[7] and despite his scant knowledge of the language, to attend the French university closest to Lithuania, the University of Strasbourg. In his second year he began to study philosophy, and at the end of his third year, encouraged by a young philosopher working at the Institute of Philosophy at Strasbourg, Gabrielle Peiffer, he applied to spend a year at the University of Freiburg to work on Husserl's newly emerging philosophy. When Levinas arrived in Freiburg in 1928, however, it wasn't only Husserl he found there. As he puts it, 'to use the language of tourists, I went to see Husserl and I found Heidegger'.[8]

Arriving in Freiburg in 1928, Levinas accidentally stumbled into one of the most dramatic moments in the early history of phenomenology. Husserl was in the middle of his last seminar series before retiring in March. But even though Husserl was still teaching and writing, Levinas had the impression of someone who had 'finished the research of his research ... there was no longer any surprise'.[9] And while extremely grateful for the attention he personally received from Husserl, it was the triumphant return of Heidegger from Marburg that gripped the young Levinas. His presence was inspiring:

Everything seemed unexpected: the marvels of his analysis of affectivity, the new access to the everyday, the difference between Being and beings, the famous ontico-ontological difference, the rigour with which all that was thought in the brilliance of the formulations, absolutely impressive.[10]

Levinas' work on Husserlian phenomenology was not abandoned, but he constantly made efforts to find 'Heideggerian elements in it'.[11] What is more, the final dissertation not only brought in Heideggerian themes but also presented phenomenology in terms of a Bergsonian discourse that *was* French philosophy at that time.[12]

With its distinctive segue between German and French thought, Levinas' prize-winning doctorate, awarded in 1929, was an important event in French philosophy and was published only a year later as *The Theory of Intuition in Husserl's Philosophy*. Add to this the fact that Husserl's two lectures given (in German) at the Sorbonne in February 1929 (attended by Levinas, Gabriel Marcel and (reportedly) Merleau-Ponty) were done into French by Levinas himself (published for the first time anywhere in 1931),[13] and one can begin to appreciate that Levinas had more than a hand in the arrival of phenomenology in France. Indeed, as Cumming notes, it was even because of Levinas that Sartre's 'conversion to Husserl' could occur without his reading Husserl at all. There is an often-told story of a meeting over drinks in 1932 at which Sartre's classmate from the *Ecole Normale Supérieure*, Raymond Aron, who was then studying Husserl's work in Berlin, apparently knocked Sartre sideways with the suggestion that, with Husserl's philosophy, '[y]ou can talk about this cocktail, and it's philosophy'. Cumming continues the famous story with a less frequently remembered coda: 'Sartre then rushed out to purchase the only full-length exposition of Husserl available in French – *The Theory of Intuition in Husserl's Phenomenology*, a dissertation which Emmanuel Levinas had written under Husserl's supervision.'[14] The Husserl who came to France in the 1930s arrived, as Sartre admitted in his own case, decisively, '*via* Levinas'.[15]

With this in view, it would seem reasonable to suppose, with Cumming, that if Sartre and Merleau-Ponty did not see that Heideggerian phenomenology involved (as Husserl himself and, for different reasons, Derrida too insisted) a profound break with Husserl's, this was in part because they were introduced to Husserl via a Levinasian text which did not perceive a rupture of any great significance between Husserl and Heidegger either, and which even assumed the steady procession from the inaugurating master to his most significant and vital disciple. Citing Levinas' dissertation, Cumming lays out the Levinasian scene-setting of Husserl and Heidegger for France very clearly:

Levinas explains that his 'objective' in the dissertation is 'to grasp' Husserl's 'fundamental and simple aspiration' and with this objective in mind he will 'not hesitate to take into account the problems posed by philosophers who are Husserl's disciples and, in particular Martin Heidegger, whose influence on the dissertation will often be recognisable.' Indeed, Levinas believes that 'the intense philosophical life which animates Heidegger's philosophy sometimes permits us to render more precise the contours of Husserl's philosophy.' For Levinas is convinced as an expositor that 'the influence of a thought on important disciples permits without doubt ... a more accurate assessment than would the laborious study of a conscientious commentator.'[16]

This reading looks very plausible. And yet perhaps the scene here is not as straightforward as Cumming sets it out, for in his contrasting account Derrida gives good reason to think that Levinas was, from the start, out of step with an epoch that he (Derrida) delimits as one characterised by a distinctive (Sartrean) way of 'reading or not reading' Heidegger, an epoch in which Husserl and Heidegger are regarded as fellow travellers.[17] Indeed, according to Derrida, in his dissertation on Husserl Levinas had *already* turned decisively 'toward Heidegger *against* Husserl'.[18] Derrida is guided here by his conviction that, already in 1930, one could detect 'a reticence' in Levinas' interpretation of Husserl of a distinctively Heideggerian kind: 'the imperialism of *theoria* [in Husserl] already bothered Levinas'.[19]

Cumming is not unaware of this evidence, but suspects Derrida's admiration for Levinas got the better of him. Levinas may have been reticent about some of Husserl's formulations, and certainly turned towards Heidegger for something he regarded as more adequate. But this is not to be construed as a turn against Husserl since the Heideggerian correction is still conceived as faithful to a distinctively Husserlian 'fundamental inspiration'. It does not concern matters *fundamental* enough to constitute a deviant break. On the other hand, however, Derrida's reading is motivated by what seems to be the equally plausible claim that what Levinas noticed in his moment of reticence – and it would seem that Levinas was alone among the first generation of French readers of German phenomenology to find it noteworthy at all – was in fact (and Levinas' own assessments notwithstanding)[20] a juncture of just such significance.

The concern is with nothing other than how we should conceptually elaborate a faithful phenomenology of perception. Commenting on Husserl's affirmation of the posteriority of science to 'the concrete and vague world of perception',[21] Levinas suggests (reticently enough) that Husserl was 'perhaps wrong to see in this concrete world, a world of perceived *objects* above all'.[22] This is hardly a side-issue, and it is striking that Levinas offers as a corrective to the Husserlian still-too-theoreticist view of perception a thought he attributes (perhaps, as Derrida rather pointedly notes, not entirely faithfully) to Heidegger: the concrete world prior to the world as grasped by science 'is in its very Being like a centre of action, a field of activity or of solicitude'.[23] And Derrida is surely right to see Levinas as moving away from Husserl here. Again fairly tentatively, conditionally, Levinas affirms that 'if' Husserl's conception of the 'existing world' as revealed in concrete life is attributed 'the mode of existence of the object given over to the theoretical glance', then 'we will have to take our leave'.[24]

The early Levinas had, then, it seems, already at least prepared the move 'toward Heidegger and against Husserl' that would much later characterise the Derridean reception of phenomenology that came to dominate France in the last quarter of the twentieth century. However, while Levinas never retracted his reticence with regard to the suspect 'imperialism of *theoria*' in Husserl, things are not so simple as far as his own developing view is concerned. For after the Second World War, and after the revelation of Heidegger's disastrous involvement in the politics of National Socialism, Levinas also (and more famously) announced his need to 'take his leave' from something he regarded as problematic in the Heideggerian approach too: 'If our reflections are in large measure inspired by the philosophy of Martin Heidegger ... they are also governed by a profound need to leave the climate of that philosophy.'[25]

Utterly understandable though such a recoil would be on political and ethical grounds, Levinas' criticisms of Heidegger's focus on entities and others as they are disclosed in Dasein's concernful dealings and solicitude (as they are disclosed, then, in an understanding of Being) are not directly shaped by the revolting facts of Heidegger's involvement with Nazism. Indeed, as we shall see in this chapter, the primary characteristic of Levinas' launching of a new departure for phenomenology in the opening phases of his groundbreaking text *Totality and Infinity* (1961) is the way it resists *both* Husserlian *and* Heideggerian conceptual forces, and does so on what can be regarded as distinctively philosophical grounds, grounds that, as we shall see, both are faithful to and yet also profoundly interrupt the inheritance of phenomenology. Thus, if Levinas' early thought develops – as a matter of fact – 'toward Heidegger against Husserl', his first mature work develops not, as it did for Sartre and Merleau-Ponty, through an attempt to *reconcile* Husserl and Heidegger, still less through a trenchant championing of Heidegger *against* Husserl, but through a dialectical negotiation of a distinctive path *between* the perceived defects of positions that are, more often than not, characteristically Husserlian on the one hand and Heideggerian on the other.

Given his general preference for Heidegger against (the still-too-Cartesian-and-theoreticist) Husserl, it is perhaps a rather convenient abstraction of Derrida's to summarise the 'proper route' of Levinas' writings as always of the form of a 'neither this ... nor that'.[26] True enough, but making it explicit that the positions to be avoided here are, in central cases, Husserlian and Heideggerian in equal measure is of more than passing methodological interest.[27] Indeed, while Levinas remained deeply indebted to both Husserl and Heidegger – and, indeed, respectful too to the phenomenological studies of Sartre, Merleau-Ponty and others – the conception of human solitude and separateness from others that he develops is achieved in a way that really is, as Derrida insists, 'new, quite new'.[28]

Derrida sang the virtues of Levinas' 'strong and faithful thought'[29] loud and long in 'Violence and Metaphysics' but, as I have noted, that essay did not precipitate a rapid rise in attention to or interest in Levinas' work by others. Towards the end of the twentieth century, however, Derrida's sustained interest in Levinas' writing seems to have provided a growing readership with a *via* to Levinas.[30] And today it is unusual to find serious readers of phenomenology who do not feel themselves obliged to make the effort 'to respond responsibly' to Levinas.[31] Levinas' profoundly difficult writings are beginning to arrive. This chapter aims to assist the movement of that beginning by following the opening phases of the new beginning in phenomenology launched by *Totality and Infinity*. Part I of the chapter focuses primarily on the themes of totality and infinity from the preface and the beginning of the first section. Part II focuses on Levinas' attempt to effect a partial 'rehabilitation of sensation' in the phenomenology of perception. Part III focuses on Levinas' distinctive account of what he conceives as our non-phenomenal openness to others.

Part I: The Levinasian thicket

Levinas' writing

It doesn't take a genius to see why it proved a mighty task to raise the profile of Levinas' thought. Open the work that Derrida introduced in 'Violence and Metaphysics' as Levinas' 'great book' and 'great work',[32] *Totality and Infinity*, and you soon realise that you are in for a very bumpy ride. Indeed, within the preface itself Levinas apologises for failing to write a proper preface: 'these preliminary lines', he ruefully suggests, 'ought to state without detours the intent of the work undertaken'.[33] No such luck. Making headway with Levinas' writing, trying to follow 'the vicissitudes of [its] chase', is, as he acknowledges, like moving through a 'thicket of difficulties where nothing guarantees the presence of game'.[34] I do not know how many times I picked up the 'great book' only to put it down again in a kind of bewildered exhaustion. While the preface identifies the book, plainly enough, as 'philosophical research'[35] engaging in 'a defence of subjectivity',[36] it is hard not to have sympathy with anyone who feels that, without having read very far at all, they have already read far enough.

Derrida – hardly an author known for his readability – also acknowledges the formidable difficulty of reading Levinas. Indeed, having noted that Levinas' text progresses through negations of a 'neither this nor that' kind, Derrida quickly adds that the conceptual options for thinking can seem so comprehensively exhausted by that process that an alternative can make its way only through 'the poetic force of metaphor'.[37] And whether that should be seriously countenanced in a work of 'philosophical research' is a serious question. Commenting on the fact that he would offer only 'a very partial reading' of Levinas' work, Derrida engages directly with the thorny issue of Levinas' deeply poeticised text in an attached footnote:

Partial not only due to the point of view chosen, the amplitude of the works, the material and other limits of the essay. But also because Levinas's writing, which would merit an entire separate study itself, and in which stylistic gestures (especially in *Totality and Infinity*) can less than ever be distinguished from intention, forbids the prosaic disembodiment into conceptual frameworks that is the first violence of all commentary. Certainly, Levinas recommends the good usage of prose which breaks dionysiac charm or violence, and forbids poetic rapture [see Levinas, *Totality and Infinity*, pp. 202–03, SG], but to no avail: in *Totality and Infinity* the use of metaphor, remaining admirable and most often – if not always – beyond rhetorical abuse, shelters within its pathos the most decisive movements of the discourse.

By too often omitting to reproduce these metaphors in our disenchanted prose, are we faithful or unfaithful? Furthermore, in *Totality and Infinity* the thematic development is neither purely descriptive nor purely deductive. It proceeds with the infinite insistence of waves on a beach: return and repetition, always of the same wave against the same shore, in which, however, as each return recapitulates itself, it also infinitely renews and enriches itself. Because of all these challenges to the commentator and the critic, *Totality and Infinity* is a work of art and not a treatise.[38]

The difference between a philosopher who does and a philosopher who does not continue the old quarrel with poetry seems to be both (in theory) endorsed and (in practice) obscured by Levinas' writing. But I think Derrida is right to eschew a commentary that would naïvely pretend to 'read through' the unusually poetic mode of composition in order thereby to reach a more prosaic conceptual framework lying behind it. The way Levinas' words are chosen, ordered and fitted together is an integral part of its real business, not something supplementary to its work of argument and demonstration. So while one should remain sensitive to the threat that recourse to metaphor can and sometimes does lead to 'rhetorical abuse', one should also resist the, I think, too easy assumption that what Dermot Moran calls the 'metaphorical exuberance' of Levinas' writing is a mark of its philosophical irresponsibility.[39]

But taking sides here is tricky. Where Derrida sees Levinas' work as accruing persuasive force from the wave-like replayings of its favoured formulations, Moran sees here merely a 'dense style and apparent abandonment of rational argument and justification in favour of repetitive, dogmatic assertions'.[40] From Moran's point of view, then, the Levinasian text is made up of little more than 'prophetic incantations and quasi-religious absolutist pronouncements' which produce nothing but 'entirely unsupported claims',[41] and Derrida's willingness to take sustained interest in a text whose 'most decisive movements' may have very little, almost nothing, to do with the (literal) meaning of words is ultimately as philosophically irresponsible as the text it applauds.[42] Both author and reader in this case are, it might be thought, involving themselves with powers of language which are at odds with basic norms of clarity and precision that should characterise philosophical writing.

I confess that I feel massively on Derrida's side on this matter, and while it is not clear to me what a demonstration would look like that could hope fairly to rule on the use of metaphor in philosophy, I take the argument in defence of approaches in philosophy that cannot be reduced to argument in the narrow sense outlined in Chapter 1 to have obvious pertinence again here. The conclusion of that chapter was that the kind of reflective clarity aimed for if one is seeking genuinely to turn people around in philosophy does not preclude, and may indeed even require, a certain demandingness in the writing itself: coming to terms with the issues discussed in the text and coming to terms with the text in which they are discussed are not, then, wholly separable tasks. So I think one can hope to do better than give in to more imaginatively challenged interpreters, and embrace the notion that Levinas, as a philosopher, chooses his words in the way poets choose their words.

That being said, however, if we are seriously to entertain as a consequence that every word counts, I do not think it necessary to affirm that *Totality and Infinity* is really 'a work of art and not a treatise', as Derrida suggests. To agree with Wittgenstein, as I take it both Derrida and Levinas implicitly do, that writing philosophy should be 'nur *dichten*' (as a *poetic composition*) is not to suppose that the way philosophy should be written is as 'nur *Gedicht*' (as a *poem*).[43] If someone finds this distinctively dense (*dicht*) way of writing irreplaceably fitting in philosophy, that does not mean that they are really writing poems, and by the same token it is not as if a proper concern with a philosophical text that is composed in this way demands that one should pay special (still less exclusive) attention to the images and metaphors that it makes use of. On the other hand, it does call for readers who are prepared to be unprepared in philosophy, prepared, in particular, not to assume that they know what it means to be an appropriately sensitive reader of every text that might, with justice, be called philosophical.

So without wishing to condemn Levinas' text to 'prosaic disembodiment', the examination of the opening waves of *Totality and Infinity* pursued in this chapter will put the question of metaphor to one side. Towards the end of the chapter this wave work will return us to issues of composition and authorship that Levinas' text both (in its writing) invites and yet arguably (in view of what is written) cannot adequately or happily acknowledge.[44] At that point we will be touching on questions (quite precisely) concerning *writing* – its structure and functioning – which will take the discussion towards what is called the 'grammatological opening' that launched the work of Jacques Derrida, and thus will take us also towards a 'beginning' that marks a crucial turning point in the inheritance of philosophy in the name of phenomenology.

The transcendence of totality

The gist of Levinas' most unpreface-like preface to *Totality and Infinity* is that a satisfactory 'defence of subjectivity' requires that we rid ourselves of the tempting idea that individuals can be reduced to mere 'bearers of forces' that belong to an objective movement of world history.[45] The tempting idea is that the real significance of what people do, the 'ultimate meaning' of their lives, depends on and must be grasped in terms of the *total context*, or, as Levinas puts it, must be 'derived from the *totality*' of history,[46] derived, that is, ultimately, from everything that will have been the case. Against this, Levinas wants reflectively to affirm that we do not need to wait for this 'judgement of history'[47] to assess the significance of our acts or the events of our lives. He wants to affirm that we can legitimately be expected to speak and act in our own name and should thus be 'ready for judgement at every moment'.[48]

For this is surely how we would like it to be. We would like to believe that, even if they fail to do so, people *can* act for good and honourable reasons and *can* be legitimately criticised when they do not. And yet the reality we see everyday seems so often to support the opposite view. We see in history people, indeed whole civilisations, parading their honour and virtue while all the time acting out of self-interest, directed not by a distinctive moral vision but by non-moral calculations that seek out the best way of getting one over on their rivals, of 'winning by every means'.[49] Moral talk in such cases is pure expedience, subservient to what Levinas calls 'politics'. So can we be sure, as Levinas puts it in his enigmatic opening line to the preface, that 'we are not duped by morality'?[50]

Classical attempts to 'defend subjectivity' have typically sought to do so by affirming the essential freedom of individuals. Levinas, however, does not regard such approaches as philosophically satisfactory. For, again, the evidence of history does not seem to be on their side. Indeed, the evidence for the view that the real movements of history have little to do with what people think they freely choose seems 'irrefutable'.[51]

The question, then, is whether we can give the lie to the idea that people's sayings and doings are ultimately just moments in an objective historical totality which encompasses them. Levinas sets the bar for finding a satisfactory response to this question as high as he can. The only tolerable approach is to find *within* the perspective which aims to grasp reality objectively, and which claims that the meaning of individual lives derives ultimately from a historical totality, a genuinely totality-busting idea. Is there a moment when the search for such an objective understanding reaches an unsurpassable limit? Can we conceive without contradiction something whose exteriority to the represented totality is not merely a relative exteriority – not something that could be encompassed in a more encompassing representation – but which is 'absolutely other', and hence, if the measure of objectivity is independence from the representation that grasps it, something 'more objective than objectivity'?[52]

Such a radically totality-busting idea can readily be found, Levinas suggests, if we attend to 'the gleam of exteriority or of transcendence in the face of the Other [*le visage d'autrui*]'.[53] In what Levinas will call 'expression', the face of the Other presents itself. But what presents itself in expression, the Other in his or her singularity, is in principle *irreducible* to the objective, visible or otherwise worldly order in which it is presented. The face, for Levinas, is not the visual countenance or visible 'facial expression' of a human being. Rather, he uses the term 'face' to capture the sense that one's own relation to the Other is not just an attentiveness to a certain body in the world but to *this particular person*. And the language of 'the face' is very natural here. Wittgenstein voices this appropriateness when he notes that 'if someone has a pain in his hand, then ... one does not comfort the hand, but the sufferer: one looks into his face'.[54] The turn towards someone's visible face that Wittgenstein describes in this remark serves as an expression on our own part for a concern for *this person* 'facing' me. Of course, this appropriateness is contingent on the fact that we do 'look into his face', and we certainly can express this special attention in other ways too. Moreover, if we did not anyway have visually distinctive faces, if, indeed, we did not have the form of face that most human beings actually do have, this way of speaking would seem far less compelling and natural. But then something else would figure for this expressive turn to the expression of the singularity of the Other. And for Levinas this too might be called (by us) the turn to the face of the Other. In any case, this turn is never to be understood as a turn to a special part of the visible body but rather to something that, for Levinas, exceeds *anything* visually or perceptibly given in the world. Indeed, with the presentation of the Other, Levinas claims, I find myself 'face to face' with an alterity that maintains a fundamental *separateness* from me that cannot be understood in merely phenomenal or spatial terms at all. In the dimension of alterity that pertains to the face of the Other there is no separating distance that I might overcome by getting closer (even *much* closer, as we shall see) or by, for example, producing a map or other representation in which, in the same space, we have (symmetrically) me 'here' and the Other in his or her particular otherness 'there'. In this respect, and this is precisely what characterises the Other as such, the Other remains beyond every 'yonder' within the total 'there' of the world or history that I can encompass in sensible experience or thought. Indeed, the alterity that is inseparable from the Other is graspable at all, Levinas suggests, only with the idea of infinity as that which (following Descartes) designates 'a relation with a being that maintains its *total exteriority* with respect to him who thinks it.'[55]

So the idea that will serve to resist the *totality* is the idea of *infinity*. But this is an 'abstract and formal' way of characterising a totality-busting point that is, Levinas thinks, pre-reflectively evident to everyone in 'the relationship of conversation'. In a sense to be explained in what follows, Levinas insists that what we encounter as the face of the Other 'exceeds' or 'overflows' any thought or idea of the Other that I might form.[56] Thus while Levinas announces the title of his book in the claim that 'the rigorously developed concept of this transcendence [of totality] is expressed by the term infinity',[57] what follows in *Totality and Infinity* is not the elaboration of an abstract idea but a meditation on the concrete overcoming of the totality that is experienced through an everyday 'welcome', a welcome that 'receives from the Other' what it essentially exceeds one's power to fully thematise or finally to get the measure of: the presentation of the Other in expression that Levinas calls 'face'.[58] In the next section I will outline Levinas' conception of the being that is open to what it is never capable of fully embracing: the human being.

The unreasonable animal

What Levinas elaborates as the concretisation of the idea of infinity, viz. the radical exteriority of the Other, has a more traditional philosophical interpretation in the idea that behind an individual's visible behaviour in the 'outside world' is 'an interior and hidden world'.[59] But this traditional (let's say Cartesian) picture of the outer and inner is not at all what Levinas has in mind with the idea of the otherness of the Other. I will examine Levinas' non-Cartesian treatment of interiority in Part II of this chapter, but it is worth stressing at this point that the concept of *expression* which articulates his analysis of the exterior manifestation to me of the Other is also conceived in robustly non-Cartesian terms. Expression is not an ongoing series of ('outer') natural and objective events in the world that can provide (for anyone who can devise an adequate theory of their causality) reliable information about the ('inner') goings-on of some 'subject of experience'.[60] On the contrary, in expression the Other, precisely, '*expresses itself*', so there is nothing 'impersonal' or 'neutral' about what is going on there.[61] That is, what is in question in this case is never simply the presence of some behavioural trait or condition in the world which is *in itself* insignificant but which can give reliable notice of significant events going on elsewhere. Rather, the behavioural matter is intrinsically expressive, intrinsically revelatory of the Other.

The concept of 'expression' that Levinas puts in place of the traditional idea of 'outward behaviour' claims to capture what can be, for (some) me, *immediately* given. However, as an essentially personal presentation it is not something available to just anyone you please.[62] On the contrary, for Levinas, what is given here is not something that can be established as obtaining independently of a distinctive *response* from me to the Other as such.[63] That is, the identification or recognition of an expression is, for Levinas, *already* a response. The revelation of an Other requires that behaviour must, in some way, be (immediately) received or encountered *as* the expression of *this particular person*.

So an expression is not simply a natural ('outer') event that gives information to someone else about some other natural (but 'inner' and 'conscious') event. Moreover, the reception of the expression as an expression is held to require already a very distinctive kind of response. How, then, should we characterise the condition of the one who is capable of receiving it? Levinas marks the distinction of the being to which the expression of the Other can be immediately given, the being that can 'welcome' or turn towards the Other as Other, by specifying it as 'a desiring being' that precisely desires what is 'invisible', desires what is 'not given' and 'of which there is no [adequate] idea'.[64] Such a being, specifically for Levinas the human being, is to be understood, then, not in terms of a distinctive array or range or patterning of worldly needs and desires that it can satisfy (or try to), but in terms of its orientation in the world by a desire that *cannot* be satisfied in the world, a desire for what is and remains 'absolutely other', a desire that one can thus call 'metaphysical'. Indeed, if metaphysics is understood (as it has been since Plato) as aiming to grasp something *beyond* our merely worldly existence, then our worldly existence is, according to Levinas, one constituted by a profoundly metaphysical desire (a 'Desire' with a capital D, as he often puts it), an essentially unsatisfiable movement towards the absolutely other.

In virtue of its articulation of a movement away from the world and history – and in particular everything that actually went on in the world in the twentieth century that put human life and human freedom in peril – Levinas acknowledges that such a Desire for 'the invisible' must look like a 'demented pretension'.[65] But, Levinas asks, isn't it precisely the human difference, what he calls the 'infinitesimal difference' between human beings and non-human animals, that we know that what took place then was 'a human misery', a kind of collapse back into 'animality'?[66] Indeed, don't we know that being able to resist or defer what is, for every human, the constant possibility of that collapse, a collapse back into a life directed only by finite needs and desires, is precisely what makes us human? And this, Levinas insists, 'implies the disinterestedness of goodness, the desire of the absolutely other or nobility, the dimension of metaphysics'.[67] Again, the idea is that what makes us human is not a distinctive formation of (in principle satisfiable) needs and desires, not therefore something that might be best protected by declaring that each human subject has the 'inalienable right' to satisfy those needs and desires and protect its 'freedom' to do so, but a Desire whose dignity or nobility resides in the fact that, in each case, it has *none* of *my* needs at its basis at all: a Desire for the absolutely other, a good and disinterested Desire that aims, concretely, at the Other.[68] The 'dawn of humanity',[69] the incomparable difference of 'man', emerges, then, for Levinas with 'the dimension of metaphysics', and hence emerges concretely as soon as there is the welcome of the Other as such, a welcome that cannot be separated radically from a disinterested desire for the Other's welfare. To be human, then, is to know that the 'instant of inhumanity' that came to pass in the twentieth century – and the Shoah is clearly to the fore here in Levinas' thought – is the always live possibility of putting what is *most* important in peril. And what is '*most* important' is precisely not a concern with events that might jeopardise *my* life. Levinas puts this delightfully, irresistibly, in the following remark from an interview:

With the appearance of the human – and this is my entire philosophy – there is something more important than my life, and that is the life of the Other. That is unreasonable. Man is an unreasonable animal.[70]

To call something unreasonable is usually a rebuke, and one might also think that Levinas is here inviting (as some of his critics suppose) an abdication of reason, an irrationalism. If we were to understand 'reason' in the manner of what Levinas identifies as 'rationalism'[71] – where 'being rational' ultimately requires that an individual should radically renounce every dimension of its particularity in the interest of a universal rational order – then, certainly, Levinas is opposed to the domination of reason. But that does not imply that, for his part, he regards the interest of respecting rather than sacrificing that particularity as 'fundamentally antagonistic to reason'.[72] On the contrary, since he affirms that reason essentially 'lives in language',[73] he holds that reason has its life in the very scene in which individuality is most profoundly realised, in the 'face to face' of conversation. And then Levinas' point about the unreasonable animal is that there could then be no covenant in reason which could found or justify one's (logically prior) finding that the life of the Other is 'more important than my life', finding that the Other 'counts more than myself'.[74]

Of course, we do not typically act in accordance with this evaluation. We know that selfishness and war are in many ways the dominant reality of human life. Nevertheless, according to Levinas no human being can ever act in complete ignorance of a certain altruistic imperative either: *we know* (we cannot not know) that the meaning of being human is inseparable from the relation expressed in the speech of the one who puts the Other first (the '*après vous*', as Levinas liked to say). The relation to the Other is, that is to say, ubiquitously haunted by an irreducibly *ethical* orientation that Levinas presents as a scene of infinite *obligation*.[75] In the next section I will examine how Levinas conceives this special status of the Other.

The otherness of Others and of things

Levinas' claim is that if the otherness of the Other is to be acknowledged we cannot account for our relation to the Other in terms restricted to what we can encounter in the world, restricted, as he puts it, to what is 'visible from the outside'.[76] The scene of the face to face is thus extremely hard reflectively to articulate without distortion, for a faithful articulation requires that we avoid construals that would present it as if from sideways on: we must resist conceiving it in terms of a relation between two independently identifiable subjects in a social space. Specifically, what we have to strive to avoid is taking up (what Sartre calls) a 'third man' perspective which would include both me and the Other:[77] a 'totalising' 'lateral view'[78] that would hope to achieve a 'synoptic gaze that encompasses them'.[79] Simon Critchley explains as follows:

When I totalize, I conceive of the relation to the Other from some imagined point that would be outside of it and I turn myself into a theoretical spectator on the social world of which I am really part, and in which I am an agent. Viewed from outside, intersubjectivity might appear to be a relation between equals, but from inside that relation, as it takes place at this very moment, you place an obligation on me that makes you higher than me, more than my equal.[80]

But wait! Even if it is accepted that the relation to the Other is in this way non-totalisable, why should we reserve that distinction for our relation to Others alone? Isn't it equally distorting to conceive the relation to other objects and things as if from sideways on? Moreover, it would not help to insist that the *esse* of the Other cannot be reduced to its *percipi* (there is, as Sartre might have said, an essential transphenomenality of every Other)[81] since that is not unique to Others either. While an Other is ontologically distinctive in that it is *another like myself*, it is not ontologically distinctive in being *other to myself*. So what is ultimately so distinctive about the appearing of the Other?

Levinas' basic response to this question is developed through the elaboration of a fundamental distinction between the objectivity of objects and the transcendence of the Other. Citing both Plato and Aristotle as forerunners to this distinction, Levinas stresses the central importance that it has for his thinking, affirming (in italics) that '*the difference between objectivity and transcendence will serve as a general guideline for all the analyses of this work*'.[82]

Levinas spells out this distinction with two tightly interwoven ideas. The first concerns the kind of appropriating power one can have over something (the power to possess), the second the kind of cognitive hold one can have on something (the power to know).

With regard to the first idea, Levinas' claim is that while the otherness of an object is not totally annulled when one becomes aware of it, the 'bond' between oneself and the object nevertheless 'does not exclude, and in reality implies, the possession of the object, or the *suspension* of its being'.[83] By contrast, in one's awareness of an Other one precisely finds 'a datum whose being can not be *suspended* by an appropriation'.[84]

The sense of 'suspension' here is left unexplained by Levinas, but it is, I think, of the same sort one finds in the expression of a 'suspended sentence' in legal contexts. In the case of the suspended being of the object, however, there is a distinctive and telling reversal of fortunes. For while a suspended sentence leaves a convicted criminal with most of his or her formal independence and liberty, the case of objects that Levinas is considering concerns, *à la* Sartre, the radical putting off of or debarment of an object from sheer being (in-itself) through its being caught up in human structures of significance. To say that something has had its being 'suspended' means that its being is no longer 'being in-itself' pure and simple. Figuratively speaking, it has lost the liberty of having its own being in-itself. By fundamental contrast, however, even a criminal who we keep behind bars or a servant who is at our beck and call absolutely resists this kind of appropriation or possession: the otherness of the Other 'remains infinitely transcendent'.[85]

The second idea clarifies the first by specifying an appropriable object as, ultimately, one which it is in my power cognitively *completely* to grasp: my idea of it is one that can 'coincide' with it or can be fully 'adequate' to it.[86] For example, if the object is a bottle of wine, then an idea of a bottle of wine is capable of being formed which fully takes the measure of such an object. Again, by contrast, the Other is precisely what resists such an all-encompassing grasp or understanding: my idea of it is 'an idea whose *ideatum* overflows the capacity of thought'.[87] Levinas' deceptively simple point here is not that the 'privacy' of experiences makes the subjective states of every Other unknowable (although, as we shall see, Levinas does seem sometimes – and mistakenly in my view – to put it that way), and more importantly it is not at all an invitation to give up every project of understanding the Other, of getting to know them better, and so to 'renounce comprehension absolutely'. No, that project remains a profoundly ethical imperative, and ideas will precisely be the instrument of understanding. Levinas' point, however, is that this instrument is *constitutionally* blunt: the understanding one arrives at can never be final and is invariably obliged to reckon with what it cannot fully reckon; namely, the fundamental '*unforseeableness* of his reaction'.[88] So, for example, one might say of an Other that he is intuitive, passionate, open-minded and lonely. And these ideas might be, in a certain way, 'spot on'. But they are not, as it were, life sentences or the last word. Ideas we have of Others leave open, and can never outrun, the possibility of being surprised.

With respect to objects, Levinas consistently affirms the broadly post-Kantian conviction that our life as lived is profoundly falsified if we conceive it as even notionally separable from the concrete relationships with the 'furnishings' of the world.[89] Indeed, the 'I' *is* at all only *as* existing or sojourning in the world where it is 'at home'. Now, as we are beginning to see, for Levinas what figure as the objective furnishings of the world are 'spread forth'[90] in a setting where they are presented as 'for me', caught up with my life, appropriated as possessions. In the world as I find it 'everything belongs to me'.[91] Thus the objects of the world, whether they resist my physical powers or not and whether they are legally owned by me or not, have their independent being (in-itself) 'suspended' under my appropriating gaze. This does not mean that 'I represent the world to myself as being for me',[92] but that the human mode of being at home in the world is, concretely, in the form of a subject-sojourning-in-the-element. For such a subject objects have an alterity that 'falls under my power',[93] 'even the stars'.[94]

The sensible experience we undergo of objects, what Levinas calls 'enjoyment', is thus conceived as both intrinsically world-involving and yet irreducibly egoistic and relative. To put it in terms of the figure favoured by Levinas, given that 'eating' has the sense of 'the transmutation of the other into the same', and this transmutation is 'the essence of enjoyment', so 'all enjoyment is in this sense alimentation'.[95] We 'eat' the other (object) and in that respect it is the other relative to me. The Other (person), by contrast, is presented precisely as *not* falling under my power: 'he is not wholly in my site' and 'escapes my grasp by an essential dimension even if I have him at my disposal'.[96] In short, the otherness of the Other cannot be appropriated, one cannot in Levinas' view 'suspend' the being of the Other: the presentation of the Other to me – the face of the Other – is the presentation of what remains absolutely and not only relatively other to me.[97]

Of course, insisting that the Other is 'absolutely other' to me cannot mean that the Other remains utterly unrelated to me. Indeed, we have already noted that it is in the relation of conversation that the 'face to face' is consummated. But this 'bond' between me and the Other, an everyday relation that Levinas calls (perhaps rather enigmatically) 'religion', is not representable as a scene of two worldly items bonded together, not representable from outside or sideways on as a totality.[98] On the contrary, it is essentially an asymmetric relation in which the Other with whom I speak transcends the egoistic and relative order of the same, so that the relationship of conversation 'maintains the distance' of a 'radical separation'.[99]

It belongs to Levinas' distinction between objectivity and transcendence that the reach of sensible experience is fundamentally circumscribed or *limited*. Such a circumscription marks that one's life involves what one might call an 'inner life'. As should already be clear, however, Levinas' view of this is profoundly antithetical to a standard Cartesian conception of interiority as a subjective realm isolated from the world outside it. Indeed, for Levinas, one's sensible life is precisely steeped in or saturated by intrinsically world-involving contents. Before returning to issues concerning our openness to the Other in Part III of this chapter, Part II will examine Levinas' elaboration of this conception of human sensibility more closely. In doing so we will be following a wave of Levinas' text that develops in explicitly critical response to the phenomenologies of Heidegger and Husserl.

Part II: Levinas contra Heidegger and contra Husserl

Leaving Heidegger

'We live from "good soup", air, light, spectacles, work, ideas, sleep etc. . . . These are not objects of representations. We live from them.'[100] So begins Levinas' elaboration of our sensible life in terms of what he calls 'living from . . .'. Although the contrast to a representationalist conception anticipates a movement of resistance to Husserl, the conception is developed in the first instance by identifying a perceived shortcoming in Heidegger's non-representational account of Dasein's encounter with entities in their readiness-to-hand. As we shall see, Levinas' objection to Heidegger here is not that his account of 'the structure of the *Zeug* as *Zeug*' is false or misleading so much as that it is partial and incomplete: what is missing, Levinas suggests, is proper attention to the sensual 'enjoyment' which 'accompanies every utilisation'.[101]

This supplementary addition to the Heideggerian account is intended to draw attention to the fact that the character of equipmentality alone does not exhaust what is given in the sensible presentation of objects. As it stands, embedding the encountered entity into structures of references and relations presents an overly abstract and formal conception. Objects are never encountered as merely 'fit for a job', but always to some degree 'present themselves to "taste", already adorned, embellished', even the hammer.[102] In Heidegger's conception, moreover, the relational involvement of the object in Dasein's dealings serves only to play up Dasein's ontological *dependence* on the world. Or, rather, it tends to occlude that dimension of our existence which, in the sensory undergoing of one's dealings (for example in 'the joy or pain of handling the hammer'), 'delineates *independence* itself'.[103] That is, the Heideggerian analysis of Dasein's Being-in-the-world passes over the sensory solitude of myself separated from the object I am involved with and dependent on, an enjoyment that, considered as a phenomenon in its own right, Levinas calls 'happiness': 'life's relation with its own dependence on the things is enjoyment – which, as happiness, is independence'.[104]

To give a Husserlian twist to a Heideggerian expression, the 'mineness' of my life is thus conceived as inseparable from a sphere of 'my pure sensuousness'. Again, this is not a Cartesian doctrine of an 'inner theatre' with a passing show of private experiences. On the contrary, what we enjoy we 'live from … ': namely, furnishings, 'good soup', bread, books, etc. Such things make up the contents of experience, such things are, for example, *what is seen by me*. But this implies also, precisely, *my seeing the object*, and this is what Levinas is insisting that we do not forget.

We need to take care not to falsify this idea. Contents are what occupy one's vision and are potential objects of knowledge. To say that, in addition, we must not forget 'seeing the object' is not to add a new object of perceptual knowledge. There is, as Levinas stresses, no internal 'vision of vision'.[105] But that should not lead us to downplay or overlook the actual going on of one's undergoing of a vision of things: 'it is not knowing but enjoyment, and, as we shall say, the very egoism of life'.[106] Or, again (in a very Wittgensteinian formulation), 'one does not know, one lives sensible qualities: the green of these leaves, the red of this sunset'.[107]

So in relation to contents which we live from, there is always also a lived enjoyment of them: 'life is *love of life*', or, somewhat more prosaically, 'the bare fact of life is never bare'.[108] And this enjoyment is not just a colouring or affective tonality that we get here and there as an extra. The supplementary addition to the Heideggerian conception aims to reach to something more fundamental than the view it supplements: enjoyment is the very 'pulsation' or 'egoism' of the 'I'.[109] In contrast to the 'religious' bond with the absolute other that is the Other, Levinas calls the happiness of enjoyment the dimension of lived sensuousness that characterises the singular 'ipseity of the I' in its world-involving 'living from … ', the 'atheist separation', the lived mode of human dependence: isolation, solitude, detachment, independence.[110]

Bringing to the fore something that we have already seen making its way into Levinas' work, I want briefly to highlight how Levinas embeds a fundamental distinction between the condition of human sensibility and a merely (purely) animal condition into his articulation of the atheist separation that marks 'a veritable *subject*'.[111] For in Levinas' thought the animal condition is always conceived as something from which human life has been distinctively and radically 'liberated'.[112] The idea here is not that the lived sensuousness of a human life is, as one might say, of a special or superior *quality* to that attained by an animal. Rather, his far more radical claim is that the animal is 'outside of happiness and unhappiness' altogether:[113] its dependent condition is wholly and through and through one of natural dependence. Heidegger famously described the animal as 'lodged' in an environment in contrast to human existence which 'inhabits' a world.[114] Levinas shares this fundamental (and not at all new) humanism even as he attempts to re-emphasise against Heidegger the irreducibility of our sensible (and so one might have thought animal) condition. Indeed, the concept of the human difference from the animal so invades every aspect of his account of the lives of the living that Levinas even questions whether non-human animals are born; they are not 'veritably born' anyway.[115] There is, that is to say, no essential break for the animal from its 'uterine existence' to its in the world presence: its dependence never achieves a condition of 'living from … ' that is 'at home with itself'; its mode of dependence is never that of solitude and independence.[116]

Levinas does not hesitate to affirm the idea of a fundamental 'gap between the animal and the human'.[117] And he regards attempts to develop a more robustly naturalistic interpretation of human life as hopeless. Indeed, on the conception of a (purely) natural life that he endorses, no addition of further natural capacities, needs or desires will lift the human out of a condition of 'enrooted' attachment to 'pure nature'.[118] At the end of this chapter I will begin to mount a challenge to Levinas' conception of animal life, but his more traditional humanism is not without plausibility in its own terms. Indeed, the idea that human life involves the transformation of a condition of sheer animal dependency into one where an individual enjoys needs that can be resisted as well as satisfied is undoubtedly compelling. It is hard not to think there is something right about the thought that 'animal needs' are, for the animal, a kind of 'immediate attack' inseparable from 'struggle and fear';[119] hard not to think that animal life is fundamentally dominated by its 'immediate and incessant contacts' with what is physiologically given;[120] hard not to think, therefore, that what animals lack is the *time* made possible by a 'postponement of dependence'.[121]

And it is hard to see how this way of 'having time' with respect to what one depends on might be accounted for in fully naturalistic terms. Indeed, Levinas' alternative would seem rather more persuasive. If the existence of the human entails 'the liberation of man breaking with the animal condition' by way of 'having time', then it seems right to insist that the human can exist *as such* only by holding itself open to what is *not* given, an openness to the unforeseeable, an openness to an 'uncharted future',[122] an absolute alterity beyond the present horizon of expectation or anticipation.[123] On this view, the human exists as human only in virtue of its anticipation of what it cannot fully anticipate, its striving towards what it cannot satisfy, through a Desire, in short, for what is absolutely other. On this view, the distinctively human mode of dependency and neediness, the independence which constitutes every human as 'a veritable subject',[124] should be understood as *already* marked and thoroughly run through by a distinctively non-natural, metaphysical Desire: for 'man' 'the physiological plane is transcended'[125] because 'the time presupposed by need is provided me by Desire'. 'Human need', for Levinas, 'already rests on Desire'.[126]

For Levinas, then, 'to be' for the human means to live a life that is not simply 'enslaved' to the world but can be said 'to have time in the midst of facts'.[127] But to live such a life is to have one's orientation in the world shaped by a fundamentally metaphysical Desire. It is, that is to say, a life that is concretely inseparable from its *openness* (without sensible awareness) *to the Other*.[128] A purely natural life, by contrast, is one which is constantly engaged in a struggle to survive, *a struggle for its own life above all*.[129] Before exploring further how, according to Levinas, a condition of sheer animal dependency can be transformed into the life of a 'veritable subject', I want to complete the dialectical turn through which Levinas' conception of human 'living from ... ' bypasses Husserl.

Leaving Husserl

Up to this point I have been focusing on that aspect of Levinas' discussion of 'living from ... ' that takes its point of departure from Heidegger's analysis of the encounter with entities in their readiness-to-hand: the supplementary addition of enjoyment. It is a complex argument in which the supplementary addition comes to supplant the original conception. To begin with Levinas affirms that 'the structure of the *Zeug* as *Zeug* and the system of references in which it has its place *do indeed* manifest themselves, in concerned handling, as irreducible to vision'.[130] But he quickly adds that these structures 'do not encompass the substantiality of objects which is always there in addition'.[131] Consideration of this additional feature points, rather, towards the dimension of enjoyment which accompanies every utilisation of things. Indeed, it is a dimension which, once acknowledged, can be seen to belong ubiquitously to human life as lived in general. For not every 'thing' we enjoy is *Zeuge*: 'the crust of bread, the flame in the fireplace, the cigarette'.[132] At this point, then, the supplement supplants. What comes into view is the fact that it is not the disclosure and utilisation of *Zeug* that distinguishes us but 'enjoying *without* utility … this is the human'.[133] And this distinctively human mode of 'being-in-the-element' is not taken into consideration by Heidegger (and of course not only Heidegger) at all.

But now, since the dimension of enjoyment is essentially an enjoyment *of* something, and since this dimension 'corresponds to what Husserl calls "the primordial sphere"',[134] the analysis of 'living from … ', even as it leaves Heidegger behind, seems to return us to a point of departure that is basically Husserlian: for enjoyment is a 'form of intentionality'.[135] However, the supplementary addition that takes us away from Heidegger also distances the analysis from Husserl's conception: *contra* Husserl (and not only Husserl), to-be-in-the-element *qua* enjoyment is 'not reducible to a representation',[136] not to be 'confused' with the form 'consciousness of'.[137] Here there is intentionality, or a representing broadly construed, *without* a representation. Indeed, that one 'lives' and does not 'know' sensible qualities is of a piece with the thought that our sensibility is not 'a moment of representation' that aims at an object, but an affective state *steeped* in the object: 'the instance of enjoyment'.[138] Enjoyment brings with it isolation and solitude, the atheist separation of the enjoying being. Yet this is precisely not a disengagement from the contents which it lives from; it does not result in a subject/object or representation/represented duality: 'To be separated is to be at home with oneself. But to be at home with oneself … is to live from … , to enjoy the elemental.'[139] The interiority of the I is inseparable from its affective openness to the world.

At bottom the basic Levinasian objection to Husserl is fundamentally the same as the objection to Heidegger: the problem with both of their accounts, for Levinas, is that they construe our being-in-the-world in terms which give primacy to what Kant calls the faculty of understanding. In Heidegger, the horizon of every encounter with beings (as such) is the understanding of Being. In Husserl, the encounter with beings (as such) presupposes an objectifying act, so that the character of objectivity of all objects is conceived as grounded in the 'creative freedom'[140] or 'pure spontaneity'[141] in which a subject projects a conceptual 'terrain' in the light of which every object shows itself. In general, Levinas is (like Sartre) profoundly hostile to the idealist consequences of the Husserlian account. Despite the progress made by the Husserlian gesture which resists positing objects as outside the reach of the experiencing subject, Husserl still winds up endorsing 'the most astonishing possibility of reducing to a *noema* [reducing to an "object-as-intended"] the very being of the existent' and so 'reducing the represented to its meaning' or 'reducing a reality to its content thought'.[142]

Levinas, by contrast, like Sartre and Merleau-Ponty, wants to 'hold on to the exteriority which the transcendental method suspends'.[143] And thus the Levinasian return to sensibility makes possible both a non-praxiological and non-theoreticist affirmation of the exteriority of objects. *Pace* Heidegger, enjoyment is not a practical relation to things, and so there is no question of reducing the world to 'a system of use-references'.[144] But, *pace* Husserl, enjoyment is not a representation of things either, and so there is no question of reducing reality to a represented reality.[145] Thus, the analysis of enjoyment as our 'primordial relation' to the material world[146] trumps both Husserl and Heidegger in one blow: there is no privilege given either to theory or to practice since 'behind theory and practice there is enjoyment of theory and practice'.[147]

Levinas calls the mode of worldly existence of the separated subject 'inhabitation'.[148] He contrasts this both with the 'da' [there] of Heideggerian Dasein (it is not a form of understanding of Being) and with the intentionality of the Husserlian transcendental subject (which is always 'a representation or founded on a representation').[149] I will conclude this part by briefly exploring Levinas' delightfully simple – but profoundly controversial – account of human inhabitation. Controversial, for, as the presupposition of the mode of existence he wants to describe, Levinas will appeal to 'those silent comings and goings of the feminine being whose footsteps reverberate the secret depths of being'.[150] Levinas' account of a human subject's existence is not only *concrete* and *sensible* but also, and extremely unusually in philosophy, *explicitly gendered*.

Leaving home

Levinas' conception of inhabitation is developed through the elaboration of another 'neither ... nor ... ' dilemma, although this time the alternatives can be lined up as Husserlian and Heideggerian only very roughly, as threatened distortions or caricatures of their views. The two alternative conceptions of inhabitation that Levinas starts with and will reject are:

1 The idea that a person comes to the world as having come to it from 'an intersideral space';[151] from an (inner) 'this side' in which he already maintains self-possession and from which he makes forays into the other (outer) 'that side'.
2 The idea that a person is already 'outside', 'brutally cast forth', as if dropped into a strange place, 'foresaken in the world'.[152]

Clearly, neither option is singly satisfactory. So Levinas concludes that there must be a starting 'being-in-position' for the human subject that is somehow 'simultaneously without and within'.[153] Levinas proposes, I think very plausibly, the concrete phenomenon of an 'intimate home' as the somewhere in the world neither purely private nor purely objective that is 'the dwelling' from which one can venture forth and to which one can return.[154]

This is an attractive resolution of the 'neither ... nor ... ' dilemma, but in some ways it serves only to heighten the question of how, on Levinas' account, an individual born a natural animal can (possibly) come to occupy a human dwelling. How can it achieve this kind of 'pulling itself together' (what Levinas calls 'recollection') in the 'intimacy of a home'?[155] The problem here is a particularly sharp one for Levinas since, on the one hand, this achievement cannot without circularity be regarded as produced through the face-to-face relation with an Other (it is what makes such a relation possible) and, on the other hand, it cannot be regarded as a merely natural event either.

Levinas' controversial answer is that 'recollection' can only occur as the result of an intimacy with a (fully fledged) Other who holds his or her otherness as a 'face' back: not the 'you [vous] of the face but the thou [tu] of familiarity'.[156] The condition of 'recollection', of pulling oneself together, is, that is to say, the discreet parental-type presence (a presence which is, Levinas suggests, 'discreetly an absence') which, by virtue of the affection felt for you, surrounds you with a sort of protective refuge from the elements.[157] This discreet 'welcome' to a home is not a matter of giving a human infant the run of the place while adults keep their distance, but of providing it with a pre-established 'field of intimacy' in the world, whether that be in a building, a tent or a cave.[158] Levinas is willing to gender his discourse on this discreetly welcoming Other by calling the alterity that is the condition of recollection 'feminine alterity', the woman.[159]

He says this, but also partially withdraws it. Since what is at issue is, roughly speaking, a social function and not a biological trait, he also insists that 'the empirical absence of the human being of "feminine sex" in a dwelling nowise affects the dimension of femininity which remains open there, as the very welcome of the dwelling'.[160] The inhabitant who already inhabits the dwelling and whose feminine presence discreetly welcomes the human infant need not, in fact, be a woman, but it is always an inhabitant who gives for the young one a secure space in which to be at home in the world.[161]

I do not want to get involved with the dispute over whether the Levinasian analysis of the woman and feminine alterity is merely metaphorical or problematically theoretical, in some way proto-feminist or purely anti-feminist. In any case, it is not, I think, to be read as proposing a *thesis*. As Simon Critchley puts it,

> [Levinas] does not claim to be providing us with new knowledge or fresh discoveries, but rather with what Wittgenstein calls *reminders* of what we already know but continually pass over in our day-to-day life. Philosophy reminds us of what is passed over in the naïvety of what passes for common sense.[162]

One might add that it also reminds us of what is passed over in the sophistication of what passes for theory. Levinas seeks to make sense of the possibility that a purely natural existence can pull itself together in a world already human. His answer is that this is not achieved either through some kind of natural or through some kind of supernatural ('magical') causality – as if putting human babies in a building, tent or cave somehow 'produces' recollection as an effect. On the contrary, his elaboration of 'recollection' is intended as self-standing and is presented simply to remind us that an ordinary human upbringing is concretely accomplished only *as* 'existence in a dwelling'.[163] And this transforming event can take place, Levinas holds, only because the one who will come to exist there receives a discreet welcome to a dwelling already inhabited by a fully human inhabitant. This is not intended as the conclusion of any kind of theory of child development. Or at least it is intended to do no more than enable us reflectively to affirm what we already know: that the condition of adult self-possession for human beings is an ordinary human upbringing. And once one acknowledges this point it seems to me that the main objection one might want to bring against Levinas is not that he presents a questionable empirical claim in unnecessarily gendered vocabulary, but that the semantic field of his gendered vocabulary (the woman's intimacy, gentleness, affection, discreet presence, reserve and so on) presents a massive distortion of the truly awful empirical reality of many million of children who, one might suspect, never had a 'discreet welcome' to a human home and yet who manage to pull themselves through and make their way. His conception of what an ordinary human upbringing must come to is, one might think, preposterously idealised.

Yet that objection, however well intentioned, is not obviously telling against Levinas. For example, even in those cases where it seems clear that children get on without any formal parental support, it is not obvious that they do so all on their own. Might not the one who functions as a 'feminine alterity' for a boy or girl on the streets of a Brazilian favela be another street child? Might not the one who functions as a 'feminine alterity' for a boy or girl constantly tormented and beaten by his or her parents be found elsewhere? Perhaps such eventualities concern a kind of human tragedy or terrible human fatality, but they need not utterly discredit the Levinasian description.

On the other hand, one might still have concerns with a conception that finds itself needing to supply such an account in the first place. Indeed it might be thought that it emerges as an issue only if one regards the transformation that takes place in an ordinary human upbringing in a quite distinctive and certainly not unproblematic way; namely, as fundamentally 'breaking with the animal condition'.[164] In Part III of this chapter I will begin to call into question the humanism that governs Levinas' conception. This will pave the way for an examination of Derrida's more thoroughgoing engagement with the humanist presuppositions in the phenomenological heritage in the next chapter.

Part III: The rehabilitation of sensation

The Other as sensibly given

The first hundred or so pages of *Totality and Infinity* that I have been focusing on can be read, as Levinas suggests, as a partial 'rehabilitation' of sensation, a rehabilitation of the experiential, sensible given.[165] While Levinas fully endorses the post-Kantian critique of the classical notion of 'the given' as brute sense-data, his focus on human sensibility suggests that the post-Kantian emphasis on the sensible-object-as-understood loses something philosophically valuable when it abandons the stress on the sensible-object-as-such. Nevertheless, his partial rehabilitation is not intended as a return to a classical conception, aiming, indeed, entirely to replace the sensualist's confused 'physiological definition of sensation' through a phenomenology of sensible life 'lived as enjoyment'.[166]

Levinas' conception of enjoyment is, I think, an excellent foil to more traditional conceptions of sensory 'data'. On the other hand, one might still worry that there remains in Levinas' account the threat that he found Husserl succumbing to: that when one stays within the dimension of experiential interiority one can find it difficult not to limit what we can make sense of to what is given in the realm of possible sensory experience. As we have seen, however, Levinas appeals to a fundamental distinction between the objectivity of sensible objects and the radical transcendence of the Other, and that distinction would seem to build the overcoming of that limitation into the basic structure of his thought.

But at what price? In the remainder of this chapter I want to explore two concerns that one might have with Levinas' account. First, that even if not shipwrecked on the reef solipsism, the insistence on the radical transcendence of the Other commits Levinas to what one might call a problematic *solitarism* in the philosophy of life. The worry here is that Levinas leaves no conceptual room for the idea of really getting close to any Other: that we are not only separate but always and everywhere fundamentally separated. And, second, that the same insistence commits Levinas to retaining what one might call a problematic (though non-classical) *sensualism* in the philosophy of perception. The worry here is that Levinas leaves no conceptual room for the idea of perceptual contents that are not the undergoing of sensory qualities that are fully present in the present. In my view, while the first concern can be satisfactorily answered by Levinas, the second cannot. His determination of, for example, 'what in the world can be seen' is, I think, not only narrow and artificial but is guided by a central feature of the very conception of experience that his rehabilitation wants to reject. In the next two sections I will follow these concerns in turn.

Sensible pleasure

In the first part of this chapter I introduced the idea of the subject's absolute separation from the Other by contrasting it to spatial distances that might be overcome by moving closer. The phenomenology elaborated here, and equally what I will identify in the next section as the *interruption* of phenomenology that it also affirms, is very powerful. However, it does leave one wondering whether his account can make sense of anything but wholly and exclusively solitary experiences. This concern with what I am calling Levinasian solitarism can be taken up by considering a topic that he explored in a lecture series from 1946/7, published as *Time and the Other*: the topic of getting really close to, indeed touching, the Other, specifically of *caressing* the Other. In this section I want to show how Levinas' partial rehabilitation of sensation avoids the pitfalls of radical solitariness that, as we shall see, mar more traditionally empiricist conceptions.

In English we have been invited to read Levinas' discussion of 'the plane on which [our] sensible life is lived' as a discourse on 'enjoyment'.[167] Now, given their usual connotations, one might well be surprised to find that the word that ('for want of a better word')[168] 'enjoyment' translates is not the more or less general French term '*plaisir*' but the typically more specific or specialised one '*jouissance*'. That is, for Levinas *jouissance* is not one affective state among others (a lovely heightened sensory delight) but that ubiquitous sensory mode in which, prior to all theoretical and practical dealings, every human 'I' undergoes its worldly sojourn.[169]

With this in view, I want to examine a distinction that Levinas draws within the realm of sensory *pleasure* (*plaisir*) that can go unmarked if we let ourselves get carried away by the delights of his general enjoyment (*jouissance*). For in a discussion where talk of just such heightened pleasure might seem obviously most appropriate, where Levinas explores the marvel of undergoing sensual pleasures with an Other, the realm of pleasure (*plaisir*) is marked by a significant internal differentiation: 'voluptuousness', Levinas insists, 'is not a pleasure [*plaisir*] like others'.[170] The pleasure (*plaisir*) of voluptuousness is not, he is saying, of a piece with other modes of pleasure (*plaisir*) in which we may, from time to time, exist our separation and solitude. On the contrary, it is a profoundly distinctive case, and that precisely because *this* solitude 'is not solitary':[171]

> A phenomenology of voluptuousness, which I am only going to touch upon here – *voluptuousness is not a pleasure like others, because it is not solitary like eating or drinking* – seems to confirm my views ... on the absence of any fusion in the erotic.[172]

I will come to the views that Levinas says are confirmed here shortly. First, however, I want to draw attention to the fact that the case of pleasure (*plaisir*) with which the voluptuous is contrasted in this passage is that of nourishment: 'eating and drinking'. Now, as we have already seen, this case is not just one among others for Levinas either. On the contrary, with respect to one's enjoyment (*jouissance*) it is typically given a generality that covers the totality of sensuous life itself. There is something like an internal torsion in Levinas' conception of the field of sensible experience at this point that raises sharply the concern with his conception of our solitariness. For since one cannot 'enjoy' the Other, since the presentation of the Other to me cannot be reduced to the phenomenal presence to me of anything simply present in the present, the idea of a sensible pleasure (*plaisir*) that is somehow irreducibly 'not solitary' seems completely senseless.

A traditional empiricist might attempt to appeal directly to Levinas' division within the domain of sensory pleasure to remove this problem, and to distinguish undergoings that are impressions of objects like hammers and cigarettes and undergoings that are impressions of Others. The trouble is, however, that an empiricist is in no position to draw such a distinction: no sensible impression that I am in a position to get can be, in itself, up to the job of giving rise to an idea of an Other. Voluptuous pleasures, for example, that mode of sensibility in which I am supposed to undergo a pleasure that is not solitary, are just a series of impressions of another body. I want to make sense of getting an idea of a pleasure that is not *my* pleasure. But, clearly, for the traditional empiricist (for whom all ideas must be derived from impressions) success in this would be total failure.[173] So the distinction is one that an empiricist is in no position to affirm.[174] Indeed, for the empiricist the problem is not simply being unsure whether the Other enjoys one's touch or not, but, in the *impossibility* of enjoying the Other's enjoyment, the very idea of 'the enjoyment of the other' has no content *whatsoever*.

As we have already noted, Levinas positively affirms a mode of presentation of the Other that is *irreducible* to anything given in sensible experience. So the empiricist's problem is not something that he has to find himself landed with at all. Nevertheless, some have felt that the Levinasian insistence on separateness and solitude still goes too far. In remaining infinitely separate from an Other even as we touch them, he has, just like the traditional empiricist, left the Other out of the picture altogether. Luce Irigaray, for one, declares that Levinas on the voluptuous is totally inadequate:

> He knows nothing of communion in pleasure ... . For Levinas, the distance is always maintained with the Other ... . This autistic, solitary love does not correspond to the shared outpouring, to the loss of boundaries which takes place for both lovers when they cross the boundaries of the skin into the mucous membranes of the body, leaving the circle which encloses my solitude to meet in a shared space, a shared breath, abandoning the relatively dry and precise outlines of each body's solid exterior to enter a fluid universe where the perception of being two persons becomes indistinct, and above all, according to another energy, neither that of the one nor that of the other but an energy produced together and as a result of the irreducible difference of sex.[175]

Irigaray wants to insist that there really is something like 'fusion' produced within heterosexual sex.[176] This fusion would come about through the material 'loss of boundaries' that takes place during a sexual encounter, a massive heightening of bodily ambiguity which ultimately resolves into a new identity: there is produced 'in us', she says, a third, 'our child'. Not the physical child of blood and bone, who may or may not come about as a result, but 'our work'. In other words, her claim is that, in this case (perhaps uniquely) there is no longer the chance (as one might say following Strawson and Wittgenstein) of individuating the pleasure of the sex-experience-as-undergone over persons: 'the perception of being two persons', she says, 'becomes indistinct'.[177] And so we should here say that what was undergone (what Irigaray calls 'that im-mediate ecstasy') is a pleasure 'neither mine nor thine', a pleasure 'transcendent and immanent to one and to the other'.[178]

Despite its phenomenological acuity concerning the significance in this case of a certain experience of 'losing oneself' in the pleasures of sex, and despite its faithful identification of material breaches of bodily integrity, Irigaray's description is not unproblematic. Indeed, isn't there a flight of fantasy here too? A reflective cover version of the idea that 'losing oneself' in this case really is a scene in which, as the Spice Girls put it, '2 Become 1'? Moreover, isn't Levinas actually right to insist that if this scene is really to be one of genuinely non-solitary pleasure (which I take it is the point of talk of fusion) there must in fact always be (at least) two (and of any sex, I would think). Of course, as we have seen, the traditional empiricist is unable to count above one here; this really does remain for him a profoundly 'solitary love'.[179] But Levinas does not regard the presentation of the Other to me as a matter of sensible enjoyment, and so, as we shall see, he does not need to make recourse to a content enjoyed in the present to justify regarding voluptuous pleasure as precisely 'not solitary'.

In order to avoid a problematic solitarism, what we need to make sense of is not the idea of having 'an impression of the Other' but of a pleasure that is *inseparable* from an orientation towards the Other as such, for example the pleasure of touching (not *somebody* but) *someone*. Levinas' beautifully under-stated example is of my caressing a hand which has been given. And he notes, surely correctly, that if I caress someone's hand it is not the 'softness or warmth of the hand' that I am aiming to touch, but the Other: the pleasure lies in touching *her* or *him*.[180] And while it is true that the Other's feeling of me feeling them is something I experience 'as pure future', as Levinas very care-fully puts it, rather than as a content enjoyed in the present, that does not mean the Other's feeling is without interest to me. Indeed, *in this moment* with the Other nothing is more interesting to me than this pure future. As Witt-genstein might put it, the 'image' of the Other's feeling is irrevocably part of the scene here, only neither as a representation nor as a sense content given in the present.[181] The situation is therefore one where, thankfully, in a moment of non-solitary intimacy we remain totally distinct, absolutely separate.[182]

If our concept of the 'privacy' of sensible experiences is non-contingently connected (grammatically connected, as Wittgenstein would put it) to the possibility of dissimulation and pretence, another way of putting the necessity of separation in this situation (one not mentioned by Levinas but certainly in keeping with his view) is in terms of the possibility of behavioural simulations such as a faked orgasm, what Derrida delightfully calls 'this feint of orgiastic ecstasy'.[183] What is at issue here is the capacity (typically of a woman, but it is not restricted in principle only to women) to put a sincere expression out of play and to put something else, a simulated expression, in its place. The moment was enjoyed perhaps, but as a moment of *joie* without *jouissance*, (general) *jouissance* without (specific) *jouissance* – and yet at that moment 'orgiastic ecstasy' is nevertheless still *expressed*. And even if voluptuous pleasure is indeed profoundly *non*-solitary (as I think it is), still the enjoyment of the Other remains, as I put it earlier, *constitutionally* open to question, and it is so even if it is accompanied by confessions of love, of ecstasy, or a cigarette. In a court of law or just talking to friends the next day, it will always be possible for the Other to declare that she or he really felt very little, almost nothing. Moreover, this is so even if 'in another mode' I had been totally certain of it.[184]

The traditional empiricist cannot even get that far. In the absence of any impression of the Other he is not even in a position to wonder whether the Other's orgasm was faked. Against this, it seems to me that the Levinasian distinction between lived and known qualities should enable us to feel comfortable with the thought that, *pace* the traditional empiricist, it is correct to say, 'I know that you are (now) coming', and wrong to say, 'I know that I am (now) coming'.[185]

What makes this proposal (also) plausible is the way it lets us see what the traditional empiricist's typical reversal of it passes over: namely, that what is *enjoyed* in one's own case is *presented* in the case of the Other, indeed presented in the dimension of what Levinas calls *expression*, presented in the 'face' of the Other. Such expression, we should remember, is not the presentation of a *merely* phenomenal form or present sensory content, not something available to just anyone you please, yet, in the situation where I respond *not* to the (mere) observable behaviour of a living thing but, out of Desire, to *the expression of an Other*, it is something I *acknowledge*; and, in that way, is precisely *not* something about which I can have no idea at all.

It is with this thought that one can get beyond the impoverished resources of the traditional empiricist conception: the alterity one is presented with in expression is not based on having present sensory experiences or impressions which are somehow in themselves non-solitary; it is rather that, with the response in which the expression of an Other is manifest, with the welcoming of the face, non-solitariness becomes part of the very fabric of our life as lived. Indeed, my acknowledgement of the Other *as* Other enters right into what I sensibly enjoy, enters, for example, right to the heart of my voluptuous pleasure.

So Levinas' distinction between objectivity and transcendence can be invoked to remove the concern that his rehabilitation of sensation leads inevitably to a problematic *solitarism*. However, as I noted at the end of the last section, there is an additional concern that is, in my view, more difficult for Levinas to answer: namely, that the same distinction builds into his conception of the limits of sensible experience a problematic *sensualism*. In the next section I will turn to that concern.

Reading the Other

The aspect of sensualism that is at issue here concerns the way it interprets human sensibility exclusively in terms of given sensory 'impressions' or 'intuitions' that are simply and fully present in the present. On such an interpretation, talk about 'seeing the Other' or 'feeling the Other' would have to be conceived as of a piece with (if no doubt more complex than) talk about 'seeing the colour of someone's eyes' or 'feeling the warmth of their breath'. Levinas' whole conception of the face as fundamentally non-phenomenal is from the start utterly opposed to such a view, and I think he is absolutely right to reject it. On the other hand, however, Levinas' counter-affirmation of a mode of presentation of the Other that is irreducible to anything given in sensible experience at all seems to me just as problematic as the rightly rejected construal of the sensualist. In my view, our aliveness to others as such – and I deliberately drop the capitalisation here in order to begin to include in the discussion our aliveness to the lives of animals, our most other others – is not something that has to be understood utterly apart from our sensible life; indeed it is not something that has to be understood utterly apart from what Levinas regards as a 'merely' animal condition. Gathering these points together, in what follows I will introduce the idea that our aliveness to others is inseparable from the perception of marks and traces of a kind that are neither simply present in the present nor exclusively human.

This claim, and the problematic character of Levinas' conception of the limits of sensible experience that I want to highlight, will take a certain amount of unpacking. However, to begin with let us ask again what, according to Levinas, is 'given' of the Other? As we have seen, Levinas resists, and I think rightly resists, the idea that the *esse* of the Other can be reduced to its *percipi*. However, Levinas' fundamental distinction between objectivity and transcendence leads him to construe what is phenomenally given of the Other in terms only of what the Other *does*: his observable 'works', his actions, gestures and (akin to the 'hatchets and drawings' of primitive humans)[186] his writing.[187] All of these are phenomenal realities which, with respect to the reality of the Other as Levinas conceives it, ultimately 'lack reality'.[188] Indeed, speech too, which is profoundly privileged by Levinas as the basic mode in which the face is presented to me, can itself be regarded merely phenomenally, as mere 'speech activity', and hence also to some degree 'dead' or lacking reality. Speech – and not the phenomenal production of a speech-activity – is the principal 'living' reality of the 'manifestation of the Other':[189] 'living man' is always determined as 'subjectivity that speaks'.[190]

173

As we shall see, Derrida was highly suspicious of this privileging of speech, and he was so even before he made the critical breakthrough to a new and generalised conception of writing in the late 1960s, highly suspicious already of a discourse that follows so closely what 'Plato says about written discourse'.[191] These suspicions are not independent of Derrida's more general sense of the need to 'resist' philosophy's most traditional determinations of 'the sensible and the intelligible',[192] determinations which conceive what is given to perception or to the intellect in terms of the presence of something fully present in the present. It is Levinas' adherence to this tradition, and in particular the distinctive narrowness of his sense of the perceived presence of the Other, that I want to track in this section.

For Levinas, the revelation of the face of the Other is a revelation *beyond* sensible experience, beyond anything perceptually available in the world. It 'breaks with the world'.[193] And thus, according to the Levinasian distinction between objectivity and transcendence, the manifestation of the Other to me 'leads us to a relation totally different from experience in the sensible sense of the term, relative and egoist'.[194] The face is not a feature of the perceived world for Levinas, the revelation of the face is a *non-phenomenon*, or a presentation of *non-presence*: 'it never becomes an image or an intuition';[195] it is 'a presentation irreducible to manifestation';[196] 'it is neither seen nor touched'.[197]

We have identified and followed a number of launches, re-launches, shifts and re-elaborations of phenomenology in the 'beginnings' discussed in this book. But with Levinas' conception of the non-phenomenal presentation of the Other the project of phenomenology seems to come up against an absolute *limit*. Simon Critchley puts the point, perhaps in overly Husserlian terms, as follows:

> If the fundamental axiom of phenomenology is the intentionality thesis, namely that all thought is fundamentally characterised by being directed towards its various matters, then Levinas's big idea about the ethical relation to the other person is not phenomenological, because the other is not given as a matter for thought or reflection [or intuition, one should add. SG]. As Levinas makes clear in an essay from 1965, the other is not a phenomenon but an enigma, something ultimately refractory to intentionality and opaque to the understanding.[198]

To my mind this way of presenting the Levinasian interruption of phenomenology is not only formulated in terms that overprivilege Husserl's conception (perhaps we could correct this by suggesting, with Derrida, that phenomenology is 'always' in some way 'phenomenology of perception')[199] but is also far too quick to accept Levinas' thought that the disclosure of the Other is enigmatic *as opposed to* (in some sense) phenomenal. Nevertheless, the idea that philosophy written in the name of phenomenology meets a decisive limit in the case of the presentation of the Other seems to me a very 'big idea' indeed, and one which it would be profoundly distorting, phenomenologically distorting, to try to overcome or reduce. On the other hand, I think there is a fundamental (and, as I have indicated, in Derrida's view fundamentally traditional) 'axiom' at work in Levinas' own construal of this limit that should not be accepted: namely, the idea that what is given in a perceptual presentation is always and everywhere the presence of something fully present in the present.

Something of the work of this axiom is evident already in the Levinasian language of 'face' and 'expression'. For while drawn from the vocabulary of our perception of living things, and especially of human beings, it refers in Levinas neither to the (visual) face nor even to any kind of (visual) 'facial expression'.[200] Such displacements are not in themselves objectionable, but in this case I think that Levinas' willingness to move away from the life in which those terms have their everyday home is problematic. I will explain this.

In view of its irreducibility to present sensory perceptions (perceptions of, say, colour and shape), Stanley Cavell has suggested that it is natural to figure the scenes in which the other is presented to me as ones in which the behaviour of a living thing is, in a certain way, 'read'.[201] Interestingly, however, Cavell strongly resists treating this idea, as he puts it, 'as a reduction'. That is, he is 'quite sympathetic' to those who would say it is merely metaphorical to affirm that '[t]he human body is a text'.[202] But it is not totally clear as a result why Cavell thinks we find the concept of reading quite so fitting here, why we are inclined, in his words, to 'retain' it in this case.[203] In Chapter 7 I will examine how Derrida develops a new and generalised notion of writing which would allow us – still without 'a reduction', I think – to appreciate the depth of that fittingness. However, as he (Derrida) recognised even before he had fully developed that new notion of writing, Levinas would have had none of this. To treat the face as in any sense a kind of 'text' would require a total inversion of what he says, an inversion which is massively resisted by his conception.[204] For Levinas, as I have indicated, writing, like 'works' or 'deeds', belongs to the phenomenal realm and thus, with respect to the reality of the Other, lacks reality: unlike speech it is not expression but mere sign, something which, like the surviving 'hatchets and drawings' of primitive humans, give us only traces of the 'subjectivity that speaks', traces of the 'living man'.

But I think Derrida was right to say that, against Levinas' partial rehabilitation of sensation, a radical 'rehabilitation of writing',[205] in the form, for example, of renewed attention to the structure of writing internal to what Levinas regarded as life-lacking speech activity, would have enormously helped the analysis of the 'presentation of the other' in terms, precisely, of *expression*. But now, such expression would be conceived neither as fundamentally linguistic nor as peculiarly human. For Derrida, as we shall see in detail in Chapter 7, expression should be regarded as 'writing' (in a generalised sense), and as such is a form or mark of life that must be capable of a repetition in the absence of the 'here and now' of its inscription. It is, Derrida will argue, a form or mark of life that thus 'constitutes itself by virtue of its iterability'.[206] And hence it is a form or mark that is, in itself, irreducible to anything that might be simply present to the eye or indeed simply present to the mind's eye.

We need to attest to our capacity to witness 'an event that entails in its allegedly present and singular emergence the intervention of an utterance that in itself can only be [iterable] in its structure'.[207] Derrida's strategy here is, as I have indicated, to undertake a radical 'rehabilitation of writing'. In doing so he attempts reflectively to come to terms with our own pre-reflective sense of our perceptual openness to others – our sense that we can, for example, see the joy or disappointment on someone's face – in a way that is not beholden to traditional philosophical delimitations of perception and recognition in terms of presence.

As I say, I will go into this in detail in Chapter 7. However, at this point we should note that Derrida's rehabilitation of writing is not a (roughly speaking, Merleau-Pontian) cancellation of the (roughly speaking, Levinasian) idea that a phenomenologically faithful articulation of our life with language must interrupt phenomenology as a philosophy of present perception. Indeed, one can even argue that an elaboration of the connections between *writing* and *self-expression* actually makes the case for that interruption all the more clearly and convincingly. Don't we know, for example, that when it comes to getting oneself across, when it comes to giving one's thoughts the best chance of 'bearing a stamp that marks them as mine',[208] 'the writer absents himself better, that is expresses himself better as other, addresses himself to the other more effectively than the man of speech?'[209] What I do *now* – express myself – can only be that if *what* I *do* now – write something – can do without my current presence, my presence in the present. However, that structural absence within the functioning of self-expression does not require us to suppose, as Levinas supposes, that a genuine presentation of others in self-expression cannot belong to the perceived world; unless, that is, we conceive perception as restricted to a subject's sensitivity to objectively present sensible qualities or properties.

But this restriction, though affirmed without question by Levinas, is not compulsory. It is one of the most striking features of Levinas' thought that it totally refuses to accept that the face of the Other might be something one could be said perceptually to see. It is surely more striking still that we do not, in our pre-reflective lives, normally refuse to do so *at all*. Making the essential point against traditional prejudices, Wittgenstein puts it like this:

> 'If you only shake free from your physiological prejudices, you will find nothing queer about the fact that the glance of the eye can be seen too.' For I also say that I see the look that you cast at someone else. And if someone wanted to correct me and say that I don't really see it, I should take that for pure stupidity.

On the other hand I have not *made any admissions* by using that manner of speaking, and I should contradict anyone who told me I saw the glance 'just the way' I see the shape and colour of the eye.

For 'naïve language', that is to say our naïve, normal way of expressing ourselves, does not contain any theory of seeing – does not show you a *theory* but only a *concept* of seeing.[210]

There is no doubt that Levinas' partial rehabilitation of sensation involves a compelling repudiation of the traditional assumption which supposes that what is perceptually 'given' in general should be grasped on the basis of the 'physiological definition of sensation' as 'simple quality'.[211] Nevertheless, I suspect that his refusal to countenance all talk of the presentation of the Other as a genuinely perceptual experience, and as a result of that his total resistance to an analysis of expression in terms of 'the body that speaks or writes',[212] reflects the fact that he does not radically repudiate the prejudice that theorises seeing as *exclusively* a matter of the visual enjoyment of present sensory contents. And he does not do so because his basic and guiding distinction between the phenomenally objective and the infinitely transcendent leaves him with no conceptual room properly to acknowledge his own normal way of expressing himself about the visual givenness of others *as* others.

But now, and finally, if we can begin to recall ourselves to our normal ways of expressing ourselves (if we can begin comfortably to accept that, for example, the glance of the eye of the other can be seen), then not only can we acknowledge a (non-figurative) sense of seeing the expression of the other but we can see our way to acknowledging something else too: namely, that we can see the expression of another animal. In the next and final chapter I will examine how, in Derrida's work, the rehabilitation of writing affords an orientation to a life with language that supports both of these points. As we shall see, while not breaking from phenomenology altogether it is an orientation which effects an interruption of it that is both more general and more radical than that effected by Levinas' account of the encounter with the Other.

7

INTERRUPTING PHENOMENOLOGY

Jacques Derrida

In the name of phenomenology

In a review of a book that spoke of a 'turn to phenomenology' in recent analytic philosophy, Ian Hacking observes that talk of phenomenology in this context typically refers to what is revealed to us from the standpoint of 'introspection', a standpoint, he rightly insists, that has little to do with the concerns of 'Husserl, Merleau-Ponty and others who are normally identified with phenomenology'.[1] Hacking also suggests that it is really no good trying to grab the title for an introspectionist method either, since 'Husserl and his descendents' explicitly insist on the crucial difference between the reflective perspective of phenomenology and the naïve objectivism of introspective psychology. Closing off any major adjustment to what might be written in the name of phenomenology, Hacking asserts that Husserl and his descendants 'now own the name'.[2]

I emphasised such a difference myself in Chapter 1, where I introduced phenomenology by saying that it is important not to conflate the idea of phenomenology as a philosophical method with an interest in phenomenology as the (supposed) 'passing show' of immediate experience. However, I am not sure I would go along with Hacking's assertion that Husserl and his descendants now own the name. Indeed, not only is the name up for grabs by philosophers who do not regard themselves as descendants of Husserl – and I cited Austin, Ryle and Wittgenstein as three good cases of that, three thinkers who are definitely not engaged in an introspectionist effort either – but in important respects Hacking's suggestion underestimates the extent to which the name has *already* been up for grabs within the inheritance of phenomenology that descends from Husserl. By taking 'beginnings' of various kinds as my point of departure I have tried to show that some of Husserl's most influential descendants have produced quite radical shifts in the inheritance of phenomenology. In particular, we have seen significant adjustments in what has been regarded as having *priority* in a phenomenological investigation.

In Chapter 3 we saw R.M. Hare distinguish the philosophical path he (with others) was taking from 'the German way' by the fact that he wanted to question whether 'statements' on 'metaphysical' topics actually mean some-thing. This question, Hare insisted, is *logically prior* to the ones that his 'German thinkers' were (still) asking. But this kind of priority complaint is not the preserve of British critics of German philosophers. Indeed, the most strik-ing adjustments within the inheritance of phenomenology that I have traced in this book are precisely adjustments in what is regarded as having priority. Inheriting something of the priority oddness of Brentano's descriptive phe-nomenology, in Husserl's mature work the priority is on the disclosure of 'the intrinsically first field of knowledge' via the phenomenological reduction. In Heidegger the priority is the clarification of Dasein's 'understanding of Being'. In Sartre the starting point is concrete 'human reality'. In Merleau-Ponty it is the world and my bodily presence in the world prior to subsequent scientific theorising. In Levinas it is the encounter with the Other. None of these is a randomly chosen beginning. On the contrary, they are points of departure that are regarded as philosophically crucial by those who take them. And the shape of phenomenology alters with the adjustments produced by these shifting departure points. In exploring this line of accomplished deviance, 'we are', as Robert Cumming puts it, 'up against philosophies which are recalcitrant each in its own different way to being lined up in a single overall history of phenomenology, within which the development of each could be fitted'.[3]

In Chapter 2 we saw that Derrida begins one of his first engagements with phenomenology by raising a question of priority too. In a reading of Husserl's launching distinction between expressive and indicative signs, Derrida com-plains that Husserl failed to ask the prior question of the nature of signs 'in general'.[4] In my view Derrida's elaboration of this new point of departure is of a fundamentally different order to those we have seen with other adjustments in phenomenology. In particular, the attempt to undertake what he calls a 'reha-bilitation of writing' is an 'interruption of phenomenology'[5] that lurches away altogether from an attempt to provide an explicitation or explication of the human subject or (to revert to the discussion of Chapter 3) any 'functional equivalent' of such a subject. Derrida steps back from an analysis centred on, for example, 'transcendental subjectivity' or 'Dasein' or 'human reality' or 'incarnate subjectivity' or 'life run through by Desire', and begins anew in an analysis which attempts to 'make explicit the experience of language'.[6]

As we shall see in this chapter, Derrida's move away from, roughly speaking, a philosophy of the (perceiving) subject and towards, roughly speaking, a phi-losophy of (written) language does not provide him only with a new way of interrupting phenomenology. In principle it effects a shift that would delimit Western philosophy in its entirety, at least insofar as that is centred on the 'great metaphysical systems' of the classical tradition.[7] As Robert Cumming notes, when Derrida endorses the 'contamination' of all uses of signs by the structure that belongs to the indicative sign called 'writing', he does not just have Husserl's preference for conceptual purity in view: 'for he would find the entire philosophical tradition puritanical – tainted by the tantalization of purity'.[8] However, Derrida does not come to this conclusion independently of his engagements with phenomenology. Indeed, appreciation of Derrida's criticisms of Western metaphysics needs to acknowledge the profound debts they retain to previous work in phenomenology, especially, but not only, work by Heidegger and Levinas. The rehabilitation of writing, the elaboration of a new 'grammatology' (science of writing), could not, Derrida suggests, but 'take the form of a critique of phenomenology',[9] but that critique is not developed from somewhere simply external to phenomenology. The 'interruption of phenomenology' that Derrida perceives in his own efforts to elaborate a new notion of writing is also faithful to a certain phenomenological legacy: it is a critique of phenomenology that is itself made 'in the name of phenomenology'.[10] As we shall see, the distinction of phenomenology for Derrida lies in the fact that it can be read both as (at times stubbornly) retaining *and* (at times radically) challenging what, following Heidegger, he takes to be the very 'ether of metaphysics' from its Greek beginnings:[11] the privilege granted to the value of *presence*. In this chapter, by following some of the beginning steps in his rehabilitation of writing I hope to show that Derrida is best understood not as ushering in the 'end' of phenomenology as a 'philosophical movement',[12] but rather as radicalising – and coming to terms with – its most powerful forces of ether-shaking 'self-interruption'.[13]

Part I: A preface to what remains to come

The truth of man

Derrida's work is stubbornly difficult to read. He challenges received wisdom without endorsing the received counter-wisdom to it. The whole fabric of our thinking can seem to become unstitched in his hands. For example, from first to last his work fundamentally challenges the widely cherished idea that human history has moved and is moving still along a basically linear path, in stages, from a state of primitive animality to one of civilised, rational and scientific humanity. And from first to last Derrida's texts relentlessly criticise the Western ethnocentrism that has dominated our understanding of that linear idea. Yet, he does not simply affirm the opposite side of that ethnocentric coin. He does not affirm, *à la* Rousseau, the nobility or innocent purity of so-called 'primitive man'. The book that many, myself included, regard as his greatest work, *Of Grammatology*, begins by calling Western ethnocentrism into question – but it ends with a critique of Rousseau.

I am going to begin this chapter with an examination of Derrida's launch of a rehabilitation of writing in that book. It launches itself, conventionally enough, with a preface, just over a page long. It is quite a conventional preface too in that (unlike the one by Levinas examined in Chapter 6) it states without more ado what the author intends to do. It does not engage, for example, with issues concerning its own genre, and it does not take up the problem that philosophers have more or less conventionally identified with philosophical prefaces – at least since Hegel asked his readers not to take him seriously in his.[14] The supposed problem with prefaces is that the '*prae-fatio*' is a saying-beforehand that is actually written-after-the-fact, after the work, and as standing outside the (real) philosophical work of the work, that real work thus being the essential '*prae-fatio*' of writing the preface. Derrida does not dwell on this logic of the preface in the preface to *Of Grammatology*. However, in an over fifty-page-long preface to a text published five years later the status of the preface does become an explicit theme, and Derrida's later remarks helpfully preface the earlier apparently more traditional ones:

> The preface announces in the future tense ('this is what you are going to read') the conceptual content or significance of what will already have been written. And thus sufficiently read to be gathered up in its semantic tenor and proposed in advance. From [this] viewpoint, which re-creates an intention-to-say after the fact, the text exists as something written – a past – which, under the false appearance of a present, a hidden omnipotent author (in full mastery of his product) is presenting to the reader as his future. Here is what I wrote, then read, and what I am writing that you are going to read. After which you will again be able to take possession of the preface which in sum you have not yet begun to read, even though, once having read it, you will have already anticipated everything that follows and thus you might just as well dispense with reading the rest.[15]

The 'pre-' of the pre-face makes the future present, a future which is in fact already written and past. One might wonder, then, whether there can be *a preface to what remains to come* that does not render what remains to come everything but 'to come'. Perhaps only if what remains to come will have always already resisted the idea of '*complete* gathering up' that a writer of a preface or indeed a writer of a metaphysical system might, beyond the preface, yearn for. Derrida will affirm that resistance.

Of Grammatology begins, as I say, with a short preface. In it Derrida tells us, very straightforwardly, what we will read and announces 'the guiding intention' of the book.[16] This he then describes in terms of the problematisation (or making problematic) of traditional approaches to the 'critical reading' of texts, consequent, it later transpires, upon considerations surrounding the status of *writing* throughout the history, especially, of philosophy. This problematisation will mount, he states, a fundamental challenge to 'classical' conceptions of the shape of human history. Indeed it will 'demand that reading should free itself ... from the classical categories of history'.[17] Although Derrida does not take this to involve a complete abandonment or rejection of 'classical norms' concerning, for example, historical periodisation, it will attempt to make problematic or enigmatic the feeling for linear historical sequence and for clearly separate and distinct stages which has, in (what we like to think of as) our modern time, become near obligatory in research that calls itself 'contemporary'. Unlike most today – that is, unlike those today who want to understand what is going on in the 'here and now' of our 'today' in terms of its subsequence to immediately preceding conditions and developments – Derrida retains something of the more classical conviction that we are under the obligation to study the classics.[18] The dead, even the long dead, are not everywhere finished, not always simply 'dead and gone', belonging to a past that is simply past and from which we can simply separate ourselves off and which we can leave behind, as definitively other than us, fundamentally non-contemporary with us. Moreover, even though the classical tradition is generally conceived today as a literary tradition, Derrida is (again up to a point classically) engaging with the more classical sense of the classical as a philosophical tradition, and specifically a philosophical tradition which constantly opens on to a conception of human life and history – a history that stands in contrast to merely natural life or natural history – as having a *definite sense*, a *delineable meaning* or shape, indeed as the unfolding of a distinctively linear trajectory: a movement in stages away from an origin and towards an anticipated 'end of man' to come. Derrida will typically regard such classical texts as in one way or another including all the great metaphysical systems of the Western canon.

Derrida's exposition of the classical tradition, and the radicalisation of phenomenology that shapes it, is launched with the elaboration of a grammatological priority. For according to Derrida the classical presumption that human life and history has, uniquely, a relatable or delineable (linear) shape (a meaning) is powerfully informed and indeed pre-programmed by a distinctive interpretation of the history of (human) *writing*. According to that interpretation there were, first, primitive pictures, then symbols, then hieroglyphics, then characters and then finally a phonetic alphabet which, for the first time, properly represents spoken sounds. The history of writing is thus conceived as a teleological and linear history in which we move from non-linear or pluridimensional marks towards an ideally linear, phonetic script. Derrida's work of 'deconstruction' aims to retrieve from the texts of the classical tradition – including some of the major phenomenological texts – an acknowledgement of an essential or structurally necessary non-linearity, the disclosure in such texts of something other than a heading-to-an-end of 'man'.

However, if, as that acknowledgement suggests, such texts already recognise (at least 'in a certain way', as Derrida often puts it) that no actual writing can attain the purely linear ideal, why are we inclined to look at the history of writing as if it were a movement towards this ideal? Perhaps because we think it *ought* to move this way. And one powerful influence (not the only one) in this regard is an appeal to a tempting analogy: namely, with that of an individual human being's mental development. In view of a reasonable assumption that human beings have undergone profound changes in their communal psychology over the course of their long-run history, it can seem very natural to configure *stages* in the development of what we call 'the history of humanity' on the model of the history of an individual mind. Indeed, early anthropology used to talk blithely of 'the childhood of mankind', of 'man' then passing through its 'adolescence' and now, at last (hooray/boo), reaching (round here anyway) full rational and scientific 'maturity'. And as a (Western) child goes through stages in learning to write properly, so – we like to think – did (Western) 'man'.

But what if we begin to read the non-linear remains left between the lines of the texts that affirm this linear picture? This requires, Derrida suggests, a form of rationality and scientificity that neither simply conforms to nor simply rejects the rationality and scientificity striven for in Western modernity[2]. With the becoming legible within the trajectory of the West of its own developmental 'mythography', we are, Derrida suggests, entering a new age of writing: an age in which Western writings themselves are beginning to conceive writing differently.[19] And as the still currently standard (rational, scientific) picture of 'what it is for such writing to be well shaped and disciplined'[20] starts to come under pressure from within, so also 'we are beginning', Derrida observes, 'to write differently' too.[21]

It was never going to be easy to defend such a turn in our time.

What I introduced in Chapter 6 under the title of Derrida's rehabilitation of writing aims to intervene at the very heart of the classical philosophical tradition as he reads it – a tradition that, in his view, still profoundly marks the movement and self-understanding of our so-called 'modern' and supposedly 'post-metaphysical' times. Derrida's own counter-time – what one might call his de-periodisation of classical history – gives him a sharp and (up to a point still) classical sense that a supposedly 'modern' thinker's most relevant predecessor can be very remote.

The point here is not merely to affirm that our memory of the past informs our inhabitation of the present. On the contrary and more radically, Derrida affirms that what is most alive and active in a time is not always something 'at present' alive or 'immediately' available to those who are at home in it, to those who live comfortably, as one says, in our time. Indeed, as we shall see, according to Derrida our picture of 'consciousness' in general,[22] a picture that Derrida identifies as one in which consciousness is 'thought only as self-presence',[23] deflects us from proper acknowledgement of structures within the heart of our situated openness to the world that cannot be reduced to what is 'at present' alive or 'immediately' available to those who are at home in it.

Conceiving consciousness in terms of self-presence remains a mark of our situation 'today'. However, it is also a mark of our time that it is not everywhere affirmed. Explicit resistance to it has if anything been growing, and Derrida (while he displays a singular initiative in this community of resistance) does not at all regard himself as alone in trying to think otherwise. Indeed, in the middle of his exploration of what he calls 'the trace' structure that belongs to writing in *Of Grammatology* – a structure where traces do not refer back to something fully present in the present but only to other traces – Derrida turns gratefully to acknowledge that his appeal to this concept of the trace in a 'deconstruction of presence' does *not* serve to distinguish his work from everything else going on today, and he positively welcomes that his discussion will receive life from the 'force' of texts and demonstrations of others. It is at this point that Derrida acknowledges a crucial debt to and a welcome inheritance from two moments within the inheritance of phenomenology, key texts by Levinas and Heidegger that run counter to the dominant philosophical privileging of presence and self-presence.[24]

But this inheritance of phenomenology is far from straightforward. Indeed, it is precisely moments of extreme self-interruption, moments where phenomenology calls itself most radically into question, that Derrida highlights and wants, in his own work, to retain and to generalise. The cases are, first, Levinas' discussion of the Other as infinitely beyond the horizon of phenomenal presence, the idea that the presentation of the Other is the presentation of an alterity that can never 'be lived in the originary or modified form of presence'.[25] The second is Heidegger's identification of the history of metaphysics as everywhere presupposing 'the meaning of Being as presence and the meaning of language as the full continuity of speech'.[26] Derrida aims to 'reconcile' these (to Levinas' mind, conflicting) ideas and to do so through a demonstration of the ubiquity in what we call 'language' and ultimately the ubiquity in what we call 'experience' in general, of structures that imply an essential and irreducible relation to an alterity that can never 'be lived in the ... form of presence'. This is what Derrida seeks to achieve through his rehabilitation of writing, and as such it aims both at calling into question the fundamental 'ether' of the classical metaphysical tradition – the privilege granted to the present – and at fundamentally interrupting phenomenology as a philosophy of the perceiving subject.

Situated rather boldly within some of the most radical textual and theoretical environments of our time,[27] the attempt 'to make enigmatic what one thinks one understands by the words "proximity", "immediacy", "presence"' that he calls the 'final intention' of the argumentation in *Of Grammatology*[28] thus aims to go back behind the most elemental motifs of our contemporary self-understanding, motifs that have, Derrida thinks, dominated Western humanity for centuries hitherto, and which have for the most part dominated phenomenology as well. Indeed, as we shall see, the intention here is to disturb even the most stubborn and radical of all classical period breakers, the break which would have traditionally marked the coming to presence of self-presence itself: 'the opposition of nature and culture, animality and humanity, etc.'.[29] Affirmation of this opposition is what he calls the 'classic humanism' of classical metaphysics.[30] At issue here, as I have already indicated in previous chapters, is a *cognitivist presumption* that there is, in the (fundamental or essential) nature of things, a distinctive *truth* of man breaking with an animal condition: a fundamental (and fundamentally unique) *meaning* of human life and history that can be discursively disclosed or revealed and brought to light.

Such a truth or meaning has, as we have seen, been regularly elucidated in terms of a teleological movement of human history (or of spirit) towards a proper 'end of man', but there are, Derrida suggests, other configurations '*of the same type*' too.[31] Derrida cites here Sartre's conception of the movement of the for-itself towards an (impossible) end of being-in-itself-for-itself,[32] as well as religious conceptions of the coming irruptive fulfilment of a determinate (if temporally radically unpredictable) messianic promise.[33] However, as I say, the crucial humanist presumption is that what would serve fundamentally to distinguish the human from all merely natural (and in that sense meaningless) life resides in a fundamental truth of man, a truth to be brought to light or revealed to man himself, 'seen' through an appropriately elaborated discursive relation of himself to himself.

According to Derrida, this humanist presumption is, in one way or another, powerfully retained in the texts that dominated the inheritance of phenomenology in the first three-quarters of the twentieth century in Germany and France, giving that inheritance a distinctive backbone around which its interrupting adjustments move. This claim is given its most sustained expression in an essay entitled 'The Ends of Man', where Derrida highlights the following iterations within phenomenology – each already touched on in this book – of the thought that there is a unique and distinctive truth or meaning to human life:[34] Husserl construes 'man' (very classically) as the *animal rational*, and thence as the unique site of the unfolding of 'a teleology of reason' in (as) human history, a movement culminating, precisely, in 'transcendental phenomenology';[35] Heidegger's 'Dasein', 'though not "man"', is nevertheless nothing other than man', and the hope to reinstate or restore 'the essence of man', to reduce the distance that today makes Dasein ontologically 'far' from its own Being (as existing in an understanding of Being), would also be 'a restoration of a dignity' for the human to the extent that, 'in the thinking and the language of Being, the end of man has been prescribed';[36] Sartre's theme (problematically translating Heidegger's 'Dasein') is 'human-reality', a theme that, in a conceptual sense, 'translated the project of thinking the meaning of man' (the classical humanist project) as the (impossible yet structurally inevitable) project to be-in-itself-for-itself, that is to say 'the project of becoming God'.[37] We might add to Derrida's list that both Merleau-Ponty and Levinas also speak unequivocally of 'man' in terms of a radical distinction from anything merely animal. While Derrida finds the resources for a reading of the philosophical heritage that aims to criticise it radically from within some of these adjustments in phenomenology, he does not leave the humanist backbone of its dominant line of inheritance in place. Indeed, Derrida's attempt to 'shake the whole edifice' of Western metaphysics is pursued by freeing up forces within phenomenology that make its own humanist backbone tremble too.[38] I will come back to this critique of humanism in Part III of this chapter. First, however, we need to examine the rehabilitation of writing more closely. To preface that examination I want briefly to introduce a line of 'faith' that Derrida will oppose to the supposed 'truth' of classical humanist conceptions of history.

The exergue

With nothing short of the metaphysical tradition as such in view, the scope of Derrida's analysis is of course far wider and even more ambitious than even this ambitious critique of phenomenology suggests. Yet it is also tempered with a modesty that deserves stressing. Wanting to 'respect classical norms' while at the same time endeavouring inventively to take steps which will make enigmatic the founding resources of Western philosophy is not something Derrida claims to be able to undertake 'without embarrassing [himself] in the process'.[39] Indeed, Derrida's work of re-reading the classical metaphysical heritage of the West cannot avoid this embarrassment. This is not simply because his work inevitably produces hard-to-bear conceptual tensions and torsions (which it does), but rather because such tensions and torsions inevitably multiply and accumulate in a text that can only be written as a kind of preface to what remains to come *beyond* any determinate teleological (or indeed any determinate messianic or eschatological) horizon of anticipation. As we shall see, Derrida's engagement with Western modernity[2] has as its guiding light an openness to a future that *cannot* be reduced to anything at present live or available in our time (irreducible, for example, to a present anticipation or expectation of a determinate future present). How such a future that *remains* always radically 'to come' (always ahead of us and beyond every horizon of anticipation) can serve as a *guide* to research pursued 'here and now' is not something that such research will be able unproblematically to articulate in the terms of philosophy's traditional guidance on the relationship between, for example, guidance and light. What guides Derrida is not the light of a vision of 'man' but the impetus or impulse (in the 'here and now') of a commitment, a promise or a pledge not to close the future within the horizon of understanding of a given epoch; to leave room 'here and now' for the coming of something altogether unanticipated and new. As he puts it, 'if there is a categorical imperative, it consists in doing everything for the future to remain open'.[40] In this section I will work towards the clarification of this thought.

Of Grammatology is divided into two parts. Part I is entitled 'Writing Before the Letter' and 'outlines a theoretical matrix'.[41] This matrix is intended to serve to justify, as far as is possible, the effort at a rehabilitation of writing. Part II is entitled 'Nature, Culture, Writing' and engages with the task of going back behind traditional Western thinking about writing in its exemplary expression in the work of Rousseau. Part I begins with a short text of just over two pages, rather enigmatically (for me at least when I first read it) entitled 'Exergue', a text which is led off by the following series of three numbered quotations, forming, Derrida says, 'a triple exergue':[42]

1 The one who will shine in the science of writing will shine like the sun. A scribe (EP, p. 87).

O Samas (sun-god), by your light you can scan the totality of lands as if they were cuneiform signs (ibid.).

2 These three ways of writing correspond almost exactly to three different stages according to which one can consider men gathered into a nation. The depicting of objects is appropriate to a savage people; signs of words and of propositions, to a barbaric people; and the alphabet to civilised people. J.-J Rousseau, *Essai sur l'origine des langues*.

3 Alphabetic script is in itself and for itself the most intelligent. Hegel, *Enzyklopadie*.

The first numbered 'exergue' of the triplet is formed from two sayings which originate from sources before even classical antiquity. They are sayings of the (ancient) ancients that Derrida sourced from one of the books by the pre-historian André Leroi-Gourhan (entitled *L'Ecriture et la psychologie des peuples* and referred to in Derrida's text just cited as 'EP') that were in view in a review essay from which *Of Grammatology* was, in its first part, worked up. Together the two ancient sayings anticipate the project of Derrida's own grammatology; mark his interest in what is historically remote; and, since we have just noted a moment of modesty, indicate the frankly astonishing extent of his ambition. The second numbered 'exergue' of the triplet represents a profoundly *ethnocentric* (by which Derrida intends to pick out analyses which affirm a certain superiority of what is called 'Western Man') and *phonocentric* (by which Derrida intends to pick out analyses which affirm a certain priority to what is called 'speech') conception of the history of writing, anticipating what Derrida will present as Rousseau's exemplary position in the epoch that he (Derrida) wants to delimit. And if we anticipate that the kind of *intelligence* supposedly unique to 'man' has been determined over and over again in the history of Western philosophy as the capacity for grasping a purely intellectual order or an ideal *logos*, then the third numbered 'exergue' in the triplet, from Hegel, anticipates that the *ethnocentric* and *phonocentric* conception is also *logocentric* (by which Derrida intends to pick out analyses which affirm a certain irreducibility of what are called 'ideal meanings').

But what is an 'exergue'? According to the *Oxford Compact English Dictionary* an 'exergue' is .... But the word is not listed there. Many readers of analytic philosophy were prepared by J.L. Austin to do philosophy with a dictionary ('quite a concise one will do')[43] – with Derrida you often need a fairly good dictionary to read him at all. Trying again, then, what is an 'exergue'? According to the *Chambers Twentieth Century Dictionary* an 'exergue' is 'part of the reverse of a coin, below the main device, often filled up by the date, etc.'. That doesn't seem to help much either. However, the subsequent etymology does: '[Fr., – Gr. *ex*, out of, *ergon*, work.]'. So those like me who are initially perplexed by the title would have been better off had they been competent users of French (the singularies of a language are a favourite theme of Derrida's), and better still had they been attentive to the Greek root of the French word which indicates that we are concerned with something on the edge of or outside the main 'work', an outwork. So the 'Exergue' is in fact another preface, another *prae-fatio*, only this time Derrida reaches for a term for it that goes back to a 'saying-beforehand' which goes back behind (or goes on behind the back of) the Latin 'saying-beforehand'.[44]

Following the triplet of quotations Derrida tells us what his point is in quoting them, or what they are 'intended ... to focus attention on'.[45] We need to read the rest of the 'Exergue' carefully because Derrida spells it out very slowly. What the 'triple exergue' announces or is intended to focus attention on is:

(a) '*not only*' a marked *ethnocentricism* connected with the concept of writing
and
(b) '*nor merely*' a marked *logocentrism* (or 'the metaphysics of phonetic writing') which, he claims controls (and yet is *also* – in a certain way – constantly challenged by)
 (i) *the concept of writing* in a world where the phoneticization of writing must dissimulate its own history
 (ii) *the history of metaphysics* which has always assigned the origin of truth in general to the *logos*, and
 (iii) the concept of science
 and
(c) '*must not only*' announce that a science of writing, grammatology, is showing signs of liberation all over the world
but, with this 'triple exergue', finally
(d) '*I would like to suggest above all*' that a science of writing runs the risk of never being established as such (there could be for it, for example, no unity of a project, no statement of method, no statement of limits and so on). And that is because the very idea of such a science as one which would liberate us from the epoch dominated by the metaphysics of phonetic writing, the very idea of this science 'is meaningful for us' only *within* that epoch and that domination.

Despite this limitation, however, the fact that Derrida had his days (his 'here and now') in that epoch too did not stop him attempting to make more or less systematic steps; it did not simply stop him in his theoretical tracks with regard to a new grammatological project. He concludes the 'Exergue' with a final (and very characteristic)

(e) '*Perhaps*' a 'patient meditation and painstaking investigation on and around what is still provisionally called writing' may still be a way of being 'faithful to a future world', a future beyond the present horizon of determinate

188

anticipation or foresight, but which nevertheless has a kind of *imminence* such that it 'proclaims itself at present'.[46]

This 'future world' would be one in which the 'the values of sign, word, and writing' which have dominated our epoch will have been 'put into question' in a radically new way.[47] However, insofar as this future remains precisely beyond the horizon of every at present anticipatable future present we also remain in the (theoretically embarrassing) situation of being guided by a future world we do not *know* and hence have to admit that 'for that future world ... for that which guides our future anterior, there is as yet no exergue'.[48]

The logic of the preface was at work all along. However, with *Of Grammatology* we have a case of a preface-like work that aims to be faithful to a future which (Derrida can only, 'here and now', hope) *will have been* prefaced by his initiative. This is Derrida's 'messianism', a messianism *without* the determinate outline of an already anticipated arrival or end; a commitment or faithfulness to a future that is, precisely, uncharted. But note: this implies, concretely, the expression of what, after Levinas, we can *also* call a turn to the other, indeed to 'the *singularity* that is always other'.[49] This does not mean that the ambition is to write a text addressed exclusively to just one particular – but unknown – person. Openness to the other is, as we saw in Chapter 6, a moment within a dimension of *ethical separation*, an acknowledgement that 'every other (one) is every (bit) other'.[50] So what Derrida aims to achieve is not an epistemological relation to something currently unknown but a way of thinking that most effectively resists – and, indeed, to find what in our heritage already resists – a reductive, universalising, *a priori* anticipation of the essential possibilities, the proper identity, of every possible other. As we shall see, unlike Levinas, Derrida will not pre-emptively prescribe that one reserves an hospitable openness only for every other that is every bit human.

The significance (and I mean that in the literal as well as in the evaluative sense of that word) of Derrida's work is thus far from assured since its production is *premised* on a commitment or pledge or profession of faith to what lies essentially 'beyond the closure of knowledge': the uncharted future, the other. Nevertheless, rather as Heidegger wagered that the question of Being is a basic and fundamental question and not empty nonsense, so Derrida (more or less blindly) wagers that his rehabilitation of writing affords the strategically most powerful context for 'the wanderings of a way of thinking' that remains 'faithful and attentive' to what resists every effort of a 'complete gathering up', a wandering which resists – and, as I say, seeks out in the very heritage it aims to criticise what already resists – an apocalyptic desire for 'once for all' completeness.[51] The rehabilitation of writing thus belongs to an insistent and philosophically dislocating strategy for an affirmation, from the inside of the heritage, of what is classically called 'finitude'. Hence it is also a discourse on death. In Part II of this chapter I will examine the central features of this rehabilitation.

Part II: The rehabilitation of writing

Situating the linguistic turn

Derrida's rehabilitation of writing takes its point of departure from a gesture that he regards as the 'philosophical movement *par excellence*', a gesture that one finds already in Plato's condemnation of writing in the *Phaedrus*,[52] and hence taking in a heritage stretching back 'at least some twenty centuries'.[53] On the other hand, however, this heritage is not a static order, and within the epoch of this philosophical movement *par excellence* Derrida identifies a shifting development which, in its dominant mode, ultimately comes to a head when the attention of 'the most diverse researches' finally turns to *language*.[54]

As we shall see, what is often referred to today as the 'linguistic turn'[55] was, in Derrida's view, a very long time coming, and far from breaking with or turning away from the classical tradition of metaphysics it was, in its innermost trajectory, its culmination; making visible, he claims, its deep structural configuration, and not at all its coming to an historical end.

Is Derrida part of this linguistic turn? Is his work a moment of it? In view of his emphasis on the need to 'make explicit the experience of language' it would seem that it is.[56] Indeed, Derrida's writings are frequently regarded, and it would seem for good reason, as an extreme example of this turn to language. His claims that a work of reading 'cannot legitimately transgress the text towards something other than it', and (more notoriously) that 'there is nothing outside the text', are deeply suggestive of the idea that his work takes the linguistic turn, even outlines a form of linguistic idealism.[57] And this is undeniable: for Derrida, the 'person writing' and everything that is normally treated as 'the real life of these existences "of flesh and bone"' is not, in his view, something 'beyond or behind' what we usually like to believe we can unproblematically circumscribe as 'so-and-so's text'.[58] On the contrary, he insists that this 'real life' is itself something 'inscribed in a determined textual system'.[59]

So it is all just language then.

If that was what Derrida was saying he might even deserve the denunciations and smears that his work has been so regularly treated to. He would be guilty of an absurd *inflation* of language. If what Derrida appeals to, in the quotations cited above, as the 'textual system' were indeed a linguistic system, we could have been done with him long before he died. But it never was that.

To begin to understand a formulation like 'there is nothing outside the text' we have first to acknowledge that the notion of 'the text' at work here does not relate to a system of language but, in a sense of 'writing' that I will examine in this part, to *a general structure of writing*. For Derrida, language, and all that we (not incorrectly) think of as belonging to language – words, sentences, signs, speech, writing (in the usual sense), rules, meaning, reference and so on – is made possible by, is 'opened by' and must ultimately be understood in terms of general structures of writing (in his new sense): 'writing thus *comprehends* language'.[60]

With this affirmation it can be seen that Derrida's thought, far from being part of a distinctively linguistic turn in philosophy, is actually working already beyond it, precisely situating it. Indeed, as we shall see, at the opening of the opening chapter to *Of Grammatology*, Derrida emphasises that he does not regard the current turn to language as *a methodological must* for a satisfactory and rigorous post-metaphysical philosophy but as more like *an historical necessity* within the metaphysical epoch which we still inhabit. Moreover, for Derrida this is an epoch which 'seems to be approaching what is really its own *exhaustion*'.[61] With the appearance in various domains of a *graphematic* turn in our time we are, he suggests, witnessing nothing less than 'a new mutation in the history of writing, in history as writing':[62]

> However the topic is considered, the *problem of language* has never been simply one problem among others. But never as much as at present has it invaded, as such, the global horizon of the most diverse researches and the most heterogeneous discourses .... The devaluation of the word 'language' itself, and how, in the very hold it has upon us, it betrays a loose vocabulary, the temptation of a cheap seduction, the passive yielding to fashion, the consciousness of the avant-garde, in other words – ignorance – are evidences of this effect. This inflation of the sign 'language' is the inflation of the sign itself, absolute inflation, inflation itself. Yet, by one of its aspects or shadows, it is itself still a sign: this crisis is also a symptom. It indicates, as if in spite of itself, that a historico-metaphysical epoch must finally determine as language the totality of its problematic horizon. It must do so ... because ... language itself is menaced in its very life ... when it ceases to be self-assured, contained, and guaranteed by the infinite signified which seemed to exceed it.
>
> By a slow movement whose necessity is hardly perceptible, everything that for at least some twenty centuries tended toward and finally succeeded in being gathered under the name of language is beginning to let itself be transferred to, or at least summarized under the name of writing.[63]

This vast historical sweep, so confidently laid out at the opening to *Of Grammatology*, establishes an orientation from which Derrida never wavered. The abrupt hostility to the contemporary inflation of language, to the so-called linguistic turn, is distinctive too. The widespread reach of that turn (which is, he suggests, much more of a 'straight ahead' than a 'turn' in our heritage) is not regarded as a fertile philosophical advance but as a kind of cultural poverty, a movement which, far from being justified by clearly articulated reasons, is characterised by its 'loose vocabulary', 'cheap seduction', 'fashion', all in all a turn marked more by 'ignorance' than a powerful new theoretical or scientific advance. On the other hand, Derrida regards this historical movement in which the sign is pushed to the fore as itself an indicative sign or a symptom: language comes to the centre of every philosophical problematic because everything that seemed solidly to render its status as essentially *un*problematic, everything that had assured us that it (language) *is* what we thought it *should* be – namely, the system of purely external or sensible signification of an order of pure intelligibility (of 'meaning' construed as pure ideality), an order traditionally grasped in terms of *the divine word* or *divine logos* – has begun to melt into air.

One might want to invoke the idea that 'God is dead' to interpret the kind of disenchanting claim that Derrida will make against this 'enchanted' conception of linguistic meaning.[64] But I would recommend reading what Derrida has to say about the history of (or as) writing, and his presentation of our present time as witnessing 'the end of the book',[65] as a new and powerful way of giving content to that rather heady slogan. Of course, the possibility of making sense of such a massive motif through the seemingly unremarkable and insignificant topic of writing can seem pretty extraordinary. But according to Derrida there are systematic and irreducible links between, on the one hand, the conception of the sign through which, still today, we generally obtain our understanding of writing and, on the other hand, 'the epoch of Christian creationism ... when these appropriate the resources of Greek conceptuality'.[66]

Central to this linkage is the classical construal of linguistic signs as the unity of a sensible signifier and an intelligible signified or meaning. While this conception of meaning need not everywhere be related to the idea of the divine *logos* of a creator God, as the 'pure face of intelligibility', it is still immediately caught up with the idea of the *logos* in general, the idea, that is, of an order of *pure* intelligibility. And this idea simply cannot be 'innocently separated' from its 'metaphysical-theological roots' in the thought of the divine *logos* which, it is written, *was* 'in the beginning': ultimately inseparable, then, from the idea of the 'word or face' of God.[67] On this view, 'the sign and divinity' thus have 'the same place and time of birth'.[68] Or again, 'the age of the sign is essentially theological'.[69] And in such an age *writing*, the very image of the material or sensible signifier *essentially* exterior to the *logos* as pure intelligibility, can only find itself 'debased'.[70]

At this point one might begin to appreciate a certain deep historical significance in the fact that it is writing and not language that is now beginning to impose itself as the gathering point for thought and research in various domains. Indeed, it would suggest that the understanding of the figure of the human, of 'man' himself, may be undergoing an epochal shift: the fundamental structures of human life and human history will begin to be conceived otherwise than in terms of the *zóon logon echon* or *animal rationale* or the creature made in God's image on its way or taking itself home on a journey towards its proper end. As I have indicated, in this humanist tradition the supposedly unique creature, 'man', is conceived as having an essence or existence that is *radically* 'opposed to animality'.[71] But when writing comes to the fore, when the possibility of meaning is acknowledged to entail the impossibility of its ideally pure ideality, when thinking the *meaning* of man can no longer be framed as a matter of grasping the (metaphysical or essential) *truth* of man (for example as the creature or living thing with the capacity for grasping the *logos* or with the capacity for reason or transcendence or language or self-presence), when we find that thinking the meaning of man can therefore no longer be elaborated in terms of a teleo-messianic promise concerning the proper *end* of man, then 'we' certainly are on another heading, indeed something other than a heading for what has traditionally been conceived as 'man'.

On the other hand, in the absence of a conception of 'man' that is 'in the running' to a uniquely human end this epochal shift might seem only to leave us standing still, left 'at the starting line'.[72] But, as Derrida affirms, it may also give one the 'strength and speed' to keep moving otherwise, doing everything one can to keep the future open, doing everything one can to resist a totalising representation of history where the future and the alterity of every other are reduced to an already anticipated arrival.

While Derrida's reassessment of writing is bound up with an effort to liberate it – and us – from the classical humanist onto-theological axiology in which it – and we – still remain, he also recognises that, in fact, within the epoch of the sign (our epoch) the sign 'writing' has not always been condemned to a kind of fallen secondariness. Within that epoch there has always also been (as one might have suspected) 'good' as well as 'bad' writing. However, what is at issue with such good writing has always been an essentially *figurative* or metaphorical sense of writing, a sense once more and at once connected with the divine *logos* (especially evident in the medieval idea of 'the book of Nature' that would be 'God's writing'), a sense of writing which precisely *defines* (and note the interesting inversion of the usual order of priority here) the *literal* meaning as a merely human tool in the sensible world: writing, as one of man's technical instruments, is the secondary supplement to speech, speech appearing here as the more ethereal (and in so-called 'inner speech', itself fundamentally *non-exterior*) and natural first signifier. Human writing, the (secondary) signifier of the (primary) signifier, is just a mark, a trace of a genuine presence, it is 'the dead letter', and has nothing to do with (or can only threaten to contaminate) the pure self-present life of spirit and the soul, nothing to do with any good writing that it is the task of literate civilised man to study and learn:

> The good writing has therefore always been *comprehended*. Compre-
> hended as that which had to be comprehended: within a nature or a
> natural law, created or not, but first thought within an eternal pre-
> sence. Comprehended, therefore, within a totality, and enveloped in a
> volume or a book. The idea of the book is the idea of a totality, finite
> or infinite, of the signifier; this totality of the signifier cannot be a
> totality, unless a totality constituted by the signified pre-exists it,
> supervises its inscriptions and its signs, and is independent of it in its

ideality .... If I distinguish the text from the book, I shall say that the destruction of the book, as it is now under way in all domains, denudes the surface of the text.[73]

The motif of the 'end of the book' is not a prediction that libraries will start closing down, but belongs to a way of coming to terms with a situation which we have, in a certain way, always already known is our own but which today is 'in the process of making itself known *as such*':[74] namely, that there never was an order of pure intelligibility, no *logos* or good writing that would be an (ideally pure) ideal presence, a pre-existing and occult (that is, hidden) 'spiritual realm' beyond what is denounced as bad (because wholly material and exterior) writing.

Equally, however, what is in the process of making itself known as such today is that everything that has been traditionally situated as fundamentally *external* to (and hence always threatening to contaminate) what has been regarded as the life of the mind proper to 'man' (for example the irreducibly 'in the world' order of marks, tracks and traces, presumed accidents of what is essential to human life and which are from that point of view non-accidentally connected to – supposedly – 'merely animal' existence) is, in fact and in principle, the very condition of possibility of that life; that, for example, 'there is no linguistic sign before writing'.[75] We have to be careful here, for Derrida's affirmation of 'writing before the letter', a textile of traces that will exceed and comprehend language, is no more an affirmation of the historical primacy of what is traditionally regarded as 'bad' writing than it is an endorsement of its metaphorical other. Rather, and beyond the opposition of good and bad writing (and so perhaps also 'beyond good and evil' as traditionally determined in general),[76] Derrida's affirmation of a turn in our time marked by the 'end of the book' is, like Nietzsche's affirmation that 'God is dead', neither a brutally bald naturalism nor a hopeless nihilism – as if human life and history are now regarded as somehow fundamentally meaningless or debased, diseased in comparison to its formerly affirmed greatness and spiritual health. As Derrida puts it, 'one can no longer see disease in substitution when one sees that the substitute is substituted for a substitute'.[77]

But this does not leave everything as it is either. Or rather – and this is a decidedly phenomenological gesture even as it interrupts its dominant inheritance – the rehabilitation of writing leaves us with no way of giving content to the idea of *criticising* or *regulating* or in general *assessing* anything that does, for an individual, give life a meaning in terms of attaining a truth that is already 'written' (for example in some kind of 'good' writing we might intuit or have revealed to us) 'outside the text'. That kind of reassuring cognitivism is not to be had – and never was even when 'Western man' lived a life which firmly presumed it was.

The point is worth emphasising that it is primarily the fundamental cognitivism with regard to the idea of the '*logos*' that is in question here. However, that does not diminish the significance of the criticism. Christian scripture has Jesus saying, 'I am the Way, the Truth and the Life', and, as Renford Bambrough stresses,

> the orthodox and traditional interpretation of this saying insists on the fundamental priority of the Truth. It is because Christianity claims to offer the truth about the nature of the world and man and God and Christ that it requires and expects of men that they should follow a particular Way and live a particular Life.[78]

Beyond this cognitivism perhaps there is still Life in the Way that takes seriously (if not literally) an idea of the divine *logos*. I imagine that the Way here would have to be *exceptionally narrow* and *profoundly one's own*; one would be walking one's own tightrope. But, really, I am in no position to judge this *at all*.

Derrida's critique of the cognitivist claims of traditional humanism is, without doubt, an extraordinary radicalisation and acceleration of the Enlightenment critique of enchanted nature and the *logos* as pure order of intelligibility. And one can readily see why the authors who Derrida finds most compelling are those who have most powerfully questioned the fundamental transcendentalism, supernaturalism and ethnocentrism of Western logocentrism – Rousseau, Marx, Nietzsche, Freud, Saussure, Husserl, Heidegger, Levinas, Austin. Some strange bedfellows here, and each can and will be criticised by Derrida for falling short in some respects, for repeating the very logocentrism they also criticise. However, for Derrida these thinkers do not stand *squarely* within the logocentrism of the Greco-Christian epoch and their importance resides in the power of their work to call into question its onto-theological roots and axiology.

This is not to say that Derrida regards himself as in a position simply to reject these roots. Indeed, as I have indicated, he retains a fundamentally phenomenological commitment to the thought that any breakthrough which would hope genuinely to '*criticize* metaphysics radically' must (can only) make (inventive) use of the resources of the metaphysical heritage we actually inhabit:[79] there is no claim to a critique from outside or from sideways on here. However, as we have seen, he does situate his work as aiming to be 'faithful and attentive' to a certain 'outside'; to an uncharted future, the other beyond the horizon of understanding that is gifted in our time. And for Derrida the fundamental lever of this radical and radically ethical criticism of metaphysics is the re-evaluation of that hitherto hardly philosophically central or philosophically unavoidable concept of writing.

According to Derrida, then, the so-called linguistic turn is not just an event (happy or not) which happened to take place not so long ago. On the contrary, he regards the emergence of the *problem* of language as belonging profoundly to the history of Western metaphysics. However, the movement of that history is also characterised by the ever more critical questioning of and uncertainty regarding the onto-theological presuppositions of traditional Western thought, and Derrida belongs to that general movement of 'enlightenment' critique too. Nevertheless, what Derrida perceives in the modern focus on language is not fertile ground for further rational and scientific critiques of pre-modern superstitions but an inconspicuous and essentially dogmatic retention of fundamental motifs of the very onto-theological metaphysical tradition that it claims to supersede: the last, most surreptitious and perhaps most lasting stand of the logocentric epoch.

On the basis of a 'theoretical matrix' that presents the axiology of this epoch as everywhere caught up in a metaphysical and ethnocentric ideal of purely phonetic writing, Derrida will make a stand against the modern inflation of the sign 'language'. And, as I have indicated, what he finds most significant and interesting is not the so-called *linguistic turn* but signs of a growing *graphematic turn* in the historical tide. For some time now people have said, 'language for action, movement, thought, reflection, consciousness, unconsciousness, experience, affectivity, etc.'. Today, however, Derrida suggests, 'we tend to say "writing" for all that and more':

> to designate not only the physical gestures of literal pictographic or ideographic inscription, but also the totality of what makes it possible; and also, beyond the signifying face, the signified face itself. And thus we say 'writing' for all that gives rise to an inscription in general, whether it is literal or not and even if what it distributes in space is alien to the order of the voice: cinematography, choreography, of course, but also pictorial, musical, sculptural 'writing'. One might also speak of athletic writing, and with even greater certainty of military or political writing in view of the techniques that govern those domains today. All this to describe not only the system of notation secondarily connected with these activities but the essence and content of these activities themselves. It is also in this sense that the contemporary biologist speaks of writing and *pro-gram* in relation to the most elementary processes of information within the living cell. And, finally, whether it has essential limits or not, the entire field covered by the cybernetic program will be the field of writing. If the theory of cybernetics is by itself to oust all metaphysical concepts – including the concepts of soul, of life, of value, of choice, of memory – which until recently served to separate the machine from man, it must conserve the notion of writing, trace, *grammè* [written mark], or *grapheme*, until its own historico-metaphysical character is also exposed.[80]

Supposing this is indeed the way things are going (and, with certain pockets of classical-meaning-emphasising resistance, it seems to me that it is even more obvious than it was in 1967 that 'we tend to say' today 'writing' and 'code' and 'programme' and 'text' rather than 'language' and 'sign' and 'meaning' in our articulation of various aspects, particularly deep aspects, of human life and history), *why* should we take the idea of a graphematic mutation any more seriously or regard it as more significant than the so-called linguistic turn? Of course, I have already begun to suggest why a graphematic turn may have profound historico-metaphysical implications. But Derrida knows that unless he offers an 'attempt to justify it'[81] his involvement in this turn within the history of (or as) writing will be guilty of precisely 'giving in to the movement of inflation' which he had denounced so trenchantly in the so-called linguistic turn.[82] So what could possibly justify it? What is it about writing, if anything, that makes it fit to be the gathering point for so many developments taking place today? In the next section I will outline the way I have come to see the shape of Derrida's justification for engaging in the graphematic turn.[83]

Writing and iterability

What we might call Derrida's 'master argument' concerning what he will call the 'iterability' of writing purports to show that 'the traits which can be recognized in the classical, narrowly defined concept of writing' are *'necessarily valid* for all signs'.[84] While this claim to generality does not, for this reason, straightforwardly change or challenge the 'usual meaning' of the word 'writing', it does put pressure on what we are inclined to say when we are asked about writing, and indeed what we are inclined to say about words of a language in general.

What, then, is the classical, narrowly defined concept of 'writing'? According to Derrida, the classical conception regards writing as, first and foremost, an instrument or technical means of communication and, indeed, 'an especially potent means of communication'.[85] What is the 'potency' that is supposed to be so specific to writing? On the classical interpretation that Derrida wants to criticise, writing emerges as a technical device when the desire or need arises to extend the field of communication to addressees who are present but who are out of range of the natural voice. Writing thus first appears in fact when the space of sociality has changed to the point that we need or want to send messages to others who are 'not only distant but outside of the entire field of vision and beyond earshot'.[86]

In his first challenge to the classical construal Derrida asks whether in fact and in principle this distance 'must be capable of being carried to a certain absoluteness of absence' if writing is to be possible. The question is then: is the absence of the addressee that is supposed to specify writing to be characterised in terms only of the distant presence of a receiver, or should the scope of this concept of absence be widened to include, at the limit, the possibility of the addressee's absolute absence – specifically, his or her death.

I write a letter and address it with a proper name. To do this is to write to an empirically determinable receiver or addressee. Of course, it is always possible that before receiving my written message this addressee or these addressees may die. Does this prevent my writing from being read? Of course not. However, Derrida does not want the obviousness of this point to be taken to reflect a commonsense supplement to the traditional view of writing. On the contrary, with the re-evaluation of the relationship of writing to absence Derrida wants radically to transform the conceptual economy in this area. I will explain this.

Note first of all that the traditional interpretation of writing does not mention the absence of the producer of the written mark who sends it away to be read elsewhere. It is clear, however, that parallel considerations must hold here too:

> To write is to produce a mark ... which my future disappearance will not in principle, hinder in its functioning .... For a writing to be a writing it must continue to 'act' and to be readable even when what is called the author of the writing no longer answers for what he has written .... The situation of the writer is, concerning the written text, basically the same as that of the reader.[87]

Derrida is not concerned here with writing or death only as empirical phenomena. Rather, his concern is with the logical possibility and not merely the physical opportunity for a written text to remain readable when the absence of the sender or the addressee is no longer a mode of presence (distant presence) but a radical or absolute absence (death). And his claim, a claim that he acknowledges as retaining a debt to Husserl's analysis of the ideality of expressive signs even as it interrupts that analysis,[88] is that the possibility of it functioning again beyond (or in the absolute absence of) the 'living present' of its context of production or its empirically determined destination is part of what it is to *be* ('here and now') a written, that is to say readable, mark: to be what it is all writing must be capable of functioning beyond the death of *any* (although of course not *every*) empirically determinable user in general. We can thus propose the following 'law' of writing: a mark that is not structurally readable – and in that sense iterable – beyond the death of the empirically determinable producer and receiver would not be writing.

The general claim, then, is that the *possibility* of 'functioning in the absence of' implied by the classical conception of writing must be capable of being brought to an *absolute* limit if writing 'here and now' is to constitute itself as such. Any event of writing or reading, if it is to take place as such 'here and now' – and hence, in this contextual event, for the message to function as such, or, in other words, to *mean* something – presumes as its condition of possibility the possibility of an iteration in the radical absence of this one – up to and including, for example, an iteration in a future that remains to come.

So, any written message is readable only to the extent that a reader can read whatever a sender could write in the radical absence of that sender: *writing can and must be able to do without the presence of the sender.* Equally, any message is readable only to the extent that a reader can read whatever the sender could write in the absolute absence of the receiver's presence: *writing can and must be able to do without the presence of the receiver.*

These two possible absences 'construct the possibility of the message itself'.[89] That is, and *pace* the classical interpretation, it is not the relative permanence of the written word (its relatively continuous presence in being) which makes iterations possible in the absence of the sender (who is present 'over here') or receiver (who is present 'over there'); rather, the written mark is precisely made to make up for these *possible absences*, made to do – to act, to function – without the presence of its producer or intended receiver.

It is with these thoughts in view that the idea of a strategic generalisation of the term 'writing' becomes forceful. According to Derrida's argument the absence that characterises writing is a function not of the fact of its relative persistence or permanence but of logically necessary preconditions of its status *as* readable writing. It is true that these preconditions are most perspicuous in the case of writing, but what if these possibilities of absence can be acknowledged to be part of the structure of *every* event of communication, no matter of what kind, whatever the species?

The idea here is that a 'singular event' that functions as a means of communication (for example an event of speech) can *be* the event it is only on condition of a necessary or structural relation to an iteration that is *another such* singular event which is *not present* at the time of its production or reception – another such event which is not what it is except in its relation to *another such* event, another such event which is not what it is except in its relation to *another such* event, and so on. Although the movement is fundamentally without limit, numbers are not accumulating here. Or, rather, the limit is: *not once.* This is what Derrida is insisting upon when he states that the 'unity of the signifying form' that is 'required to permit its recognition' in any 'here and now' 'only constitutes itself by virtue of its iterability'.[90]

There are two major points to bring out here. First, it goes along with this thought that 'for a word to *be* at all is for it *to be used*'.[91] Second, and subsequently, it brings into prominence that the possibility of a written mark functioning *again* in the absence of the current presence of its user or its current context of use is not just a supplementary benefit of writing, but internal to its *being* the 'writing' it is. In every case, an event of writing (and now, let us say, *no matter what kind*) thus breaks away from its determinable author or producer or context of production. *What* I *do* now must, in its iterability, be sufficiently detachable from what I do *now* for it to *be* the writing it is 'here and now'.

Now, precisely because what is recognised in the case of writing is, in this way, made to do without (any particular) me and without (any particular) here and now, it also gives itself to be experienced (each time) by (any) me as possessing a transcendent identity, a meaning. But this is an idea of a here-and-now-expressed-in-the-event meaning, that is, given the structural irreducibility of the relation to *another such* event internal to (every) such event 'here and now', a kind of illusion of transcendence, an experience or interpretation of a pure and present ideal identity that comes with the territory but which is never given: 'a kind of structural lure, what Kant would have called a transcendental illusion'.[92]

In *Limited Inc.* Derrida takes up a potential counterexample to the idea that writing has a constitutively necessary relation to the possibility of absence: John Searle's example of 'a shopping list for myself'; something that can function, Searle supposes, in the presence of its recipient and without requiring any relation to his or her absence. In what could be read as the beginning of a commentary on the first paragraph of Wittgenstein's *Philosophical Investigations*, Derrida offers the following reminder/rejoinder:

> *At the very moment* 'I' make a shopping list, I know (I use 'knowing' here as a convenient term to designate the relations that I necessarily entertain with the object being constructed) that it will only be a list if it implies my absence, if it already detaches itself from me in order to function beyond my 'present' act and if it is utilizable at another time, in the absence of my-being-present-now.[93]

And this same structure would be evident even if I just kept the list in my head, or repeatedly said it out loud as I went along. Such events too, Derrida will argue, are, in their iterability, 'writing' in his new sense. The factually late emergence of what we usually call writing, the eventual emergence of a relatively permanent mark that can do without the current presence of a determinable sender or recipient, should not mislead us here. For that emergence is *possible* because, in principle, the possibility of this absence is part of the logical structure of *any* sign, linguistic or not, human or not, in general; part of the conditions of possibility of any 'means of communication' in general. And this is why we might speak of a 'writing before the letter' that makes what we normally call 'the written letter' possible. According to Derrida, then, language – and not just language – must be grasped as 'a possibility founded on the general possibility of writing'.[94]

That this structure is most perspicuous in writing provides a *raison d'être* for its generalisation, but taking and retaining the old name 'writing' also ensures an effective intervention into the fabric and axiology of the heritage that has hitherto dominated the issue. A fundamental motif of that fabric is that it relegates writing to a position of debased secondariness: the graphic representation of the phonetic representation of signified senses or ideal thought-contents or meanings. If, however, anything that could function as a means of communication must possess, in its iterability, the structure of writing, the traditional conception of the linguistic sign must give way to an understanding of generalised 'writing', a conception of marks that are, in their essential iterability, *irreducible to anything that can be simply present in the present*. The metaphysical tradition of presence and the Greco-Christian idea of an underlying ideal rational order or pure ideal *logos*, potentially present to the properly adjusted understanding, finds itself dislocated by resources internal to its own construction. Hence the form of argument is deconstruction, not simply the proposal of a new or rival construction

In this section I have followed Derrida's attempt to call into question the very idea of the linguistic 'sign' or 'word' as something to be construed in terms of the unity of or relation between an outer or in any case *sensible* representation or expression ('signifier') and an inner or in any case *ideal* thought-content or meaning ('signified'). Working within the conceptuality of the tradition we are brought to see a profoundly therapeutic point to affirming, against the dominant logocentric construction of the tradition, that *anything that accompanied writing* (anything that would seem to give these supposedly 'dead' marks 'life') *would just be more writing*. There is in this critique, in a formulation I will have to clarify in a moment, a 'reduction *of* meaning – that is, of the signified'.[95]

While this formulation risks misunderstanding, it puts Derrida's argument into a relation to phenomenology that is fundamental to it. For insofar as phenomenology has involved a commitment to achieving a 'reduction *to* meaning'[96] – 'literally a Husserlian proposition',[97] as Derrida notes, but this is a project still visible in Heidegger's attempt to make explicit, precisely, 'the *meaning* of Being' through a 'reading of the text Dasein'[98] – Derrida's rehabilitation of writing will necessarily take the form of 'a critique of phenomenology'.[99]

I will examine the ethical core of this critique of phenomenology in the next section. However, as I say, Derrida's contrasting effort at a 'reduction *of* meaning' could easily be misunderstood. Indeed, it invites – and has invited – the idea that Derrida's deconstructive thought (presumably incoherently) proposes the *elimination* of the very idea of 'meaning'. And there are remarks which would seem to support an eliminativist reading of Derrida on meaning. For example, he (presumably incoherently) writes that 'writing literally means nothing'.[100] Remarks like this make it seem that Derrida wants to make theoretical claims that would conflict with a life with language that is (I would think) irreducibly committed to talk of 'meaning'. However, as should now be clear, the conception of writing outlined by the argument from iterability does not aim to eliminate ordinary (and hence iterable) talk of 'meaning' but to criticise the classical conception of meaning that is embedded in the idea of an event of speech that would express an ideally pure presence, a pure ideality that would be fully present in the present. Indeed, as Derrida immediately goes on to insist in the passage from 'The Ends of Man' I have been citing, to affirm the 'reduction *of* meaning' is *not* a matter of 'erasing or destroying meaning' but 'a question of determining the possibility of meaning on the basis of a "formal" organisation which in itself has no meaning'.[101] This '"formal" organisation' is, we now see, the system of general 'writing', or, as he puts it in *Of Grammatology*, 'a determined textual system', in which our life has its inseparable life.[102] Purity, on the other hand, the ideal purity of a pure ideality or classical meaning, is never to be had in the present event of such writing. The irreducible singularity of every such event, the specific 'here and now' of marks put into play, could not emerge as such (as a singular event of writing) unless 'the eventhood' of this event was 'in itself . . . repetitive or citational in its structure, or rather, since those two words may lead to confusion: iterable'.[103] Geoffrey Bennington frames the nerve of Derrida's response to a tradition 'tainted by the tantalization of purity' in the following formulation:

> What might look like a negative contingency which might affect or compromise the ideal purity of an event is integrated into the description of that event as a condition of possibility which is simultaneously the condition of the *a priori* impossibility of the event's ever achieving that ideal purity.[104]

As Derrida puts it elsewhere, 'contrary to what phenomenology . . . has tried to make us believe' and, indeed, more generally, 'contrary to what our desire cannot fail to be tempted to into believing', 'the thing itself [the present "meaning"] always steals away'.[105]

Throughout this chapter, and indeed throughout this book, I have wanted to highlight the involvement of the phenomenological philosophers whose starting points I have been examining in a wider tradition of Western humanism. In the next and final part of this chapter I want to draw some of the themes of this book together by examining further the critique of classical humanism that shapes Derrida's interruption of phenomenology and indeed shapes his deconstruction of the classical tradition in philosophy in general.

Part III: Deconstructing humanism

The difference between humans and animals

The system of interpretation of writing that has dominated in the age of the sign is, I think, fundamentally and powerfully disrupted by Derrida's argument from iterability. In a rare methodological clarification he describes his deconstruction as an 'intervention' that effects 'a reversal . . . and a general displacement' of the traditional evaluative hierarchy which privileges speech over writing.[106] However, in a gesture which I have suggested belongs profoundly to the legacy of phenomenology, we can now see that this deconstruction of the traditional logocentric construction does not 'destroy structures from the outside'; on the contrary, it is 'not possible and effective . . . except by inhabiting those structures' in a novel way.[107] Indeed, as we have seen, Derrida's discussion works on that structure by putting to work acknowledged (but marginalised) predicates from within it against the evaluative order that has traditionally dominated it. So this deconstructive reading is not simply a 'destroying of the tradition' at all but rather an affirmation of what in the heritage 'has always resisted the prior organization of forces . . . the dominant force organizing the hierarchy that we may refer to, in brief, as logocentric'.[108]

Thus in Derrida's work a graphematic turn 'makes known as such' a movement of *logocentric construction* which, in fact and in principle, has always also been a movement vulnerable to *graphematic deconstruction*. However, as I have also tried to stress, to affirm the ubiquity of writing and the text is not to suggest that reality is (really just) a system of notation. The general text is not a structure of language but that 'textual' whereabouts in which our life has its inseparable life, a whereabouts never altogether separable from but never altogether reducible to the where(ver)abouts 'where we believe we are'.[109]

So the idea of inscription within a text belongs to an attempted specification or clarification of the structure of world-inhabitation that marks the life and history of human beings, or, more precisely, that marks a life with language. In fact, however, part of that effort aims also to show that it is not applicable to human beings alone. The elaboration of this structure in terms of the mark and trace deliberately aims to be hospitable to non-human animal life, and thus deliberately aims to resist the humanism of the logocentric heritage. The critique of humanism is an aspect of Derrida's thought that, while clearly permeating it, is often more operational than thematic, more implicit than worked out. However, as we have seen, he is particularly keen to stress and to distance himself from the stubborn humanism that traverses the phenomenological inheritance of philosophy to which he is most indebted, a humanism he sees underpinning phenomenological conceptions of the 'life-world', of the 'there' and (patently) of 'human-reality'. It is appropriate, then, to finish the examination of Derrida's interruption of phenomenology with this theme. For it is in the lines of this enormous and enormously complex field that Derrida's radicalisation of phenomenology also displaces the backbone of its dominant inheritance.

From the start Derrida was clear that his work of deconstruction was pitted against 'the opposition of nature and culture, animality and humanity, etc.'.[110] But what resources are there for taking any new steps in this area? As I have indicated, Derrida's most continuous gesture is to deploy terms that are not marked out for human use alone, terms that might thus 'free the space for another discourse on "the animal"'.[111] It would be a mistake, however, to regard Derrida as attempting to forge a conventionally naturalistic alternative to traditional humanism. Indeed, as so often in his work, his steps retain a considerable respect for the tradition he wants to criticise. To help situate Derrida's thought on this topic I want to start off with a conception that is, in my view, very close to his own but which, perhaps, takes philosophical risks – risks of conceptual purity – that Derrida would ultimately want to question. The conception is presented in a fascinating passage I have already referred to by Cora Diamond:

> The difference between human being and animals is not to be discovered by studies of Washoe or the activities of dolphins. It is not

that sort of study or ethology or evolutionary theory that is going to tell us the difference between us and animals: the difference is, I have suggested, a central concept for human life and is more an object of contemplation than observation (though that might be misunderstood; I am not suggesting it is a matter of intuition). One source of confusion here is that we fail to distinguish between 'the difference between animals and people' and 'the differences between animals and people'; the same sort of confusion occurs in discussions of the relationship of men and women. In both cases people appeal to scientific evidence to show that 'the difference' is not as deep as we think; but all that such evidence can show, or show directly, is that the differences are less sharp than we think. In the case of the difference between animals and people, it is clear that we form the idea of this difference, create the concept of the difference, knowing perfectly well the overwhelmingly obvious similarities.[112]

This comes from the best attempt I know to affirm without reservation the idea of a distinctive difference between human beings and other animals. But appreciation of its novelty requires that we situate it within and against the background of the tradition it helps to expose. That tradition is clearly in view in Derrida's elaboration of the logocentric heritage. Indeed, he has defined logocentrism as 'first of all a thesis regarding the animal, the animal deprived of the *logos*, deprived of the "*can-have-the-logos*"'.[113] It is the logocentric epoch which has made Diamond's affirmation possible, but it is an epoch dominated by a view of the human difference from which her affirmation must also be, as far as possible, disentangled.

For reasons I will come back to shortly, while I do not think that the dominant idea of the human difference is simply rooted in 'theoretical' resources, we can follow Derrida's identification of the Greek and Christian sources of the logocentric epoch into the terrain of this theme by taking our theoretical cue from the corresponding Greek and Christian determinations of the uniqueness of *homo animalis* identified by Heidegger; the anthropology of classical humanism: the conception of the human as the *zōon logon echon* (*animal rationale*) and the creationist conception of the human as made in God's image.

The Western idea of the human difference has been worked on and worked over – made something of – by a humanist tradition that is, I think, fundamentally rooted in these two sources. However, it is clear that certain aspects of this classical tradition are now losing their common appeal. In particular, many today are beginning to think that the idea that the human difference is something we humans have *discovered* to be the case (through either metaphysical investigations or revelations, in any case as 'an object of observation', as Diamond puts it) should not be sustained. Derrida, like Diamond, is firmly located among those who are *not content* with that idea.

However, there is a position taken by many others of those who recoil from classical humanism which is, in Derrida's (and Diamond's) view, just as unsatisfactory. The recoil position regards the idea that we have discovered this abyssal difference as a *factual error* on our part, the residue of less enlightened times when we had not got our understanding of nature and ourselves as natural creatures right. Today, some think, we have the power, the theoretical power, to get things right, and regard it as well established that, in fact, we are just another species of living thing, a living thing that ultimately differs from other living things only by degree.

In many of his texts, and most directly in his late essay 'The Animal that Therefore I Am (More to Follow)', Derrida attempts to negotiate a path between the logocentric discontinuism of classical humanism and the biologistic continuism of modern naturalism. On the one hand, he rejects the classical humanist assumption that the difference of which it speaks is something we have discovered to be the case. He rejects, that is, the idea that there is a truth of man (a distinctive meaning to human life and history) that would *justify* talk of a radical break between the animal and human. On the other hand, however, he also rejects the modern naturalist assumption that the traditional Western understanding of this radical break or difference is simply the result of a *defective* means of establishing what is the case, something that has been overcome by the understanding of nature and ourselves as natural creatures provided by modern naturalism. To insist that there is 'homogeneous continuity' where we clearly find an undeniable 'abyssal rupture' really is, Derrida thinks, simply 'too asinine [*bête*]'.[114]

I think Derrida is right to attack both targets. However, in what looks like an exhaustive either/or situation (the human condition as either a fundamental break from every animal condition or in a fundamental continuity with it), his wanting to take on both fronts seems to leave no room for an alternative. In my view, Derrida's route between classical humanism and modern naturalism is forged through an analysis which rejects the shared premise that serves as the fulcrum for the traditional seesaw. Consistent with the basic trajectory of the deconstruction of logocentrism, Derrida identifies at the problematic heart of both the classical humanist and the modern naturalist accounts the same fundamental *cognitivism* with regard to proper appreciation of the human difference. Both claim that a proper grasp of its significance is ultimately, *decisively*, a matter of our having adjusted our beliefs to how things really are. This, I want to suggest, is what Derrida resists. Indeed, he wants to resist quite generally the temptation to affirm in theoretical reflection what David Wiggins has called the appearance of a 'naïve cognitivism' in our 'unphilosophical' understanding of meaning and value.[115] Not that a philosophically enlightened thinker – for example a thinker who is attracted to the idea that the *difference* between humans and animals is 'more an object of contemplation than observation' – is going to give up on the idea that 'the *differences* between higher and lower forms of life' are real or to suppose that they are simply fictitious. On the contrary, such a thinker can comfortably accept that they are even *objective*. However, this thinker 'will not back down from [the] denial that these differences are *decisive*' with respect to the significance we attach to them in the creation of the concept of the difference. As Wiggins puts it:

> Such differences may be important to us. But they depend for their significance upon a framework that is a free construct, not upon something fashioned in a manner that is answerable to how anything really is.[116]

This anti-cognitivist conception is, I think, the crucial presupposition for dismounting the seesaw between classical humanism and modern naturalism. In 'The Animal that Therefore I Am (More to Follow)' Derrida's alternative is elaborated on the basis of a trenchant objection to the modern naturalist's view. As I have noted, modern naturalism typically repudiates classical humanism on the basis of an affirmation of objective continuity. Derrida contests the modern naturalist's conception of the facts in this area. In his view, the objective differences between different forms of life are not mere variations on a single (hence fundamentally general) 'animal' theme but involve a plethora of distinctive and sometimes quite singular life-structures. The claim here is clearly not that naturalism is in itself an intolerable position. In fact, Derrida's fundamental objection to modern naturalism is that its recoil from humanism effectively retains the classical humanist's old singular/general category of 'the animal'. Attention to what is objective requires that we avoid this corralling 'crime against animality' and properly 'take into account a multiplicity of heterogeneous structures and limits'.[117] For Derrida, then (unlike for either the classical humanist or the modern naturalist), there is no general 'animal condition' but a rough weave of differences and similarities among different things we call 'alive'. In view here is a differential field with 'structural breaks' and 'ruptures', not a space in which differences are always differences of degree.

Of course, Derrida's (let's say) reformed naturalism is pitted equally against the classical humanist's conception of an objective oppositional duality between pure animal life, on the one hand, and human life as animal life transformed, on the other. However, as should be clear, the emphasis on structural breaks also allows him to retain a sympathetic if critical ear to the classical humanist's objections to modern naturalism. This is particularly evident in a passage of discussion in 'The Animal that Therefore I Am (More to Follow)' devoted to one of the classical humanist's own basic concepts: the condition of being naturally naked. Consider the scene of a man in his birthday suit observed by his companion cat.[118] From the inside of this relation (it really is Derrida and his little cat), Derrida wants fully to acknowledge with the classical humanist that we do not simply have here, in the same time and space, one nude creature standing face to face with another nude creature. The differences between the ways in which each is affected by an other whose own modes of being affected are other than the other one means that there is a kind of phenomenological '*contretemps*' here. Or, rather, it means that we cannot really speak without more ado of a single phenomenological 'here' here at all.[119]

The classical humanist will agree with the emphasis on discontinuity – but will want to explain the human appreciation of this scene in terms of the human having overcome a purely animal condition. And, indeed, the kind of scene that Derrida describes is itself central to this story of overcoming. For the classical humanist, that human beings (now) exist (for the most part) in non-nudity is due precisely to their having come, uniquely, into possession of a form of (self-)knowledge that opens the human on to its own exposed presence in the world as *this individual*, as Adam for example.

Derrida does not ridicule this conception or ignore its depth. However, from the inside of an appreciation of the '*contretemps*' he questions the picture of the natural condition that it presents. On the one hand, yes, the naked man is *affected* by his capacity to be naked, and so is (generally) 'no longer naked'. On the other hand, however, since the cat is totally *unaffected* by its being naked it 'does not exist in nakedness' either. Thus, while holding on to the idea of a radical discontinuity, Derrida calls into question the classical humanist's conception of nudity as the natural condition for which the existence in non-nudity of human beings would be the unique (and not simply natural) exception. Affirming an objective internal differentiation of affective capacities, Derrida identifies instead '*two nudities without nudity*' in this naked (or not so naked) scene:[120] 'the animal would be *in* non-nudity because it [does not feel] it is nude, and [nude] man *in* nudity to the extent that he is no longer nude'.[121]

'Existence in nudity' is not, therefore, the concept of the general natural condition for animals. Indeed, from inside the human relation to the animal other it finds clear application only to certain conditions of the being that is not typically nude. The classical humanist's idea of animal nudity and human non-nudity – the very emblem of the significance the classical humanist attaches to the idea of the human *difference* – doubtless relates to objective *differences*, but, according to Derrida, it is an attempt to present in objective or 'in the world' terms a difference that is both *central* to human life (to its 'face') and yet, in those objective terms, strictly unpresentable, non-phenomenal (though, as Cora Diamond stresses, this is not to suggest that it is 'a matter of intuition'). As we shall see, without wishing (with the modern naturalist) to eliminate the concept of the human difference at all, Derrida urges us carefully to reflect on what has become of the 'face' of human life in the wake of a heritage whose dominant force 'we may refer to, in brief, as logocentric'.

Beyond the truth of man

The idea that human life has special significance, or (as the basic Greco-Christian thematisation of this special significance has it) the idea *that human life has broken from an animal condition in such a way that every human life has an incomparable uniqueness*, never was something that 'we as a species ever (as we say) found or discovered'.[122] A *fortiori* it is not an error simply to be corrected by a better theory of nature either. Indeed, what is at issue here is the result of processes of a kind that Darwin himself regarded as *contrasting* markedly with the kinds of forces which are originary in natural history: namely, 'unconstrained inventive processes'.[123] Of course, unlike the splendidly deliberate work of unnatural selection that fascinated Darwin and which gave rise to numerous new pigeon varieties, the inventive processes which have given rise to the construction upon which depends the significance we attach to the idea of the human difference were, as Wiggins (not unproblematically but bearably) puts it, 'gradual, unconscious and communal'.[124]

Derrida does not doubt that human groups have always identified themselves in ways which include an elaboration of a concept of the human difference, a difference that will always be drawn one-sidedly between 'what calls *itself* man and what *he* calls the animal'.[125] Moreover, he regards it as naïve to think that such constructions belong only to so-called 'primitive man', or 'man in an age of superstition'. Indeed, as should be clear, the 'process of *linearisation*' of the history of writing,[126] the process more conventionally called simply *civilisation*, was never a merely theoretical conception. Articulating the founding 'mythography' of modern^2 humanity, it is deeply embedded in the historical development and globalisation of Western technical-scientific culture.

Indeed, in Derrida's view the elaboration of this mythography in and as the history of the modern^2 self-understanding has had fundamental and objective consequences for both animals and humans. *On the one hand* (the animal hand), and speaking 'from the heart',[127] Derrida claims that 'no one could deny that [an alteration in the human relation to animals] has been accelerating, intensifying, no longer knowing where it is going, for about two centuries, at an incalculable rate and level';[128] 'no one can deny the *unprecedented* proportions of the subjection [of animals to the well-being of man]' that is taking place in our time.[129] Yet, according to Derrida, we live today mostly in denial, indeed in a denial of what, in other contexts – in particular, in contexts in which our relation to animals is quite distinctively not to 'animals in general' but is an aliveness to *this creature with a life* – our own speaking hearts would find intolerable. So ultimately, despite the alteration in human relations to animals that marks contemporary modernity^2,

> no one can deny seriously, or deny for very long, that men do all they can in order to dissimulate this cruelty [of the subjection of animals] or to hide it from themselves, in order to organise on a global scale the forgetting or misunderstanding of this violence that some would compare to the worst cases of genocide (there are also animal genocides: the number of species endangered because of man takes one's breath away).[130]

And it is not only a question of driving certain species to extinction either. In 'monstrous' conditions, certain other species are given a 'virtually interminable survival' in the process of their 'industrial ... production, breeding and slaughter'.[131]

On the other hand (the human hand), this dissimulation and disassociation from what, in the kind of context of human relations with animal others mentioned above, no one can deny is obviously telling of modern[2] humanity too. Talk of an abyssal difference between the human and animal is an expression of the special significance we attach to the idea of the human, and that is no more an error than it is an error to mourn the loss of a friend. But no one can deny, or deny for very long, that this abyssal difference has a crossable frontier. For example, the concepts through which we express central-to-human relationships, concepts like friendship or fellowship or companion-ship, are not marked for human use only, but are, as Cora Diamond puts it, distinctively '*labile*'.[132] Inside an acknowledgement (from the heart) of the finite, mortal existence of another living being, we slip across the frontier of the human difference. In what we might call the *iteralability* of concepts char-acteristic of human responses to other human beings we (tres)pass beyond the human. In this process the idea of the human difference is *not* effaced. To be sure, it 'no longer forms a single indivisible line'; instead we might say that along multiple paths of the *iteralability* of our life with such concepts it forms, as illustrated by the '*two* nudities', 'more than one internally divided line'.[133]

And yet, in a time when a life containing talk of the human difference seems more than ever content to 'violate' the 'compassion' and 'pity'[134] through which, across and even in view of the difference, such *iteralability* finds paths to animals, it is becoming increasingly difficult for that slip-across to seem other than a merely sentimental slip-up. But the fact that a human being chooses his or her words as 'words from the heart', and wants, for example, to mark *this cat's* 'unsubstitutable singularity',[135] is not a mistake or error that stands in need of correction through a proper appreciation of a fundamentally unique truth of man. Nor need such words be spoken in naïve ignorance of objective facts about, for example, an individual animal's membership of a genus or species. On the contrary, it simply goes to show how that *iteralabile* talk actually enters our lives; it shows us 'the shape – the "face" – that life containing such talk has'.[136] It is, precisely, the 'face' of that life that is altered by the '*unprecedented* proportions' of 'the subjection of the animal' that dom-inates modern[2] life today. Indeed, as David Wiggins notes, part of the unease that many feel about factory farming, intensive livestock rearing, the general spoliation of nature and the extinction of innumerable animal species is that they show us modern[2] men and women, as in a mirror, as at certain points akin to a form of life we might well think 'profoundly alien': akin, that is, to an animal with 'no non-instrumental concerns and no interest in the world con-sidered as lasting longer than the animal in question will need the world to last in order to sustain the animal's own life'.[137] Such a life, we should note, is no preface to what remains to come *at all*.

Closing words

In this book I have focused on various 'beginnings' in which the challenge to inherit philosophy in modern[2] times is launched and re-launched in the name of phenomenology. I would not have written this book if I did not think that spending time with that inheritance, the challenge of coming to terms with it, was not time well spent. Not surprisingly my view here is not unconnected with my own experience of receiving a philosophical inheritance.

A great swathe of philosophy today, perhaps particularly in the English-speaking world, is marked by what I have called its modernist[1] character. It is pursued in ways that seem confident about knowing what philosophy is (or should be) and how to go about it. What I have learned above all from phenomenology is that 'we philosophers' – we who risk taking the title of philosophy for our own work – are all, in Husserl's words, at every stage 'philosophical beginners'. This is not at all to suggest that one needs to experience oneself as at every moment bereft, lost and alone, or as at every moment standing before some yawning abyss. That perhaps remains the best picture of every inheritance as a moment of radical responsibility, perhaps also the best picture of the connectedness of responsible discourse with truthfulness. But it does not make the inheritance of philosophy a heroic moment. It makes it your moment.

In the course of this chapter I have suggested that Derrida's work constitutes a particularly sharp disruption or interruption of the inheritance of phenomenology. However, I take Derrida to belong to this family of philosophical beginners too. Indeed, with respect to the issue of beginnings he is, in my view, a particularly faithful and diligent member of it. That is, his step back from phenomenology as a philosophy of the subject (or equivalent) is also a radicalisation of phenomenology's modernism[1], an affirmation of the unendingly *questionable* character of whatever one does in the name of 'philosophy' or in response to its history. This situation, what Derrida calls the situation or experience of an 'irreducible *aporia*', is not the same as being faced with (as it were) a 'mere *aporia*'.[138] What Derrida attempts to do is not to solve puzzles of the intellect or find new theoretical solutions to old philosophical problems. Rather, his whole effort is aimed at helping us responsibly to *endure* in reflection what in practice we more or less naïvely endure every day, indeed as our everyday itself: namely, a life with language. Of course, this reflection on naïvety is itself a movement within that life, a moment (one would hope) of some kind of enlightenment or awakening with respect to previous naïvety, and so also involves a transformation of (oneself with respect to) such a life, a transformation of (oneself with respect to) one's heritage. In philosophy this means one renders oneself anew as a reader of one's heritage. One may hope to become a better reader.

Derrida sums up his fears – and implied hopes – with regard to his readers in the following passage:

> Because I still like him, I can foresee the impatience of the bad reader: this is the way I name or accuse the fearful reader, the reader in a hurry to be determined, decided upon deciding (in order to annul, in other words to bring back to oneself, one has to wish to know in advance what to expect, one wishes to expect what has happened, one wishes to expect (oneself)). Now, it is *bad*, and I know of no other definition of the bad, it is bad to predestine one's reading, it is always bad to foretell. It is bad, reader, no longer to like retracing one's steps.[139]

To revert to the terms of Stephen Mulhall's discussion of philosophical modernism[1], Derrida retains the hope that his readers will not be 'in the grip of a picture' of what it is for philosophical writing 'to be well shaped and disciplined',[140] a 'picture' that shuts out the future, shuts out the opening to another inheritance, something else that we might also be prepared to call 'philosophy'. Or, indeed, call 'phenomenology'.

Similarly concerned that we may unwittingly fall back on inappropriate interpretive keys for reading a philosophical score that is performing something new, Merleau-Ponty specifically warned against concluding too quickly that we know what is emerging in the developments that are bringing phenomenology into being.[141] While this is something I completely endorse, a central aim of this book has been to challenge one of the interpretive leitmotifs that has dominated *within* these developments: the conception that construes the ongoing inheritance of phenomenology as the formation of a unified 'phenomenological movement'. But this only goes to reinforce Merleau-Ponty's good point; namely, that our inherited ways of coming to terms with philosophical texts can stand in the way of letting us become good readers of philosophy, including philosophy written in the name of phenomenology. Coming to terms with these (in various ways) extraordinary philosophical resources cannot but involve readers learning to find their inherited philosophical resources an obstacle as well as an interpretive aid in reading them.

The reader's interpretive task is not utterly hopeless, however, even if it is never utterly over. A serious contribution to a renewal of philosophy will itself offer guidance to becoming a reader of that contribution and hence will incite one to embrace 'retracing one's steps' in order to make steps anew. I am grateful to the texts of phenomenology for inciting me and continuing to incite me to interrupt the readers I have been.

NOTES

Introduction

1 John McDowell, *Mind and World*, Cambridge, Mass.: Harvard, 1994, p. 94. McDowell also calls the kind of thinking at issue here 'constructive philosophy' (ibid., p. 95), which nicely brings to the fore the generally deconstructive character of phenomenology with respect to the dominant philosophical tradition in our time.

2 McDowell, *Mind and World*, p. 76.

3 McDowell, *Mind and World*, p. 73.

4 McDowell, *Mind and World*, p. 73.

5 McDowell, *Mind, Value and Reality*, Cambridge, Mass.: Harvard, 1998, p. 175.

6 Edmund Husserl, *The Idea of Phenomenology*, The Hague: Martinus Nijhoff, 1970, p. 19.

7 Mary Warnock, *The Philosophy of Sartre*, London: Hutchinson, 1965, p 12.

1 What is phenomenology?

1 Maurice Merleau-Ponty, *Phenomenology of Perception*, London: Routledge, 1962, p. viii and p. xxi.

2 Merleau-Ponty, *Phenomenology of Perception*, xxi.

3 Merleau-Ponty, *Phenomenology of Perception*, xiv.

4 Derrida, 'Hospitality, Justice and Responsibility', in R. Kearney and M. Dooley (eds), *Questioning Ethics: Contemporary Debates in Philosophy*, London: Routledge, 1999, p. 81.

5 This title is defended by David Wood in *Thinking after Heidegger*, Cambridge: Polity Press, 2002, p. 27. My sympathy for Wood's characterisation will be evident in my presentation of Derrida's 'interruption' of phenomenology in Chapter 7 of this book.

6 'You could say of my work that it is "phenomenology"' (Ludwig Wittgenstein, *Recollections of Wittgenstein*, Rush Rhees (ed.), Oxford: Oxford University Press, 1984, p. 116).

7 'I think it might be better to use, for this way of doing philosophy, some less misleading name than those given above – for instance "linguistic phenomenology", only that is rather a mouthful' (J.L. Austin, 'A Plea for Excuses', in *Philosophical Papers*, Oxford: Clarendon, 1979, p. 182).

8 'Though it is entitled *The Concept of Mind*, it is actually an examination of multifarious specific mental concepts ... . The book could be described as a sustained essay in phenomenology, if you are at home with that label' (Gilbert Ryle, 'Phenomenology versus *The Concept of Mind*', in *Collected Papers*, London: Hutchinson, 1971, p. 188).

9 Although they are far less shy about their indebtedness to and affinity with classical studies in phenomenology from mainland Europe, it should be noted that there is also a very lively and influential approach in cognitive science, known as 'the embodied mind', which carries phenomenological philosophy into the heart of present-day concerns in English-language cognitive science and philosophy of mind. The most important contributions here are from Hubert Dreyfus, Andy Clark and Francisco Varela.

10 Bernard Williams, 'Contemporary Philosophy: A Second Look', in N. Bunnin and E.P. Tsui-James (eds), *The Blackwell Companion to Philosophy*, Oxford: Blackwell, 1996, p. 27. Williams' discussion concerns what he takes many analytic philosophers to find 'most convincing'. I will examine what might be thought of as crucial here – the role of a certain form of argument in philosophy – later in the chapter.

11 It is very important to contrast an anti-scientist stance from an anti-science stance. The former is hostile to the intrusion of the kinds of method employed in natural science into areas where (by the lights of the phenomenological philosopher) they really do not belong. There is no suggestion that they do not belong anywhere – which is what someone hostile to science as such would think. This contrast will become most pointed when we examine some of the work of Merleau-Ponty.

12 Martin Heidegger, *Being and Time*, Oxford: Blackwell, 1962, p. 50.

13 Edmund Husserl, *The Idea of Phenomenology*, The Hague: Martinus Nijhoff, 1970, p. 11.

14 Heidegger, *Being and Time*, p. 51.

15 Joseph J. Kockelmans (ed.), *Phenomenology*, New York: Doubleday Anchor, 1967, p. 25.

16 Not here anyway.

17 Heidegger, *Being and Time*, p. 50. I will explore this maxim in the final section of this chapter.

18 Heidegger, *Being and Time*, pp. 62–63.

19 See Husserl, *Cartesian Meditations*, The Hague: Martinus Nijhoff, 1970, pp. 28 and 58–60.

20 Husserl, *The Idea of Phenomenology*, p. 11.

21 Husserl, *The Idea of Phenomenology*, p. 32.

22 Husserl, *Cartesian Meditations*, p. 32. This point also indicates one of the major motivations for Husserl's regarding possibility as higher than actuality.

23 Perhaps because he is keen on the idea of phenomenology as a nascent philosophical system, Maurice Merleau-Ponty disputes this view. Looking always, as we shall see in Chapter 5, to try to reconcile the differences between Husserl and Heidegger, Merleau-Ponty explains the absence with the suggestion that Heidegger's conception of human existence in terms of 'being-in-the-world' in fact appears 'only against the background of the phenomenological reduction' (Merleau-Ponty, *Phenomenology of Perception*, p. xiv). Although there is more to be said about this issue, I do not find Merleau-Ponty's suggestion convincing – and nor would Husserl. Indeed, as we shall see in Chapter 3, Husserl thought it was obvious that Heidegger neither undertook nor even properly understood the philosophical significance of the phenomenological reduction.

24 D. Moran, *Introduction to Phenomenology*, London: Routledge, 2000, p. 3. See also pp. 180, 202, 309 and 318.

25 Moran, *Introduction to Phenomenology*, p. 316.
26 Heidegger, 'What is Metaphysics?', in *Basic Writings*, ed. D. F. Krell, London: Routledge, 1993, p. 94.
27 Moran, *Introduction to Phenomenology*, p. 309.
28 Heidegger, 'The End of Philosophy', in *Basic Writings*, ed. D. F. Krell, London: Routledge, 1993, p. 436.
29 Stephen Mulhall, *Inheritance and Originality: Wittgenstein, Heidegger, Kierkegaard*, Oxford: Oxford University Press, 2001.
30 Stanley Cavell, *The Claim of Reason: Wittgenstein, Skepticism, Morality, and Tragedy*, Oxford: Oxford University Press, p. 3.
31 Mulhall, *Inheritance and Originality*, p. 1.
32 Mulhall, *Inheritance and Originality*, p. 2.
33 Mulhall, *Inheritance and Originality*, p. 13.
34 Mulhall, *Inheritance and Originality*, p. 13, italics mine.
35 Williams, 'Contemporary Philosophy: A Second Look', p. 27.
36 Stephen Mulhall has put it to me in conversation that we can get to something like this idea from his own account if, instead of emphasising (as I have done) that in the modernist[1] condition 'there are *no* given philosophical conventions', we emphasise that 'there are no *given* philosophical conventions'.
37 Williams, 'Contemporary Philosophy: A Second Look', p. 27.
38 Moran, *Introduction to Phenomenology*, p. 21.
39 J.P Moreland in his (wonderfully entitled essay) 'Should a Naturalist be a Supervenient Physicalist', in *Metaphilosophy*, vol. 29, nos. 1/2, January/April 1998, p. 37.
40 Husserl, *Idea of Phenomenology*, p. 19.
41 Williams, 'Contemporary Philosophy: A Second Look', p. 27.
42 Wittgenstein, *Philosophical Investigations*, Oxford: Blackwell, 1958, §128.
43 Heidegger, *Being and Time*, p. 61.
44 Heidegger, *Being and Time*, p. 50.
45 Austin, 'A Plea for Excuses', in *Philosophical Papers*, Oxford: Clarendon Press, 1979, p. 189.
46 Heidegger, *Being and Time*, p. 50.
47 Given that I see the strength or force of phenomenology as residing less in the formation of a unified movement and more in its prolific capacity for self-interruption, I am happy to exploit the sense of résumé as both 'a summary of some matter' and (typically without acute accents) as 'an event in which one begins or takes up a matter again after an interruption'.
48 I am indebted to Stephen Mulhall in an early draft of his 'Philosophy's Hidden Essence' (published in *Wittgenstein at Work*, E. Ammereller and E. Fischer [eds], Routledge, 2004) for pointing me towards this way of putting things. To complicate my admission, however, and as it were in self-defence, I think that the final formulation of 'what phenomenology is' that I 'advance' at the end of this chapter is (and should be) more like an 'indigenous' part of an exposition and not just a free-floating 'thesis'.
49 Merleau-Ponty, *Phenomenology of Perception*, p. x. Cf. Wittgenstein, *Philosophical Investigations*, §109: 'We must do away with all *explanation*, and description alone must take its place.'
50 Husserl, *Idea of Phenomenology*, p. 4, italics in original.
51 Husserl, *Cartesian Meditations*, p. 151, italics in original.
52 Heidegger, *Being and Time*, p. 59.
53 Austin, 'A Plea for Excuses', p. 182.
54 Husserl, *Ideas*, p. 39. I should note that this is not a procedure that appeals to 'common sense'. This is not at all what phenomenologists do. It is not a matter of

NOTES

what the 'common man' would say if you asked him but of what this man is saying –
and doing – when you do *not* ask him. As we shall see, the *unreliability* of the
common man as a 'witness' in his own case is part of the motivation and difficulty
of phenomenology. I am indebted to Daniel Whiting for reminding me of the
importance of this point.

55 Merleau-Ponty, *Phenomenology of Perception*, p. vii.
56 Heidegger, *Being and Time*, p. 207.
57 McDowell, *Mind, Value and Reality*, Cambridge, Mass.: Harvard University Press,
1998, p. 208.
58 Cora Diamond, 'Throwing away the Ladder', in *The Realistic Spirit*, Cambridge,
Mass.: MIT Press, 1996, p. 185.
59 McDowell, *Mind and World*, p. 176. I discuss the text in which this turn of phrase
occurs later in the chapter.
60 McDowell, *Mind and World*, Cambridge, Mass: Harvard University Press, 1994,
p. 73.
61 Method in phenomenology gets its significance from its relation to this point. See,
for example, Husserl, *Cartesian Meditations*, p. 84. For further elucidation of this
idea of shifts of focus within the insider standpoint see David Wiggins on the
method of 'moral phenomenology' in 'Truth, Invention and the Meaning of Life' in
Needs, Values, Truth, Oxford: Blackwell, 1987.
62 Henri Poincaré, *The Value of Science*, New York: Dover, (1914) 1958. It should be
noted that, for Poincaré, the problem with the notion of a reality beyond what we
conceive of as reality is not that it is nonsense but that it 'would for us be forever
inaccessible'. A *totally* unphenomenological conception.
63 Jean-Paul Sartre, *Being and Nothingness*, London: Methuen, 1958, p. xxi.
64 Husserl, *Logical Investigations*, 'Introduction, Volume Two', London: Routledge,
1970, p. 252; Heidegger, *Being and Time*, p. 50.
65 Williams, 'Contemporary Philosophy: A Second Look', p. 27.
66 John Cottingham cites this central feature of Socrates' way of thinking, and helpfully stresses, as many forget to do, that this is not incompatible with his also
avoiding a certain kind of conclusion or conclusiveness (in a contribution repro-
duced after G. Bennington, 'For the Sake of Argument (Up to a Point)', in S.
Glendinning (ed.), *Arguing with Derrida*, Oxford: Blackwell, 2001, p. 52). Even so,
one might still wonder, with Geoffrey Bennington, whether Socrates is really following the argument wherever it went or only 'where he wants [it] to go' (ibid.).
67 Cora Diamond, 'Anything but Argument?', in *The Realistic Spirit*, Cambridge, Mass.:
MIT Press, 1996, p. 292.
68 Diamond, 'Anything but Argument?', p. 293.
69 In ordinary moral philosophy the procedures in question typically aim at producing,
through argument, a rigorously developed and coherent system of moral thinking.
Ongoing issues of interest and debate will thus be the formulation and testing of
principles, the removal of counterintuitive results, the rebuttal of counterexamples
and so on.
70 Diamond, 'Anything but Argument?', p. 305.
71 Diamond, 'Anything but Argument?', p. 305. It should be noted that in asking this
question Diamond is implicitly seeking to keep her (moral) thinking on the same
plane as (and not sideways on to) the 'insider' responses she wants critically to
examine.
72 Diamond, 'Anything but Argument?', p. 305.
73 Diamond, 'Anything but Argument?', p. 306.
74 Cora Diamond, 'Having a Rough Story about What Moral Philosophy Is', in *The
Realistic Spirit*, p. 374.

75 Diamond, 'Having a Rough Story about What Moral Philosophy Is', p. 374.

76 According to Diamond, the excision of imagination from moral philosophy isn't simply a shortcoming in a moral philosopher, but a radical 'closing off' of oneself to oneself as a thinking, feeling, being, a blindness to one's own appreciation and involvement in what it is to be human quite generally (C. Diamond, 'The Importance of Being Human', in D. Cockburn (ed.), *Human Beings*, Cambridge: Cambridge University Press, 1991, p. 45. fn. 18).

77 The principle targets are: Heidegger and his talk of 'letting be' (despite the fact that this sometime member of the Nazi party regards 'just living along' as an inauthentic mode of concern (Heidegger, *Being and Time*, p. 396)); Sartre and his talk of anxiety and despair (despite the fact that he has a radically 'action-centred' conception of human reality); Levinas and the suggestion that the face of the other can leave one silenced (despite the fact that for Levinas one is thereby called to respond to the other – it is egocentric concerns that are silenced); and, oh so often, Derrida and, for example, his claim that justice 'is always in excess with respect to right', despite the fact that he says this means that 'there is always an urgency to act', not that 'it doesn't matter what you do since it is never enough'.

78 Wittgenstein, *Philosophical Investigations*, §124.

79 Jacques Derrida, 'Politics and Friendship', in *Negotiations*, E. Rottenberg (ed.), Stanford: Stanford University Press, 2002, p. 169.

80 Wittgenstein, *Philosophical Investigations*, §108.

81 See Cora Diamond, 'Wittgenstein and Metaphysics', in *The Realistic Spirit*, p. 35.

82 Crispin Wright, *Truth and Objectivity*, Oxford: Harvard University Press, 1993, p. 202.

83 As Wright puts it, his account of truth, though 'minimalist', does '*not* imply Quietism and [is], to the contrary, at the service of resistance to it' (Wright, 'Comrades against Quietism', *Mind*, 107, 1998, p. 185).

84 McDowell, *Mind and World*, p. 175.

85 McDowell, *Mind and World*, p. 176.

86 McDowell, *Mind and World*, p. 176.

87 For extremely helpful presentations of this argument, see David Finkelstein, 'Wittgenstein on Rules and Platonism', in *The New Wittgenstein*, eds A. Crary and R. Read, Routledge, 2000; and see also Stephen Mulhall, *Inheritance and Originality*, pp. 97–102.

88 McDowell, *Mind and World*, p. 176.

89 McDowell, *Mind and World*, p. 176.

90 Wiggins, 'Truth, Invention, and the Meaning of Life', p. 100.

91 Compare André Gide's 'Preface' to *The Immoralist*: 'In art there are no problems that are not sufficiently solved by the work of art itself' (London: Penguin, 1960, p. 8).

92 Regarding the distribution of talent here as uneven is, in a certain way, to depart from the classical ideal in which philosophical competence belongs to us all in virtue of the fact that we are all rational creatures. Ordinary philosophical argument thus appears as *normative* for all, even if only *convincing* for a small few. See Diamond, 'Wittgenstein and Metaphysics', p. 26.

93 'But enough of such topsy-turvy theories! No theory we can conceive can mislead us with regard to the *principle of all principles: that very primordial dator Intuition is a source of authority for knowledge, that whatever present itself in "intuition" in primordial form* (as it were in its bodily reality), *is simply to be accepted as it gives itself out to be, though only within the limits in which it then presents itself*' (Husserl, *Ideas*, p. 83, italics in original).

94 Husserl, *Logical Investigations*, 'Introduction, Volume Two', p. 252.

95 I am indebted to R.D. Cumming, *Phenomenology and Deconstruction*, Chicago: Chicago University Press, 1991–2001, vol. 1, p. 37, for this point.

96 I do not want to suggest that literary efforts are of no interest to phenomenology; indeed, four of the thinkers whose texts are explored in this book reached to works of the creative imagination as having an important contribution and even *affiliation* with their own work: Heidegger with poetry; Sartre and Derrida with literary fiction; Merleau-Ponty with painting. For Husserl, however, the affiliation is with geometry; for Levinas it is (perhaps) Talmud scholarship and the Hebrew Bible. I should also stress that it is not part of my understanding of phenomenology that it *should* take imaginative literature as its affiliate or model. In fact, as far as my presentation goes, the affiliate is (a certain vision of) moral philosophy.

97 Merleau-Ponty, *Phenomenology of Perception*, p. xx.

98 Austin, 'A Plea for Excuses', p. 181.

2 The emergence of phenomenology

1 Merleau-Ponty, *Phenomenology of Perception*, p. xxi.

2 Merleau-Ponty, *Phenomenology of Perception*, p. viii.

3 Gilbert Ryle, 'Phenomenology', in *Collected Papers*, London: Hutchinson, 1971, p. 171.

4 Martin Heidegger, *The Basic Problems of Phenomenology*, Bloomington: Indiana University Press, 1982, p. 328.

5 The '*work*' (Husserl's italics) of 'phenomenological philosophy' is outlined in these terms in the foreword to the second edition of Husserl's *Logical Investigations* (pp. 43–50). As we shall see in Part II of this chapter, Husserl's first Logical Investigation opens with an analysis aimed at disentangling an 'ambiguity' in the term 'sign'. Husserl writes elsewhere of 'yet another dangerous ambiguity' that we need to protect ourselves against if we are to avoid 'a very closely besetting confusion' (Edmund Husserl, *Ideas: General Introduction to Pure Phenomenology*, trans. W.R. Boyce Gibson, London: Collier-Macmillan, 1962, p. 285).

6 Husserl's statement in italics in 'Philosophy as Rigorous Science' (original text 1911, included in *Phenomenology and the Crisis of Philosophy*, New York: Harper Torchbooks, 1965), is characteristic: '*The stimulus for investigation must start, not with philosophies, but with issues [Sachen] and problems.*' This Husserlian proposition is cited by Heidegger ('The End of Philosophy', in *Basic Writings*, ed. D.F. Krell, London: Routledge, 1993, p. 439) as giving voice to a crucial aspect of the phenomenological resistance to the ordinary philosophy of our time expressed in the call back 'to things themselves' [*Sachen selbst*].

7 A.D. Smith, *Husserl and the Cartesian Meditations*, London: Routledge, 2003, p. 1.

8 Gilbert Ryle, 'Phenomenology versus *The Concept of Mind*', in *Collected Papers*, London: Hutchinson, 1971, p. 181.

9 Ryle, 'Phenomenology versus *The Concept of Mind*', p. 181.

10 Ryle, 'Phenomenology', in *Collected Papers*, p. 168.

11 Jean-Paul Sartre, *Situations*, trans. B. Eisler, New York: Fawcett, 1965, vol. 9, p. 70.

12 Edmund Husserl, *Cartesian Meditations*, trans. D. Cairns, The Hague: Martinus Nijhoff, 1970, p. 11.

13 Husserl, *Cartesian Meditations*, p. 2.

14 See Husserl, *Ideas*, p. 55.

15 Edmund Husserl, *The Crisis of European Sciences and Transcendental Phenomenology*, trans. D. Carr, Evanston: Northwestern University Press, 1970, p. 378.

16 Husserl, *Crisis*, p. 290.

17 Husserl, *Crisis*, p. 378. Husserl's conception of 'man' is discussed by Derrida in his essay 'The Ends of Man' (*Margins of Philosophy*, London: Harvester Wheatsheaf, 1982). I will return to this discussion in Chapter 7, but see note 18 here too.

18 Derrida notes that in the *Crisis* 'Husserl distinguishes between three levels and three stages of historicity: culture and tradition as human sociality in general; European culture and the theoretical project (science and philosophy); the conversion of philosophy into phenomenology' (Derrida, 'The Ends of Man', p. 123).

19 Smith, *Husserl and the Cartesian Meditations*, 2003, p. 7.

20 Cumming, *Phenomenology and Deconstruction*, vol. 3., pp. 3–4.

21 Husserl, *Logical Investigations*, vol. 2, pp. 255–56.

22 Husserl, *Logical Investigations*, vol. 2, p. 256.

23 Husserl, *Logical Investigations*, vol. 2, p. 256.

24 Husserl, *Logical Investigations*, vol. 2, p. 256.

25 Husserl, *Crisis*, p. 389.

26 Cumming, *Phenomenology and Deconstruction*, vol. 1, p. 7.

27 Smith, *Husserl and the Cartesian Meditations*, p. 11.

28 In a personal communication, A.D Smith notes that the reference to 'Existenz' in the paragraph following the 'dream' remark might support Cumming's speculation. But, he adds, 'it also suggests Jaspers'. And the reference to 'world-view' philosophy that soon follows suggests both Jaspers and Dilthey. An inundating torrent is unlikely to be formed by a single deviant.

29 Cumming, *Phenomenology and Deconstruction*, vol. 1, p. 7.

30 Cumming, *Phenomenology and Deconstruction*, vol. 1, p. 29.

31 Husserl, *Cartesian Meditations*, p. 1.

32 Husserl, *Logical Investigations*, foreword to second edition: 'My *Logical Investigations* were my "break-through", not an end but rather a beginning' (p. 43).

33 Moran, *Introduction to Phenomenology*, p. 59, my emphasis.

34 Husserl, *Cartesian Meditations*, p. 14.

35 One can come to this conclusion independently of the longstanding assumption. See the final chapter of Glendinning, *On Being with Others: Heidegger–Derrida–Wittgenstein* (London: Routledge, 1998), especially pp. 142–47.

36 The idea here is often illustrated with the fiction that is called 'the Mary case'. Mary is a scientist who was blind from birth but who has pursued theoretical investigations into the physiology and neuro-physiology of colour perception. Let's suppose that Mary knows everything there is to know about the physical and neural processes bound up with the perception of red things. What does she know about red vision? 'What doesn't she know?' her colleagues might reply. Well, she doesn't know *what it is like* to see red. This is the subjectivity of the mental, and it seems radically 'invisible' to scientific studies of the brain.

37 Husserl, *Logical Investigations*, vol. 2, p. 554.

38 Franz Brentano, *Psychology from an Empirical Standpoint*, London: Routledge, 1995, p. 5.

39 Brentano, *Psychology from an Empirical Standpoint*, p. 77.

40 Brentano, *Psychology from an Empirical Standpoint*, p. 19.

41 Franz Brentano, *Descriptive Psychology*, London: Routledge, 1995, p. 163.

42 See Husserl, *Logical Investigations*, vol. 1, p. 115–16; and *Cartesian Meditations*, p. 83. For an anticipation of contemporary interpretations of the self-refuting nature of sceptical arguments (to the effect that 'the argument [the sceptic] uses ... presupposes precisely that which it denies in its own theses'), see Husserl, *Ideas*, p. 208.

43 Brentano, *Psychology from an Empirical Standpoint*, p. 88. Cited in Husserl, *Logical Investigations*, vol. 2, p. 554.

44 The idea that our 'access' to the phenomena is always and essentially in the form of a 'consciousness *of* something' can come to appear more problematic if, like Heidegger, one highlights that it is to conceive that access as *fundamentally* a mode of *knowledge* of something or other. As we shall see in Chapter 3, in Heidegger's view knowledge (as such) *presupposes* a more basic state of our being, one which involves something one could still call 'access to entities within the world' but which is not itself a kind of 'knowing' them: the basic state of our being that he calls 'being-in-the-world'. A connected question is whether assuming that all forms of mental functioning (including knowing) are 'sub-species of a *summum genus* called "consciousness of ... "' (Ryle, 'Phenomenology', p. 176) commits one to 'an egocentric metaphysics' that is encumbered with an irredeemably 'egocentric *predicament*': the threat of scepticism and solipsism. I will return to this in Part III of this chapter.

45 See Heidegger, *Being and Time*, §17.

46 See Derrida, *Speech and Phenomena: And Other Essays on Husserl's Theory of Signs*, Evanston: Northwestern University Press, 1973, *passim*.

47 Husserl, *Logical Investigations*, vol. 1, p. 275.

48 See Christopher Norris, *Deconstruction: Theory and Practice*, London: Methuen, 1982, pp. 44–45.

49 As we shall see in Chapter 6, this idea recurs in Levinas' conception of the face and expression.

50 Husserl, *Logical Investigations*, vol. 1, p. 269.

51 Husserl, *Logical Investigations*, vol. 1, p. 269.

52 Derrida, *Speech and Phenomena*, p. 20.

53 Heidegger, *Prolegomena zur Geschichte des Zeitbegriffs*, cited in translation by Cumming, *Phenomenology and Deconstruction*, vol. 3. p. 121.

54 Husserl, *Logical Investigations*, p. 278.

55 Husserl, like many Anglophone philosophers of language who follow Grice, will deny that cases such as 'smoke means fire' are cases of 'meaning' in the sense he wishes to isolate. As we shall see, the presence of smoke will, on Husserl's analysis, be a clear case of an 'indication' of fire.

56 Although it has analogies with inference, Husserl does not want to suggest that there is an inferential structure in view here: it is not a piece of reasoning that takes us from A to B. On the other hand it is not a baldly causal associative relation either. Following Brentano, he calls it a relation of 'motivation', a habitual disposition that is an established 'connection among our convictions', so that, for example, on seeing A someone might, without more ado, 'confidently expect' B – and might be wrong to do so.

57 Husserl, *Logical Investigations*, p. 274.

58 Husserl, *Logical Investigations*, p. 269.

59 Husserl, *Logical Investigations*, p. 277.

60 Note that what is 'first' heard here too is not 'dead' sounds or marks but spoken words or communicative speech, sounds 'endowed ... with sense' (Husserl, *Logical Investigations*, p. 277).

61 Husserl, *Logical Investigations*, p. 278. (Pronoun details in the original have been modified here for simplicity's sake.)

62 Husserl, *Logical Investigations*, p. 279.

63 Husserl, *Logical Investigations*, p. 282.

64 Husserl, *Logical Investigations*, p. 285.

65 Husserl, *Logical Investigations*, p. 285.

66 In view of this conception Husserl is sometimes read, not wholly inappropriately, as affirming a form of Platonism. However, the basic idea is only that 'what *I* think', if

it is to be a case of me having a thought at all, must be regarded as intrinsically a content of a possible act of *anyone's* thinking.

67 As Wittgenstein puts it: 'When someone says the word "cube" to me, for example, I know what it means ... I *understand* it' (Wittgenstein, *Philosophical Investigations*, Oxford: Blackwell, 1958, §139).

68 Husserl, *Logical Investigations*, p. 279.

69 Derrida, *Speech and Phenomena*, p. 22.

70 Derrida, *Speech and Phenomena*, p. 22.

71 Husserl, *Logical Investigations*, p. 332.

72 Husserl, *Logical Investigations*, p. 332.

73 Derrida, *Speech and Phenomena*, p. 22.

74 Derrida, *Speech and Phenomena*, p. 3.

75 An 'eidetic' reduction is evident in Husserl's procedure of compiling examples (the slave's brand, the nation's flag, chalk marks on a wall) not to show a motley multiplicity of non-expressive signs but to identify an *invariant* essence that marks an 'essential distinction' to expressive signs, in this case the essence of indication. An anticipation of the phenomenological *epoché* that leads to the phenomenological reduction of 'externality' in general is broached in the 'bracketing' of commitments to 'in the world' items outside the subjective field. Husserl's later appreciation that the sense of 'externality' that belongs to the totality of the existing world in general is *itself* to be grasped as an intended objective ideality would require that the regress to the interiority of a single 'thinking being' of the first Logical Investigation go through its own eidetic reduction to arrive at the 'solitude' of the 'transcendental ego': the transcendental ground of intersubjectivity and (hence) also of the sense of the objectivity of the existing world in general. I will not be exploring Husserl's attempt to develop a method (the method of 'free variation') to achieve the eidetic reduction in this chapter, concentrating instead on the phenomenological reduction as it is developed in *Cartesian Meditations*. Interested readers might consult Paul MacDonald's presentation of the method for achieving the eidetic reduction in *Descartes and Husserl: The Philosophical Project of Radical Beginnings*, Albany: SUNY, 2000, ch. 7.

76 Derrida, *Speech and Phenomena*, p. 27.

77 Cumming, *Phenomenology and Deconstruction*, vol. 3, p. 127.

78 It is in the discussion of the car indicator that Heidegger notes that 'Dasein is *always* in some fashion or other directed and on its way' (Heidegger, *Being and Time*, pp. 78–79).

79 I will explore this idea in Chapter 7.

80 It is very important to note that what is called into question is Husserl's *understanding* of such an inquiry – not (as in Quine, for example) a naturalistic rejection of the very idea of such an inquiry. That is, the kind of 'in the world' considerations Heidegger and Derrida wish to bring in to an account of the functioning of signs is very different from the kind of 'empirical' considerations that a naturalistically inclined philosopher might want to look at or invoke. In particular, they are not aiming to appeal to the facts as conceived by natural science, or facts about how things typically happen, or about causal mechanisms in the brain. Rather, they want to draw our attention to the way structures of significance in general have an *irreducibly* 'in the world' basis. I am grateful to Daniel Whiting for urging me to stress this point.

81 Derrida, *Speech and Phenomena*, p. 30.

82 Derrida, *Speech and Phenomena*, p. 31.

83 I will examine Heidegger's general analysis of equipment in Chapter 3.

84 Heidegger, *Being and Time*, p. 108.

85 Derrida, *Speech and Phenomena*, p. 21. Derrida's emphasis on gesture here will be subordinated in his developed argument to the indicative signs we call 'writing'. When I explore that argument in Chapter 7 I will also be able to clarify the methodological character of 'deconstruction' in terms of its reversal and displacement of traditional philosophical hierarchies.

86 Heidegger, *Being and Time*, p. 108. Translation partly modified consistently with Cumming's correction in *Phenomenology and Deconstruction*, vol. 3, p. 121.

87 See Cumming, *Phenomenology and Deconstruction*, vol. 3, p. 123.

88 This is rather oddly translated by Macquarrie and Robinson as 'symptoms', doubly oddly since they had earlier distinguished them (see Heidegger, *Being and Time*, p. 52). On the other hand, one might see them here as picking up on something in the semantics of 'symptom' that closely relates to *Husserl's* understanding of indicative signs: namely, that it concerns signs which point towards something which does not (in the present or immediately) show itself.

89 See Heidegger, *Being and Time*, p. 108.

90 The theological background to this conception of the intelligibility of the word ('the *logos*') is the focus of Derrida's 'deconstruction' of 'logocentrism' that will be explored in Chapter 7.

91 Although they are essentially intentional objects they are also, as we have seen, essentially shareable. As noted above, the idea here is not that such objects are baldly Platonic items but that they must be regarded as intrinsically contents of possible acts of (anyone's) thinking.

92 This distinction has also been proposed by others. See, for example, John Searle, *Intentionality*, Cambridge: Cambridge University Press, 1983, pp. 167–68.

93 I go through the steps that take these ideas from the epistemological doubts expressed here (*uncertainty* concerning the presence of experiences that are not my experiences) to the more devastatingly solipsistic conclusion (affirmation of the impossibility of *making sense* of experiences that are not my experiences) in Glendinning, *On Being with Others*, ch. 1.

94 Husserl, *Cartesian Meditations*, p. 151. I will return to Husserl's commitment to our pre-reduction understanding of the world on pp. 57–58.

95 Sartre, *Being and Nothingness*, London: Methuen, 1958, p. 223.

96 Heidegger, *Being and Time*, p. 122. On the battle of the giants see *Being and Time*, p. 21.

97 Husserl, 'Phenomenology and Anthropology', cited and translated by Cumming, *Phenomenology and Deconstruction*, vol. 3, p. 230.

98 A.D. Smith, who stresses the communal character of Husserl's conception of phenomenology, also specifies it as a distinctively ethical community. See Smith, *Husserl and the Cartesian Mediations*, p. 7. In Chapter 4 I will explore the way this kind of conception is affirmed in Jean-Paul Sartre's moral phenomenology.

99 Husserl, *Cartesian Meditations*, p. 14.

100 Cited in Derrida, 'Geschlecht: Sexual Difference, Ontological Difference', *Research in Phenomenology*, 13, 1983, p. 66.

101 Husserl, *Cartesian Meditations*, p. 7. As in Chapter 1, I will refer to the distinctive 'modernist outlook' of phenomenology (its concern with the question of how even to begin in philosophy) as its modernism[1] and will contrast this with the modernity[2] of post-Enlightenment Western scientific culture.

102 The lurch is in part a shift to a different argument *type*: from appealing to (roughly speaking) 'the Cartesian idea of science … grounded on an absolute foundation' (Husserl, *Cartesian Meditations*, p. 11) to developing a transcendental argument about the presuppositions of knowledge in general. Or, better: a shift to seeing how an argument type of the second kind can realise the intended outcome of the first. I

am indebted to John Cottingham for helping me see the significance of this shift, and also for giving me access to his personal writings on Husserl's first Cartesian Meditation. I will refer to some of his criticisms of Husserl's reading of Descartes in these notes.

103 Husserl, *Cartesian Meditations*, p.18.

104 Smith, *Husserl and the Cartesian Meditations*, pp. 21–22.

105 John McDowell, 'Two Sorts of Naturalism', *Mind, Value and Reality*, p. 171. I am not suggesting that McDowell's step back and Husserl's step back are the same. The latter is a radicalisation of the former precisely in that the latter steps back from (without annulling) *every* step back that we might, in the natural attitude, engage in.

106 Smith, *Husserl and the Cartesian Meditations*, p. 23.

107 'It must be possible for the "I think" to accompany all my representations; for otherwise something would be represented in me which could not be thought at all, and that is equivalent to saying that the representation would be impossible, or at least would be nothing to me' (Kant, *Critique of Pure Reason*, London: Methuen, 1933, B131).

108 Husserl, *Cartesian Meditations*, p. 19.

109 Husserl, *Cartesian Meditations*, p. 23.

110 Husserl, *Cartesian Meditations*, p. 23.

111 Husserl, *Cartesian Meditations*, p. 24. John Cottingham thinks that Husserl is wrong to specify the mind here as 'human' since Descartes reserves this anthropological status exclusively 'for the mind–body complex'. According to Cottingham, then, Husserl should have stuck to saying that 'Descartes infers the existence of a pure thinking substance, a *mens sive animus*, from the certainty of his existence as a thinker.' I do not think this correction seriously affects Husserl's concern that Descartes' *acceptance* of the ego is fatally 'positional'; accepting it as that region of reality we can be certain of. But Cottingham's complaint has legs, as we shall see.

112 Husserl, *Cartesian Meditations*, p. 25.

113 Husserl, *Cartesian Meditations*, p. 25. Cottingham's complaint noted in note 111 can make a return here. For it is clear that Descartes could defend himself with the point that you can't have 'cogitationes' of any kind without a 'real substance' to do the cogitating. Husserl, however, attempts to 'trump' that point by urging an *epoché* with respect to whatever this bit of real stuff might be.

114 Husserl, *Cartesian Meditations*, p. 26.

115 Husserl, *Cartesian Meditations*, p. 25.

116 Heidegger, *Being and Time*, p. 249.

117 Husserl, *Cartesian Meditations*, p. 26.

118 Husserl, *Cartesian Meditations*, pp. 136–37. It is worth noting that, like the analysis of expression, the isolation of a sphere of 'my pure sensuousness' will recur strongly in the work of Levinas (see Chapter 6).

119 Husserl, *Cartesian Meditations*, p. 84.

120 Husserl, *Cartesian Meditations*, p. 84.

121 Husserl, *Cartesian Meditations*, p. 83.

122 Husserl, *Cartesian Meditations*, p. 83.

123 Husserl, *Cartesian Meditations*, p. 83.

124 Husserl, *Cartesian Meditations*, p. 83.

125 Husserl, *Cartesian Meditations*, p. 83.

126 Husserl, *Logical Investigations*, vol. 2, pp. 255–56.

127 Husserl, *Cartesian Meditations*, p. 84.

128 Husserl, *Cartesian Meditations*, p. 83.

129 Husserl, *Cartesian Meditations*, p. 83.

130 Husserl, *Cartesian Meditations*, p. 137.

131 Husserl, *Cartesian Meditations*, p. 137; and see also p. 154.
132 Heidegger (rightly in my view) pins just this way of putting things to the Husserlian project in 'The End of Philosophy', p. 440.
133 Husserl, *Cartesian Meditations*, p. 137.
134 We should note that Husserl regards the dominant, sedimented tradition of philosophy that has come down to us as 'historically degenerate' (Husserl, *Cartesian Meditations*, p. 139). For Husserl the inaugural and authentic sense of first philosophy has (to borrow a Heideggerian formula) been forgotten, and requires reactivation. For further discussion of this sense of a radically non-traditional tradition, see Simon Critchley, *A Very Short Introduction to Continental Philosophy*, Oxford: Oxford University Press, 2001, pp. 68–72.
135 Husserl, *Cartesian Meditations*, p. 148.
136 As we shall see in Chapter 6, this point will be brought to the fore in Levinas' conception of the encounter with the other person.
137 Husserl, *Cartesian Meditations*, p. 150.
138 Wittgenstein, *Philosophical Investigations*, §124.
139 Husserl, *Cartesian Meditations*, p. 151.
140 Husserl, *Cartesian Meditations*, p. 157.
141 Husserl, *Cartesian Meditations*, p. 157.
142 Merleau-Ponty, *Phenomenology of Perception*, p. xi.
143 Heidegger, *Being and Time*, p. 254.

3 Phenomenology as fundamental ontology

1 As before I will refer to what Dermot Moran calls the distinctive 'modernist outlook' of phenomenological investigations as its modernism[1] and will contrast this with the modernity[2] of post-Enlightenment Western scientific culture.
2 Heidegger, *Being and Time*, p. 21
3 The unfinished condition of *Being and Time* is discussed by David Farrell Krell in his 'General Introduction' to Heidegger's *Basic Writings*, pp. 16–25.
4 Heidegger, *Being and Time*, p. 60
5 Heidegger, *Being and Time*, p. 62. 'Dasein' is a standard term for 'existence' (in general) in German philosophy. It is left in German in most translations of Heidegger but could be literally rendered as 'Being-there'. Heidegger reserves this term for designating the kind of entity that we (human beings) are. I will more fully introduce this idea in due course.
6 Heidegger, *Being and Time*, p. 60.
7 John Sallis, *Delimitations: Phenomenology and the End of Metaphysics*, Bloomington: Indiana University Press, 1986, p. 99. See also Stephen Mulhall, *Inheritance and Originality*, Oxford: Oxford University Press, 2001, pp. 185–96.
8 Heidegger, *Being and Time*, p. 21.
9 Heidegger, *Being and Time*, p. 21.
10 Heidegger, *Being and Time*, p. 23 [*Rätsel*, translated as 'enigma'].
11 Heidegger, *Being and Time*, pp. 21–23.
12 Heidegger, *Being and Time*, p. 21.
13 Heidegger, *Being and Time*, p. 21.
14 Heidegger, *Being and Time*, p. 21.
15 R.M. Hare 'A School for Philosophers', *Ratio*, vol. 2, no. 2, 1960, p. 114–15.
16 Hare, 'A School for Philosophers', p. 117. As we shall see in Part III of this chapter, the basic challenge to the 'old ways' of philosophy posed by the Vienna Circle turns on the proposal that meaningful statements are exclusively of one or two kinds: they are either (directly or indirectly) verifiable statements about reality or

they are statements which concern the role of linguistic signs. Nonsense is produced either (a) if a logically well-formed statement is unverifiable or (b) if one violates the rules of logical grammar.

17 Heidegger, *Being and Time*, p. 21.

18 We have to be careful when throwing around labels like 'metaphysical'. As we shall see in Part II of this chapter, Heidegger has a distinctive understanding of what philosophy as metaphysics is. And (ironically, rather like Hare) it is something that he wishes to establish a distance from.

19 Heidegger, *Being and Time*, p. 158.

20 Cora Diamond, 'The Importance of Being Human', in *Human Beings*, p. 60.

21 I will return to issues around theories of meaning in Part III of this chapter.

22 Heidegger, *Being and Time*, p. 1.

23 Heidegger, *Being and Time*, p. 1.

24 It is worth noting that this supposed 'fact' itself seems to get asserted (as such) only on the basis of an acknowledged-to-be problematic principle from Aquinas: 'An understanding of Being is already included in conceiving anything which one apprehends as an entity.'

25 Heidegger, *Being and Time*, p. 25.

26 Heidegger, *Being and Time*, p. 25.

27 Hare, 'A School for Philosophers', p. 108.

28 Heidegger, *Being and Time*, p. 25.

29 Wittgenstein, *Philosophical Investigations*, §89.

30 Wittgenstein, *Philosophical Investigations*, §89.

31 Heidegger, *Being and Time*, p. 69.

32 Heidegger, *Being and Time*, p. 59.

33 Wittgenstein, *Philosophical Investigations*, §129.

34 Quoted from Augustine's *Confessions* in Heidegger, *Being and Time*, p. 69.

35 That the shift of theme is actually superficial is evident from the fact that Heidegger, like Augustine, regards a certain way of being in *time* as characterising the *fundamental* meaning of a finite human existence (see Heidegger, *Being and Time*, p. 38).

36 Heidegger, *Being and Time*, pp. 24–25.

37 Heidegger, *Being and Time*, p. 25.

38 Heidegger, *Being and Time*, p. 24.

39 On Wittgenstein's use of the idea of a 'picture' as a casual, pre-theoretical – and not in itself incorrect – response out of which theoretical 'ideas' that are in various ways inadequate and distorting can readily grow, see Stephen Mulhall, *Inheritance and Originality*, pp. 36–38.

40 Heidegger, *Being and Time*, p. 39.

41 Heidegger, *Being and Time*, p. 47.

42 Heidegger, *Being and Time*, p. 47.

43 Heidegger, *Being and Time*, p. 40.

44 Heidegger, *Being and Time*, p. 25.

45 I am grateful to Ali Shahrukhi for suggesting this approach to me.

46 Section 6 is entitled 'The Task of Destroying the History of Ontology' (Heidegger, *Being and Time*, pp, 43–44).

47 Heidegger, *Being and Time*, p. 43.

48 Heidegger, 'The End of Philosophy', p. 432.

49 'Philosophy – what we call philosophy – is metaphysics getting under way' (Heidegger, 'What is Metaphysics?', p. 110).

50 Wittgenstein, *Philosophical Investigations*, §89.

51 Heidegger 'What is Metaphysics?', p. 106. This conception of metaphysics is (perhaps not surprisingly) perfectly summarised by Kant:

> All pure *a priori* knowledge ... has in itself a peculiar unity; and metaphysics is the philosophy which has as its task the statement of that knowledge in this systematic unity. Its speculative part, which *has especially appropriated this name*, [is] what we entitle *metaphysics of nature*, [it is the part] which considers everything in so far as *it is* (not that which ought to be) by means of *a priori* concepts.
> (Kant, *Critique of Pure Reason*, London: Methuen, 1933, A845 B873)

That philosophy which Kant here calls 'metaphysics of nature' is what is at stake in the discourses on philosophy and the end of philosophy in Heidegger's work.

52 Heidegger, 'The End of Philosophy', p. 436.
53 Austin, 'Ifs and Cans', in *Philosophical Papers*, p. 232.
54 Heidegger, 'The End of Philosophy', p. 434–35.
55 Heidegger, 'The End of Philosophy', p. 434. The idea of a coming *terminus* of philosophy does not imply the complete coming to a halt of philosophical activity. However, the claim would be that such activity will become a kind of unending repetition of the pretty-much-the-same.
56 See, for example, Husserl, *Ideas*, p. 57.
57 Husserl, *Ideas*, p. 58.
58 Heidegger, *Being and Time*, p. 10.
59 Heidegger, *Being and Time*, p. 9.
60 In *Being and Time* Heidegger offers the following list of examples of 'regions of Being': 'Nature, space, life, Dasein, language, and the like' (Heidegger, *Being and Time*, p. 29). He also identifies the following 'sciences' as having undergone 'crises' in the articulation of their basic concepts (crises, that is, in what is identified as constituting the Being of the entities in that area): mathematics, physics, biology, the historiological human sciences and theology (Heidegger, *Being and Time*, pp. 29–30).
61 Heidegger, *Being and Time*, p. 10.
62 Heidegger, *Being and Time*, p. 10.
63 Heidegger cites Husserl on transcendental subjectivity as the 'sole absolute being' in 'The End of Philosophy', p. 440.
64 Heidegger, *Being and Time*, p. 11.
65 Heidegger, *Being and Time*, p. 33.
66 Heidegger, *Being and Time*, p. 35:

> If to Interpret the meaning of Being becomes our task, Dasein is not only the primary entity to be interrogated; it is also that entity which already comports itself, in its Being, towards what we are asking about when we ask this question. But in that case the question of Being is nothing other than a radicalisation of an essential tendency-of-Being which belongs to Dasein itself – the pre-ontological understanding of Being.

67 Heidegger, *Being and Time*, p. 254.
68 Heidegger, 'The End of Philosophy', p. 433.
69 Heidegger, 'The End of Philosophy', p. 435.
70 Joanna Hodge, *Heidegger and Ethics*, London: Routledge, 1995, p. 21.
71 Heidegger, *Being and Time*, p. 7.
72 Heidegger, *Being and Time*, p. 6.
73 Heidegger, 'What is Metaphysics?', p. 95.
74 Heidegger, 'The End of Philosophy', p. 437.
75 Husserl, *Psychological and Transcendental Phenomenology*, cited by Cumming in *Phenomenology and Deconstruction*, vol. 3, p. 51.

76 Heidegger, *Being and Time*, p. 89.
77 Heidegger, *Being and Time*, p. 33.
78 Heidegger, *Being and Time*, p. 89.
79 Merleau-Ponty, *Phenomenology of Perception*, London: Routledge, 1962, p. xiv.
80 Heidegger, *Being and Time*, p. 233.
81 Heidegger, *Being and Time*, p. 233.
82 Heidegger, *Being and Time*, p. 235.
83 Derrida, '"Eating Well", or the Calculation of the Subject', in E. Cadava *et al.* (eds), *Who Comes after the Subject*, London: Routledge, 1991, p. 98.
84 Derrida, 'Violence and Metaphysics', p. 110. The formulation 'new, quite new' is nicely disconcerting. In some cases, if something is only 'quite' new it is not thought really to be new *at all*. But Heidegger's Dasein is not just a repetition of the old 'subject' idea. It really is quite new! Even if it is disconcerting, Derrida's formulation is just right for measuring the deviations internal to the inheritance of phenomenology.
85 Heidegger, 'The End of Philosophy', p. 440. Heidegger has Husserl explicitly in his sights with this formulation.
86 Heidegger was less than impressed by the general focus by readers on his analytic of Dasein: 'Philosophy could hardly have given a clearer demonstration of the power of this oblivion of Being than it has furnished us by the somnambulistic assurance with which it has passed by the real and only question of *Being and Time*' (W. Kaufmann (ed.) *Existentialism from Dostoevsky to Sartre*, p. 35).
87 Husserl, *Logical Investigations*, vol. 2, pp. 255–56.
88 Heidegger, *Being and Time*, p. 63. This formulation strikes me as fundamentally similar to Husserl's (equally impersonal) acknowledgement of the 'further difficulty' internal to the phenomenological inquiry touched on at the start of Chapter 2.
89 Heidegger, *Being and Time*, p. 67.
90 Heidegger, *Being and Time*, p. 67.
91 Stephen Mulhall, *Heidegger and Being and Time*, London: Routledge, 1996, p. 31.
92 Heidegger, *Being and Time*, p. 48. As Stephen Mulhall notes, the Christian anthropology also represents 'us' as 'reaching yearningly beyond our creaturely existence' and this desire for transcendence is retained in Heidegger's 'idea of Dasein as transcendent' (Stephen Mulhall, *Philosophical Myths of the Fall*, Princeton: Princeton University Press, 2005, pp. 46–47). If we add that the possession of the 'logos' remains in view with Heidegger's conception of the constitution of Dasein's 'there' as characterised primordially by '*discourse*' (Heidegger, *Being and Time*, p. 172), it becomes clear that his 'fundamental ontology' does not so much '*detach*' itself from the tradition or reject it as 'radically rethink' it (Mulhall, *Philosophical Myths of the Fall*, p. 47). See note 93 for a further point on this rethinking of the sources of our current self-understanding.
93 This is a term Heidegger comes to use more frequently after *Being and Time*, especially after the writing of the 'Letter on Humanism' (prepared for publication in 1947), but the idea is not new to the later writings. Heidegger's own position is (by his own admission) an original kind of (and hence rethought) 'humanism' (Heidegger, 'Letter on Humanism', *Basic Writings*, p. 245), a position evident in his saying of classical humanism that it did not set man's '*humanitas*' too high but rather 'not ... high enough' (ibid., pp. 233–34). In this section, by humanism I mean the classical humanism that Heidegger works through but does not endorse.
94 Heidegger, 'Letter on Humanism', pp. 228–29.
95 Heidegger, 'Letter on Humanism', p. 227.
96 Heidegger, *Being and Time*, p. 33.
97 Heidegger, *Being and Time*, p. 78.

 98 Heidegger, *Being and Time*, p. 33.
 99 Heidegger, *Being and Time*, p. 98.
100 Heidegger, *Being and Time*, p. 69.
101 Husserl, *Cartesian Meditations*, p. 78.
102 Husserl, *Cartesian Meditations*, p. 78.
103 Heidegger, *Being and Time*, p. 69.
104 Heidegger, *Being and Time*, p. 84.
105 Heidegger, *Being and Time*, p. 72.
106 Heidegger, *Being and Time*, p. 33.
107 Heidegger, *Being and Time*, p. 58.
108 Heidegger, *Being and Time*, p. 58.
109 Heidegger, *Being and Time*, p. 267
110 Heidegger, 'What is Metaphysics?', p. 94.
111 Simon Critchley, *A Very Short Introduction to Continental Philosophy*, Oxford: Oxford University Press, 2001, p. 91.
112 Heidegger, 'What is Metaphysics?', p. 93.
113 Heidegger, 'What is Metaphysics?', p. 102.
114 Heidegger, 'What is Metaphysics?', p. 94, translation modified.
115 Heidegger, 'What is Metaphysics?', p. 95.
116 Herman Philipse, *Heidegger's Philosophy of Being*, Princeton: Princeton University Press, 1998, pp. 9–10.
117 Heidegger, 'What is Metaphysics?', p. 96.
118 Moreland, 'Should a Naturalist be a Supervenient Physicalist', p. 37.
119 Heidegger, 'What is Metaphysics?', p. 96.
120 Heidegger, 'What is Metaphysics?' p. 96.
121 Heidegger, 'What is Metaphysics?' p. 96.
122 Heidegger, *Being and Time*, p. 26.
123 Philipse, *Heidegger's Philosophy of Being*, p. 10.
124 Philipse, *Heidegger's Philosophy of Being*, p. 10.
125 Philipse, *Heidegger's Philosophy of Being*, p. 10.
126 Philipse, *Heidegger's Philosophy of Being*, p. 10.
127 Heidegger, 'What is Metaphysics', p. 95.
128 Philipse, *Heidegger's Philosophy of Being*, p. 11.
129 Philipse, *Heidegger's Philosophy of Being*, p. 11.
130 Heidegger, 'What is Metaphysics?', p. 97. Note that 'logic' here means, as it always does in Husserl too, 'the logic of science'.
131 Heidegger, 'What is Metaphysics?', p. 97.
132 Heidegger, 'What is Metaphysics?', p. 97.
133 Heidegger, 'What is Metaphysics?', p. 97.
134 Heidegger, 'What is Metaphysics?', p. 99.
135 Heidegger, *Being and Time*, p. 175.
136 Heidegger, 'What is Metaphysics?', p. 99.
137 Heidegger, 'What is Metaphysics?', p. 100.
138 Philipse *Heidegger's Philosophy of Being*, p. 11. Heidegger, 'What is Metaphysics?', p. 100. Philipse acknowledges Heidegger's appeal to *Angst*, but his presentation of the point seems deliberately to obscure matters by immediately connecting it to Heidegger's attempt to conceive every negative phenomenon as 'grounded in the not that springs from the nihilation of the nothing' (Heidegger, 'What is Metaphysics?', p. 105). I mention this difficult idea here only because Heidegger's affirmation of it is far from being simply external to the scene that unfolds between Philipse's interpretation and his (Heidegger's) text. For this scene itself speaks for Heidegger's pointed challenge to the idea that negation (the logicist's exclusive basic function)

is the 'sole or [even] leading' form of 'nihilative behaviour'. As Heidegger puts it, 'unyielding antagonism and stinging rebuke have a more abysmal source than the measured negation of thought' (ibid.). The phenomenological rejection of the logicist conception will be to the fore in Chapter 4 too when I look at what Sartre calls *négatités*. I will try, in the notes to that chapter, to say a little more about Heidegger's infamous and difficult formulations concerning 'the nihilation of the nothing'.

139 Philipse, *Heidegger's Philosophy of Being*, p. 14.
140 Heidegger, 'What is Metaphysics?', p. 101.
141 Heidegger, *Being and Time*, pp. 231–32.
142 Heidegger, *Being and Time*, p. 119.
143 Philipse, *Heidegger's Philosophy of Being*, p. 187.
144 Philipse, *Heidegger's Philosophy of Being*, p. 230.
145 Philipse, *Heidegger's Philosophy of Being*, p. 229.
146 Philipse, *Heidegger's Philosophy of Being*, p. 485, fn. 65.
147 Philipse, *Heidegger's Philosophy of Being*, p. 384.
148 Heidegger, 'What is Metaphysics?', p. 110.
149 Sartre, *Being and Nothingness*, p. 559.
150 Philipse, *Heidegger's Philosophy of Being*, p. 386.
151 Philipse, *Heidegger's Philosophy of Being*, p. 267.
152 Philipse, *Heidegger's Philosophy of Being*, p. 268.
153 Heidegger, 'What is Metaphysics?', p. 106.
154 Philipse, *Heidegger's Philosophy of Being*, p. 374.
155 Heidegger, *An Introduction to Metaphysics*, p. 10.
156 Heidegger, *An Introduction to Metaphysics*, pp. 37–38. Heidegger situates Europe (and Germany as 'situated in the centre' of Europe) as the privileged site for a future spiritual 'awakening' and America and Russia as the major forces of ongoing spiritual 'decline':

> This Europe, in its ruinous blindness forever on the point of cutting its own throat, lies today in a great pincers, squeezed between Russia on one side and America on the other. From a metaphysical point of view, Russia and America are the same; the same dreary technological frenzy, the same unrestricted organization of the average man.
>
> (ibid., p. 37)

We should remember, however, that in the same lecture series Heidegger would praise 'the inner truth and greatness of this movement of [National Socialism] (namely the encounter between global technology and modern man)' (ibid., p. 199) – a rather more classic case of Europe 'cutting its own throat' I would think.

157 Heidegger, *An Introduction to Metaphysics*, p. 42. While Heidegger regards restating the question as belonging to 'the fundamental conditions for an awakening of the spirit' and 'indispensable if the peril of world darkening is to be forestalled' (ibid., p. 50), he stresses, surely correctly, that 'philosophy can never directly supply the energies and create the opportunities and methods which bring about an historical change' (ibid., p. 10). Nevertheless, he does think that original philosophical questioning can initiate a 'profound transformation' (ibid., p. 10) and 'a new beginning' (ibid., p. 39):

> It spreads only indirectly, by devious paths that can never be laid out in advance, until at last, at some future date, it sinks to the level of a commonplace, but by then it has long been forgotten as original philosophy.
>
> (ibid., p. 10)

In Chapter 7 we will see that this relation to the possibility of something radically new taking place 'at some future date' becomes a centrepiece of Derrida's ambition for philosophy.

158 See Heidegger, *An Introduction to Metaphysics*, p. 20. The way spiritual, political and religious themes get caught up in the adventures and misadventures of Heidegger's Being question are explored in Derrida's fascinating essay *Of Spirit: Heidegger and the Question*, Chicago: University of Chicago Press, 1989.

4 Existential phenomenology

1 Sartre, *Being and Nothingness*, p. 4. See also Robert Cumming, *Phenomenology and Deconstruction*, vol. 1, p. 149, citing Sartre's view of *Being and Nothingness* as an attempt to produce a (rudimentarily dialectical) 'synthesis of Husserl's non-dialectical consciousness . . . with the dialectical project . . . which we find in Heidegger'.

2 'We wanted to start out with the concrete as a whole' (Sartre, *Questions de méthode*, Paris: Gallimard, 1960, p. 22). Cited in English translation with commentary and further references in Cumming, *Phenomenology and Deconstruction*, vol. 2, p. 29.

3 Sartre, *Situations*, New York: Fawcett, 1965, p. 154. Cited in Cumming, *Phenomenology and Deconstruction*, vol. 4, p. 93.

4 McCulloch, *Using Sartre: An Analytical Introduction to Early Sartrean Themes*, London: Routledge, 1994, p. ix. While a faithful Heideggerian would certainly quarrel with the very idea of a philosophy of *mind*, McCulloch's thought is that it is precisely confusions about what it is to have something (as we say) 'in mind' or 'before the mind' that Sartre aims to dispel.

5 Cumming, *Phenomenology and Deconstruction*, vol. 3, p. 243.

6 Sartre, *Being and Nothingness*, p. 15.

7 Derrida, 'Response to Baldwin', in S. Glendinning (ed.), *Arguing with Derrida*, Oxford: Blackwell, 2000., p. 107.

8 Sartre, *Being and Nothingness*, p. 16.

9 Sartre, *Existentialism and Humanism*, London: Methuen, 1973, p. 55.

10 E.g.: 'Anguish in fact is the recognition of a possibility as *my* possibility' (Sartre, *Being and Nothingness*, p. 35).

11 E.g.: 'Anguish . . . [means that] when a man commits himself to anything . . . he is not only choosing what he will be . . . but is . . . deciding for the whole of mankind' (Sartre, *Existentialism and Humanism*, p. 30).

12 Sartre, *Being and Nothingness*, p. xxi.

13 Sartre, *Being and Nothingness*, p. xxi.

14 The phenomenalist view Sartre rejects is one which aims to 'reduce' (or translate without residue) claims about how things *are* to claims about how things (do or might) *seem* to some perceiver. It is to suppose that, 'for all those bodies which compose the mighty frame of the world, . . . their being is to be perceived or known' (Berkeley, 'Nothing Outside the Mind', in J. Cottingham (ed.), *Western Philosophy: An Anthology*, p. 93). While, naturally enough, Sartre first sets his sights on Berkeley, it is important to note that he has an eye fixed firmly on Husserl too, making the point that 'Husserl and his followers' have the same position as Berkeley when, 'after having effected the phenomenological reduction, they treat the *noema* [the intentional object] as unreal and declare that its *esse* is *percipi*' (Sartre, *Being and Nothingness*, p. xxvi). There is no methodological equivalent to the phenomenological reduction in Sartre any more than there is in Heidegger. On the other hand, Sartre retains – and so has to cope with the consequences of retaining – the Husserlian emphasis on consciousness and intentionality.

15 Sartre, *Being and Nothingness*, p. xxxiv.

16 Sartre, *Being and Nothingness*, p. xxxvi.

17 Sartre, *Being and Nothingness*, p. 9.

18 Heidegger, *Being and Time*, p. 54. This conception concerns what shows itself as the ontology of everyday thought and talk: tables, chairs, cafés, vases, people ... the whole array of what Sartre (following Heidegger in 'What is Metaphysics?') calls 'existents' (things which, in some way or other, *are*).

19 McCulloch, *Using Sartre*, p. 97. McCulloch also explores what he calls the 'elements of idealism' in Sartre's thought, but is, I think, too willing to see 'traces' in it of a conflicting 'transcendental idealism' (ibid., p.117). In my view, McCulloch underestimates the importance of his own good distinction between 'what occurs or not' and 'what is significant (to us)' (ibid., p. 114) in his reading of Sartre.

20 Sartre, *Being and Nothingness*, p. xl.

21 See Cavell, *The Claim of Reason*, p. 45. I develop Cavell's distinction between being *so* and *being* so myself in Glendinning, *On Being With Others*, ch. 8.

22 McCulloch, *Using Sartre*, p. 117.

23 Sartre, *Being and Nothingness*, p. xxvii.

24 Sartre, *Being and Nothingness*, p. xxvii.

25 Sartre, *Being and Nothingness*, p. xxvii.

26 Sartre, *Being and Nothingness*, p. xxxii.

27 Sartre, *Being and Nothingness*, p. xxix.

28 The idea of a 'thetic' awareness concerns the intentional theme of consciousness. Correspondingly, a 'non-thetic' awareness is a consciousness whose theme is still only implicit or pre-reflective.

29 Sartre, *Being and Nothingness*, p. xxix.

30 Sartre, *Being and Nothingness*, p. xxix.

31 Sartre, *Being and Nothingness*, p. xxix.

32 McCulloch, *Using Sartre*, p. 101. See Sartre, *Being and Nothingness*, p. xxix: 'every positional consciousness of an object is at the same time a non-positional consciousness of itself'.

33 Sartre notes that 'Heidegger expressed very well' the idea of 'a being which is existence through and through', citing Heidegger's remark that, for Dasein, 'the "how" (*essentia*) of this being ... must be conceived in terms of its existence (*existentia*)' (Sartre, *Being and Nothingness*, p. xxxi). Quite apart from the massive shift from Dasein existing so that its own Being is an issue for it to consciousness as self-presence, what Sartre does not seem to recognise is that the *sense* of 'existence' for Dasein is precisely *contrasted* with the traditional understanding of existence; namely, as 'presence'. I will come back to Sartre's use of the Heideggerian formula in the lecture on moral phenomenology in Part III of this chapter.

34 Sartre, *Being and Nothingness*, p. xxxiii.

35 Sartre, *Being and Nothingness*, p. xxxviii.

36 The title harks back to Descartes' ontological proof of the existence of God, the argument which purports to establish God's *existence* as following from the idea of God's *perfection*. The Sartrean variant aims to show that 'consciousness implies in its Being a non-conscious and transphenomenal Being' (Sartre, *Being and Nothingness*, p. xxxviii). Levinas will also appeal to an ontological proof in his discussion of (what is essentially) the transphenomenal Being of the other person.

37 Sartre, *Being and Nothingness*, p. xxxvii.

38 Sartre, *Being and Nothingness*, p. xxxvii.

39 Sartre, *Being and Nothingness*, p. xxxvii.

40 Sartre, *Being and Nothingness*, pp. xxxvi–ii.

41 Sartre, *Being and Nothingness*, p. xxxvii.

42 Sartre, *Being and Nothingness*, p. xxxvii.

43 McDowell, *Mind and World*, p. 176.
44 Sartre, *Being and Nothingness*, p. xlii.
45 Sartre, *Being and Nothingness*, p. xxiv.
46 If the 'phenomena in the ordinary sense' are 'existents' or 'objects', the phenomena at issue for Sartre's phenomenology at this point are not phenomena in this sense *at all* but the appearing of the Being of these phenomena: phenomena of Being.
47 Sartre, *Being and Nothingness*, pp. 29–45.
48 Sartre, *Being and Nothingness*, p. xxiv.
49 Sartre, *Nausea*, pp. 179–80.
50 Sartre, *Nausea*, p. 181.
51 Sartre, *Nausea*, p. 182.
52 Sartre, *Nausea*, pp. 182–83.
53 Sartre, *Being and Nothingness*, p. xxiv.
54 Sartre, *Nausea*, p. 184.
55 Sartre, *Being and Nothingness*, p. xxxviii.
56 Sartre, *Being and Nothingness*, p. 9.
57 I am inclined to agree with Robert Cumming in thinking that 'not-Being' is a more accurate translation of *néant* in Sartre's title than 'nothingness' (Cumming, *Starting Point*, p. 328, fn. 57). However, it is probably too close visually to the term 'non-Being' (*non-être*), which Sartre also uses, so in what follows I will leave the Barnes translation as it is. The basic structure is this: *non-être* relates to beings (things) as *néant* relates to Being. Or, again, *non-être* concerns what is not the case and *néant* is (as it were) the Being of what is not the case. Of course, what is not the case has no Being, which is why we might want to speak instead (as Cumming would prefer) of the not-Being of what is not the case, rather than the (more mysterious?) nothingness of what is not the case. I am grateful to Christina Howells for walking through this with me.
58 Sartre, *Being and Nothingness*, p. xxxix.
59 Sartre, *Being and Nothingness*, p. 4.
60 Sartre, *Being and Nothingness*, p. 4.
61 Sartre, *Being and Nothingness*, p. 38.
62 Sartre, *Being and Nothingness*, p. 7.
63 In fact, this is precisely what Wittgenstein seems to suggest about the logical space of the world at the start of the *Tractatus* (1.11–1.2).
64 Sartre, *Being and Nothingness*, p. 9. By an 'intuition' here Sartre simply means a perceptual experience.
65 Sartre, *Being and Nothingness*, pp. 10–11.
66 Sartre, *Being and Nothingness*, p. 9.
67 Sartre, *Being and Nothingness*, p. 11.
68 A.J. Ayer cited in Maurice Cranston, *Sartre*, London: Oliver & Boyd, 1962, p. 48.
69 Sartre, *Being and Nothingness*, p. 24.
70 Sartre, *Being and Nothingness*, p. 16. Sartre also uses the non-projectivist metaphor of nothingness as a 'worm' coiled 'in the heart of Being'. This is in order to stress that negative realities are not 'extra-mundane' but remain 'within the limits of the real' (ibid., p.21).
71 This conception would suppose that the phenomenon of Being-in-the-world could be grasped as the product of a synthetic 'gluing' together of the two regions of Being that were analytically separated out in the introduction.
72 Sartre finds the contrasting idea of total symmetry in both Hegel and Heidegger. He also reads Heidegger in 'What is Metaphysics?' as treating non-Being as 'beyond the world' (Sartre, *Being and Nothingness*, p. 17), as something (unlike Sartrean *négatités*) precisely *extra-mundane*. This reading of Heidegger is, I think, clearly wide

of the mark. As we saw in Chapter 3, 'the Nothing' in Heidegger is not 'beyond the world' but is the 'nothing' of the world itself. I will return to this theme again in note 81.

73 Sartre, *Being and Nothingness*, p. 17.
74 Sartre, *Being and Nothingness*, p. 17.
75 Sartre, *Being and Nothingness*, p. 18.
76 Sartre, *Being and Nothingness*, p. 24.
77 Sartre, *Being and Nothingness*, p. 24.
78 Sartre, *Being and Nothingness*, p. 104.
79 Sartre, *Being and Nothingness*, p. 218.
80 If one thinks of concept possession as akin to a capacity for navigating (in various ways) in Being, and if one thinks of entities in the world as what we encounter in such navigation, then (as I have already indicated) there is no room for a gap between a navigating 'scheme' on the one hand and the 'world' one encounters on the other. One might think, however, that Sartre opens up a new gulf between 'scheme' and 'Being'. This is not so. In nausea we get a sense that we are only at home in Being because we are at home in the world. There is no stepping outside one's scheme of meaning here – but a collapse of meaning. That is, one does not see that our concepts do or do not correspond to anything in reality – one loses one's way about one's concepts altogether. I am grateful to Daniel Whiting for discussion of this point.
81 Hazel Barnes helpfully notes that the neologism *'néantise'* does not suggest the English term 'annihilate' (destroy) but rather something like 'nihilate' – because 'the fundamental meaning of the term is "to make nothing"' (Sartre, *Being and Nothingness*, p.17, fn. 11). We come here to what looks like a major point of difference between Heidegger's anti-subjectivist analytic of Dasein and Sartre's anthropological humanism, a difference which could be put thus: for Sartre there takes place a distinctive phenomenological event *among beings* when 'Man nihilates', while for Heidegger Dasein exists only in an openness to 'the Nothing' which, *in that event* (itself an event in Being), 'itself nihilates' (Heidegger, 'What is Metaphyscs?', p. 103, see also Heidegger, 'Letter on Humanism', p. 261). I will make a further effort at clarifying this infamous 'statement' in a short note on Merleau-Ponty's conception of our historical thrownness in Chapter 5, note 20.
82 Sartre, *Being and Nothingness*, p. 23.
83 Sartre, *Being and Nothingness*, p. 24.
84 The idea of 'man' is not only problematic because of its androcentrism but also, following Heidegger, because of what one might call its humanist anthropologism. On this conception we are always thinking of 'man' not only as male but, as it were, as the creature that (through revelation or discovery) we regard as uniquely distinctive, standing tall above all 'the animals'. For this reason I would prefer to hold the word 'man' in inverted commas throughout. However, for the sake of tidiness, and since Sartre's thought is, for the most part, utterly inside this anthropologistic conception, I will not keep doing so.
85 It is important to note that Sartre's understanding of freedom, which he takes to be the standard 'technical and philosophical concept' (Sartre, *Being and Nothingness*, p. 483), must be contrasted with what he takes to be the point of view of common sense or of 'the empirical and popular concept' of freedom (ibid.). The latter concept, which admits of differences of degree, is connected with getting (or being able to get) what one wants. This is *not* what Sartre is saying. To say we are free in his sense does not mean we can always get what we want. No, Sartre understands by freedom 'autonomy of choice'. So he is not at all suggesting that we can do or be whatever we want, but that it is intrinsic to our lives that *wherever we have more*

than one possibility open to us (and that is, in his view, *everywhere*) nothing *forces* us to take one route (to pursue one project) rather than another – in each case the choice is always our own and our own alone.

86 Sartre, *Existentialism and Humanism*, p. 28.

87 Sartre, *Existentialism and Humanism*, p. 28

88 That Sartre begins at a step 'already a step beyond' mere animality is perhaps implicit in (and would have been obvious to his listeners with) his recourse to the word 'man' here. The semantics of the today more generally accepted (because more obviously gender-neutral) term 'human being' would not mark this step so obviously since it offers far less opposition to talk about 'us' before 'we' had (as the idea has it) emerged from a *purely* natural order. The price (a good price it might be thought) of making use of the less gendered name for 'us' has thus been a kind of naturalisation of our self-conception. I will return to issues concerning human animality in Chapter 7.

89 Heidegger, 'Letter on Humanism', p. 230.

90 Heidegger emphasises this idea too in the 'Letter on Humanism', insisting that 'the essence of man consists in his being more than merely human' (Heidegger, 'Letter on Humanism', p. 245). John McDowell, who has argued for a somewhat similar conception of human beings as possessed of a man-made ('second') 'nature', indicates how this changeover for the human to becoming fully (hu)'man' introduces a totally new order of evaluative significance into human life: 'The alteration in one's make-up that opened the authority of nature to question is precisely the alteration that has put the dictates of virtue in place as authoritative' (McDowell, *Mind, Value and Reality*, p. 189).

91 I mean this conclusion to resonate with the title of an essay by Jacques Derrida entitled 'The Animal That, Therefore, I Am (More to Follow)' (*Critical Inquiry*, 28, 2002) which I will explore in Chapter 7. Obviously that title is already intended to pick up on the famous Cartesian formula 'I think therefore I am', the formula that Sartre explicitly endorses in *Existentialism and Humanism* as 'the only theory compatible with the dignity of man, it is the only one which does not make man into an object' (Sartre, *Existentialism and Humanism*, p. 45). No animals there.

92 It is worth noting that the emerging or coming about of the initial 'upsurge' of 'man' out of a purely animal condition is not something that Sartre is concerned to explain or engage with here, or indeed anywhere else. And I do think there are problems with this indifference. The worry, as one might put it, is not how something could come out of nothing, but how nothing could come out of something. Sartre might say that he does not need to explain how it came about only to describe what is the case. However, if it is completely unclear how the sort of entity Sartre says we are could possibly have come to be at all, one can only begin to wonder if we can really be the sort of entity he says we are.

93 'God makes man according to a procedure and a conception, exactly as the artisan manufactures a paper-knife, following a definition and a formula. Thus each individual man is the realisation of a certain conception which dwells in the divine understanding' (Sartre, *Existentialism and Humanism*, p. 27).

94 Sartre, *Existentialism and Humanism*, p. 45.

95 Heidegger, 'Letter on Humanism', p. 230.

96 Sartre, *Existentialism and Humanism*, p. 50.

97 Sartre, *Existentialism and Humanism*, p. 45.

98 Sartre, *Existentialism and Humanism*, p. 46.

99 Sartre, *Existentialism and Humanism*, p. 50.

100 Sartre, *Existentialism and Humanism*, p. 54.

101 Sartre, *Existentialism and Humanism*, p. 56.

102 Wiggins, 'Truth, Invention and the Meaning of Life', p. 91.
103 I am grateful to Philip Stratton-Lake for drawing my attention to the importance of this objection to Sartre.
104 Wiggins, 'Truth, Invention and the Meaning of Life', p. 100.
105 Wiggins, 'Truth, Invention and the Meaning of Life', p. 101.
106 McDowell, *Mind, Value and Reality*. p. 155.
107 Emmanuel Levinas, *Totality and Infinity*, Pittsburgh: Duquesne University Press, 1969, p. 21. I will introduce Levinas' thought on this issue in Chapter 6.
108 With this McDowellian notion of (the possibility of) moral objectivity in view, it becomes important to see that the challenge to Sartre is not brought because he makes no room for the idea that moral judgements are supported by 'reality as it is in itself'. He certainly doesn't make any room for that idea, but then that is not *so* controversial. The question is, rather, whether he can make room for the idea that some moral judgements are in *any* significant respect in better shape than any others. One has to be careful not to conflate these notions of objectivity. Sartre obviously gives up the first, but if he gives up on even the possibility of the second his work cannot stand as an essay in moral phenomenology. I am grateful to Daniel Whiting for impressing on me the importance of this distinction.
109 Sartre, *Existentialism and Humanism*, p. 29.
110 Sartre, *Being and Nothingness*, p. 553.
111 Sartre, *Being and Nothingness*, p. 553.
112 Sartre, *Existentialism and Humanism*, p. 42.
113 Max Deutscher, *Genre and Void: Looking Back at Sartre and Beauvoir*, Aldershot: Ashgate, 2003, p. 59.
114 Sartre, *Existentialism and Humanism*, p. 30.
115 Sartre, *Existentialism and Humanism*, p. 52.
116 Sartre, *Existentialism and Humanism*, p. 52.
117 Sartre, *Existentialism and Humanism*, p. 52.
118 Cranston, *Sartre*, p. 80.
119 Peter Caws, *Sartre*, London: Routledge, 1979, p. 119.
120 Warnock, *Sartre*, p. 131.
121 Immanuel Kant, *Foundations of the Metaphysics of Morals*, Indianapolis: Bobbs-Merill, 1949, second section, p. 39.
122 'Man cannot be sometimes slave and sometimes free; he is wholly and forever free or he is not free at all' (Sartre, *Being and Nothingness*, p. 441; see also p. 550).
123 Sartre, *Existentialism and Humanism*, p. 31. It is clearly a good thing that Sartre does not actually take a Kantian route, since those who are convinced that he *does* are understandably quick to point up the massive shortcomings in his defence of it: there is a general consensus that Sartre provides almost nothing: 'no arguments' (Warnock, *Sartre*, p. 131) or only 'the most perfunctory arguments' (Cranston, *Sartre*, p. 82), and Caws finds 'the examples are unconvincing' (Caws, *Sartre*, p. 119) and thinks that 'Sartre's use of moral generalisation is a matter more of evangelistic rhetoric than of philosophical reasoning' (ibid., p. 120). This is the point at which Sartre's later denunciation of the lecture 'as an error' (Cranston, *Sartre*, p. 82) is often dragged up – as if Sartre wasn't more or less constantly disowning his own work.
124 Sartre, *Existentialism and Humanism*, p. 39.
125 Sartre, *Existentialism and Humanism*, p. 49.
126 Sartre, *Existentialism and Humanism*, p. 31.
127 Sartre, *Existentialism and Humanism*, pp. 31–32.
128 Sartre, *Existentialism and Humanism*, p. 38. In Chapter 7 I will return briefly to the question of religion in the context of an epoch in which the idea that we inhabit a cosmos that bears its maker's mark is no longer a matter of course for us.

129 Sartre, *Being and Nothingness*, p. 520, Sartre's italics. The interplay between the singular 'a' and the general 'man' is clearly crucial. The 'who' that I am is always irreducibly caught in this interplay.
130 Sartre, *Existentialism and Humanism*, p. 32. Word order slightly amended for readablility.
131 Caws, *Sartre*, p. 121.
132 Sartre, *Existentialism and Humanism*, p. 30.
133 So far from being an addition creating 'an error', these ideas come straight out of Sartre, *Being and Nothingness*.
134 Sartre, *Existentialism and Humanism*, pp. 52–53.
135 I am indebted to Gordon Finlayson for highlighting the significance of this concept for contemporary moral thinking. See Finlayson, 'Adorno on the Ethical and the Ineffable', *European Journal of Philosophy*, vol. 10, no. 1, 2002, pp. 1–25.
136 Sartre, *Existentialism and Humanism*, p. 36
137 Sartre, *Existentialism and Humanism*, p. 48.
138 Sartre, *Existentialism and Humanism*, p. 67. Cf. Sartre, *Being and Nothingness*, p. 510.
139 Sartre, *Being and Nothingness*, p. 439; Sartre, *Existentialism and Humanism*, p. 34.
140 Merleau-Ponty, *Phenomenology of Perception*, p. xix.

5 Phenomenology of perception

1 Merleau-Ponty, *Phenomenology of Perception*, London: Routledge, 1962, p. xxi.
2 Merleau-Ponty, *Phenomenology of Perception*, p. viii.
3 Merleau-Ponty, *Phenomenology of Perception*, p. xxi.
4 Merleau-Ponty, *Phenomenology of Perception*, p. xx.
5 The term 'facticity' is elaborated by Heidegger in terms of what he calls 'the "factuality" of the fact of one's own Dasein' (Heidegger, *Being and Time*, p. 82). The point is grammatically to distinguish the factuality of such facts from the factual occurrence of something merely present-at-hand. The facticity of existence is not just the obtaining of some state of affairs but concerns the kind of *phenomenological event* in Being that occurs when there is Dasein.
6 Merleau-Ponty, *Phenomenology of Perception*, p, xiv.
7 Merleau-Ponty, *Phenomenology of Perception*, xiv.
8 Merleau-Ponty, *Phenomenology of Perception*, p. 3.
9 Daniel Thomas Primozic, *On Merleau-Ponty*, Belmont: Wadsworth/Thomas Learning, 2001, p. 9.
10 Merleau-Ponty, *Phenomenology of Perception*, p. vii.
11 On the other hand, Merleau-Ponty's account certainly *incorporates* (brings into its body) all five of the phenomenological 'theses' I (perhaps somewhat unfaithfully) extracted in Chapter 1.
12 Merleau-Ponty, *Phenomenology of Perception*, p. viii, italics in original.
13 Merleau-Ponty notes that 'the chief gain' of phenomenology over traditional philosophical inquiry is that it has 'united extreme subjectivism and extreme objectivism in its notion of the world' (Merleau-Ponty, *Phenomenology of Perception*, p. xix).
14 Merleau-Ponty, *Phenomenology of Perception*, p. vii.
15 Merleau-Ponty, *Phenomenology of Perception*, pp. vii–iii.
16 Merleau-Ponty, *Phenomenology of Perception*, pp. xx–xxi.
17 Merleau-Ponty, *Phenomenology of Perception*, p. xxi. As we shall see, this is a gesture that is also fundamental to Derrida's understanding of his 'wanderings' on the theme and history of writing.
18 Merleau-Ponty, *Phenomenology of Perception*, p. xxi.

19 Merleau-Ponty, *Phenomenology of Perception*, p. xxi.

20 As a final effort to gloss Heidegger's infamous formulation about the nihilating nothing, it should be noted that the phrase 'the world worlds' is a Heideggerian coinage (from 1919) which is (for the reasons given in Chapter 3 concerning *that in the face of which anxiety is anxious*) structurally and thematically equivalent to the phrasing of the expression 'the nothing itself nihilates'. As Moran notes, the 1919 formulation aims to avoid supposing that the 'event' thought here is the work of an 'ego' (Moran, *Introduction to Phenomenology*, p. 205). As I noted in Chapter 4, note 81, in the context of Sartre's appropriation of Heideggerian resources, precisely the same point is involved in Heidegger's more (in)famous formulation from the inaugural lecture. There is, as we shall see, an emphasis on our 'thrownness' into a world and history in Merleau-Ponty which is deeply sympathetic to this kind of critique of idealistic philosophies of the subject.

21 In Chapter 1 I cited Socrates as a crucial figure within the modernist[1] conception of the self-responsible philosopher *arguing with others*. Merleau-Ponty gave a central place to Socrates in his inaugural lecture at the Collège de France, published under the title *In Praise of Philosophy* in 1953. See Primozic, *On Merleau-Ponty*, pp. 33–35, for some well-selected passages from that text.

22 Merleau-Ponty, *Phenomenology of Perception*, p. xxi. It is at this point that Merleau-Ponty cites the French heroes of 'modern thought' listed at the start of this chapter.

23 Merleau-Ponty, *Phenomenology of Perception*, p. vii.

24 Merleau-Ponty, *Phenomenology of Perception*, p. vii.

25 Merleau-Ponty, *Phenomenology of Perception*, p. xiv.

26 As Robert Cumming rather wryly notes, for those like Merleau-Ponty who encountered what they were waiting for, it seems that what they had been waiting for 'determined in considerable measure what they got' (Cumming, *Phenomenology and Deconstruction*, vol. 1, p. 62). Still we shouldn't suppose that Merleau-Ponty subscribes to the view that, as far as the interpretation of texts is concerned, one can find anything one wants or that anything goes. His basic point is, rather, that our cultural history provides us with the resources for interpreting texts: that is, they are not read *at all* without being read from a historically emergent interpretive standpoint. And his further point is that the history of philosophy has been particularly productive in providing for itself the interpretive resources for understanding its own productions. Merleau-Ponty is urging us not to conclude too quickly that we know what is emerging in the movement that is bringing phenomenology to being. I will have more to say on what Merleau-Ponty finds there in Chapter 7.

27 Merleau-Ponty, *Phenomenology of Perception*, p. 146.

28 I will explore Merleau-Ponty's reasons for recommending saying 'I *have* a body' rather than 'I *am* my body' or 'This body *is* mine' in Part III of this chapter.

29 The idea of being 'outside oneself' that is captured with the image of '*ek-static*' standing in the world is something Merleau-Ponty borrows from Heidegger's conception of Dasein's being 'already outside alongside' entities in the world and of Dasein's temporalising *ek-static* stretch.

30 Merleau-Ponty, *Phenomenology of Perception*, p. 52.

31 Merleau-Ponty, *Phenomenology of Perception*, p. viii.

32 Merleau-Ponty, *Phenomenology of Perception*, p. viii.

33 Merleau-Ponty, *Phenomenology of Perception*, pp. viiii–ix. The same point is made again in the introduction when he states that it is 'the pre-scientific life of consciousness' alone that can 'endow scientific operations with meaning and to which the latter always refer back' (ibid., pp. 58–59).

34 For Merleau-Ponty this Heideggerian conception is 'no more than an explicit account of the *"natürlicher Weltbegriff"* or the *"Lebenswelt"* which Husserl, towards the end of his life, identified as the central theme of phenomenology' (Merleau-Ponty, *Phenomenology of Perception*, p. vii). As we have noted already, this was *not* Husserl's judgement. He regarded Heidegger's analytic of Dasein as Being-in-the-world as a 'transposition' of his genuinely transcendental phenomenology 'into the anthropological', and hence as a profound *misunderstanding* of his phenomenology, involving a shift 'backward from the level' which was its 'entire meaning to overcome'.

35 Heidegger, *Being and Time*, pp. 54–55.

36 Cited in Heidegger, *Being and Time*, p. 22.

37 Merleau-Ponty, *Phenomenology of Perception*, p. xvi.

38 Merleau-Ponty, *Phenomenology of Perception*, p. viii.

39 Merleau-Ponty, *Phenomenology of Perception*, p. viii.

40 Merleau-Ponty, *Phenomenology of Perception*, p. viii.

41 Merleau-Ponty, *Phenomenology of Perception*, p. xv.

42 Merleau-Ponty, *Phenomenology of Perception*, p. ix.

43 Thomas Baldwin, 'Introduction', in *Maurice Merleau-Ponty: Basic Writings*, T. Baldwin (ed.), London: Routledge, 2004, p. 12.

44 Baldwin, 'Introduction', p. 12.

45 The analytic *locus classicus* for the attack on 'the myth of the given' is Wilfred Sellars' essay *Empiricism and the Philosophy of Mind*, an essay brilliantly developed in John McDowell's *Mind and World*. Both authors acknowledge a phenomenological heritage in their positions.

46 Merleau-Ponty himself writes of 'guarding against myths' involved in 'empiricist doctrines' which attempt to construct perception from meaningless sensations (Merleau-Ponty, *Phenomenology of Perception*, p.23).

47 Baldwin, 'Introduction', p. 14.

48 Merleau-Ponty, *Phenomenology of Perception*, p. 9.

49 Baldwin, 'Introduction', p. 20.

50 Baldwin, 'Introduction', p. 20.

51 Baldwin, 'Introduction', p. 20.

52 A scientific study of a river conducted today would have to incorporate calculations derived from theorems in fluid dynamics. However, that only shows that the investigation cannot even give itself an understanding of the fact that it is 'about a fluid', let alone that it is 'about a river'. As Peter Smith notes (in *Explaining Chaos*, Cambridge: Cambridge University Press, 1988, ch. 5), it is a 'stubbornly unreviseable' feature of even the very best theories in fluid dynamics that it grasps fluids in terms of what, in fact, they are not: namely, as 'perfect continua'.

53 Baldwin, 'Introduction', p. 12.

54 Baldwin, 'Introduction', p. 21.

55 Baldwin, 'Introduction', p. 21.

56 Baldwin, 'Introduction', p. 21.

57 I have developed this comparison myself in Glendinning, 'Perception and Hallucination', *Journal of the British Society of Phenomenology*, vol. 29, no. 3, pp. 314–18.

58 Merleau-Ponty, *Phenomenology of Perception*, pp. 23–24. Referring to 'the cultural apparatus' that his education and experience have provided him with, Merleau-Ponty invokes the idea of 'all the primary thoughts which contribute to my perception or to my present conviction' (ibid., p. 61). The similarity of this picture to Wittgenstein's *On Certainty* conception is striking. Indeed, one might borrow and concur with here Merleau-Ponty's own judgement that, with regard to 'the type of clarification' aimed for by Gilbert Ryle 'along with Wittgenstein', 'I do not see much that separates us' (Merleau-Ponty, *Texts and Dialogues*, p, 66).

59 Merleau-Ponty, *Phenomenology of Perception*, pp. x–xi. This is also a very Wittgensteinian point. Indeed, by drawing on our everyday ways of talking, Merleau-Ponty also offers a rather Wittgensteinian defence of it as well, noting that 'ordinary experience draws a clear distinction between sense-experience and judgement. It sees judgement as the taking of a stand, as an effort to know something . . .; sense-experience, on the contrary, is taking appearance at its face value, without trying to possess it and learn its truth' (Merleau-Ponty, *Phenomenology of Perception*, p. 34). A good illustration of the distinction here is Müller-Lyer's optical illusion (ibid., p. 6). The perceptual illusion is so powerful that it is still given visually as lines which are 'neither of equal nor unequal length' (ibid., p. 6), 'even if I *know*' (ibid., p. 34) they are, objectively speaking, of equal length.

60 Merleau-Ponty, *Phenomenology of Perception*, p. ix.

61 Merleau-Ponty, *Phenomenology of Perception*, p. ix.

62 Merleau-Ponty, *Phenomenology of Perception*, p. xiii.

63 Merleau-Ponty, *Phenomenology of Perception*, p. ix.

64 Merleau-Ponty, *Phenomenology of Perception*, p. ix.

65 Merleau-Ponty, *Phenomenology of Perception*, p. ix.

66 Merleau-Ponty, *Phenomenology of Perception*, p. xi.

67 Merleau-Ponty, *Phenomenology of Perception*, p. xii.

68 Merleau-Ponty, *Phenomenology of Perception*, p. xiii.

69 Merleau-Ponty, *Phenomenology of Perception*, p. 57. Word order altered for convenience.

70 Merleau-Ponty, *Phenomenology of Perception*, p. 11.

71 Merleau-Ponty, *Phenomenology of Perception*, p. xix.

72 Merleau-Ponty, *Phenomenology of Perception*, p. xiii.

73 Sartre, *Being and Nothingness*, p. 439; Sartre, *Existentialism and Humanism*, p. 34.

74 Merleau-Ponty, *Phenomenology of Perception*, p. xix.

75 Merleau-Ponty, *Phenomenology of Perception*, p. xvii.

76 Merleau-Ponty, *Phenomenology of Perception*, p. 40.

77 Merleau-Ponty, *Phenomenology of Perception*, p. 31.

78 Merleau-Ponty, *Phenomenology of Perception*, p. 39.

79 Merleau-Ponty, *Phenomenology of Perception*, p. 10.

80 Merleau-Ponty, *Phenomenology of Perception*, p. 40.

81 Merleau-Ponty, *Phenomenology of Perception*, p. 39.

82 Merleau-Ponty, *Phenomenology of Perception*, p. 41.

83 Merleau-Ponty, *Phenomenology of Perception*, p. 49.

84 Merleau-Ponty, *Phenomenology of Perception*, p. 49.

85 Merleau-Ponty, *Phenomenology of Perception*, p. 39.

86 Merleau-Ponty, *Phenomenology of Perception*, p. 57.

87 Merleau-Ponty, *Phenomenology of Perception*, p. 49.

88 Merleau-Ponty, *Phenomenology of Perception*, p. 57. As he puts it earlier, the focus on 'living experience' is not a retreat to some 'incommunicable impression' (ibid., p. 5).

89 Merleau-Ponty, *Phenomenology of Perception*, p. 5.

90 Merleau-Ponty, *Phenomenology of Perception*, p. 63.

91 Merleau-Ponty, *Phenomenology of Perception*, pp. 23–24.

92 Merleau-Ponty, *Phenomenology of Perception*, p. 54.

93 Merleau-Ponty, *Phenomenology of Perception*, p. 62.

94 Merleau-Ponty, *Phenomenology of Perception*, p. 58.

95 Merleau-Ponty, *Phenomenology of Perception*, p. xiv.

96 Merleau-Ponty, *Phenomenology of Perception*, p. 6.

97 Merleau-Ponty, *Phenomenology of Perception*, p. 29. Cf. Wittgenstein's 'Stand roughly there' in *Philosophical Investigations*, §88.

98 Merleau-Ponty, *Phenomenology of Perception* p. 11. See also ibid., pp. 5 and 8 for further examples of perceptually ambiguous and context-dependent cases.

99 Merleau-Ponty, *Phenomenology of Perception*, p. 24.

100 Merleau-Ponty, *Phenomenology of Perception*, p. 23.

101 Merleau-Ponty, *Phenomenology of Perception*, pp. 23–24.

102 Merleau-Ponty, *Phenomenology of Perception*, p. 24.

103 Husserl introduces the idea of the *noema* to conceptualise the intentional directedness of consciousness towards specific (intentional) objects. Rather like a Fregean sense (at least on Dummett's reading of that), it is to be thought of as the route to the object. See Dermot Moran, *Introduction to Phenomenology*, pp. 155–60.

104 Merleau-Ponty, *Phenomenology of Perception*, p. 31.

105 Merleau-Ponty, *Phenomenology of Perception*, p. 63. 'Ambiguous' is to be understood here as suggesting that *what we perceive* is often many layered, context-dependent and pretty vague. Merleau-Ponty's suggestion, then, is *not* that the perception of 'something or other' is ambiguous in the sense of having a content that can be grasped either as *this* determinate 'something' or *that* determinate 'other' – although perceptually ambiguous figures like this are by no means excluded either (see Merleau-Ponty, *Phenomenology of Perception*, p. 34) – but that no rigorously determinate or determinable *this* or *that* is given at all.

106 Merleau-Ponty, *Phenomenology of Perception*, p. 60.

107 This idea, again, is 'the prejudice of the objective world' (Merleau-Ponty, *Phenomenology of Perception*, p. 58), or, perhaps better, 'the prejudice of determinate being' (ibid., p. 51, fn. 1).

108 Merleau-Ponty, *Phenomenology of Perception*, p. 55.

109 Merleau-Ponty, *Phenomenology of Perception*, p. 56.

110 Merleau-Ponty, *Phenomenology of Perception*, p. 56.

111 Merleau-Ponty, *Phenomenology of Perception*, p. 52.

112 Merleau-Ponty, *Phenomenology of Perception*, p. 90.

113 Merleau-Ponty, *Phenomenology of Perception*, p. 92.

114 Merleau-Ponty, *Phenomenology of Perception*, p. 92.

115 I cannot find this conception in Merleau-Ponty's dialectical cruise around distorting interpretations of the body in objective thought, but it seems to me to belong on the menu of inadequate options. The image is clearly in view in Wittgenstein's *Tractatus* conception of 'the subject' that is not '*in* the world' (5.632–35.633).

116 Merleau-Ponty, *Phenomenology of Perception*, p. 92.

117 Merleau-Ponty, *Phenomenology of Perception*, p. 92. Note the equivocation in the use of 'it' here to refer to the world. For in Merleau-Ponty's contrary conception the world is precisely *not* 'the objective world' of traditional philosophical thought but the ever-present and *strictly non-objectual* 'horizon' of one's life (ibid., p. 92). In his first book, *The Structure of Behaviour*, Merleau-Ponty offers an excellent football field analogy to help rethink the 'relationship to the world' involved here, a relationship that cannot be theorised in terms of an object for consciousness:

> To the player in action the football field is not an 'object'. It is pervaded by lines of force (the yard lines, those which demarcate the 'penalty areas') and articulated in sectors (for example, the 'opening' between members of the team) .... The player becomes one with the field and feels the direction of the 'goal'.
>
> (Merleau-Ponty, *The Structure of Behaviour*, London: Methuen, 1965, p. 168)

Here, as Robert Cumming nicely puts it, 'goal-directed action belongs to the relational context of the field' (Cumming, *Phenomenology and Deconstruction*, vol. 2,

p. 102) and hence provides a kind of literal figuration of existence as Being-in-the-world.

118 Merleau-Ponty, *Phenomenology of Perception*, p xiii.

119 Merleau-Ponty, *Phenomenology of Perception*, p xiii.

120 Merleau-Ponty, *Phenomenology of Perception*, p. 151.

121 Merleau-Ponty, *Phenomenology of Perception*, p. 150.

122 Merleau-Ponty, *Phenomenology of Perception*, p. 139.

123 Merleau-Ponty, *Phenomenology of Perception*, p. 150.

124 Merleau-Ponty, *Phenomenology of Perception*, p. 55.

125 Merleau-Ponty, *Phenomenology of Perception*, p. 55.

126 See Merleau-Ponty, *Phenomenology of Perception*, p. 151.

127 Merleau-Ponty, *Phenomenology of Perception*, p. 55.

128 Merleau-Ponty, *Phenomenology of Perception*, p. 63. It is noteworthy that in discussion with Gilbert Ryle (whose *The Concept of Mind* Merleau-Ponty stated he knew and had 'worked with') Merleau-Ponty raised the question whether, in a parallel fashion, philosophical investigations of language should not 'have recourse … to an immanent study of linguistic phenomena for which certain parts of linguistic science might be the rough sketch' (Merleau-Ponty, *Texts and Dialogues*, pp. 66–67).

129 Merleau-Ponty, *Phenomenology of Perception*, p. 63.

130 This is the topic of ch. 6 of Pt One of Merleau-Ponty, *Phenomenology of Perception*.

131 Merleau-Ponty, *Phenomenology of Perception*, p. 174.

132 Merleau-Ponty, *Phenomenology of Perception*, p. 174.

133 Merleau-Ponty, *Phenomenology of Perception*, p. 174.

134 As should be clear, Merleau-Ponty's distinction between 'being' and 'having' is not an invitation to suppose (as it is often supposed he is recommending) that 'I am my body' (see Primozic, *On Merleau-Ponty*, p. 17, and John Wild, 'Forward' to *Structure of Behaviour*, p. xv). Indeed, one of the reasons that he explores the sense of possession involved in 'having a body' through an analysis of bodily expression and 'having a language' is that the identification of the subject with the body produces just the kind of misleading objectification he wants to avoid. That is, it is precisely because he totally accepts Descartes' idea that I am not merely externally related to my body 'as a pilot to his ship' that he wants to *retain* the ordinary expression 'I have a body' (see, for example, Merleau-Ponty, *The Structure of Behaviour*, pp. 208–11). What commentators are rightly recognising, then, is that it is misleading to think that 'having a body' designates a simple proprietary relationship. However, what the objectifying identification fails to acknowledge is that a (different) sense of possession is nevertheless still in play here: a sense of possession (Merleau-Ponty's 'having') which indicates an internal and not a merely external relation. It is a central aspect of this internal relation, the relation captured with the idea of the body as the visible *expression* of a concrete ego, that Merleau-Ponty aims to make explicit through an investigation of someone's 'possession of language'.

135 'The hat is mine' will thus go along with the list: 'The hat is brown', 'The hat is old', 'The hat is stolen', 'The hat is smelly'. The idea at issue in 'I have an idea' can also belong to such a predicative list: 'The idea is old', 'The idea is stolen', 'The idea is good', 'The idea is original', 'The idea is mine'. But the best way of expressing the truth condition of the last one is with reference to the fact that I was the first to *have* it.

136 I was once pointedly rebuked for mistaking someone's wife for a hat by the German philosopher Eike von Savigny, when I thought to criticise him for ordering food for his wife at a restaurant by saying 'My wife will have the steak.' Maybe he could have let her speak for herself, but Eike was speaking for everyone on this occasion. No, his point to me was that the sense of 'my' in this case ('My wife … ') indicated

a relation not a propriety possession. So he was not suggesting ownership of something (as he might with a hat) but publicly presenting (celebrating) his relation to someone (his wife). Merleau-Ponty's schema would mark this distinction, and help one avoid mistaking a wife for a hat, by rendering the sense of 'my' involved in 'my wife' with the sentence 'I have a wife' and not the (dubious) sentence 'The wife is mine'.

137 Merleau-Ponty, *Phenomenology of Perception*, p. 175.
138 Merleau-Ponty, *Phenomenology of Perception*, p. 175.
139 Merleau-Ponty, *Phenomenology of Perception*, p. 176.
140 Merleau-Ponty, *Phenomenology of Perception*, p. 176.
141 Merleau-Ponty, *Phenomenology of Perception*, p. 176, italics in original.
142 Merleau-Ponty, *Phenomenology of Perception*, p. 176.
143 Merleau-Ponty, *Phenomenology of Perception*, pp. 176–77, italics in original.
144 Merleau-Ponty, *Phenomenology of Perception*, p. 177.
145 Merleau-Ponty, *Phenomenology of Perception*, p. 180.
146 Merleau-Ponty, *Phenomenology of Perception*, p. 183. As we have seen, a similar point is made by Derrida at the outset of *Speech and Phenomena*, when he notes that the rehabilitation of the indicative sign will allow us to see that 'the spoken word, whatever dignity or originality we still accord it, is but a form of gesture' (Derrida, *Speech and Phenomena*, p. 21). I will come back to Derrida's (in fact rather different) treatment of this idea in Chapter 7.
147 Merleau-Ponty, *Phenomenology of Perception*, p. 182.
148 Merleau-Ponty, *Phenomenology of Perception*, p. 183.
149 Merleau-Ponty, *Phenomenology of Perception*, p. 182. As he also puts it, 'speech in the speaker does not translate ready-made thought, but accomplishes it' (ibid., p. 178). There is here a '*thought in speech* the existence of which is unsuspected by intellectualism' (ibid., p. 179). In general, then, Merleau-Ponty's basic claim against intellectualism is that 'the thinking subject must have its basis in the subject incarnate' (ibid., p. 193).
150 Merleau-Ponty, *Phenomenology of Perception*, p. 183.
151 Merleau-Ponty, *Phenomenology of Perception*, p. 24.
152 Merleau-Ponty, *Phenomenology of Perception*, p. 58. We should note that this 'immediate object' is not an immediate object for just anyone you please. Again we must remember that, for Merleau-Ponty, *culture* informs perception from its roots. Thus, for example, when I see (immediately) a particular gesture as 'angry' or 'threatening' this is not perceived by me 'as the colour of the carpet' is, and the gestures of people from different cultures indicate how people with the same 'anatomical apparatus' can learn to 'use their bodies' differently and with different expressive meaning (ibid., p, 189). I develop (and mildly criticise) Merleau-Ponty's thought here in Glendinning, *On Being with Others*, pp. 140–44.
153 Merleau-Ponty, *Phenomenology of Perception*, p. 351. The worry (from the other side, as it were) that this conception leaves the other in some way *too* present to me, too much part of the *visible* 'outer' world as it is given to me, is something that will be alive when we look at Levinas' account of the 'face to face' relation to the other person in Chapter 6. That Merleau-Ponty is not himself closed off to this worry about making the other too visibly there is clear from his discussions of 'the truth in solipsism' in the chapter of *Phenomenology of Perception* that this quotation comes from (Pt Two, ch. 4, 'Other Selves and the Human World'). Merleau-Ponty's important idea that the meanings that are 'imminent to the behaviour' of a living body are not 'really contained in them' is explained in the next section.
154 See Moran, *Introduction to Phenomenology*, p. 403. It is worth noting that *The Structure of Behaviour* comes to its conclusion with a section called 'Is there not a Truth of Naturalism?' (Merleau-Ponty, *The Structure of Behaviour*, pp. 201–20).

155 I am indebted to conversations with Matthew Bell for this idea.

156 Raimond Gaita defends this view of the relation between science and philosophy at length in *The Philosopher's Dog*, London: Routledge, 2003.

157 Merleau-Ponty, *Phenomenology of Perception*, p. 190.

158 The distinction here between 'the difference' and 'the differences' between human beings and other living things is drawn from Cora Diamond's paper 'Eating Meat and Eating People', in *The Realistic Spirit*, Cambridge, Mass.: MIT Press, 1996. I will return to it briefly shortly and at greater length in Chapter 7.

159 Merleau-Ponty, *Phenomenology of Perception*, p. 151.

160 Merleau-Ponty, *Phenomenology of Perception*, p. 87.

161 Merleau-Ponty, *Phenomenology of Perception*, p. 189.

162 By humanism here I mean a position which assumes that talk of 'the difference' between humans and other living things (as opposed to 'the differences' between them) is *justified* by the fact that there is a real (observed or revealed) break in being between human beings and every other living thing, a break which establishes human beings, uniquely, as something more or other than a 'mere' (pure) living thing.

163 Merleau-Ponty, *Phenomenology of Perception*, p. 87.

164 Merleau-Ponty, *Phenomenology of Perception*, p. 58.

165 Merleau-Ponty, *Phenomenology of Perception*, p. 189.

166 Merleau-Ponty, *Phenomenology of Perception*, p. 194.

167 So the binary distinction that Merleau-Ponty appeals to is not so much between nature and culture as it is between a purely natural life and a natural life everywhere informed by culture.

168 I am indebted to Daniel Whiting for discussion of this issue as it arises in Merleau-Ponty.

169 Baldwin, 'Introduction', p. 9.

170 Merleau-Ponty, *Phenomenology of Perception*, p. 186.

171 Merleau-Ponty, *Phenomenology of Perception*, p. 186.

172 Merleau-Ponty, *Phenomenology of Perception*, p. 186.

173 Merleau-Ponty, *Phenomenology of Perception*, p. 187.

174 Merleau-Ponty, *Phenomenology of Perception*, p. 187.

175 Merleau-Ponty, *Phenomenology of Perception*, p. 188.

176 Merleau-Ponty, *Phenomenology of Perception*, p. 197.

177 The basic claim of a serious alternative would seem to me fairly clear: namely, that many non-human animals are not simply or purely creatures *without* culture. And I do not regard it as at all implausible to suppose (and empirically to test) that there are symbolic cultures within non-human animal lives too. With the movement from the non-human to the human there is, to be sure, *a transition within this field of culture* sufficiently radical that one might want to call it 'a transition from quantity to quality'. So rejecting Merleau-Ponty's dualism does not imply that one winds up affirming a baldly natural (and, as Derrida will put it, 'asinine') biologism or continuism. On the other hand, acknowledging the existence of genuinely objective *differences* within the continuity of the field does not imply either that one could specify something like an 'origin of man' that would mark (in the nature of things) a fundamental or radical rupture and *difference* with all animal nature. I will return to this in Chapter 7.

6 Phenomenology and the Other

1 Emmanuel Levinas, *Is It Righteous to Be?: Interviews with Emmanuel Levinas*, J. Robbins (ed.), Stanford: Stanford University Press, 2001, p. 29.

2 Levinas, *Is It Righteous to Be?*, p. 44.
3 Levinas, *Is It Righteous to Be?*, p. 80.
4 Levinas, *Is It Righteous to Be?*, p. 80.
5 I am here insinuating Cumming's summary of the French reception of German phenomenology (Cumming, *Phenomenology and Deconstruction*, vol. 1, p. 96) into the place opened up by Derrida's cautious adoption of a convention to 'call "France" ... the non-empirical site of a movement, a structure and an articulation of the question "of man"' (Derrida, 'The Ends of Man', in *Margins of Philosophy*).
6 Cumming, *Phenomenology and Deconstruction*, vol. 1, p. 96.
7 Levinas, *Is It Righteous to Be?*, p. 28.
8 Levinas, *Is It Righteous to Be?*, p. 32.
9 Levinas, *Is It Righteous to Be?*, p. 33.
10 Levinas, *Is It Righteous to Be?*, p. 33.
11 Levinas, *Is It Righteous to Be?*, p. 37.
12 Levinas, *Is It Righteous to Be?*, p. 31.
13 This is the text that we have in English as the *Cartesian Meditations*. The book is an expanded version of Husserl's Sorbonne lectures, and despite being given first in German it was published for the first time anywhere in Levinas' French edition (co-edited with Gabrielle Peiffer).
14 Cumming, *Phenomenology and Deconstruction*, vol. 1, p. 88–89.
15 Cumming, *Phenomenology and Deconstruction*, vol. 1, p. 89.
16 Cumming, *Phenomenology and Deconstruction*, vol. 1, p. 89.
17 Derrida, 'The Ends of Man', p. 115.
18 Derrida, 'Violence and Metaphysics', p. 108.
19 Derrida, 'Violence and Metaphysics', p. 104.
20 We should note that, despite Derrida's interventions, Levinas never rejected his early idea that 'Husserl's philosophy already stated the Heideggerian problems of Being and beings' (Levinas, *Is It Righteous to Be?*, p. 37).
21 This affirmation must have shone like the sun for the developing Merleau-Ponty.
22 Cited by Derrida, 'Violence and Metaphysics', p. 108.
23 Cited by Derrida, 'Violence and Metaphysics', p. 108.
24 Cited by Derrida, 'Violence and Metaphysics', p. 107.
25 Levinas, *Existence and Existents*, The Hague: Martinus Nijhoff, 1978, p. 19.
26 Derrida, 'Violence and Metaphysics', p. 112.
27 In fairness, this is not something Derrida can be said to have missed. Indeed, 'Violence and Metaphysics' *begins* by emphasising how deeply Levinas' thought reaches into Western philosophy, and suggests that 'it reaches a height and a level of penetration in its dialogue in which the Greeks – and foremost among them the Greeks named Husserl and Heidegger – are called upon to respond' (Derrida, 'Violence and Metaphysics', pp. 102–03).
28 Derrida, 'Violence and Metaphysics', p. 110. As I noted in Chapter 3, the formulation 'new, quite new' is somewhat disconcerting, taking away in one gesture what is given in the other, but fundamentally appropriate to the shifting sequence in the inheritance of phenomenology.
29 Derrida, 'Violence and Metaphysics', p. 109.
30 See R. Bernasconi and S. Critchley (eds), 'Editors' Introduction', in *Re-Reading Levinas*, Bloomington: Indiana, 1991, which explicitly acknowledges that the reception of Levinas has been, at least in the first instance, largely determined by 'the reception of Levinas *via* Derrida' (p. xii.).
31 Bernasconi and Critchley, 'Editors' Introduction', p. xvii.
32 Derrida, 'Violence and Metaphysics', pp. 104 and 114.
33 Levinas, *Totality and Infinity*, p. 29.

34 Levinas, *Totality and Infinity*, p. 29.
35 Levinas, *Totality and Infinity*, p. 29.
36 Levinas, *Totality and Infinity*, p. 26.
37 Derrida, 'Violence and Metaphysics', p. 112.
38 Derrida, 'Violence and Metaphysics', p. 103, fn. 7.
39 Moran, *Introduction to Phenomenology*, pp. 352–53.
40 Moran, *Introduction to Phenomenology*, p. 352.
41 Moran, *Introduction to Phenomenology*, p. 352.
42 This is not to say that Derrida is everywhere confident of having a good ear for Levinas' formulations. For example, he openly admits that he cannot make any headway at all with some types of proposition. 'Finally, let us confess our total deafness to propositions of this type: "Being occurs as multiple, and as divided into Same and Other. This is its ultimate structure" (*Totality and Infinity*).' (Derrida, 'Violence and Metaphysics', p. 158.) Yes, let's confess that.
43 Wittgenstein's remark is 'Philosophie dürfte man eigentlich *nur dichten*', which Winch (I think fairly) rendered in the first edition of *Culture and Value* as 'philosophy ought really to be written only as a *poetic composition*' (Wittgenstein, *Culture and Value*, trans. P. Winch, Oxford: Blackwell, 1980, p. 24).
44 I take it that this is what Derrida is (double-)gesturing at when he notes that the questions he raises in the course of his reading of Levinas are not to be thought of as objections but as 'questions put to *us* by Levinas' (Derrida, 'Violence and Metaphysics', p. 104).
45 Levinas, *Totality and Infinity*, p 21.
46 Levinas, *Totality and Infinity*, p. 22.
47 Levinas, *Totality and Infinity*, p. 23.
48 Levinas, *Totality and Infinity*, p. 25.
49 Levinas, *Totality and Infinity*, p. 21.
50 Levinas, *Totality and Infinity*, p. 21.
51 Levinas, *Totality and Infinity*, p. 24.
52 Levinas, *Totality and Infinity*, p. 26.
53 Levinas, *Totality and Infinity*, p. 24. The English-language translators of Levinas typically differentiate the French words *autrui* (the other person) and *autre* (otherness in general) by capitalising the former, giving us rather impressive looking English expressions like 'the face of the Other' for the somewhat less remarkable French expressions '*le visage d'autrui*'. Levinas himself capitalises both on occasion to get the impressive effect in French, but that cannot survive the translation convention.
54 Wittgenstein, *Philosophical Investigations*, §286.
55 Levinas, *Totality and Infinity*, p. 50.
56 Levinas, *Totality and Infinity*, pp. 50–51.
57 Levinas, *Totality and Infinity*, p. 24–25.
58 Levinas, *Totality and Infinity*, p. 50–51.
59 Levinas, *Totality and Infinity*, p. 200.
60 'The presentation of the face, expression, does not disclose an inward world previously closed, adding thus a new region to comprehend or to take over' (Levinas, *Totality and Infinity*, p. 212).
61 Levinas, *Totality and Infinity*, p. 51.
62 This formulation is from J.L. Austin's essay 'Other Minds' (in *Philosophical Papers*, Oxford: Clarendon, 1979, p. 85), but it fits well with what Levinas has to say about the manifestation of the face of the Other.
63 This formulation derives from McDowell (see McDowell, 'Criteria, Defeasibility and Knowledge', *Proceedings of the British Academy*, vol. LXVIII, 1983, p. 462), but

like the Austin line above it is fitting for Levinas' idea that approaching an Other
as such 'is to welcome his expression' (Levinas, *Totality and Infinity*, p. 51).
64 Levinas, *Totality and Infinity*, p. 34.
65 Levinas, *Totality and Infinity*, p. 35.
66 Levinas, *Totality and Infinity*, p. 35.
67 Levinas, *Totality and Infinity*, p. 35.
68 'The absolutely other is the Other' (*L'absolument Autre, c'est Autrui*) (Levinas,
Totality and Infinity, p. 39).
69 Levinas, *Totality and Infinity*, p. 77.
70 Levinas, quoted in 'The Paradox of Morality', trans. A. Benjamin and T. Wright, in
R. Bernasconi and D. Wood (eds), *The Provocation of Levinas: Rethinking the Other*,
London: Routledge, 1998, p. 172.
71 Levinas, *Totality and Infinity*, p. 208.
72 Levinas, *Totality and Infinity*, p. 208.
73 Levinas, *Totality and Infinity*, p. 208.
74 Levinas, *Totality and Infinity*, p. 247.
75 This infinite obligation to *this* Other is, of course, compromised as soon as there is
another Other, and according to Levinas that means that the incalculable ethical demand is compromised *right from the start* since the singularity of *every* human
(as an example, precisely, of the uniquely human) means that 'the third party
looks at me in the eyes of the Other' (Levinas, *Totality and Infinity*, p. 213).
Nevertheless, for Levinas *political* issues of distributive justice and equality would
have no weight in our thinking unless they were calculated against the background
of (or were not constantly haunted by) the incalculable *ethical* obligation to the
Other.
76 Levinas, *Totality and Infinity*, p. 35.
77 Sartre, *Being and Nothingness*, p. 231.
78 Levinas, *Totality and Infinity*, p. 290.
79 Levinas, *Totality and Infinity*, p. 53.
80 Simon Critchley, 'Introduction', *Cambridge Companion to Levinas*, eds R. Bernasconi
and S. Critchley, Cambridge: Cambridge University Press, 2004, pp. 13–14.
81 The existence of the other cannot, Sartre insists, be measured 'by means of the
knowledge we have of him' (Sartre, *Being and Nothingness*, p. 224).
82 Levinas, *Totality and Infinity*, p. 49, emphasis in original.
83 Levinas, *Totality and Infinity*, p. 49.
84 Levinas, *Totality and Infinity*, p. 198.
85 Levinas, *Totality and Infinity*, p. 194.
86 Levinas, *Totality and Infinity*, p. 51.
87 Levinas, *Totality and Infinity*, p. 49.
88 Levinas, *Totality and Infinity*, p. 199. The connections to Wittgenstein's way of
articulating the asymmetry of the first and third person are explored by Bob
Plant in his excellent *Wittgenstein and Levinas: Ethical and Religious Thought*
(London: Routledge, 2004). I think Plant is right to see important parallels.
However, at the end of this chapter I will want to draw attention to a difference between them over questions concerning the 'visibility' of the Other, a
difference that is in my view bound up with Levinas' way of elaborating the
object/Other difference in terms of the objectivity/transcendence distinction.
89 Furnishings [*meubles*] is Levinas' occasional term for the moveable 'medium-sized
dry goods' that philosophy tends to let stand for things in general. Levinas goes
along with this only as long as we acknowledge that such things 'emerge from a
background' (Levinas, *Totality and Infinity*, p. 130), what he calls the 'elemental' in
which we are 'steeped' and in which we 'bathe' (ibid., p. 132), which is not itself a

moveable dry good. This sensible background is not a presented or represented 'something' that we enjoy but the 'horizon within which I live' (ibid., p. 137): 'In my position there is not the sentiment of localization, but the localization of my sensibility' (ibid., p. 138).

90 Levinas, *Totality and Infinity*, p. 135.
91 Levinas, *Totality and Infinity*, p. 37.
92 Levinas, *Totality and Infinity*, p. 137.
93 Levinas, *Totality and Infinity*, p. 38.
94 Levinas, *Totality and Infinity*, p. 37.
95 Levinas, *Totality and Infinity*, p. 111.
96 Levinas, *Totality and Infinity*, p. 39.
97 As Levinas famously puts it, the only way I can achieve power over the other is by acknowledging my absolute lack of power, 'renounc[ing] comprehension absolutely' and thus annihilating him. 'The Other is the sole being I can wish to kill' (Levinas, *Totality and Infinity*, p. 198).
98 Levinas, *Totality and Infinity*, p. 40. I am grateful to Robert Eaglestone for drawing my attention to the fact that this designation is (*perhaps*, I will still add) not so very enigmatic: the word 'religion' is, as the dictionary says, '*perh*. conn. with *reli-gāre*, to bind'.
99 Levinas, *Totality and Infinity*, p. 40.
100 Levinas, *Totality and Infinity*, p. 110.
101 Levinas, *Totality and Infinity*, p. 110.
102 Levinas, *Totality and Infinity*, p. 110.
103 Levinas, *Totality and Infinity*, p. 110.
104 Levinas, *Totality and Infinity*, p. 112.
105 Levinas, *Totality and Infinity*, p. 112.
106 Levinas, *Totality and Infinity*, p. 112.
107 Levinas, *Totality and Infinity*, p. 135.
108 Levinas, *Totality and Infinity*, p. 112.
109 Levinas, *Totality and Infinity*, p. 113.
110 Levinas, *Totality and Infinity*, p. 115.
111 Levinas, *Totality and Infinity*, p. 116.
112 Levinas, *Totality and Infinity*, p. 116.
113 Levinas, *Totality and Infinity*, p. 146.
114 Heidegger, 'Letter on Humanism', p. 230.
115 Levinas, *Totality and Infinity*, p. 134.
116 Levinas, *Totality and Infinity*, p. 147.
117 Levinas, *Totality and Infinity*, p. 149.
118 Levinas, *Totality and Infinity*, p. 116–17. This is essentially the same point I raised in the context of discussing Merleau-Ponty's attempt to affirm both a privative naturalism and a fundamental humanism. As indicated in the main text, what needs to be questioned here is the conception of 'the animal' and of 'pure nature' that is operative in this account. I will come back to this in Chapter 7.
119 Levinas, *Totality and Infinity*, p. 116.
120 Levinas, *Totality and Infinity*, p. 116.
121 Levinas, *Totality and Infinity*, p. 116.
122 Levinas, *Totality and Infinity*, p. 117.
123 Levinas, *Totality and Infinity*, p. 117.
124 Levinas, *Totality and Infinity*, p. 116.
125 Levinas, *Totality and Infinity*, p. 115.
126 Levinas, *Totality and Infinity*, p. 117.
127 Levinas, *Totality and Infinity*, p. 117.

128 At this point Levinas' analysis broaches a suggestive if difficult thought, developed most directly and most forcefully in *Time and the Other* (Pittsburgh: Duquesne University Press, 1987), that the relation to the future one cannot anticipate, the unforeseeable future as 'absolute other', is opened up concretely in the relationship to other people (ibid., p. 80). As he puts it, 'the condition of time lies in the relationship between humans, or in history' (ibid., p. 79); or, again, 'it seems to me impossible to speak of time in a subject alone, or to speak of a purely personal duration' (ibid., p.77). The relation to the Other *is* a relation to an uncharted future. It is, therefore, the fundamental condition of *being in time*.

129 There is no doubt that for Levinas the Other who I am infinitely obliged to must be another *like myself*, another human, and *not* a merely animal other. The most sustained critical engagement with Levinas on the question of the alterity of the other animal is John Llewelyn's 'Am I Obsessed by Bobby?', in *Re-Reading Levinas*, eds R. Bernasconi and S. Critchley, pp. 234–45. I will very briefly engage with this issue myself in the final section of this chapter and return to it more directly in Chapter 7.

130 Levinas, *Totality and Infinity*, p. 133. It is I think telling that Levinas regards the ready-to-hand as escaping the locus of the visible. There is a prejudice here that I will explore in the final section of this chapter and which Heidegger (and Derrida after him) seem to me rightly to want to remove: namely, the assumption that what is given to perception is always and everywhere the presence of something simply present.

131 Levinas, *Totality and Infinity*, p. 133.
132 Levinas, *Totality and Infinity*, p. 133.
133 Levinas, *Totality and Infinity*, p. 133.
134 Levinas, *Totality and Infinity*, p. 67. Word order modified for fluency.
135 Levinas, *Totality and Infinity*, p. 122.
136 Levinas, *Totality and Infinity*, p. 135.
137 Levinas, *Totality and Infinity*, p. 137.
138 Levinas, *Totality and Infinity*, p. 136.
139 Levinas, *Totality and Infinity*, p. 147.
140 Levinas, *Totality and Infinity*, p. 124.
141 Levinas, *Totality and Infinity*, p. 125.
142 Levinas, *Totality and Infinity*, p. 127.
143 Levinas, *Totality and Infinity*, p. 127.
144 Levinas, *Totality and Infinity*, p. 133.
145 Levinas, *Totality and Infinity*, p. 133.
146 Levinas, *Totality and Infinity*, p. 149.
147 Levinas, *Totality and Infinity*, p. 113.
148 Levinas, *Totality and Infinity*, p. 138.
149 Levinas, *Totality and Infinity*, p. 122.
150 Levinas, *Totality and Infinity*, p. 156.
151 Levinas, *Totality and Infinity*, p. 152.
152 Levinas, *Totality and Infinity*, p. 152.
153 Levinas, *Totality and Infinity*, p. 152.
154 Levinas, *Totality and Infinity*, p. 153.
155 Levinas, *Totality and Infinity*, p. 153.
156 Levinas, *Totality and Infinity*, p. 155.
157 Levinas, *Totality and Infinity*, p. 155.
158 Levinas, *Totality and Infinity*, p. 156.
159 Levinas, *Totality and Infinity*, p. 155.
160 Levinas, *Totality and Infinity*, p. 158.

161 It might be added, *pace* Simone de Beauvoir in *The Second Sex* (Harmondsworth: Penguin, 1984, p. 16), that the feminine alterity is not, for Levinas, an attenuated or second-rate mode of subjectivity but 'is comprehensible and exercises its function of interiorization only on the ground of *the full human personality*' (Levinas, *Totality and Infinity*, p. 155, italics added).

162 Critchley, 'Introduction', *Cambridge Companion to Levinas*, p. 7.

163 Levinas, *Totality and Infinity*, p. 154.

164 I am grateful to Kathleen Lennon for helping me find this way of framing the worry with Levinas' account.

165 Levinas, *Totality and Infinity*, p. 188.

166 Levinas, *Totality and Infinity*, p. 187.

167 Levinas, *Totality and Infinity*, p. 187.

168 Stella Sandford, 'Levinas in the Realm of the Senses: Transcendence and Intelligibility', *Angelaki*, vol. 4, no. 3, 2000, p. 63.

169 'The I exists as separated in its enjoyment, that is, as happy', says Levinas (*Totality and Infinity*, p. 63). Levinas seems to demand we acknowledge that even when things are going badly and we are, as we say, unhappy, we are still hot with sensation, and this serves to remind us (lest we forget it) that when we are living, even barely living, we are not dead.

170 Levinas, *Time and the Other*, p. 89.

171 There is a distinction here, then, which, as Stella Sandford has noted, 'is elided in the implication of eros in the account of *jouissance*' (Sandford, 'Levinas in the Realm of the Senses', p. 64).

172 '[L]*a volupté n'est pas un plaisir comme un autre, parce qu'elle n'est pas un plaisir solitaire comme le manger ou le boire*' (Levinas, *Time and the Other*, p. 89, italics added to the English translation).

173 Levinas puts it as follows: if we 'could possess, grasp and know the Other, it would not be Other' (Levinas, *Time and the Other*, p. 90). The traditional philosopher would concur. Indeed, I think Levinas' inference from the logical impossibility of *undergoing* ('possessing') the other's experience to the impossibility of *knowing* what the other undergoes is a very traditional idea – and an error. I will return to this in the final section.

174 It is a measure of the importance to Levinas of this distinction that he sees a profound fault when we confuse the two, which I suspect we do more or less constantly, more or less comically, identifying what he calls 'the ridiculous and tragic image of devouring in kissing and biting' (Levinas, *Existence and Existents*, p. 43, cited in Sandford, 'Levinas in the Realm of the Senses', p. 64).

175 Luce Irigaray, 'Questions to EL', in *Re-Reading Levinas*, eds R. Bernasconi and S. Critchley, Bloomington: Indiana, 1991, p. 111.

176 'Fusion' is Levinas' word, but Irigaray's translator also talks about a 'fusion of syntax' in Irigaray's work of words which 'poetically echoes the fusion of bodies' (Irigaray, 'Questions to EL', p. 118).

177 The thought is that we individuate (token) sensations 'over persons' (see, for example, P. Strawson, *Individuals*, London: Methuen, p. 41).

178 Irigaray, 'Questions to EL', p. 111.

179 Irigaray, 'Questions to EL', p. 111. 'Solitary sex', Irigaray should have said. There is a big difference here.

180 Recall again Wittgenstein, *Philosophical Investigations*, §286: 'If someone has a pain in his hand . . . one does not comfort the hand, but the sufferer: one looks into his face'.

181 Recall again Wittgenstein, *Philosophical Investigations*, §300: 'The image of pain certainly enters into the language-game [with the words "he is in pain"] in a sense; only not as a picture.'

182 I am grateful to Annabel Herzog for discussion of Levinas and Irigaray on these matters.

183 Derrida, 'History of the Lie: Prolegomena', in *Without Alibi*, P. Kamuf (ed.), Stanford: Stanford University Press, 2002, p. 37.

184 Derrida, 'Typewriter Ribbon', in *Without Alibi*, P. Kamuf (ed.), Stanford: Stanford University Press, 2002, p. 111.

185 Compare, Wittgenstein *Philosophical Investigations*, p. 222.

186 Levinas, *Totality and Infinity*, p. 181.

187 Levinas, *Totality and Infinity*, p. 182.

188 Levinas, *Totality and Infinity*, p. 181.

189 Levinas, *Totality and Infinity*, p. 182.

190 Levinas, *Totality and Infinity*, p. 182.

191 Levinas, *Totality and Infinity*, p. 181.

192 Derrida, 'Différance', in *Margins of Philosophy*, trans. A. Bass, London: Harvester Wheatsheaf, 1982, p. 5.

193 Levinas, *Totality and Infinity*, p. 194.

194 Levinas, *Totality and Infinity*, p. 193.

195 Levinas, *Totality and Infinity*, p. 297.

196 Levinas, *Totality and Infinity*, p. 200.

197 Levinas, *Totality and Infinity*, p. 194.

198 Critchley, 'Introduction', *Cambridge Companion to Levinas*, p. 8.

199 Derrida, *Speech and Phenomena*, p. 104

200 We saw this movement away from expressive behaviour in Husserl too. The critique outlined there can, I think, be replayed against Levinas here.

201 Cavell, *The Claim of Reason*, p. 356.

202 Cavell, *The Claim of Reason*, p. 363.

203 Cavell, *The Claim of Reason*, p. 45.

204 Derrida, 'Violence and Metaphysics', p. 126.

205 Derrida, 'Violence and Metaphysics', p. 127.

206 Derrida, 'Signature Event Context', p. 10.

207 Derrida, 'Signature Event Context', p. 16.

208 Wittgenstein, *Philosophical Investigations*, preface.

209 Derrida, 'Violence and Metaphysics', p. 127.

210 Wittgenstein, *Zettel*, second edition, Oxford: Blackwell, 1991, §223.

211 Levinas, *Totality and Infinity*, pp. 187–88.

212 Levinas, *Totality and Infinity*, p. 206.

7 Interrupting phenomenology

1 Ian Hacking, 'A New Way to See a Leaf', *New York Review of Books*, 7 April 2005, vol. LII, no. 6, p. 70.

2 Ian Hacking, 'A New Way to See a Leaf', p. 70, fn. 1.

3 Cumming, *Phenomenology and Deconstruction*, vol. 1, p, 125.

4 'By proposing from the start a radical dissociation between two heterogeneous kinds of sign, between indication and expression, he has not asked what is meant by a sign *in general*' (Derrida, *Speech and Phenomena*, p. 23).

5 Derrida, 'Hospitality, Justice and Responsibility', in R. Kearney and M. Dooley (eds), *Questioning Ethics: Contemporary Debates in Philosophy*, London: Routledge, 1999, p. 81.

6 Derrida, *Points de suspension*, Paris: Galilée, 1997, p. 387.

7 Derrida, 'The Ends of Man', p. 134.

8 Cumming, *Phenomenology and Deconstruction*, vol. 3, p. 104.

9 Derrida, 'The Ends of Man', p. 134.

10 Derrida, 'Hospitality, Justice and Responsibility', p. 81.

11 Derrida, 'Différance', p. 16.

12 With Derrida's work in view, Robert Cumming asserts that 'we are aware' in our time 'of phenomenology as having by and large come to an end, as philosophical movements do' (Cumming, *Phenomenology and Deconstruction*, vol. 1, p. 166).

13 Derrida, 'Hospitality, Justice and Responsibility', p. 81. Derrida is reflecting on Levinas' comment that 'when phenomenology addresses the question of the other it interrupts itself', but he inscribes these remarks in the context of a discussion of his own relation to phenomenology: 'self-interruption' is, he insists, 'another name' for the internal division and difference that he identifies in the structure of all writing (ibid.).

14 'Don't take me seriously in a preface. The real philosophical work is what I have just written.' Hegel, cited by Gayatri Chakravorty Spivak in her 'Translator's Preface' to *Of Grammatology*, p. x.

15 Derrida, 'Outwork, Prefacing', in *Dissemination*, London: Athlone Press, 1981, p. 7.

16 Derrida, *Of Grammatology*, p. lxxxix.

17 Derrida, *Of Grammatology*, p. lxxxix.

18 This obligation has its mythological origin in the answer Zeno reportedly received from the Delphic Oracle, which was 'Take on the colour of the dead' and which Zeno interpreted to mean 'Study the ancients.' The traditional – classical – way of understanding this is as a call to reveal through the exegesis of strictly unprecedented texts an original or ideal exemplary meaning. Derrida, however, goes back to the ancients precisely to disrupt that classical idea. Derrida wants to acknowledge that we never reach an origin that would dispose of precedents and will never find in a supposedly original text anything other than a tissue of precedents.

19 Derrida, *Of Grammatology*, p. 87.

20 Mulhall, *Inheritance and Originality*, p. 1.

21 Derrida, *Of Grammatology*, p. 87.

22 Derrida, *Of Grammatology*, p. 70. I am using the term 'picture' here in the Wittgensteinian sense introduced in Chapter 3. A (more or less spontaneous, pre-reflective and not in itself incorrect) 'picture' contrasts with (more or less theoretical, developed and typically distorting) 'ideas' that are 'rooted' in it. See Wittgenstein, *Philosophical Investigations*, §1.

23 Derrida, 'Différance', in *Margins of Philosophy*, London: Harvester Wheatsheaf, 1982, p. 16.

24 Derrida, *Of Grammatology*, p. 70. It is interesting to compare Derrida's acknowledgement of others in *Of Grammatology* to more typical modes of acknowledgement. Books written these days, including this one, are usually prefaced by long slews of grateful acknowledgements thanking everyone for everything but the errors. But note that Derrida's list of acknowledgements occurs *within* his text and does not just precede it. For Derrida, the debt to others has become of methodological and not merely personal significance. One might compare this to Gilbert Ryle's book *The Concept of Mind*. That text famously has no footnotes at all and no texts by others are appealed to (not even by Descartes). Less well known is that the book has no acknowledgements either. He says too that he is 'primarily' trying to 'get some disorders out of my own system', and is only 'secondarily' interested in helping others (G. Ryle, *The Concept of Mind*, Harmondsworth: Penguin, 1990, p. 11). One might also recall here Ryle's response (often misreported) at a conference on analytic philosophy in France in the late 1950s, where, upon being asked whether his position was 'strictly in agreement' with 'the programme outlined at the beginning of the century by Russell and refined by Wittgenstein and some others',

he vehemently replied: '*I certainly hope not*' (Ryle, quoted in *Texts and Dialogues with Merleau-Ponty*, p. 69.) The methodological significance of this remark is important. Despite his resistance to the Cartesian 'myth' of consciousness, Ryle's text is constructed with a strong sense of its author as fundamentally *solitary*, as the resident, as it were, of an inner fortress. Derrida seems to be far less of an inner fortress, more a point of confluence, a node.

25 Derrida, *Of Grammatology*, p. 70. As Derrida notes elsewhere, Levinas 'found his way' through a 'break within phenomenology' opened up by Husserl's analysis of the alter-ego in the fifth Cartesian Meditation (Derrida, 'Hospitality, Justice and Responsibility', p. 71).

26 Derrida, *Of Grammatology*, p. 70.

27 Because the analysis of the trace opens on to a 'deconstruction of consciousness' conceived as self-presence, Derrida regards his work as belonging to a movement of thought in our time that includes not only Levinas and Heidegger but also Nietzsche, Freud and, indeed, various contemporary scientific fields, 'notably biology' (Derrida, *Of Grammatology*, p. 70).

28 Derrida, *Of Grammatology*, p. 70.

29 Derrida, *Of Grammatology*, p. 70.

30 Derrida, 'Geschlecht II', in *Deconstruction and Philosophy: The Texts of Jacques Derrida*, ed. J. Sallis, Chicago: Chicago University Press, 1987, p. 168.

31 Derrida, 'Force of Law: The "Mystical Foundation of Authority"', in D.G. Carlson, D. Cornell and M. Rosenfeld (eds), *Deconstruction and the Possibility of Justice*, London: Routledge, 1992, p. 25, emphasis in original.

32 On what Sartre calls this 'useless passion' that man is in projecting itself to be God (i.e. desiring to attain 'to the dignity of the in-itself-for-itself'), see Sartre, *Being and Nothingness*, p. 615.

33 Derrida, 'Force of Law', p. 25.

34 Derrida, 'The Ends of Man', in *Margins of Philosophy*, London: Harvester Wheatsheaf, 1982.

35 Derrida, 'The Ends of Man', pp. 122–23.

36 Derrida, 'The Ends of Man', pp. 127–34.

37 Derrida, 'The Ends of Man', pp. 115–16.

38 'To make something tremble in its entirety' and 'to shake the whole' translates Derrida's use of the French '*solliciter*'. See Derrida, 'Différance', translator's footnote 18, p. 16.

39 Derrida, *Of Grammatology*, p. lxxxix.

40 Derrida, *A Taste for the Secret*, p. 83.

41 Derrida, *Of Grammatology*, p. lxxxix.

42 Derrida, *Of Grammatology*, p. 3. We might note that the short foreword inserted before the opening chapter of Pt II closes by making the point that the inclusion of Levi-Strauss' texts in 'an introduction to "the age of Rousseau"' 'will be somewhat more than an exergue' (Derrida, *Of Grammatology*, p. 100).

43 Austin, 'A Plea for Excuses', p. 186.

44 Derrida, *Limited Inc.*, pp. 45 and 109, fn. 3.

45 Derrida, *Of Grammatology*, p. 3.

46 All the quotations here are from the exergue to Pt I of Derrida, *Of Grammatology*, pp. 3–5.

47 Derrida, *Of Grammatology*, p. 5.

48 Derrida, *Of Grammatology*, p. 5.

49 Derrida, 'Force of Law', p. 25.

50 Derrida explores the quasi-tautological 'dictum' '*tout autre est tout autre*' at length in *The Gift of Death*, Chicago: Chicago University Press, 1995, ch. 4.

51 The phrase is from Wittgenstein's engagement with the quest for radical completeness and finality in philosophy, traditionally taken up as 'the question of essence', in Wittgenstein, *Philosophical Investigations*, §92. I explore this dream of systematic completeness further, and with further help from Derrida, in Glendinning, 'Wittgenstein's Apocalyptic Librarian', in *Wittgenstein and the Future of Philosophy: A Reassessment after 50 Years*, eds R. Haller and K. Puhl, Vienna: Hölder-Pichler-Tempsky, 2002.

52 Derrida, *Limited Inc.*, p. 8.

53 Derrida, *Of Grammatology*, p. 6.

54 Derrida, *Of Grammatology*, p. 6.

55 The idea is that, in recent times, philosophical problems, especially problems in philosophy of mind and epistemology, came to be regarded as fundamentally problems *about* language, or at least problems whose solution was fundamentally *dependent upon* a correct analysis of language. It is, again, a question of *priority*.

56 Derrida, *Points de suspension*, p. 387.

57 Derrida, *Of Grammatology*, p. 158.

58 Derrida, *Of Grammatology*, p. 159.

59 Derrida, *Of Grammatology*, p. 160.

60 Derrida, *Of Grammatology*, p. 7.

61 Derrida, *Of Grammatology*, p. 8.

62 Derrida, *Of Grammatology*, p. 8.

63 Derrida, *Of Grammatology*, p. 6.

64 I draw on Weber's concept of 'disenchantment' from John McDowell's discussion of the progressive 'disenchantment of nature' that he (I think rightly) takes as belonging to 'the time of the rise of modern science' (McDowell, *Mind and World*, p. 70). Derrida does not extend that disenchantment to language in the sense of suggesting that word-books are as devoid of meaning as the 'book' of nature (cf. ibid., p. 71). However, without denying that one finds an intelligibility in something when writing is read, he does challenge the enchanted conception of that intelligibility. As we shall see, what he says will have implications for our understanding of a word-book too as a 'container' – held between two covers – for *a* given meaning, or for a *given* meaning, or for a given *meaning*.

65 Derrida, *Of Grammatology*, p. 6.

66 Derrida, *Of Grammatology*, p. 13.

67 Derrida, *Of Grammatology*, p. 13.

68 Derrida, *Of Grammatology*, p. 14.

69 Derrida, *Of Grammatology*, p. 14.

70 Derrida, *Of Grammatology*, p. 12.

71 Derrida, 'Geschlecht II', p. 165.

72 Derrida, 'Force of Law', p. 26.

73 Derrida, *Of Grammatology*, p. 18.

74 Derrida, *Of Grammatology*, p. 9.

75 Derrida, *Of Grammatology*, p. 14.

76 Derrida, *Of Grammatology*, p. 314.

77 Derrida, *Of Grammatology*, p. 314.

78 Renford Banbrough, *Reason, Truth & God*, London: Methuen, 1969, p. 86.

79 Derrida, *Of Grammatology*, p. 19.

80 Derrida, *Of Grammatology*, p. 9.

81 Derrida, *Of Grammatology*, p. 9.

82 Derrida, *Of Grammatology*, p. 9.

83 What follows summarises a line of interpretation that I have been exploring for some time now concerning writing and iterability. The most sustained treatment can be found in Glendinning, *On Being with Others*, chs 5–7.

84 Derrida, *Limited Inc.*, p. 9.
85 Derrida, *Limited Inc.*, p. 3.
86 Derrida, *Of Grammatology*, p. 281.
87 Derrida, *Limited Inc.*, p. 8.
88 As we saw in Chapter 2, Husserl's reductions aim to reveal, within what he conceives of as pure expression, a relation to an object; namely, the intending of an objective ideality. One is, as it were, face to face with an essentially repeatable and sharable ideality. Derrida insists that he is 'very interested in and indebted to Husserl's analysis of idealization. One could say that I "borrow" from him while leaving him at a certain point' (Glendinning, *Arguing with Derrida*, p. 103). And what he borrows is the thought that repeatability is an essential characteristic of *all* expressive signs – and ultimately whether they are 'expressions' in Husserl's restricted sense or not.
89 Derrida, *Limited Inc.*, p. 50.
90 Derrida, *Limited Inc.*, p. 10.
91 This is of course a very Wittgensteinian lesson. Indeed, the quotation here is from the conclusion of an explicitly Wittgensteinian approach to language in Phil Hutchinson and Rupert Read, 'Memento: A Philosophical Investigation', in *Film as Philosophy*, R. Read and J. Goodenough (eds), London: Palgrave Macmillan, 2005, p. 76. It is worth further noting, as the authors do, that since 'language does not exist external to its use … it cannot, in John McDowell's phrase, be viewed from sideways on' (ibid.).
92 Derrida, *Positions*, p. 33. Kant defines a transcendental illusion by contrast to empirical illusions of the sort 'in which a bungler might entangle himself through lack of knowledge' or a 'lack of attention' (Kant, *Critique of Pure Reason*, A297–98, B354).
93 Derrida, *Limited Inc.*, p. 49.
94 Derrida, *Of Grammatology*, p. 52.
95 Derrida, 'The Ends of Man', p. 134.
96 Derrida, 'The Ends of Man', p. 134.
97 Derrida, 'The Ends of Man', p. 134.
98 Derrida, 'The Ends of Man', p. 126.
99 Derrida, 'The Ends of Man', p. 134.
100 Derrida, *Positions*, p. 14.
101 Derrida, 'The Ends of Man', p. 134.
102 I am grateful for discussions with Daniel Whiting on this interpretive issue. I stress here the inseparability of our life from a life with signs (in general) in order to highlight that, for Derrida, it is not only that an individual becomes a 'speaking subject' by 'making its speech conform to the system of the rules of language' but that one cannot even conceive of a 'presence to itself of the subject' 'before speech or signs' (Derrida, 'Différance', p. 16).
103 Derrida, *Limited Inc.*, pp. 17–18.
104 Geoffrey Bennington, *Interrupting Derrida*, London: Routledge, 2000, p. 139.
105 Derrida, *Speech and Phenomena*, p. 104. Translation altered, after J.D. Caputo, 'The Economy of Signs in Husserl and Derrida', in John Sallis (ed.), *Deconstruction and Philosophy: The Texts of Jacques Derrida*, Chicago: University of Chicago Press, 1987, p. 109.
106 Derrida, *Limited Inc.*, p. 21.
107 Derrida, *Of Grammatology*, p. 24.
108 Derrida, *Limited Inc.*, p. 21.
109 Derrida, *Of Grammatology*, p. 70. Translation altered, after G. Bennington, 'Deconstruction and the Philosophers (The Very Idea)', in *Legislations: The Politics of Deconstruction*, London: Verso, 1994, p. 162.

110 Derrida, *Of Grammatology*, p. 70.
111 Glendinning, *Arguing with Derrida*, p. 108.
112 Diamond, 'Eating Meat and Eating People', p. 324.
113 Derrida, 'The Animal that Therefore I Am (More to Follow)', *Critical Inquiry*, vol. 29, 2002, p. 396.
114 Derrida, 'The Animal that Therefore I Am', p. 398.
115 Wiggins, 'Truth, Invention and the Meaning of Life', p. 125. We saw this in Chapter 5 in Merleau-Ponty's cognitivist construal of what he rightly regards as 'the view that we ordinarily take of language, as being in a peculiar category' (Merleau-Ponty, *Phenomenology of Perception*, p. 190).
116 Wiggins, 'Truth, Invention and the Meaning of Life', p. 124.
117 Derrida, 'The Animal that Therefore I Am', p. 416.
118 Derrida, 'The Animal that Therefore I Am', p. 374.
119 I explore this kind of scene of meeting the animal other in similar terms in Glendinning, 'From Animal Life to City Life', *Angelaki*, vol. 5, no. 3, 2000.
120 Derrida, 'The Animal that Therefore I Am', p. 374.
121 Derrida, 'The Animal that Therefore I Am', p. 374.
122 Wiggins, 'Truth, Invention and the Meaning of Life', p. 124.
123 Wiggins, 'Truth, Invention and the Meaning of Life', p. 124.
124 Wiggins, 'Truth, Invention and the Meaning of Life', p. 124.
125 Derrida, 'The Animal that Therefore I Am', p. 398.
126 Derrida, *Of Grammatology*, p. 86.
127 Derrida, 'The Animal that Therefore I Am', p. 369.
128 Derrida, 'The Animal that Therefore I Am', p. 393.
129 Derrida, 'The Animal that Therefore I Am', p. 394.
130 Derrida, 'The Animal that Therefore I Am', p. 394.
131 Derrida, 'The Animal that Therefore I Am', p. 395.
132 Diamond, 'Eating Meat and Eating People', p. 329. Diamond pointedly notes that 'the most familiar extensions [of modes of thinking characteristic of our responses to human beings to animals] involve moral concepts like charity and justice'.
133 Derrida, 'The Animal that Therefore I Am', p. 399.
134 Derrida, 'The Animal that Therefore I Am', p. 397.
135 Derrida, 'The Animal that Therefore I Am', p. 378.
136 Diamond, 'The Importance of Being Human', p. 60.
137 Wiggins, 'Truth, Invention and the Meaning of Life', p. 102.
138 Derrida, *Aporias*, trans. T. Dutoit, Stanford: Stanford University Press, 1993, p. 78.
139 Derrida, *The Post Card*, Chicago: University of Chicago Press, 1987, p. 4.
140 Mulhall, *Inheritance and Originality*, p. 1.
141 Merleau-Ponty, *Phenomenology of Perception*, p. viii. See Chapter 5.

BIBLIOGRAPHY

Austin, J.L., 'A Plea for Excuses', in *Philosophical Papers*, Oxford: Clarendon, 1979.
——, 'Ifs and Cans', in *Philosophical Papers*, Oxford: Clarendon, 1979.
——, 'Other Minds', in *Philosophical Papers*, Oxford: Clarendon, 1979.
——, *How to Do Things With Words*, Oxford: Oxford University Press, 1980.
Baldwin, Thomas (ed.), 'Introduction', in *Maurice Merleau-Ponty: Basic Writings*, London: Routledge, 2004.
Banbrough, Renford, *Reason, Truth & God*, London: Methuen, 1969.
Bass, Alan, 'Introduction', in Jacques Derrida, *Writing and Difference*, London: Routledge, 1978.
Beauvoir, Simone de, *The Second Sex*, trans. H. M. Parshely, Harmondsworth: Penguin, 1984.
Bennington, Geoffrey, 'Derridabase', in Geoffrey Bennington and Jacques Derrida, *Jacques Derrida*, Chicago: Chicago University Press, 1993.
——, 'Deconstruction and the Philosophers (The Very Idea)', in *Legislations: The Politics of Deconstruction*, London: Verso, 1994.
——, *Interrupting Derrida*, London: Routledge, 2000.
——, 'For the Sake of Argument (Up to a Point)', in S. Glendinning (ed.), *Arguing with Derrida*, Oxford: Blackwell, 2001.
Berkeley, George, *The Principles of Human Knowledge*, Glasgow: Collins, 1962.
Bernasconi, Robert and Simon Critchley (eds), 'Editors' Introduction', in *Re-Reading Levinas*, Bloomington: Indiana, 1991.
Bernasconi, R. and D. Wood (eds), *The Provocation of Levinas: Rethinking the Other*, London: Routledge, 1998.
Brentano, Franz, *Psychology from an Empirical Standpoint*, trans. A.C. Rancurello, D.B. Terrell and L.L. McAlister, London: Routledge, 1995.
——, *Descriptive Psychology*, trans. B. Müller, London: Routledge, 1995.
Caputo, John D., 'The Economy of Signs in Husserl and Derrida', in John Sallis (ed.), *Deconstruction and Philosophy: The Texts of Jacques Derrida*, Chicago: University of Chicago Press, 1987.
——, *Demythologizing Heidegger*, Bloomington: Indiana University Press, 1993.
Cavell, Stanley, *The Claim of Reason: Wittgenstein, Skepticism, Morality, and Tragedy*, Oxford: Oxford University Press, 1979.
Caws, Peter, *Sartre*, London: Routledge, 1979.
Cohen-Solal, Annie, *Sartre: A Life*, London: Heinemann, 1985.

Cranston, Maurice, *Sartre*, London: Oliver & Boyd, 1962.

Critchley, Simon, 'Introduction', in S. Critchley and W. Schroeder (eds), *A Companion to Continental Philosophy*, Oxford: Blackwell, 1998.

——, 'Remarks on Derrida and Habermas', *Constellations*, vol. 7, no. 4, December 2000.

——, *A Very Short Introduction to Continental Philosophy*, Oxford: Oxford University Press, 2001.

——, 'Introduction', in R. Bernasconi and S. Critchley (eds), *Cambridge Companion to Levinas*, Cambridge: Cambridge University Press, 2004.

Cumming, Robert Denoon, *Human Nature and History: A Study of the Development of Liberal Political Thought*, 2 vols, Chicago: Chicago University Press, 1969.

——, *Starting Point: An Introduction to the Dialectic of Existence*, Chicago: Chicago University Press, 1979.

——, *Phenomenology and Deconstruction*, 4 vols, Chicago: Chicago University Press, 1991–2001.

Davidson, Donald, 'On the Very Idea of a Conceptual Scheme', in *Inquiries into Truth and Interpretation*, Oxford: Clarendon, 1984.

Derrida, Jacques, *Speech and Phenomena: And Other Essays on Husserl's Theory of Signs*, trans. D.B. Allison, Evanston: Northwestern University Press, 1973.

——, *Of Grammatology*, trans. Gayatri Chakravorty Spivak, Baltimore: Johns Hopkins University Press, 1974.

——, 'Violence and Metaphysics', in *Writing and Difference*, trans. A. Bass, London: Routledge, 1978.

——, *Dissemination*, trans. B. Johnson, London: Athlone Press, 1981.

——, 'The Ends of Man', in *Margins of Philosophy*, trans. A. Bass, Chicago: Chicago University Press, 1982.

——, 'Différance', in *Margins of Philosophy*, trans. A. Bass, London: Harvester Wheatsheaf, 1982.

——, 'The Time of a Thesis', in A. Montefiore (ed.), *Philosophy in France Today*, Cambridge: Cambridge University Press, 1983.

——, 'Geschlecht: Sexual Difference, Ontological Difference', trans. R. Berezdivin, *Research in Phenomenology*, 13, 1983.

——, *Positions*, trans. A. Bass, London: The Athlone Press, 1987.

——, *The Post Card*, Chicago: University of Chicago Press, 1987.

——, 'Geschlecht II', in *Deconstruction and Philosophy: The Texts of Jacques Derrida*, ed. J. Sallis, Chicago: Chicago University Press, 1987.

——, 'Signature Event Context', trans. S. Weber and J. Mehlman, in *Limited Inc*, G. Graff (ed.), Evanston: Northwestern University Press, 1988.

——, *Limited Inc.*, G. Graff (ed.), Evanston: Northwestern University Press, 1988.

——, *Of Spirit: Heidegger and the Question*, trans. G. Bennington and R. Bowlby, Chicago: University of Chicago Press, 1989.

——, '"Eating Well", or the Calculation of the Subject', in E. Cadava, P. Connor and J.-L. Nancy (eds), *Who Comes after the Subject*, London: Routledge, 1991.

——, 'Force of Law: The "Mystical Foundation of Authority"', in D.G. Carlson, D. Cornell and M. Rosenfeld (eds), *Deconstruction and the Possibility of Justice*, London: Routledge, 1992.

——, *Aporias*, trans. T. Dutoit, Stanford: Stanford University Press, 1993.

——, *The Gift of Death*, trans. D. Wills, Chicago: Chicago University Press, 1995.

——, *Points de suspension*, Paris: Galilée, 1997.

——, 'Faith and Knowledge', trans. S. Weber, in J. Derrida and G. Vattimo (eds), *Religion*, Cambridge: Polity Press, 1998.

——, 'Hospitality, Justice and Responsibility', in R. Kearney and M. Dooley (eds), *Questioning Ethics: Contemporary Debates in Philosophy*, London Routledge, 1999.

——, 'I Have a Taste for the Secret', in J. Derrida and M. Ferraris (eds), *A Taste for the Secret*, Cambridge: Polity Press, 2001.

——, 'Response to A.W. Moore', in S. Glendinning (ed.), *Arguing with Derrida*, Oxford: Blackwell, 2001.

——, 'Response to Baldwin', in S. Glendinning (ed.), *Arguing with Derrida*, Oxford: Blackwell, 2001.

——, 'Response to Mulhall', in S. Glendinning (ed.), *Arguing with Derrida*, Oxford: Blackwell, 2001.

——, 'Politics and Friendship', in E. Rottenberg (ed.), *Negotiations*, Stanford: Stanford University Press, 2002.

——, 'The Animal that Therefore I Am (More to Follow)', trans. D. Wills, *Critical Inquiry*, vol. 29, 2002.

——, 'History of the Lie: Prolegomena', in P. Kamuf (ed. and trans.), *Without Alibi*, Stanford: Stanford University Press, 2002.

——, 'Typewriter Ribbon', in *Without Alibi*, P. Kamuf (ed. and trans.), Stanford: Stanford University Press, 2002.

Deutscher, Max, *Genre and Void: Looking Back at Sartre and Beauvoir*, Aldershot: Ashgate, 2003.

Diamond, Cora, 'The Importance of Being Human', in D. Cockburn (ed.), *Human Beings*, Cambridge: Cambridge University Press, 1991.

——, 'Throwing away the Ladder', in *The Realistic Spirit*, Cambridge, Mass.: MIT Press, 1996.

—, 'Anything but Argument?', in *The Realistic Spirit*, Cambridge, Mass.: MIT Press, 1996.

——, 'Wittgenstein and Metaphysics', in *The Realistic Spirit*, Cambridge, Mass.: MIT Press, 1996.

——, 'Having a Rough Story about What Moral Philosophy Is', in *The Realistic Spirit*, Cambridge, Mass.: MIT Press, 1996.

——, 'Eating Meat and Eating People', in *The Realistic Spirit*, Cambridge, Mass.: MIT Press, 1996.

Finkelstein, David, 'Wittgenstein on Rules and Platonism', in A. Crary and R. Read (eds), *The New Wittgenstein*, London: Routledge, 2000.

Finlayson, Gordon, 'Adorno on the Ethical and the Ineffable', *European Journal of Philosophy*, vol. 10, no. 1, 2002.

Gaita, Raimond, *The Philosopher's Dog*, London: Routledge, 2003.

Gide, André, *The Immoralist*, London: Penguin, 1960.

Glendinning, Simon, *On Being with Others: Heidegger–Derrida–Wittgenstein*, London: Routledge, 1998.

——, 'Perception and Hallucination', *Journal of the British Society of Phenomenology*, vol. 29, no. 3, 1998.

——, 'From Animal Life to City Life', *Angelaki*, vol. 5, no 3, 2000.

——, 'Much Ado about Nothing', in *Ratio*, vol. XIV, no. 3, 2001.

——, 'Wittgenstein's Apocalyptic Librarian', in R. Haller and K. Puhl (eds), *Wittgenstein and the Future of Philosophy: A Reassessment after 50 years*, Vienna: Hölder-Pichler-Tempsky, 2002.

257

——, 'What is Phenomenology?' *Think*, no. 7, 2004.

——, 'The End of Philosophy as Metaphysics', in T. Baldwin (ed.), *The Cambridge History of Philosophy 1870–1945*, Cambridge: Cambridge University Press, 2004.

——, 'Language', in J. Reynolds and J. Roffe (eds), *Understanding Derrida*, London: Continuum, 2004.

——, '*Le Plaisir de la lecture: Reading the Other Animal*', *Parallax*, vol. 12, no. 1, 2006.

——, 'Merleau-Ponty: The Genius of Man', in T. Baldwin (ed.), *Reading Merleau-Ponty*, London: Routledge, 2007.

Hacking, Ian, 'A New Way to See a Leaf', *New York Review of Books*, 7 April 2005.

Hammond, Michael, Jane Howarth and Russell Keat, *Understanding Phenomenology*, Oxford: Blackwell, 1980.

Hare, R.M., 'A School for Philosophers', *Ratio*, vol. 2, no. 2, 1960.

Heidegger, Martin, *An Introduction to Metaphysics*, trans. R. Manheim, New Haven: Yale University Press, 1959.

——, *Being and Time*, Oxford: Blackwell, 1962.

——, *The Basic Problems of Phenomenology*, trans. A. Hofstadter, Bloomington: Indiana University Press, 1982.

——, 'What is Metaphysics?', in *Basic Writings*, ed. D.F. Krell, London: Routledge, 1993.

——, 'The End of Philosophy and the Task for Thinking', in *Basic Writings*, ed. D.F. Krell, London: Routledge, 1993.

——, 'Letter on Humanism', in *Basic Writings*, ed. D.F. Krell, London: Routledge, 1993.

Hodge, Joanna, *Heidegger and Ethics*, London: Routledge, 1995.

Howells, Christina (ed.), 'Conclusion', in *Cambridge Companion to Sartre*, Cambridge: Cambridge University Press, 1992.

Husserl, Edmund, *Ideas: General Introduction to Pure Phenomenology*, trans. W.R. Boyce Gibson, London: Collier-Macmillan, 1962.

——, 'Philosophy as Rigorous Science', in *Phenomenology and the Crisis of Philosophy*, New York: Harper Torchbooks, 1965.

——, *The Idea of Phenomenology*, trans. W.P. Allston and G. Nakhnikian, The Hague: Martinus Nijhoff, 1970.

——, *Cartesian Meditations*, trans. D. Cairns, The Hague: Martinus Nijhoff, 1970.

——, *The Crisis of European Sciences and Transcendental Phenomenology*, trans. D. Carr, Evanston: Northwestern University Press, 1970.

——, *Logical Investigations*, 2 vols, trans. J.N. Findlay, London: Routledge, 1970.

Hutchinson, Phil and Rupert Read, '*Memento*: A Philosophical Investigation', in R. Read and J. Goodenough (eds), *Film as Philosophy*, London: Palgrave Macmillan, 2005.

Irigaray, Luce, 'Questions to EL', trans. M. Whitford, in R. Bernasconi and S. Critchley (eds), *Re-Reading Levinas*, Bloomington: Indiana, 1991.

Kant, Immanuel, *Critique of Pure Reason*, trans. N.K. Smith, London: Methuen, 1933.

——, *Foundations of the Metaphysics of Morals*, trans. T. K. Abbot, Indianapolis: Bobbs-Merill, 1949.

Kaufmann, Walter (ed.), *Existentialism from Dostoevsky to Sartre*, New York: Meridian, 1956.

Kockelmans, Joseph J. (ed.), *Phenomenology*, New York: Doubleday Anchor, 1967.

Levinas, Emmanuel, *Totality and Infinity*, trans. A. Lingis, Pittsburgh: Duquesne University Press, 1969.

——, *Existence and Existents*, trans. A. Lingis, The Hague: Martinus Nijhoff, 1978.

——, *Time and the Other*, trans. R.A. Cohen, Pittsburgh: Duquesne University Press, 1987.

——, *Is it Righteous to Be?: Interviews with Emmanuel Levinas*, J. Robbins (ed.), Stanford: Stanford University Press, 2001.

Llewelyn, John, 'Am I Obsessed by Bobby?', in R. Bernasconi and S. Critchley (eds), *Re-Reading Levinas*, Bloomington: Indiana, 1991.

MacDonald, Paul, *Descartes and Husserl: The Philosophical Project of Radical Beginnings*, Albany: SUNY Press, 2000.

McCulloch, Gregory, *Using Sartre: An Analytical Introduction to Early Sartrean Themes*, London: Routledge, 1994

McDowell, John, 'Criteria, Defeasibility and Knowledge', *Proceedings of the British Academy*, vol. LXVIII, 1983.

——, *Mind and World*, Cambridge, Mass.: Harvard University Press, 1994.

——, *Mind, Value and Reality*, Cambridge, Mass.: Harvard University Press, 1998.

Merleau-Ponty, Maurice, *Phenomenology of Perception*, trans. C. Smith, London: Routledge, 1962.

——, *The Structure of Behaviour*, trans. A.L. Fisher, London: Methuen, 1965.

——, *Texts and Dialogues with Merleau-Ponty*, H. Silverman and J. Barry (eds), New York: Humanities Press, 1992.

Moran, Dermot, *Introduction to Phenomenology*, London: Routledge, 2000.

Moreland, J.P., 'Should a Naturalist Be a Supervenient Physicalist', *Metaphilosophy*, vol. 29, nos. 1/2, January/April 1998.

Mulhall, Stephen, *Heidegger and Being and Time*, London: Routledge, 1996.

——, *Inheritance and Originality: Wittgenstein, Heidegger, Kierkegaard*, Oxford: Oxford University Press, 2001.

——, *Philosophical Myths of the Fall*, Princeton: Princeton University Press, 2005.

——, 'Philosophy's Hidden Essence', in E. Ammereller and E. Fischer (eds), *Wittgenstein at Work*, Routledge, 2004.

Norris, Christopher, *Deconstruction: Theory and Practice*, London: Methuen, 1982.

Philipse, Herman, *Heidegger's Philosophy of Being*, Princeton: Princeton University Press, 1998.

Plant, Robert, *Wittgenstein and Levinas: Ethical and Religious Thought*, London: Routledge, 2004.

Plato, *The Republic*, trans. D. Lee, Harmondsworth: Penguin, 1974.

Poincaré, Henri, *The Value of Science*, New York: Dover, (1914) 1958.

Polt, Richard, *Heidegger: An Introduction*, London: UCL Press, 1999.

Primozic, Daniel Thomas, *On Merleau-Ponty*, Belmont: Wadsworth/Thomas Learning, 2001.

Royle, Nicholas, *Jacques Derrida*, London Routledge, 2003.

Ryle, Gilbert, 'Phenomenology versus *The Concept of Mind*', in *Collected Papers*, London: Hutchinson, 1971.

——, 'Phenomenology', in *Collected Papers*, London: Hutchinson, 1971.

——, *The Concept of Mind*, Harmondsworth: Penguin, 1990.

——, *Texts and Dialogues with Merleau-Ponty*, H. Silverman and J. Barry (eds), New York: Humanities Press, 1992.

Sallis, John, *Delimitations: Phenomenology and the End of Metaphysics*, Bloomington: Indiana University Press, 1986.

Sartre, Jean-Paul, *Being and Nothingness*, trans. H.E. Barnes, London: Methuen, 1958.

——, *Questions de méthode*, Paris: Gallimard, 1960.

——, *Nausea*, trans. R. Baldick, Harmondsworth: Penguin, 1965.

——, *Situations*, trans. B. Eisler, New York: Fawcett, 1965.

——, *Existentialism and Humanism*, trans. P. Mairet, London: Methuen, 1973.

Searle, John, *Intentionality*, Cambridge: Cambridge University Press, 1983.

Sellars, Wilfred, *Empiricism and the Philosophy of Mind*, Cambridge, Mass.: Harvard University Press, 1997.

Smith, A.D., *Husserl and the Cartesian Meditations*, London: Routledge, 2003.

Smith, Peter, *Explaining Chaos*, Cambridge: Cambridge University Press, 1988.

Spivak, Gayatri Chakravorty, 'Translator's Preface', in Jacques Derrida, *Of Grammatology*, Baltimore: Johns Hopkins University Press, 1974.

Sandford, Stella, 'Levinas in the Realm of the Senses: Transcendence and Intelligibility', *Angelaki*, vol. 4, no. 3, 2000.

Strawson, Peter, *Individuals: An Essay in Descriptive Metaphysics*, London: Methuen, 1959.

——, 'Imagination and Perception', in R.C.S. Walker (ed.), *Kant on Pure Reason*, Oxford: Oxford University Press, 1982.

Warnock, Mary, *The Philosophy of Sartre*, London: Hutchinson, 1965.

Wiggins, David, 'Truth, Invention, and the Meaning of Life', in *Needs, Values, Truth*, Oxford: Blackwell, 1987.

Wild, John, 'Forward', in Maurice Merleau-Ponty, *The Structure of Behaviour*, London: Methuen, 1965.

Williams, Bernard, 'Contemporary Philosophy: A Second Look', in N. Bunnin and E.P. Tsui-James (eds), *The Blackwell Companion to Philosophy*, Oxford: Blackwell, 1996.

Wittgenstein, Ludwig, *Philosophical Investigations*, trans. G.E.M. Anscombe, Oxford: Blackwell, 1958.

——, *Tractatus Logico-Philosophicus*, trans. D.F. Pears and B.F. McGuinness, London: Routledge, 1961.

——, *Culture and Value*, trans. P. Winch, Oxford: Blackwell, 1980.

——, *Recollections of Wittgenstein*, Rush Rhees (ed.), Oxford: Oxford University Press, 1984.

——, *Zettel*, second edition, Oxford: Blackwell, 1991.

Wood, David, *Thinking after Heidegger*, Cambridge: Polity Press, 2002.

Wright, Crispin, *Truth and Objectivity*, Oxford: Harvard University Press, 1993.

——, 'Comrades against Quietism', *Mind*, 107, 1998.

INDEX